Patty (& Steve)

Thank you for your support of ou[r] ministry. We so appreciate you and Steve... your faithfulness to the Chaplaincy Ministry, and your contribution to the Blanket Ministry... it touches everyone = staff, administration, & patients.

God bless & keep you & your household,

Donna & Chuck

Matt. 6:33

MW00619954

# CHOOSING THE GOOD PORTION

# CHOOSING THE GOOD PORTION

## Women of the Orthodox Presbyterian Church

*Edited by*
*Patricia E. Clawson*
*and Diane L. Olinger*

The Committee for the Historian
of the Orthodox Presbyterian Church
Willow Grove, Pennsylvania

Printed in the United States of America

# Contents

## Part Two: Choosing to Build, 1950s–1960s

## Part Three: Choosing to Serve, 1970s–1980s

## Part Four: Choosing to Live for Christ, 1990s–2000s

# Introduction:
# Why These Stories?

## *Patricia E. Clawson*

The Orthodox Presbyterian Church, as it is called today, was formed in 1936 under the leadership of J. Gresham Machen, John DeWaard,[1] Bruce Hunt, and other seminary professors, pastors, missionaries, and ruling elders. These forefathers in the faith stood against a denomination that had diluted its view of the Word of God to that of the word of men. In the 1920s and '30s, some presbyteries and seminaries of the Presbyterian Church (USA) no longer required ministers to acknowledge Jesus as God nor to share Christ's saving work with those dying on the mission field without hope. Such apostasy prompted the establishment of Westminster Theological Seminary in 1929 and the Independent Board of Presbyterian Foreign Missions in 1933. Three years later, Machen was defrocked from the office of minister for "disloyalty" to the PCUSA. On June 11, 1936, the Lord used these biblically-minded defenders of the faith to give birth to the Presbyterian Church of America, later renamed the Orthodox Presbyterian Church.[2]

Recalling our heritage reminds us of who we are within Christ's church. Books, articles, lectures, and even a Historian DVD retell

1 Although John DeWaard was not present at the First Assembly, his letter was read to that assembly about the founding of his new church. He joined the Wisconsin Presbytery and was on the rolls of the Second General Assembly, which met five months later in 1936.

2 The Presbyterian Church of America changed its name to the Orthodox Presbyterian Church on February 9, 1939, because of a lawsuit by the Presbyterian Church (USA).

how the OPC began through the fidelity of those godly men. But the OPC's story doesn't end there. Those men had wives, mothers, sisters, daughters, and friends who encouraged, supported, and suffered alongside them while they witnessed our church blossom and grow.

The Minutes of the First Assembly that met at Philadelphia's New Century Club on that June day in 1936 recorded the names of 50 women who stood with 34 ministers, 17 elders, and 27 laymen to become constituting members of what we now know as the OPC. A photo of the Second General Assembly, held five months later, shows 39 women, all wearing hats, sitting among 95 determined men. These ladies supported their pastors' difficult decisions to leave their pulpits, pensions, and parsonages to serve in a new denomination where the gospel revealed in God's Word was, and would continue to be, the gospel preached. Little has been written about these women of whom it might be said, they "labored side by side with me in the gospel" (Philippians 4:3).

This book profiles some of these mothers in the faith and their spiritual offspring whose service over the decades has helped to mold the OPC into what it is today. Recording the stories of those who are at rest with the Lord and those edging toward glory hopefully will encourage younger generations of women to steadfast service and sacrifice for the sake of Christ.

Most of these narratives have never been put in print before. This became apparent while researching the biographies of husbands and wives for features posted daily on our OPC.org website: *Today in OPC History.* To pen short sketches on most OPC sisters requires serious sleuthing. Writing about early OPC women became complicated because few are still with us, and those who knew them often can't recall those long ago days. Although brief records are available on our ministers in the OPC's *Ministerial Register,* information about their wives is limited to when they married and died. A notable exception, the Committee on Foreign Missions compiles profiles on missionary spouses. The OPC's 50th anniversary book, *The Orthodox Presbyterian Church 1936-1986,* also offers some stories about the contribution of women. Nuggets of their service can be found scattered throughout the books celebrating the OPC's 75th anniversary, other works published by the Committee for the Historian, and various articles featured over the years in *The Presbyterian Guardian* and *New Horizons in the Orthodox Presbyterian Church.*

When I first wrote features for *Today in OPC History* as the editorial assistant/ office secretary for the Committee on Christian Education, I often left the OPC administrative offices and visited a friend in skilled care. Grace Elizabeth Mullen was in her last weeks of a ten-year battle with cancer. For more than a decade we had shared a pew during evening worship at Calvary OPC in Glenside, Pennsylvania. Grace was our denomination's first archivist and knew more about its history than almost anyone. Sharing stories with her regarding the women I was writing about brought Grace a taste of the outside world.

Lying in her hospital-type bed, Grace scarcely had energy to eat and was in great pain, yet her eyes lit up whenever I mentioned a subject's name. Invariably she told me new facts about that person. One night I mentioned how much I appreciated the sacrifices made by Pauline "Polly" Gaffin, one of our first missionaries to China and Taiwan. After World War II when the Communists made their dangerous push through China, Polly's husband, Dick, returned to Shanghai alone, leaving her in New Jersey to care for their children by herself for more than two and a half years. Grace sat up and excitedly shared how close she and her mother were to the Gaffins during that time as both families lived and worshipped in Wildwood, New Jersey. "What a marvelous person 'Aunt Polly' was," Grace exuded. Then she leaned forward, looked intently into my eyes, and said, "Pat, I think you should write a book about Polly."

Stunned by her suggestion, I stammered that I couldn't. But her words percolated in my mind. With little available information on OPC women and few left who knew our early pioneers, would our church forget all that God had done through these women's lives? Although I questioned my ability to write a whole book on Polly Gaffin, I knew many writers together could author one book about these special saints.

As the idea germinated, one day I asked my boss, Danny Olinger, who serves as both the general secretary of the Committee on Christian Education and the president of the Committee for the Historian: "Do you think the Committee for the Historian would be interested in publishing a book on women in the OPC?"

Danny, who also had experienced difficulty in researching stories on OPC women, supported the idea. He directed me to pitch a proposal to the full Committee for the Historian, which unanimously approved the idea. Danny's wife, Diane, with whom I had collaborated on several articles and who had served on the editorial board of the *Ohio State Law Journal*, agreed to co-edit the book. Out of more than 65 OP women given the opportunity to contribute to this volume, 55 of OPC heritage researched and wrote a chapter for this book. In an effort to feature sisters from throughout the OPC, we requested recommendations from many, including all 17 presbytery stated clerks. From 81 original suggestions and our own research emerged 93 women's stories that became part of this collection.

Only a handful of the thousands of godly women with whom God has blessed the OPC in its first 80 years are highlighted. Since no single volume could hold all of their stories, we selected a few women to represent what God has done in the lives of missionaries, pastors' wives, seminary spouses, single women, those who contributed to their congregations behind the scenes, those who helped to start churches, taught VBS, reached out to different cultures, struggled in their faith, offered hospitality, lost a loved one, and those whose husbands were in harm's way. If only we were able to share the profiles of all the special women in the OPC!

Grace's suggestion was the impetus for this book. The women profiled lived by faith, often in difficult circumstances. These humble-hearted saints didn't balk at doing the hard thing to serve the church in many ways—all in the midst of God's sanctifying work in their lives.

We hope their stories will do more than entertain. As you read what God has done in these women's lives, reflect upon their service and sacrifices for the sake of Christ and his church. Challenge yourself to grow in your service to our Father by supporting the OPC's work within your congregation and beyond your church doors. These women were ordinary saints whom God used in often extraordinary ways. May we, too, have such servant hearts.

Since each of these stories was written to stand alone, certain background information about Machen and the start of the OPC has been repeated in several stories.

To give a historical perspective to this work, we sought to have at least a 20-year gap between the major events recorded in these women's lives and the time of publication in 2016. Yet some of those featured in the later chapters are still in the midst of their labors for the Lord, and the events surrounding their lives are closer at hand. We felt their stories warranted the shortened historical timeframe. For these women and those who penned all of the stories, the Lord is in the midst of his sanctifying work in our lives. As the years go by, if some of us stumble on our way to glory, please pray that God would "right" us and complete his sanctifying work within us.

This book's title, *Choosing the Good Portion: Women of the Orthodox Presbyterian Church,* comes from Luke 10:38–42, where Jesus was welcomed by Martha into her home. She busily fixed a meal for her many guests, but was "distracted" in her efforts. Her sister Mary appears to have helped her, then "left" to sit with the disciples at their master's feet and listen to his teaching. Martha was intent on "much serving" which perhaps meant fixing a substantial meal for the guests, so she complained to Jesus that Mary had "left" the serving to her. Mary may have thought what she helped to prepare was adequate. Jesus told Martha that "one thing (was) necessary" and Mary "(has chosen) the good portion."

With a heart for service, Martha had viewed feeding Jesus as more important than the spiritual nourishment Christ was providing.

She forgot the need to listen to Jesus before doing what he says. "The good portion offered to those who welcome Christ to their home isn't the service they give him but what they receive from him. He gives you a place at his feet with his disciples. He gives you himself.... To give to Christ you must first receive from him."[3]

This story may be frustrating to those of us who identify more with Martha. While her desire to provide sustenance for those sitting at Jesus' feet was important, Mary chose first to receive direction from God's Word—the foundation for all service. The women featured in this book are like Martha, who served the church with tremendous zeal. Yet even more important, they reflect Mary's love for God's Word as the reason and guide for all service. Like our forefathers in the faith, these women chose the good portion.

3  Douglas B. Clawson, "The Good Portion." Sermon preached on April 16, 2000, at Grace OPC in Hanover Park, Illinois.

# Part One

# Choosing to Sacrifice
# 1930s–1940s

# 1

# Mary "Minnie" Machen: Building a Foundation

## *Katherine VanDrunen*

Mary "Minnie" Machen was not technically a woman of the Orthodox Presbyterian Church. She died five years before the OPC was established. But she was a remarkable Presbyterian woman who had profound influence upon her son, J. Gresham Machen. He was instrumental in the formation of Westminster Theological Seminary in Philadelphia, the Independent Board for Presbyterian Foreign Missions, and what would be called the Orthodox Presbyterian Church—all three biblically conservative alternatives for early 20th-century Presbyterians still holding to the historical tenets of Reformed Christianity.

Born on June 17, 1849, in Macon, Georgia, Minnie was the only daughter of John Jones Gresham and Mary Baxter Gresham. Her father powerfully influenced the community and home in which Minnie was raised. John Gresham was a prominent churchman, served in local and state leadership positions, owned two plantations, and helped to establish the first manufacturing company in Georgia. Minnie maintained a close relationship with her father and named her second son after him. Her father lived long enough to know his grandsons during their visits to Macon and his frequent visits to Arthur and Minnie's home in Baltimore.

Standard instruction in the Gresham home included the Psalms, the Ten Commandments, and the Westminster Shorter Catechism. Minnie was raised in First Presbyterian Church, which

a contemporary in Macon recalled: "We went to Sunday
School of course.... I was tak-
en to church as soon as I could
sit alone.... Dr. Clisby was a
Presbyterian of the old school,
who delivered deep theological
sermons of an hour to an hour
and a half." As a young adult
Minnie taught Sunday school.
One of her students later wrote
that her teachings "have had a
refreshing influence on my life,
and maturing years affect the
heart with livelier gratitude to
her."[1]

Mary "Minnie" Machen (photo
provided courtesy of Barry Waugh,
presbyteriansofthepast.com, from
the 1842 Inn, Macon, Georgia)

After preparation at pri-
vate schools, Minnie graduated
from Macon's Wesleyan Female
College with honors in 1865. This was the first women's college
to provide a curriculum comparable to colleges for men, but did
so for the important role these women would play training their
children intellectually and morally. Through English Literature,
Mathematics, and Natural, Mental, and Moral Philosophy women
would learn their role in society as part of "a rational, divinely or-
dered universe." Latin and French would train their minds. Therefore, in the conservative context of antebellum Georgia, Wesleyan
Female College was innovative in its goal to train women at the
level of men, but remained traditional in its vision.

Minnie was an excellent student and avid learner all her life,
particularly loving botany, astronomy, the classics, and Victorian

---

1 John T. Boufeuillet, "Three Notable Georgia Women," *Atlanta Journal,*
January 7, 1932; and Eugenia Blount Lamar, *When All Is Said and Done*
(Athens: University of Georgia, 1952), 34–35.

literature. In 1903 she published *The Bible in Browning* with Mac-Millan. She also wrote articles for the *Southern Presbyterian* and the *Central Presbyterian*. She entertained notable people, such as US President Woodrow Wilson, Johns Hopkins University President Daniel Coit Gilman, and Princeton President Francis L. Patton. Taking advantage of the cultural and intellectual opportunities in Baltimore, Minnie regularly attended the opera, theater, and university lectures. She was described by the same former Sunday school student as having "an ideal home in Baltimore. There lovers of culture and of holy things caught new inspiration. Her high appreciation of the beautiful in nature and art added much to the esthetic, educational, and spiritual life of Baltimore."[2]

Minnie met her future husband, Arthur Machen, while visiting her maternal aunt Sarah Baxter Bird. Educated in the university town of Athens, Georgia, Minnie's aunt became an antebellum plantation mistress who suffered widowhood and poverty after the Civil War. An inheritance from her uncle allowed her to relocate with her two children to a prestigious neighborhood in Baltimore. She joined Franklin Street Presbyterian Church, where Arthur had rented a pew for his mother and sister when they fled Virginia during the war. Of the organizing pastor, Stuart Robinson, Arthur wrote: "He applies a sound manly intellect, and all the energy of one who goes about his work as being in truth [God's] very work."[3]

After the war, when the northern Presbyterian Church demanded an oath of loyalty to the federal government, Franklin Street's new pastor, J. J. Bullock, led the formation of the Presbytery of Patapsco in the southern Presbyterian Church. Other border state pastors and congregations joined him. He addressed his congregation: "All history attests that the Church that neglects her own proper work and undertakes to do the work of Caesar is wholly

2  Boufeuillet.
3  Arthur Machen to Lewis Machen, January 7, 1854, and April 22, 1854, quoted in Arthur W. Machen, *Letters of Arthur W. Machen with Biographical Sketch* (Baltimore, 1917), 220–21.

untrustworthy, unfaithful to herself and to her great Head and King." Bullock's Franklin Street Church filled with southern expatriates in the years following the war and formed a close community, including the Machens and extended family, Johns Hopkins professor Basil Gildersleeve, and Woodrow Wilson when in town.[4]

Arthur and Minnie's courtship letters are filled with their shared interest in spiritual and intellectual pursuits. In one letter, Arthur wrote about studying creation: "[Scientists] believe in the ether because without its existence they know not how to account for certain phenomena; and yet how tremendous the phenomena which can only be accounted for upon the assumption that there is a God and that Christ was God manifest in the flesh!" He went on to an analysis of the word "unsearchable" from Ephesians 3:8, "the unsearchable riches of Christ," and the proper attitudes Christians should have when studying the works of such scientists of his day as Charles Darwin and Thomas Huxley. Of this letter, Arthur's grandson noted: "This, indeed, was the climate of scholarship in which Uncle [J.] Gresham [Machen] was reared and sheds some light, I believe, on his insistence on free and open study."[5]

Arthur and Minnie also corresponded about a woman's intellectual capabilities and Minnie's fear that marriage would stifle her studies. It is clear that Arthur loved Minnie as much for her intelligence as for her beauty and charm. He expressed the intellectual partnership they would share, along with his library.

Arthur's respect for Minnie made it possible for him to leave much of their children's intellectual and spiritual instruction in her very capable hands while he continued to build his legal career.

---

4 J. J. Bullock, *J. J. Bullock's Address to His Congregation at the Franklin Street Church, Baltimore, Giving His Reasons for Dissolving His Connection with the Old School General Assembly of the Presbyterian Church, June 12, 1866* (Baltimore, 1866), 5, quoted in Harold M. Parker Jr., "Much Wealth and Intelligence: The Presbytery of Patapsco," in Parker's *Studies in Southern Presbyterian History* (Gunnison, CO: B&B, 1979), 27.

5 Arthur W. Machen Jr. to Ned B. Stonehouse, December 9, 1954, private collection.

Through Minnie's training, Gresham had a deeper understanding of Scripture by age 12 than many of the seminarians he later taught. She taught each son and any other young person staying with them by using personalized questions and lessons from the Bible and catechism each Sunday afternoon. She was also active in their academic lives, frequently visiting their schools, interacting with their teachers, reading and critiquing their papers (even in their college years), and regularly discussing their future plans.

Part of the family character was formed by Civil War experience. Although Minnie's father had opposed secession, he supported the Confederacy by providing manufactured goods and food to the army at a reduced price, and defending Macon as part of a group too old to officially join the army. However, when his only healthy son, Thomas, was conscripted, John worked to get him reassigned to the engineer corps in Macon, and told him to "run as hard as you can crack it" if in danger of capture. Minnie and her mother helped at the hotel converted into a hospital, but Minnie, while still a student, wrote a letter of protest when a plan called for Wesleyan College also to become a hospital. Many extended family members fought and suffered. Therefore, Minnie would identify herself as southern, and her sons would be raised in this influence, reinforced by extended family. In addition, because John Jones Gresham did not invest in Confederate bonds for himself or the other institutions who entrusted their funds to him (such as the Presbyterian Oglethorpe College), those institutions stayed solvent after the war while many failed. Minnie's inheritance also helped fund her son Gresham's work, including Westminster Theological Seminary.

Minnie and her son Gresham maintained a very close relationship. Sending a copy of his *The Virgin Birth of Christ*, she wrote to Wesleyan College: "Naturally, I am proud to have a son who has the will and the ability to write an exhaustive, creative treatise on this great Theme.... In presenting this book, I am offering to my alma mater, to whose fostering care I owe so much, one of the greatest measures of my life." Just a few months before her death in 1931

she again wrote: "I am proud of all my sons, but of this one especially as a Defender of the Faith." Minnie took obvious pride in and
encouraged all three sons, but especially Gresham, with whom she
shared a zeal for the truth of the Bible. Their frequent correspondence spanned 30 years, and when possible Gresham joined her for
summers in New England during her 15 years of widowhood. She
understood and encouraged him in his struggles against liberalism.
Developments at Franklin Street Church under Rev. Harris Kirk
gave her first-hand experience. By the early 1920s Minnie noted in
her diary that sermons were often about non-biblical issues such as
church renovation, stained glass windows, and even the "new psychology." She noted "objectionable" missions sermons and sermons
"devoid of religion." She responded to such sermons with a hunger
for the gospel.[6]

Gresham wrote of Minnie: "I do not see how anyone could
know my mother well without being forever sure that whatever else
there may be in Christianity the real heart of Christianity is found
in the atoning death of Christ." This echoes his dying words, less
than six years after his mother's death in October of 1931, "I'm so
thankful for active obedience of Christ. No hope without it."[7]

The rich legacy Minnie Gresham Machen passed down included southern Presbyterian orthodoxy, a strong sense of the church's
distinct role in the world, and a love for honest intellectual inquiry.
Her parents had instilled traditional habits of piety—such as church
attendance and personal study of the Bible and catechism—all of
which laid a foundation for studying the world (e.g., science) and
secular literature with the presuppositions of the truth of the Bible
firmly in hand. Such formation of her character enabled her to
establish a household and educate her sons to love knowledge gen-

6 Minnie Machen to Dr. Quillian, May 27, 1930, and Minnie Machen to
Miss Loyal, June 10, 1931, Minnie Gresham Machen alumni file, Wesleyan
College.
7 J. Gresham Machen, "Christianity in Conflict," in Vergilius Ferm, ed.,
*Contemporary American Theologians: Theological Autobiographies* (New York:
1932), 1: 148.

erally and the Scriptures especially.

Machen's fight to preserve the biblical church, to distinguish the church from the world, to seek the truth diligently and devotedly, and to demand fairness and honesty stems from his heritage and upbringing. Both his father Arthur Machen and his grandfather John Gresham were described with these traits, along with the lawyer Arthur's "exceptional ability to understand and argue the relevant points of the law," and John's "faults tempered by his sense of right and Christian grace." Machen grew up in a home full of books, intellectual inquiry, and a deep-seated Christian faith.

J. Gresham Machen went on to lead the fight for such important tenets as biblical inerrancy and the supernatural truth of the virgin birth as he struggled to preserve the basic biblical foundation of Christian doctrine in the Presbyterian Church during the 1920s and 1930s. He gained the respect of many outside the church for his intellectual acumen, unshakeable message, and his demand that his opponents be upright in their attacks. The academic community noted the depth, breadth, and clear scientific reasoning of Machen's writings.

As early as the 1920s, Machen recognized a growing presence within the Presbyterian Church of what, 50 years prior, was being taught by "avowed opponents of Christianity." When the broader church shifted from doctrine (which could arguably be disproved scientifically) to practicality (acting out Christian principles in the world), the result was denial of any supernatural element in Scripture, including the virgin birth of Christ and his resurrection. In 1923 Machen wrote *Christianity and Liberalism* to teach the people of the Church that denying the supernatural, atoning work of Christ constituted a different religion from Christianity.

By the 1920s the Presbyterian Church held three streams of thought: conservatives who believed in the inerrancy of Scripture and adhered to the Westminster Confession of Faith, liberals or modernists who wished to broaden the definition of "Christian" to include those who did not believe in basic biblical doctrines of the historic Protestant church, and moderates who were personally conservative but (in a quest for unity and peace) were willing to work with the liberals. Machen pled for leaders in the Presbyterian Church to uphold the biblical and confessional standard on which it was founded. He saw this as the only way to be truthful and honest.

Princeton Seminary, the historic stalwart of conservative Reformed biblical teaching and where Machen taught from 1906–1929, felt the strain of these conflicts within Presbyterianism. When the seminary was reorganized to shift power to a liberal leaning board of directors, and professors were required to sign an oath of loyalty to the new seminary policy of inclusiveness, Machen and three other professors resigned. Westminster Theological Seminary, founded by Machen, opened in the fall of 1929 with 50 students.

The controversy in the church was not over. In 1934 Machen headed the formation of an independent foreign missions board after realizing that the Presbyterian board was doing nothing about the liberal missionaries who were preaching and teaching anti-Christian principles. The liberals responded by pressing Machen's presbytery to try him as a schismatic and remove him from the denomination.

The presbytery tried and convicted Machen without allowing him to speak in his defense.[8] When the Presbyterian Church then moved to emphasize denominational loyalty rather than doctrinal steadfastness when examining future ministers, it was clear that Machen and those who agreed with him were no longer welcome. Machen led the establishment of the Orthodox Presbyterian Church in 1936.

The Independent Board for Presbyterian Foreign Missions was largely composed of non-Presbyterian fundamentalists who agreed

---

8 More particularly, they did not allow him to introduce evidence in his defense if it concerned the Auburn Affirmation, the soundness of the Board of Foreign Missions, or the Princeton/Westminster controversy, all of which were central to Machen's position. See Ned B. Stonehouse, *J. Gresham Machen: A Biographical Memoir* (Willow Grove, PA: Committee for the Historian of the OPC, 2004), 434.

with Machen concerning the basic biblical doctrines of the church but held a strong pietistic, premillennial stance. After the trial, it was soon clear that Machen's understanding of Christian liberty, eschatology, and church polity were too different from the majority, and he was no longer wanted on the Board.

An example of Machen's character is shown in his interactions with China missionary Pearl S. Buck, whom he had used as an example of the modernist ideology he was fighting against. He wrote to her to explain he was not attacking her as a person but the views of Christianity she was teaching. She in turn respected him as a fierce and intelligent combatant, standing for what he believed and stating it clearly, accurately, and consistently, fighting for his convictions "through every change in time and human thought." [9]

Former students recalled Machen's humor and clowning, but also his generosity with anyone struggling academically and his hospitality toward students. In his classroom prayers he humbly acknowledged "in the simplest language the multitude of divine mercies channeled through the infinite merit of the Son of God" and displayed "a quality of child-like wonder, a tenderness, a naked honesty and humility."[10]

Princeton Seminary colleague Geerhardus Vos described Machen as "a profound scholar," but more importantly "a great man of God, and a true defender of our Christian faith."[11] Another Princeton colleague, Caspar Wistar Hodge, called him a personal friend whom he loved, and "the greatest theologian in the English-speaking world."[12] A Presbyterian minister described him as a man "of intense convictions and wonderful courage ... a man of principle ... who gave his heart wholly and unreservedly to the Lord

---

9 Pearl S. Buck, "Tribute," Machen Collection, Princeton Seminary.

10 Henry W. Coray, *J. Gresham Machen: A Silhouette* (Grand Rapids: Kregel, 1981).

11 *Presbyterian Guardian* 3 (January 23, 1937): 189, http://opc.org/cfh/guardian/Volume_3/1937-01-23.pdf.

12 Ibid.

Jesus Christ."[13]

Machen died January 1, 1937, in North Dakota. Exhausted and already ill, he had traveled west to encourage three new OPC congregations, but only was able to preach at one.

Minnie Gresham Machen instilled in her son Gresham a deep understanding of the biblical principles on which the Reformed faith of the Presbyterian Church was founded. Gresham's heritage also taught him that the church has a distinct role in the world to spread the gospel message, and that honest intellectual inquiry was not to be feared, but embraced. We see that she used her own training to establish an intellectual and spiritual household, where love of knowledge generally and Scripture especially were taught through example and instruction. Minnie Machen's influence on her son continues to have a lasting impact on all who seek to participate in and preserve the biblically sound beliefs and teachings of the Reformed faith. Our prayer is that the Lord would bless our efforts as mothers to continue this tradition of raising our covenant children in the faith through the help of the Orthodox Presbyterian Church.[14]

**Katherine VanDrunen** *is the Reference Librarian at Westminster Seminary California. She is a member of Escondido OPC and lives in that city with her husband, David, and son, Jack. She is currently working on turning into a book her PhD dissertation entitled* Foothills of the Matterhorn: Familial Antecedents of J. Gresham Machen.

---

13  Ibid. (quoting Rev. Maitland Alexander).
14  For further reference, see Stonehouse, *J. Gresham Machen*. My dissertation expands on this and adds information from various archives, and Minnie's personal diary.

# 2

# Hattie DeWaard:
# Doing What's Right

## *Mary Jo Miller*

She was raised in one denomination, followed her husband into another, and they were driven to a third. My mother, Hattie Smitter DeWaard, was fiercely loyal, but her loyalty was not the kind that thinks, "My church, right or wrong," nor even "My husband, right or wrong." She was among those women who stood beside their husbands and in their churches, committed to the principles of the historic Reformed faith at a time of great stress and confusion. She was privileged to be part of the Orthodox Presbyterian Church during its first 52 years.

Hattie was born on July 26, 1895, on a Michigan farm along the Grand River. Her parents, Jacob and Elsie Smitter, came from the Netherlands. They brought with them a heritage of staunch Calvinism and convictions about sacrificing for their faith. Jacob's sister and her husband had a neighboring farm. As the two families grew, a problem became apparent. J. R. Brink, missionary-at-large for Classis Grand Rapids of the Christian Reformed Church, remembered:

> Sometime during the year 1901 or 1902, a certain Mr. Smitter came to our Seminary, and requested that students be sent to Plainfield, to preach on Sunday evenings. He stated that they were living some nine miles from their church, and as they were unable to attend regularly, or send their children to

catechism classes (this was several years before the general use of automobiles) the latter were not getting what they needed.

This request was granted, but presented quite a problem, as the students had to be called for with horse and buggy, and an 18 mile round trip back of a dobbin (farm horse) was something to be reckoned with, especially as it had to be repeated again to return the student.

The first student to preach at Plainfield was called for by Mr. Smitter. But on the way back they were involved in an accident. The horse caught one of his hoofs in a street car cable opening and broke his leg. The result was they had to walk the next 7 miles to the home of Mr. Smitter.

It was a bad start, and the horse was no doubt a major loss, but the story didn't end there. Every week Jacob went to get a student preacher from Calvin Seminary. The two families were joined by others in the community each Lord's Day. They found an abandoned church building to renovate. There were ten families on the rolls when Louis Berkhof conducted the organizing service for the new church in 1906.[1] This Christian Reformed Church, with its active young people's group and emphasis on good teaching, was Hattie's church home.

Her parents put a high priority on education, but when, at the age of 24, Hattie wanted to go into nurses' training, she met stiff opposition. Along with many of their generation, her parents thought nursing was demeaning for a nice girl. Hattie, however, had a vision of it as kingdom service and was not dissuaded, even though her father offered to buy her a piano if she would stay home.

Nursing school was hard, with unaccustomed academic work, long hours, frequent night duty, and emotional cost. She never forgot the pain of seeing new mothers die from the influenza pandemic after World War I. She graduated and became a registered nurse in 1921. Although she only worked full time for a few years,

1  Louis Berkhof was a professor and later president of Calvin Seminary from 1906 to 1944. His *Systematic Theology* is still in use.

she went back to part-time nursing at various times until she was almost 80.

While still in training, Hattie was part of the local church in spite of her irregular schedule. She remembered coming off duty at the hospital, knowing she was late for church, but running all the way to get there in time for the sermon from R. B. Kuiper.[2] At Sunday evening hymn sings she met John DeWaard, a Calvin pre-seminary student. They were both from large farm families with immigrant parents committed to the Reformed faith. They both loved canoeing, long walks, and singing the Psalms in Dutch. At first, Hattie attempted to discourage John's strong interest as she was absorbed in her training. Their four-year courtship was marked by difficulties and separations. They learned to share decision-making and financial choices long before they could get married.

One difficult decision was John's choice of seminary. His classis pressed him to continue at Calvin, and he felt an obligation to those who had furthered his education so far. Yet the prospect of studying under a faculty that included Robert Dick Wilson, J. Gresham Machen, and Geerhardus Vos, made Princeton Seminary a strong draw.

As they corresponded about this, Hattie wrote, "I wish you were here with me tonight so we could talk more about you going to Princeton. In your letter today I feel that you have not yet decided. I hate the thought of not seeing you, but I do so want to see you go."

He wrote back: "You will always help me decide, as you are doing now ... I am convinced that my darling would do what she thought was best for me, even to the extent of sacrificing her own interests."

Perhaps the deciding factor was the example of his close friend,

2 R. B. Kuiper was pastor of Sherman Street Christian Reformed Church from 1917 to 1923. Later he served as president of Calvin College, professor at Westminster Theological Seminary, and president of Calvin Seminary.

Cornelius Van Til,[3] because a few days later Hattie got this letter: "Tuesday evening Van Til was here. He is absolutely going to Princeton and I am as surely going with him. You are destined to be alone for a long time."

In 1922, with several friends from Calvin, John left for New Jersey. Hattie worked in Grand Rapids and sent money when she could. Midway through his studies at Princeton, they were married on November 22, 1923. Their first child, Leona, is

John and Hattie DeWaard on their wedding day, November 22, 1923

said to have been pushed in her baby carriage by Dr. Vos.

In 1925 the elders of First Presbyterian Church in Cedar Grove, Wisconsin, wrote to Princeton Seminary for suggestions about possible candidates for their pulpit. Dr. Vos gave them John DeWaard's name. John was well matched to this largely Dutch farming community, speaking their language and understanding their work. Many years later a man from Cedar Grove said, "John DeWaard was the best pastor we ever had. He put on his overalls and helped with the haying." At the age of 33, John was finally able to provide a home for his Hattie. And it was a lovely home: a gracious two-story parsonage right next to a four-year-old church building with stained glass windows and an Austin organ. Though now in a new denomination, Hattie found the faith and practice she knew from childhood.

Four more little DeWaards were born during the Cedar Grove years. It was a good place for a happy childhood. They all went

3 Cornelius "Kees" Van Til, was John's classmate in preparatory school, college, and seminary. Their friendship was a lifelong comfort to both.

to the same one-room school. They went sledding on cold winter nights and saw the Aurora Borealis. In summer, when the truck went by on its way to the canning factory, they would run behind, snatching at the vines spilling out and eating the tender young peas.

In addition to raising her own family, Hattie found time to help other mothers. The local doctor often called on her to assist with births, usually home births in those days. Her children remember her being called in the middle of the night to drive to some distant farm. At harvest time she might be paid with a bushel of apples.

But there were gathering clouds. John's diligence in teaching his people began to lead to conflict. When humanism was found in Sunday school material provided by the denomination, when missionaries supported by the Presbyterian Church were promoting a social gospel, when men were being ordained who did not believe in the virgin birth of Christ, the congregation in Cedar Grove heard about it from their pastor. When he raised such issues at presbytery, he was rebuked. Twenty-five members of the congregation signed a petition to presbytery requesting his removal from their pulpit because they were uncomfortable with his criticisms. A vote of confidence from 372 others, however, showed that most of the congregation understood the seriousness of these issues.

As the conflict progressed from congregation to presbytery to general assembly, the pressure increased at home too. In later years, Hattie admitted that sometimes she simply became irritated at the constant drama when all she was trying to do was keep her busy family clean and fed. Yet it never seems to have occurred to her that the trouble could have been avoided. She knew John was right to fight. She also knew the probable consequences. As they discussed the future and possible loss of income, she made him promise not to be swayed by that consideration: "Don't forget, I can always get work as a nurse."

One Monday morning when she was in the basement doing laundry, John came down from the study with a letter in his hand. "If I send this, we will lose everything." They didn't need to discuss it further. They both knew that he would lose his job, the pension, and their home. "Just do what's right, John," she said, going on with her work.

The end of his 15-year pastorate at First Presbyterian Church was public and dramatic. Nineteen-year-old Edna Voskuil told it this way:

> On June 7, 1936 Rev. DeWaard did not lead a disorderly secession from the house of God. He did not ask us, nobody else asked us or even hinted to us to walk out of the church when Mr. Whitney was to declare the pulpit vacant. I walked out because I could not remain to see such a terrible thing in God's house, to see our beloved pastor, our spiritual guide, who had always preached the whole gospel as contained in the Scriptures, who dared to stand up for Jesus our only Savior, who loved the blessed truth more than himself or his position, or honor among his fellowmen, who had taught me in his Bible classes, torn from us so unreasonably.

As John left his pulpit after the benediction that morning, he was simply heading to his study. He did not choose to stay and listen to the presbytery's declaration that he was no longer allowed to preach in the Presbyterian Church. Hattie got up and followed him because she couldn't help but stand with him. Twelve-year-old Leona was startled to find herself left alone in the pew with the younger children. She got up too, and they all went after their mother and father. More than 300 people walked out that morning, leaving behind the building they had sacrificed to build.

The following Sunday they met in the village hall/fire station. Leona remembers that service: "There were no hymn books, but we sang our hearts out." The elders quickly organized, called Mr. DeWaard as pastor, joined the new denomination we now know as the Orthodox Presbyterian Church, and began digging the basement of a new church building.

At home, things changed too. The family moved to a farm house without indoor plumbing or telephone. Hattie baked bread in the wood burning stove, and John raked out the coals each evening.

The outhouse caught fire one night—maybe one of the children had been playing with those coals! The whole family formed a bucket brigade and saved the barn. There was no sense of hardship as the family settled down. Leona still remembers thinking, "Daddy was brave and Mother was good."

On the national level there was opportunity and optimism in the new denomination. In 1939 a Dutch Reformed group in Rochester, New York, joined the OPC. In the same city were several large Presbyterian Churches. It was thought that as modernism grew, many from these churches would seek out the OPC, and the seed group could become an important witness for historic Presbyterianism under the right leadership. John DeWaard would be just the man for the job.

In 1940 John accepted the call to Memorial Church in Rochester. The DeWaards appreciated the better educational opportunities for the children, but it was a difficult move. They left a place where they had been deeply loved. They came to a congregation that had not been a part of the fight which had consumed them. The influx of people seeking a true Presbyterian church didn't materialize. There was, perhaps, a sense of anticlimax. Hattie felt she was not quite what a pastor's wife was expected to be in this new community. But the domestic partnership was a solace to both of them. John still grew vegetables and fruit, and Hattie still canned and preserved much of what they ate. If Hattie as a nurse took a night duty case, John fixed the kids' lunches and mopped the floor. The older children started college, and the younger ones took music lessons.

World War II was a time of upheaval for everyone and, while John's application to serve as a chaplain was rejected because of his age, Hattie responded to the urgent call for nurses by returning to hospital work. Naturally, she found herself again caring for new mothers and babies. When, at the age of 48, she became a patient on the maternity floor herself, she and baby Mary received the very best of care from her admiring co-workers.

Mother was not an outstanding housekeeper, believing that a

vase of flowers from the garden would distract from a little dust. Her linen closet however, was a model of hospital tidiness, and she was often called upon to pull out the sheets for visitors. There were visiting seminary and denominational colleagues as well as family. When John Murray, from Westminster Seminary, was a guest, she darned his socks because, she said, "He has no wife." But in earlier Cedar Grove days she put her foot down when another bachelor, J. Gresham Machen, left his shoes outside his door for polishing, according to a European custom. John did the honors that time.

An autocratic old lady also visited. This was Miss Marguerite Montgomery. Over the years she was a frequent dinner or afternoon guest, but when she was between housekeepers, she came for extended stays. She had an interest in Westminster and enjoyed discussing ecclesiastical issues with Dad. Her desire to memorialize her only brother eventually resulted in the Montgomery library building at the seminary. On her death in 1958 she left her home to Mother and Dad. Mother remarked that God doesn't always use pensions to provide for his children.

Perhaps Mother's favorite guests were the young couples who came to meet with the pastor. Many of the young people, whose world had broadened by social changes during the war years, were dating outside of Reformed circles. Instead of scolding, Dad insisted on careful instruction of both partners before he would marry them. Mother had an affinity for those who were new to the Reformed faith, and warmly welcomed these new friends. Eventually these couples formed a network of young families in the church. When Dad retired in 1959, they gathered to celebrate with him.

But before that year was out, God took him home. He had gone to Canada, where he was in demand as pulpit supply because he could preach in Dutch. On Sunday morning he was found to have died during the night of heart failure. Mother was a widow at the age of 64. It wouldn't be true to say she couldn't get along without Dad. Her strong independence and the principles she shared with him made her long widowhood very productive. One goal they had shared was the education of the children, and she worked hard to assure that the two youngest finished college after their father died. But the loss of his spiritual leadership and his wise, discerning companionship was immense. When she believed that a sister denomination was starting to adapt to the world as the Presbyterian Church had done, her distress sometimes spilled over into harshness. She missed him very much.

In her final years, Mother returned to Michigan. Friends of those years remember her deep love for the Orthodox Presbyterian Church, especially for young churches and young people. Her brother, Lee Smitter, told her about a little mission work in the country and the abandoned church building he had found for their use. It was not far from where they had grown up. Perhaps they were thinking of their father's example. She spent hours driving around the area making contacts and did all she could to encourage those responsible to seek the help of the Orthodox Presbyterian Church. In time she had the joy of going to Spencer Mills OPC with a car full of grandchildren.

In 1976 Mother's interest in young churches took her on a visit to Maine, where she had sweet fellowship with the congregation of the little church in Rockport. There were old friends to keep up with too, and she continued to exchange letters and visits with Kees and Rena Van Til. When Rena was recovering from surgery, Mother went to stay with her for a while and came home with a vivid little story of Kees fixing breakfast for the ladies, then standing at the foot of the stairs singing, "When morning gilds the skies, my heart awaking cries, May Jesus Christ be praised.... THE OATMEAL'S READY!"

Those last years also brought some very fulfilling new friendships. A young Cal Cummings introduced her to Edie Hodge.[4] Edie later said,

> I loved your mother and can't thank God enough for her wonderful testimony of God's grace in her life. She certainly was a

---

4 Cal and Edie Cummings have served as missionaries in Japan.

blessing to me, a young, ignorant, newly converted Christian who needed lots of counsel and wisdom from God's Word. Not coming from a Christian home, I wanted to know more about how she raised her children, and what a Christian family looked like. I also wanted to understand the Reformed faith, of which I knew nothing, coming from a non-church background.

In 1977 Bill and Pat Dennison moved to Grand Rapids. Bill's admiration for Cornelius Van Til won Mother's heart immediately. They enjoyed many good talks, and when Dr. Van Til made his last trip to Grand Rapids, they shared the excitement of hearing him preach one more time. Pat was a faithful visitor even as my mother's health failed. She told me:

> I would visit with our two children to help brighten her day. I hoped to teach our children how to serve the elderly ... We would sit in her living room and she would quote Scripture by memory and tell of the early struggles in the church and how she tried to be a supportive wife to your father at a time when things were very tough. I loved her steadfastness, her resilience, her stubbornness.

Pat was still visiting Mother during the last few days of her life.

From childhood, Mother knew the promises of Scripture to be "true and firm in every part." Yet, what she believed so passionately, she sometimes struggled to know personally. A sense of unworthiness often plagued her. Her hunger for the ministry of the Word intensified. The day she died, November 25, 1988, she saw the Bible in a visiting pastor's hand, pushed away her lunch tray, and asked him to read. The pastor was Douglas Clawson and the passage was Revelation 21.

At her funeral this hymn was sung:

> By grace I am an heir of heaven. Why doubt this, oh my
>     trembling heart?
> If what the scriptures promise clearly is true and firm in every
>     part,

This also must be truth divine: by grace a crown of life is
mine.[5]

**Mary Jo Miller,** *the youngest of the six DeWaard children, lives in
Wheaton, Illinois, with her husband, Jerry. A lifelong member of the
Orthodox Presbyterian Church, Mary was baptized by her father at
Memorial Church in Rochester and now belongs to Grace Church in
Hanover Park.*

5 Hymn 584, *Trinity Hymnal* (Philadelphia: Great Commission Publications, 1961).

# 3

# Mary Rothwell,
# Nellie Rothwell,
# Mary Shillito Stevenson,
# Beatrice Shillito,
# Marguerite Montgomery,
# Anna Rath,
# and Gertrude Mead:
# The Grace of Giving

*Judith M. Dinsmore*

The offering plate comes around every Sunday, and every Sunday, Christians give. Without giving, the Orthodox Presbyterian Church would cease. Indeed, without giving, the OPC would never have been. Founded in 1936, the church struggled to gain financial footing in the middle of the Great Depression, and closely linked to its fate was the stability of Westminster Theological Seminary, founded in 1929. If one shook, the other did, too. And in the '30s, both were shaking. Several women of means, intimately involved with the OPC since its inception, stepped into the gap and gave generously to both institutions, sometimes making a crucial difference. Other women, similarly convinced that the OPC's doors must stay open despite the costs, gave not of their abundance but of their lack, donating all in bequests. All the women whose stories follow were cultivators of the grace of giving, heeding the apostle Paul's words: "But just as you excel in everything ... see that you also excel in this grace of giving" (2 Cor. 8:7).

### Mary Rothwell and Nellie Rothwell: "Spiritual Backbone"

Nellie and Mary Rothwell had been members of Forest Presbyterian Church (USA) in Middletown, Delaware, for their whole lives when in 1932 their church acquired a new pastor, a recent graduate of Westminster Theological Seminary named Robert Graham.[1] He would have been a young man compared to the Rothwell sisters when he arrived, and in his memoir Graham remembered "Forest Church" and "the Rothwells" in the same breath. "Outstanding among the saints in that church were the elderly Rothwell sisters, Mary and Nellie, who, altho[ugh] wanting in physical beauty were rich in the beauty of soul and Christian fortitude." Both sisters, Graham wrote, were interested and up-to-date on the affairs of the PCUSA. "[Mary] who was blind taught the adult class and Nellie, as her eyes, kept her informed on the apostasy which was moving in rapidly over the entire Presbyterian Church in the USA."

The "apostasy" that concerned the Rothwells, which included the PCUSA's landmark support of the Auburn Affirmation in 1923,[2] had also led J. Gresham Machen to leave his professorship at Princeton Seminary, long a bastion of the Reformed faith but now accepting equivocation on orthodoxy. Machen then founded Westminster Theological Seminary in 1929. The Rothwell sisters quickly became zealous supporters of the seminary.

Then in 1933 matters came to a head again, this time sparked by

1 "Today in OPC History—Robert Graham, March 28," OPC, http://opc.org/today.html?history_id=141.
2 The Auburn Affirmation claimed to protect the unity and liberty of the Presbyterian Church and was signed by over 1,200 ministers. It denied the right of the church to establish certain fundamental truths as tests of theological orthodoxy. These truths included the virgin birth of Christ, his substitutionary atonement and bodily resurrection, and miracles.

policies adopted by the PCU-SA's foreign missions board. Machen and others formed the Independent Board of Presbyterian Foreign Missions on the reasoning that the PCUSA's was no longer biblically sound. The fallout from this parachurch board and the subsequent discipline of Machen lasted years— and eventually resulted, in 1936, in the formation of the OPC (originally called the Presbyterian Church of America).

Mary and Nellie Rothwell

Back in Middletown, Delaware, the Rothwell sisters and their fellow congregants knew exactly where they stood. Graham wrote, "When ... the Independent Board for Presbyterian Foreign Missions was established, the Rothwell sisters stood with their pastor and greatly strengthened him in leading Forest Church to stand behind the Independent Board. When the crisis came [the formation of the OPC] ... the members of old Forest Church almost unanimously voted to withdraw from the PCUSA."

But the Rothwell sisters' support did not end there. Leaving the PCUSA meant that Forest Church would lose their building, so Nellie and Mary stepped in. "It was the Rothwell sisters who spurred us on to build a church at once by informing us on the day we were evicted from Forest that they were giving us two fine lots at Rehoboth Beach, Del[aware], to our new church."[3] The church was renamed Grace OPC, and Mary broke the ground for the new building.[4]

3 Robert Graham, *My Presbyterian Pilgrimage*, courtesy of Margaret Duff.
4 *Presbyterian Guardian* 6 (March 1939): 59, http://www.opc.org/cfh/guardian/Volume_6/1939-03.pdf.

However, Mary and Nellie Rothwell were not members of Grace for long. Mary passed away in December 1938, two years after Grace OPC was founded. When Nellie contracted lobar pneumonia a month later leading to her death in 1939, she called Robert Graham to her bedside. "She wanted me to have a Will drawn up at once with all to the [OPC—then called PCA] and $1,500 to our new Grace Church," he wrote.[5]

The sale of their personal goods amounted to some $5,000. However, the will also included a hundred-acre farm in the country near Middletown. Graham ran it in tandem with a tenant-farmer for a year, but then sold it to the farmer. Graham remembered, "Mr. Marsden in a letter of appreciation to me from the Committee [on Home Missions and Church Extension] said that the Rothwell bequest undoubtedly saved the church from bankruptcy. Missionaries at that time were receiving a very small part of their already very small salary."

A June report from the Committee on Home Missions and Church Extension contains this delighted note: "All back salaries and allowances, including those owed for the period prior to May 31, 1937, have been paid. This was made possible through the receipt of the personal estate of Miss Nellie Pryce Rothwell ... It is the cause of great rejoicing to note that the committee entered upon the present fiscal year with no obligations which it was unable to meet."[6]

And in a later report, more details were provided: "The legacy of Miss Nellie Pryce Rothwell, a faithful member of the Grace Orthodox Presbyterian Church of Middletown, Delaware, has been paid in full to the committee as residuary legatee. The proceeds from the sale of the Rothwell farm, after all charges against it were paid, amounted to $10,355.38. The committee, believing that it was Miss Rothwell's intention that the Committee on Foreign Missions

5  Ibid.

6  "Home Missions Report," *Presbyterian Guardian* 7 (June 25, 1940): 180, http://opc.org/cfh/guardian/Volume_7/1940-06-25.pdf.

should share in the estate, granted $2,500 of this amount to the Committee on Foreign Missions. Of the remaining $7,855.38, $2,900 was invested in a mortgage and two loans, $568.33 was used for survey and extension work, $323.54 was used for Jewish work, $382.60 is on hand, and the remaining $3,680.91 was used to meet monthly deficits in general missionary expenses, in accord with the committee's expanded budget."[7]

The Rothwells gave financially to the OPC at a critical time in its history—but they also gave so much more than money. After Nellie passed away, Graham is quoted in the *Presbyterian Guardian*, "I shall miss them because of the encouragement they gave me in times of discouragement ... For five years it has been my privilege to meet with them 20 minutes before the morning service for a time of prayer for the services of the day. Any pastor who has had two such persons as these in his congregation will realize how great is our loss."[8]

"In a very unobtrusive way," Graham later reflected in his memoir, "these humble sisters were the spiritual backbone of the church."[9]

### Mary Shillito Stevenson and Beatrice Shillito: More than Socialites

Mary Shillito Stevenson was born in 1883 in Cincinnati, Ohio, and her sister, Beatrice, was born one year later, in 1884. Their father was president of the Shillito Department Store and their mother, according to a newspaper of the time, was "considered one of Cincinnati's most beautiful women."[10] Although members of Cincinnati's leading society, the sisters gracefully became so much

7 "Home Missions Report," *Presbyterian Guardian* 9 (June 25, 1941): 183, http://opc.org/cfh/guardian/Volume_9/1941-06-25.pdf.

8 *Presbyterian Guardian* 6 (March 1939): 59, http://www.opc.org/cfh/guardian/Volume_6/1939-03.pdf.

9 Robert Graham, *My Presbyterian Pilgrimage*, courtesy of Margaret Duff.

10 *Cincinnati Enquirer*, July 7, 1929, http://cincinnati.newspapers.com/newspage/100502805/.

more than simply socialites—they became, each in their own way, agitators for a cause they believed in wholeheartedly: the Orthodox Presbyterian Church.

On October 23, 1917, at the age of 34, Mary married Frank H. Stevenson, pastor of Covenant-First Presbyterian Church of Cincinnati. A promising graduate of Princeton Seminary and an associate of J. Gresham Machen, Frank did not hesitate to align himself with the conservative voices inside the PCUSA. When Westminster Theological Seminary was founded in 1929, Frank was the first chairman of its board of trustees, serving until 1932. A contemporary of Frank's later wrote that "[Frank] was the guiding spirit in the administrative policies of the seminary. His large experience as an executive served to prepare him in a peculiar way for the tasks of steering the ship through the rough seas of the worst financial depression that this country has ever seen, and which overtook America only one month after Westminster was founded. Much credit must be given to him for guiding the seminary in a remarkable way, so that the infant institution remained free of debt."[11] He died suddenly of a heart attack in 1934, at only age 51.[12]

Now widowed, Mary Stevenson did not just sit at home dressed in black. In spring 1935 she and Beatrice were aware of the PCUSA trial of Machen in Trenton, New Jersey, for matters related to the formation of the Independent Board. He was found guilty and eventually suspended from ministry.[13] That sparked the sisters to action.

Later that year, when the general assembly of the PCUSA met in Cincinnati, Mary was an active part of a Christian Assembly formed in Cincinnati in reaction to the proceedings of the general

---

11  Edwin Rian, *Presbyterian Conflict* (Grand Rapids: Eerdmans, 1940), 59.

12  *Journal News* (Hamilton, OH), August 3, 1934, http://www.newspapers.com/newspage/36171281/.

13  D. G. Hart and John Muether, "The Word of God versus the Word of Man," *Fighting the Good Fight*, Part 1, http://www.opc.org/books/fighting/pt1.html.

assembly, although such attempts were "most unusual."[14] The Christian Assembly, as they dubbed themselves, hoped to be a medium through which Bible-believing Christians could protest the modernism overrunning the PCUSA.[15] Beatrice—who was "very earnest"—was named the assistant secretary.[16] Those who joined did not do so lightly. It was stigmatizing to so protest. The assembly quickly fizzled, but when a local chapter of the similar but better-organized Presbyterian Constitutional Covenant Union, based in Philadelphia, was founded in Cincinnati in October 1935, both Beatrice and Mary were on the front lines. Beatrice once again acted as secretary, and Mary hosted some of the meetings in her home. These two organizations, and the rallies and meetings they held, were crucial forerunners to the founding of the OPC and a highly visible challenge to the PCUSA. They also signaled to other key leaders inside the conservative movement, such as Machen, Charles Woodbridge, and Edwin Rian, that Cincinnati would welcome and support them. Machen later wrote, "I am tremendously impressed with the opportunities in Cincinnati. It strikes me as one of the greatest privileges that I have had."[17] Mary and Beatrice were both present at Machen's unsuccessful appeal in Syracuse, New York, in June 1936.

And yet, standing with Machen and the other conservatives did not come without its costs. Convinced of the PCUSA's errors, including defrocking Machen who was a close friend of hers and her late husband's, Mary decided to leave the PCUSA congregation

14 Elizabeth Buckner, "History of the Formation of the Trinity Presbyterian Church of America," presented orally at First Anniversary Banquet, Cincinnati, Ohio, June 28, 1937.
15 Ibid. Buckner recorded, "This Assembly's enactments were so controlled by its Modernist leaders that Dr. Machen and other like-minded individuals were openly flaunted; and those who were members of the Independent Board for Presbyterian Missions were later ejected from the Assembly."
16 Ibid.
17 J. Gresham Machen, letter to Rev. Everett C. DeVelde, August 1936, OPC archives.

in Cincinnati, Covenant-First, even though her husband had pastored it for 13 years and her family had worshipped there for five generations. As a member of Cincinnati's elite, Mary's move would not have gone unnoticed or uncriticized. She composed a compelling letter to its leadership explaining her decision: "How can I help but love every member of that dear church?" she wrote. "However … the constant refusal of the General Assembly to admit the presence of modernism and to take measures of reform concerning it, has led me to sever relations with the Presbyterian Church in the U.S.A."[18] By so doing, Mary "sacrificed all that was dearest to her heart in tender church associations, in order to testify to the world the strength of the convictions she professed."[19]

Mary became a member of newly established Trinity OPC in Cincinnati, whose organizing pastor was Everett C. DeVelde. De-Velde, a member of Westminster's first graduating class, had left Princeton when Machen left. In 1939 DeVelde proposed to the Fifth General Assembly that their name be changed to the Orthodox Presbyterian Church. A name-change was necessary because of a lawsuit brought against them that claimed their first name, Presbyterian Church of America, was too similar to Presbyterian Church (USA).[20] Tradition has it that it was Mary Shillito Stevenson and Beatrice Shillito who suggested the new name to DeVelde. While there is no documentary proof that the Shillito sisters came up with the name "OPC," it's at the very least a good guess that they were promoting it, given their connections and frequent correspondence with Machen and DeVelde at the time.[21]

---

18 "Mrs. Frank H. Stevenson Gives Her Reasons," *Presbyterian Guardian* 3 (December 12, 1936): 109, http://www.opc.org/cfh/guardian/Volume_3/1936-12-12.pdf.

19 Elizabeth Buckner, "History of the Formation of the Trinity Presbyterian Church of America," presented orally at First Anniversary Banquet, Cincinnati, Ohio, June 28, 1937.

20 "Today in OPC History—Everett C. DeVelde Sr., May 19" Orthodox Presbyterian Church, http://opc.org/today.html?history_id=189.

21 Machen had written of his preference for the word "orthodox." See J.

Now fully committed to the small band of the OPC, Mary continued to use her social standing to aid it; she travelled, headed up fundraising campaigns, and often addressed ladies' teas or meetings. She also opened her home for presbyteries and assemblies. In one *Presbyterian Guardian* article, her home was described as "an oasis of relaxation after the tension of the assembly."[22]

She was unswervingly loyal to the seminary, as evidenced in a letter to Carl McIntire, founder of the Bible Presbyterian Church, after he implied the opposite, "My love for Westminster Seminary and all that it stands for and the little I am able to do for it does in no way make me presume to dictate to those whom I revere and honor and whom I consider to be the greatest teachers and scholars of the Bible in the Protestant world today … reassure your readers of my full confidence and unswerving loyalty to the Faculty and the Seminary."[23] Her loyalty was so intact, she was part of a 1937 campaign to raise one million dollars for the seminary.[24] Mary established the Frank H. Stevenson Fellowship in 1935 ($1,500 for the purposes of studying abroad, a significant amount for the time)[25] and the Frank H. Stevenson Graduate Scholarship, both in memory of her husband.[26] She was active as president of the Women's Auxiliary of Westminster Theological Seminary until two years before her death in Cincinnati in 1962 at the age of 81.[27]

---

Gresham Machen, "What Is Orthodoxy?" *Presbyterian Guardian* 1 (November 4, 1935): 38, http://opc.org/cfh/guardian/Volume_1/1935-11-04.pdf.

22 "Other Assembly Events," *Presbyterian Guardian* 7 (June 25, 1940): 186, http://opc.org/cfh/guardian/Volume_7/1940-06-25.pdf.

23 Letter to Carl McIntire, June 29, 1937, OPC archives.

24 See "Machen Memorial Fund Committee Announces Plans and Appointments, *Presbyterian Guardian* 3 (March 27, 1937): 247, http://opc.org/cfh/guardian/Volume_3/1937-03-27.pdf.

25 The first recipient was E. J. Young.

26 See Robert S. Marsden, excerpt from *The First Ten Years* (Philadelphia: OPC Committee on Home Missions and Church Extension, 1946), http://www.opc.org/books/FirstTenYears.html.

27 See *Presbyterian Guardian* 31 (March 1962): 38, http://opc.org/cfh/guardian/Volume_31/1962-03.pdf.

Beatrice Shillito, like her sister, was a socialite-turned-activist, although unlike her sister, she never married. Active her whole life in clubs, associations, guilds, committees, and societies, Beatrice was appalled that those in the PCUSA cared so little for their own forms of governance: "[It is a] sad spectacle of the extreme indifference and smug satisfaction of the people in the pews in so many cities, as they do not know one thing about what has been taking place in their own denomination, and do not even show as much concern as is always shown in political parties, or civic organizations, or men's and women's clubs when drastic changes are under way ... The measures taken and the methods used in the U.S.A. church would never have been accepted in the business world nor law courts as I know them."[28]

She, like her sister, left Covenant-First (PCUSA) in Cincinnati, explaining in a letter to its pastor that, "I give thanks to Almighty God that in these radical and destructive days I can join such a sincere and consecrated group as I find in the [OPC]."[29] Beatrice was enrolled as a constituting member of the new denomination.[30]

Now in the OPC, Beatrice's administrative work proliferated. She and Mary served on the finance committee of the brand-new OPC congregation in Cincinnati. Described as an "indefatigable worker," Beatrice also gave generously, "taking over many expenses of the new organization [the OPC] very privately, but with great effect ... and, with her never failing cheer, has assisted us wonderfully."[31] Beatrice and Mary conferred with Machen on which sermons to give on a visit to Cincinnati in 1936.[32] Beatrice remembered

---

28  Letter to Rev. Frank R. Elder, Covenant-First Presbyterian Church, August 18, 1936, OPC archives.

29  Ibid.

30  Minutes of the First Assembly of the PCA (now OPC), June 11, 1936: 5.

31  Elizabeth Buckner, "History of the Formation of the Trinity Presbyterian Church of America," presented orally at First Anniversary Banquet, Cincinnati, Ohio, June 28, 1937.

32  Letter from J. Gresham Machen to Rev. Everett C. DeVelde, June 1936, OPC archives: "As Miss Shillito will probably explain to you, she and Mrs.

later that "Dr. Machen wrote to me in Cin[cinnati] when our orthodox church started there and I had entire charge of its publicity then vital to Dr. Machen and his cause."[33] When the church broke ground on its new property in 1939, it was purchased by Beatrice as acting chairman of the financial committee of the new church. At that point, three-fourths of the funds needed for the new building had been raised by the congregation, at least in part through the fundraising skills of Beatrice herself.

In the 1950s, after the Cincinnati church closed its doors, Beatrice joined the Bible Presbyterian Church and directed her efforts and finances there. In her 70s, Beatrice stood by what she had always maintained: "What was smoldering in Dr. Machen's day has now burst into flames. I thank the good Lord for letting me live to see it."[34] Beatrice died in Cincinnati, Ohio, in 1964 at the age of 80.

## Marguerite Montgomery: A Vision for Education

If you've ever been inside the library at Westminster Theological Seminary in Philadelphia, chances are you've heard of Marguerite Montgomery. The three-story stone building which now houses several valuable collections was made possible through the estate of Marguerite Montgomery, in honor of her brother, James.

Born in 1861, Marguerite was the great-granddaughter of Rochester, New York's founder, Nathaniel Rochester. Never marrying, she was of considerable means thanks to her inheritance and various real estate ventures. She served on the Independent Board for Presbyterian Foreign Missions, but, out of theological concerns, resigned after Machen was ousted as president.[35] Marguerite was

---

Stevenson and I had a conference about my forthcoming sermons [in Cincinnati]."

33 Letter to Carl McIntire, July 18, 1959, courtesy of Princeton Theological Seminary Library.

34 Ibid.

35 See Edwin Rian, *The Presbyterian Conflict*, Appendix, note 27, http://opc.org/books/conflict/appendix.html.

enrolled as a constituting member of the OPC (then called PCA)[36] and became a member of Covenant OPC in Rochester.

Also a member of the Independent Board, Rev. John DeWaard became a close friend of Marguerite's. When DeWaard became pastor of a nearby sister church, Memorial OPC, which didn't have a manse, she gave him and his family a spacious house. In later years, when her health failed, she stayed with De-Waard and his family for extended visits. When she passed away, she left her own home and its contents to them.

Marguerite Montgomery and Mary Clements

In 1949, when Covenant OPC began construction on a new 220-person church building, Marguerite was not only on the building committee, she broke the first shovelful at the ground-breaking ceremony—at 88 years of age![37] One could surmise that she contributed generously to the new building, as well as turning over the first dirt.

Marguerite's financial generosity helped other churches in the young denomination as well. Rev. John Galbraith pastored Geth-semane PCA/OPC in Philadelphia from 1937–1940. At first the church rented "a little storefront where the walls sweated in the wintertime from the heat," but as the church grew, they wanted

---

36 Minutes of the First General Assembly of the PCA (now OPC), June 11, 1936: 5.

37 "Church Building to Be Erected on Hoover Drive," *Greece Press*, Greece, New York, May 5, 1949, http://fultonhistory.com/newspapers%206/ Greece%20NY%20Press/Greece%20NY%20Press%201948%20-%20 1950%20Grayscale/Greece%20NY%20Press%201948%20-%201950%20 Grayscale%20-%200136.pdf.

to buy property.[38] Marguerite is one of the people Galbraith asked to consider loaning money for the purchase. She replied, "Well, before I give you an answer, I am going to come and hear you preach."[39] He must have passed the test, because she did indeed loan the money.

From the very beginning of the OPC, however, Marguerite was especially interested in Westminster, perhaps because of her own talents as a historian and scholar (she founded a society for women in Rochester called the American History Class, at which they listened to lectures). She travelled to the seminary regularly, for commencement exercises and graduations, and served for years as vice-president of its Women's Auxiliary.[40] In 1939 Marguerite funded a scholarship at Westminster in her brother's name. According to the seminary's minutes, two scholarships for graduate study, plus free tuition and free room, at the amount of $300 each, were to be awarded, as well as two scholarships for undergraduate study in slightly lesser amounts. The James H. Montgomery Scholarship Fund is still in existence today.

Marguerite maintained a close correspondence with Paul Woolley, then serving as the seminary's registrar and secretary. Whenever a particular need arose, Paul would write to Marguerite, asking for the funds to cover perhaps a dry season for the *Presbyterian Guardian* or an unexpected emergency at the seminary. He would also let her know if there was a student who needed a sponsor; correspondence from the 1940s demonstrates that Marguerite paid for the schooling and housing of at least three seminary students and their families: George Willis, Elmer Dortzbach, and Earl E. Zetterholm—each becoming an OPC minister. She also funded the publication and binding of the doctoral thesis of Fred Klooster, nephew of Cornelius Van Til and son-in-law of John DeWaard. By

38 Recording of interview by Charles Dennison of John Galbraith on December 13, 1990, OPC Archives.

39 Ibid.

40 See *Presbyterian Guardian* 27 (April 15, 1958): 58–59, http://www.opc.org/cfh/guardian/Volume_27/1958-04-15.pdf.

the tenth year of the seminary, she had donated over $24,000 to it—and that doesn't include her gifts to individual students![41] She did like to keep informed of both the seminary's and the *Presbyterian Guardian*'s financial state, and was wary of giving unless she knew exactly why, and for what purpose.

In her final years, Marguerite returned to St. Luke's Episcopal Church, longing to hear the liturgy of her youth. However, upon her death in 1958, she left an estate worth over a million dollars, of which two-thirds was bequeathed to Westminster (totaling a little in excess of $510,000)[42], again in honor and memory of her brother.

The money was used to build a library, a dire need for the seminary. "The present library of Westminster Seminary is regarded as one of the finest theological collections in the area," the *Presbyterian Guardian* reported in 1958. "It is housed, however, in a building which is completely full and which is very far from fireproof." It was so flammable, in fact, that its then-librarian, Arthur Kuschke, would leap out of bed whenever he heard a fire truck in the middle of the night and rush to the window to check if it was the seminary library that was burning. "The erection of the new building will mark a very real advance in the life of the Seminary," the *Presbyterian Guardian* article concluded.[43] It was finished and dedicated on May 22, 1963.

Marguerite, no doubt, would have been delighted.

## Anna Rath: "Gracious, Loving, Kind"

Anna K. Rath was a Midwesterner. Born in Wisconsin in 1867 to a German Reformed pastor and his wife, Anna later moved to

41  See letter from Paul Woolley to Marguerite Montgomery, December 29, 1947, courtesy of Westminster Theological Seminary.

42  See Minutes of Westminster Theological Seminary Board of Trustees Meeting, October 13, 1959, courtesy of Westminster Theological Seminary.

43  "Westminster Trustees Plan Montgomery Memorial," *Presbyterian Guardian* 27 (November 15, 1958): 152, http://opc.org/cfh/guardian/Volume_27/1958-11-15.pdf.

Anna K. Rath

Dubuque, Iowa, where she met and married Edward Rath in 1891. Edward's father, also a German immigrant, had founded a hugely successful meat-packing business that Edward eventually oversaw, quickly taking the company to new heights.[44] By 1910, after a move to Waterloo, Iowa, Edward and his partner had "grown the company to the fourth-largest slaughterhouse in Iowa."[45] Despite his wealth and success, however, Edward, a Presbyterian, was described as being an "unselfish and retiring man."[46] He passed away in 1930, leaving a sizable fortune to his wife. This was also the beginning of the Great Depression, and Anna was not slow in doing good.

George Haney, pastor of First OPC in Waterloo in the late '50s, remembered in an interview, "I lived in the manse and the people next door said one day, 'We understand that Mrs. Rath is in your church.' One lady said, 'What a wonderful woman that woman is,' and, 'You know during the Depression years she was well known for what she did here in Waterloo.' She said, 'I know of instances where people needed coal, or they needed food, and they would call Mrs. Rath and they would tell her about the need. And if they needed a ton of coal, she would call up the coal company and say deliver it to such and such an address. And if there was a

44 Rebecca Conrad, "Bringing Home the Bacon," Tall Grass Historians, http://www.cityofwaterlooiowa.com/images/PlanningZoning/pdf/bringin-homethebacon.pdf.
45 Ibid.
46 History of Black Hawk County, Iowa, and Its People, vol. C (Chicago: S. J. Clarke, 1915), ebook, http://archive.org/stream/historyofblackha02hart/historyofblackha02hart_djvu.txt.

need for food, she would go out to the grocery store and buy a supply of food and then come in her chauffeur-driven car and deliver that food to that home.' "[47]

A personal friend of Dr. Machen, with whom she corresponded, Anna also gave prolifically to Westminster Theological Seminary, as recorded by Rev. Robert S. Marsden, former general secretary of OPC Foreign and Home Missions. Marsden wrote for Anna's obituary: "After the death of Dr. Machen in 1937, when everyone was tempted to discouragement and it looked as if the whole Westminster/Orthodox Presbyterian movement might well fail, she made contributions of thousands of dollars per year for a number of years and, from all human points of view, the missions work and the Seminary might well have failed without her help."[48] Paul Woolley, acting as registrar and secretary of the seminary, wrote of Anna's help in the operating expenses of the *Presbyterian Guardian* "for some time now."[49]

When Waterloo formed its own OPC church in 1939, Anna became one of the nine original charter members. A history of that church records: "Almost from the very beginning of our efforts to found a work in Waterloo and during the years that followed, we were deeply indebted to Mrs. Anna K. Rath who graciously opened her home for our group. Sunday morning worship, midweek prayer and Bible study, and Saturday morning Bible classes for children were all held in her home during the unsettled years of our early history."[50] Continuing this pattern of hospitality, Anna opened her home to the Presbytery of Wisconsin for its fall presbytery meeting

---

47 George Haney, interview with Charles Dennison, http://www.opc.org/feature.html?feature_id=31.

48 "Anna K Rath," *Presbyterian Guardian* 29 (January 11, 1960): 8, http://www.opc.org/cfh/guardian/Volume_29/1960-01-11.pdf.

49 Letter from Paul Woolley to Marguerite Montgomery, June 10, 1947, courtesy of Westminster Theological Seminary.

50 Rev. Edward Wybenga, "A History of the Waterloo Orthodox Presbyterian Church," *History Christ Church Cedarloo*, unpublished.

in 1941.[51]

In July 1945 Anna responded to a request from the seminary for financial help, "I have been favored with visits from Messrs. Van Til, Stonehouse and Rian and may also see Mr. Marsden before the end of this month. In view of the fact that my resources have been considerably reduced, I am obliged to consider most carefully any further gifts to the causes which these men represent."[52] However, at Christmastime in 1945, Anna still gave three hundred shares of Rath Packing Company common stock to the seminary.[53]

Even though she had a position of beneficence, Anna was approachable and also vigorously concerned with higher things. As George Haney recounted, before he moved to Waterloo, "I had a picture in my mind of this well-to-do lady, and I thought, how am I going to relate to this? And I can remember the pleasant surprise when I met her, one of the godliest women that I have ever met in the course of my ministry. Gracious, loving, kind." Anna died at 92 years of age in Waterloo, Iowa, in the winter of 1960.

## Gertrude Mead: A Woman's Mite

Born in 1872, Gertrude F. Mead grew up on a farm in Central Pennsylvania, "more at home with the wild things in the woods, than with people," as she later described herself. After marrying in 1901 and living in Pittsburgh for some years, she and her husband moved back to their hometown: Clearfield, Pennsylvania. Their only child, a daughter, died three years later. Gertrude became a successful school teacher, and eventually taught in the public schools of Lumber City, Clearfield, Lawrence Township, and Ellwood City, Pennsylvania.[54]

51 "Presbytery of Wisconsin," *Presbyterian Guardian* 10 (November 25, 1941): 141, http://opc.org/cfh/guardian/Volume_10/1941-11-25.pdf.

52 Letter from Anna Rath to John P. Clelland, July 6, 1945, courtesy of Westminster Theological Seminary.

53 Letter from Anna Rath to Westminster Theological Seminary, December 17, 1945, courtesy of Westminster Theological Seminary.

54 *Progress* (Clearfield, PA), February 9, 1957, http://www.newspapers.com/

Her husband, who spent summers with Gertrude in Clearfield but went south for the winters due to the climate, passed away in 1934. Two years later, Gertrude, a member of Clearfield Presbyterian Church, attended the First Assembly of the OPC (then called PCA) in Philadelphia, where she was enrolled as a constituting member.[55] Upon her return, she became a charter member of Calvary OPC in Middletown, Pennsylvania, promptly gave

Gertrude Mead in 1955

$1,000 to the brand-new denomination, and then repeated the gift two months later. She also gave generously to her local congregation; in the throes of the Great Depression, the need around her was likely dire. In 1937 the pastor of Calvary, Robert Marsden, wrote, "We ended last month with all bills paid and just $3.00 in the church treasury. That is working pretty close, but thus far the Lord has supplied all our needs as they have arisen."[56]

In the middle of World War II, Gertrude continued to give, perhaps with a sense of urgency. She wrote her "ideas, or should I say, convictions," to the *Woman's Home Companion* in February of 1944. "I am 72 years old and have now seen three wars," she declared. "I am praying that God will bless our country and that we may not lose our Christian civilization." That same year, she gave $2,108.33 to the OPC's Committee on Home Missions and Church Extension.

---

image/?spot=3356275.
55 Minutes of the First Assembly of the PCA (now OPC), June 11, 1936: 5.
56 Letter from Robert Marsden to Gertrude Mead, December 7, 1937, OPC archives.

She moved from Clearfield to Middletown in the fall of 1952. In 1956, mindful both of her own age and the thought that Christ could return at any moment, she was still in the business of giving. "I cannot tell you how much I appreciate your generosity," wrote John Galbraith, general secretary of the Committees on Home Missions and Church Extension and Foreign Missions. However, he continued, "I think I should caution you not to use your capital … it seems to me that it is small enough as it is. Of course, you're quite right that the Lord may return before you die, then you would have saved that money in vain. However while it is true that He may come soon, we cannot presume that He will…. I do not want to see you place yourself in any difficult financial circumstances."

Sound advice to be sure, although with customary determination, Gertrude circumvented it, and by the time she passed away in 1957 at age 85, she had but "meager possessions," the sale of which all went to the Committee on Foreign Missions, as she had provided for in her will.[57] As the *Presbyterian Guardian* noted, Calvary Church of Middletown had "suffered a real loss in the death of Mrs. Gertrude F. Mead."[58] The next year, at general assembly, the moderator was presented with a beautiful new glass gavel, donated by Gertrude F. Mead.[59] Despite her meager possessions and life on a teacher's salary, Gertrude never stopped giving.

## Gracious Giving

Financial giving, even among women of prominence like these, is still difficult to trace—as, perhaps, it should be. Countless women

---

57 Rev. Robert Graham, *My Presbyterian Pilgrimage*, courtesy of Margaret Duff.
58 "Orthodox Presbyterian Church News," *Presbyterian Guardian* 26 (March 15, 1957): 15, http://www.opc.org/cfh/guardian/Volume_26/1957-03-15.pdf.
59 See "General Assembly Meets in Oostburg, Wisconsin," *Presbyterian Guardian* 27 (June 15, 1958): 89–90, http://www.opc.org/cfh/guardian/Volume_27/1958-06-15.pdf.

throughout the OPC's history undoubtedly didn't even tell their left hands about their generosity, let alone the rest of us. And financial generosity doesn't always take the form of donations and bequests. Sometimes, instead, it looks like a pastor's wife who takes a job in order to augment her family's income. Sometimes it's a gifted secretary or administrator who works for scant pay in the employ or service of the church when she could be receiving higher wages elsewhere. Sometimes it takes the form of groceries and household goods purchased for the purpose of hospitality. All these forms of generosity, and so many more, are beyond the scope of this chapter. But the stories of Nellie and Mary Rothwell, Mary Shillito Stevenson, Beatrice Shillito, Marguerite Montgomery, Anna Rath, and Gertrude Mead, who gave not just to their local church but notably to the denomination as a whole, demonstrate that all who have freely given of themselves, their time, and their money to the OPC, are not walking alone. Instead, they join a beautiful heritage of women who, often quietly, and certainly graciously, for the glory of God excelled in the grace of giving.

**Judith M. Dinsmore** *grew up attending Bethel OPC in Carson, North Dakota, and still regards Bethel as an extension of her family. Now working as an editor in Pittsburgh, Judith and her husband, Nathan, are members of Providence PCA in Robinson Township, Pennsylvania.*

# 4

# Lillian Young:
# Mourning with Joy

## *Jean Gaffin*

In 1929 a professor at Princeton Seminary, J. Gresham Machen, left that theological institution after it succumbed to the liberalism of what is now the Presbyterian Church (USA) and founded Westminster Theological Seminary in Philadelphia. Among its first graduates was my father, Edward Joseph "Joe" Young, who received his diploma in 1935. After he returned from graduate work in Leipzig, Germany, in 1936, he taught for 33 years in the Old Testament department at Westminster. I grew up as part of the seminary community and later my husband, Richard B. Gaffin Jr., would teach biblical theology and systematic theology at Westminster for over 45 years.

During my dad's student years at Westminster, he met my mother, Lillian Grant Riggs, a woman who had suffered the loss of both her intended and her new husband. God used Joe's love for her to help her move beyond these tragedies and embrace the life God had prepared for her.

Born in 1907 in Philadelphia, Lillian was the third child of James and Clara Riggs. She had two older brothers and a younger sister. Lillian had it easy while growing up; she was attractive and athletic, a star for her high school teams in Abington, Pennsylvania. In her high school yearbook was written:

Who won the silver cup at the Cheltenham Track Meet? Who

was the star fullback of the hockey team? Who captained the girls' basketball team? Who played with a dislocated shoulder through more than half the Jenkintown game? Enough said! Lil Riggs, Senior president of the Basketball and Tennis Clubs, a member of the Hockey, Glee, Hiking, and Swimming Clubs, and manager of girls' track. For four years, Lillian has been an outstanding figure in girls' athletics, not only because of her playing ability but also because of her conspicuous loyalty to Abington.

Lillian never had thoughts of college since her dad felt strongly that a woman's place was in the home. So she studied home economics in high school and as an adult bore the fruit of that preparation, becoming an outstanding seamstress, knitter, cook, and gardener.

Lillian lived in a nominal Christian home, and was a very "moral" young woman, but the gospel had never penetrated her heart. Her first engagement at 21 was (in her words) to a "fine, Christian young man," which to her may have meant he was a very good person. Before they were married, Lillian got the tragic news that her fiancé, Wilson, had been killed in an automobile accident.

Naturally such an experience was sobering. A few years later she fell in love again and married a charmer named John "Bud" Borden. My brother, Davis A. Young, tells their story in his biography of our father:

> In Bud, Lillian had made a dream catch. Blond, handsome, and athletic, Bud Borden was the textbook example of a man's man and ladies' man…. Bud and Lillian were madly in love. Lillian said that "We simply packed bags, went off one day, drove to Butler, Pennsylvania" where they were married in the Presbyterian Church on September 3, 1932. In December Bud went deer hunting in the wilderness of the Allegheny Mountains in western Pennsylvania…. Later that day came a phone call that Bud had been shot in the wilds and was seriously wounded…. Within hours Lillian, her father, and brother-in-law drove to the town of St. Mary's. The next morning Lillian went

immediately to the hospital. Bud was unconscious, but when Lillian spoke to him he looked clearly at her, said "Hello, hon. You sure do get the tough breaks," and closed his eyes again… The funeral director put Lillian along with Bud's remains on a train bound for Philadelphia. Alone with her thoughts through the dark night, listening to the metallic rhythm of the wheels clacking on the rails, Lillian could think of nothing but Bud coming home in a box somewhere on the train.[1]

She wrote:

> I think that night had a definite effect on my later life. I was a truly heart-broken young woman. I did not recover from this hurt very easily. The pain was real, an indescribable thing. One feels almost hollow, but at the same time there is a vast weight that simply will not diminish.[2]

For the second time in a few short years, the bitter sting of the death of someone she loved had visited Lillian.

Lillian was only in her mid-20s. Her once carefree heart was now dealing with very difficult circumstances. We are not sure at what point she came to understand the gospel or why she started going to a Presbyterian church, first at Mt. Carmel Presbyterian Church (USA) in Glenside, Pennsylvania, and later at Calvary Presbyterian Church in neighboring Willow Grove. We do know that after professing faith she became a regular attender on Thursday evenings at the Philologus Club, which means "lover of the word." It was a group of younger women who would gather for dinner, prayer, and Bible study, with the goal of reaching other women with the gospel. Invited to teach were ministers and students at Westmin-

---

1 This quotation is from the unpublished manuscript of the biography of E. J. Young written by my brother, Davis A. Young. This manuscript was a background source for this chapter. An edited version of the biography is forthcoming from the OPC's Committee for the Historian.
2 Ibid. Lillian's words and recollections here and below are taken from personal letters.

ster. My dad, E. J. "Joe" Young, was a young seminarian who took on the task and fell in love with Lillian, then president of the group. He first noticed her when she asked him a serious theological question!

As he gained courage, Dad wooed this very reluctant widow with promises of taking her to Germany where he would be doing graduate work. He insist-

Lillian and E. J. Young

ed that the change would help her heal and that she would even learn to love him. One of their few dates was to Coney Island, New York, where they went on the Cyclone—then one of the highest roller coasters in the country. Her long black hair had been pinned up and by the end of the ride every pin became dislodged. She loved the ride, feeling a little like her old self again, able to have fun. His persuasive skills eventually convinced her to marry him, and they did so on July 25, 1935.

He whisked her off to Germany to do further study, but first they drove to San Francisco where she met his family and he took a contentious presbytery exam to enter the ministry in the Presbyterian Church (USA). He passed, but not without a sizeable portion of presbyters complaining that he was too rigid and conservative, given his association with Westminster and J. Gresham Machen. A large number of those presbyters had been influenced by the theological liberalism in the church that denied the truth of Holy Scripture, the virgin birth of Christ, his miracles, his atoning sacrifice, and his resurrection.

While they were in Germany, Lillian aimed to be a good wife. As time went on, "their life together was beautiful. 'We truly cared for each other in a very deep sense,' she wrote. When they were out with other people their eyes would seek each other out and they were always aware of one another. When Joe Young came out with one of his timely, spontaneous jokes, his eyes would seek out Lillian, and if she were laughing then he would feel that he had hit the mark."[3]

Lillian had a great sense of humor, and she loved playing pranks on Dad when they were on their honeymoon in Leipzig. "I have lots of fun teasing him," she wrote.

> I guess being alone so much goes to my head or something. I'm always thinking up some trick or other, and the last few nights I've been hiding his pajamas. As he scurries around looking for them I inform him whether he's hot or cold. One night I tied them to the chandelier. The ceiling being high they were out of the range of vision. He had a great time standing in the middle of the floor with apparently no hiding place in sight, and me saying he was very hot. We giggle like a couple of 14 year olds. Last night I put the hair brush in the bed which added to the fun. He enjoys it all as much as I, tho' he stands around and says, 'What a life![4]

They had good times together including a short winter trip to Italy. And since Hitler was in ascendency, they had many observations about where Germany seemed to be heading. A very good writer, Lillian recorded her impressions of Hitler: "Hitler spoke of the hate-filled might of our Jewish enemies, and declared it responsible for hundreds of deaths, then without batting an eye he added, 'I must state that our movement has never murdered and never attacked anyone.'"[5]

Back home from Germany, Joe changed his credentials to the newly formed Presbyterian Church of America, later to become the Orthodox Presbyterian Church. Lillian attended some of the earliest general assemblies of the OPC and often commented on how much she enjoyed listening to the commissioners debating

3  Ibid.
4  Ibid.
5  Ibid.

doctrinal issues.

I was born that fall when Dad started his teaching in Old Testament at Westminster. Lillian always felt that she was not quite adequate to being a professor's wife since she lacked a college education. But she was very bright, an eager learner, and well read. She was very supportive of Dad." He, of course, much more informed and brilliant than I, had my sincere heartfelt support in all his labors, and theological encounters."[6] She didn't always have an easy time of it because he travelled a lot and she stayed home with me and my brother Davis, who arrived four years later.

As a young seminary wife, she participated in the Westminster Wives Club, headed at the time by Mrs. R. B. Kuiper whose idea was that each wife would develop a doctrinal paper and present it to the others. Naturally, Lillian quaked at the responsibility, but fulfilled it quite admirably.

Many of those seminary wives were also members at Germantown Orthodox Presbyterian church, which our family joined when I was eight. Among them were Dorothy Sloat, Winigrace Stonehouse, Rena Van Til, and Helen Woolley. That church became the current Calvary OPC in Glenside in the 1950s, and newer faculty wives also attended, like Jean Clowney and Grace Kline.

Grace, whose husband, Meredith Kline, taught Old Testament along with my father, was close to my mom. The Klines built a home right next to ours. Although differing on some points in the interpretation of Genesis 1 and 2, Drs. Young and Kline nevertheless had a cordial relationship.

As I became school age, Lillian was part of the group that gathered in Thelma Greiner's living room to hear Dr. Cornelius Van Til present a plan to start a Christian day school in the Willow Grove church. As secretary of the group, Lillian was quite active in the nuts and bolts of getting the school up and running. I was enrolled in the first year, 1943, as a second grader. The school, Willow Grove Christian Day School, later became part of Phila-

6 Ibid.

delphia-Montgomery Christian Academy, still in existence today.

What set Lillian apart was her strong devotion to the Ortho-dox Presbyterian Church, particularly in its local form. During the early World War II years, she would walk my brother in a stroller, while I trotted alongside, about a mile, to get a trolley to get to the church in Willow Grove because Dad sometimes preached at other churches.

We had no car for a while when we moved membership to the Germantown church and took the trolley to get there. I remember her seeing to it that I got on a trolley on Saturday morning to attend catechism classes at the YMCA where the church met.

Lillian never missed a church service without good cause. Setting an example for us, she and Dad saw that we were at Sunday school each week, morning and evening service, and as I got older, the women's missionary society meetings. Lillian sang alto in the church choir. Attending church functions to her was necessary to build our faith and to encourage others and the pastor, too. It wasn't legalism with her, but a privilege, denied to so many in this world, to be hearing God's Word from the Reformed perspective.

Lillian also attended the women's presbyterial meetings where the emphasis was on missions and missionaries in the OPC. We knew about the names and locations of every denominational missionary.

Hospitality was also a hallmark of her character. We often invited seminarians and missionaries for dinner. She believed in a linens-and-best-china approach to company, something I have long since jettisoned in favor of informality, but I think she actually was on to something that we have lost today. She planted a garden on a quarter-acre each summer, canning and freezing fruits and vegetables. Guests often enjoyed wonderful food, such as homemade rhubarb-strawberry pie.

At one point for six months she took care of a baby whose mother was suffering from what we now call post-partum depression.

At the church fun nights or women's events, she loved acting in skits, even writing them. She often had parties in which she arranged games to challenge attendees. One favorite was hiding about 20 objects around the room that would meld into the background. She always had an open home for Dave and me to invite friends over. Mom and Dad's friends were invited for a musical evening as Dad played the cello, Meredith Kline the violin, and Howard Porter, a ruling elder at Calvary in Glenside, the piano. Others came from time to time. We cut our teeth on classical music at our house, but Mom also loved all the popular music from her youth—think Scott Joplin.

She and Dad loved travel. One of her favorite times was a trip to Eritrea in 1963 where Dad spoke at the graduation of John Mahaffy (now OPC pastor in Oregon) from the home school of the Eritrean missionary children. I have a painting she did of a tree that the Herbert Bird and Francis Mahaffy children enjoyed climbing there. She wrote about this experience in "Far Away School," published in the *Presbyterian Guardian*.[7]

Her eye was keen for what was beautiful. Besides enjoying oil painting in later years, she collected antiques and art glass, especially vases. She and her younger sister, Margaret, enjoyed attending auctions and flea markets searching for bargains and sometimes selling pieces. Both my brother and I inherited a lot of beautiful pieces. Feeding and identifying birds also gave her delight as she admired God's world immensely.

Lillian was a reserved person who struggled with migraines and bouts of depression. Her life, while marked by much joy in her family and her activities, was also marked by suffering. The early loss of two men she loved and being the wife of a very public person were probably harder on her than she realized. She so admired Dad that she would regularly joke with Dave and me that Dad was going to have a mansion in heaven and she would be in a hovel. Dad naturally disabused her of that.

7 *Presbyterian Guardian* 33 (February 1964): 24, http://opc.org/cfh/guardian/Volume_33/1964-02.pdf.

I think she was a valiant person as she dealt with her difficulties. It was very important to her to glorify God. Lillian was in so many ways a quiet blessing to those who knew her. She once told me that she was a melancholic personality. Such Christians have tenderness, a love for beauty, a strong moral compass, and ironically often a good sense of humor. Yet they are troubled by this present evil age, by sin and its ramifications. They are driven to the Savior for hope as they feel the opposite pull toward depression. William Cowper, the great hymn writer, was such a person. His lyrics often focused on God lifting us from depression: "When comforts are declining, he grants the soul again a season of clear shining, to cheer it after rain."[8]

When the Lord suddenly took Dad with a heart attack on Valentine's Day 1968 at age 60, Lillian was once again a widow. For a few years she had a woman teacher live with her, and later she came to live with us. She died of pneumonia in May 1991 at 83, her final three years in Quarryville Presbyterian Retirement Community suffering from dementia. We are grateful that now she is with the Lord who makes all things new.

**Jean Gaffin** *is the wife of Richard B. Gaffin Jr., retired systematic and biblical theology professor at Westminster Theological Seminary. Jean has written and taught Bible studies and has served as a conference speaker. For 18 years she was the business manager/controller at Phil-Mont Christian Academy and wrote a history of the school in 2012. She and her husband attend Grace OPC in Vienna, Virginia. The Gaffins have had three children, a married son in Virginia, a married son in Michigan, and a daughter now with the Lord. They have nine grandchildren.*

---

8 Willian Cowper, "Sometimes a Light Surprises," *Trinity Hymnal* (Suwanee, GA: Great Commission Publications, 1961), no. 520.

# 5

# Katharine Hunt:
# With Weakness and Fear
# and Much Trembling

## *Kathryn P. Muether*

Imagine a knock on the door as you are finishing breakfast. It is the police, and they have come to arrest your husband for his public Christian convictions. You have good reason to suspect that he is headed for torture and ultimately death. As you struggle to maintain your composure through the screams and cries of your young children, you come to the awareness that your next words to your husband will possibly be the last you will ever speak to him. What would they be?

Chances are they would be unlike those of Kathy Hunt, who told her husband to be sure to take with him warm underwear.

Underwear? Psychologists might liken that response as the coping device of denial. But they would be wrong. Mrs. Hunt's words to her husband were fixed in the context of her complete assurance that his life was in God's hands, as well as her life and their children's. And that confidence liberated her, in the trauma of this episode—indeed throughout her life—to focus her calling on serving her husband, her family, and the mission of her church in quiet, routine, and even mundane ways.

In their book, *The Korean Pentecost and the Sufferings Which Followed*, William Blair and Bruce Hunt describe the remarkable growth of the Reformed faith in Korea through the first three-quarters of the twentieth century.[1] By 1976 Protestant Christianity in Korea grew to over 2.6 million adherents, even as Koreans survived five wars. Katharine Blair Hunt, daughter and wife of the co-authors, born in Pyengyang on August 3, 1904, during the first of those wars, came to embody the spiritual growth that comes through severe testing. The daughter of pioneering Presbyterian missionaries, she grew up on the mission compound, and at the age of 13 she came to America to finish high school in Kansas. After attending Park College (Missouri), she taught high school in Missouri for three years, and then returned to Korea and taught in the same school for missionary children that she had attended.

Bruce Hunt also was born and raised in Korea and attended the same school, although a year ahead of Kathy. He came to America in 1919 to attend Wheaton College and then Rutgers University, from which he graduated. He continued his studies at Princeton Theological Seminary. Upon graduating in 1928, he returned to Korea under the Presbyterian Church (USA) Board of Foreign Missions. While serving in Chunju he became engaged to Kathy, and they were married on September 27, 1932, in the gymnasium of the school where they had both attended. As Kathy later related, "Since both of us were children of the mission, and Bruce had [been] a bachelor long enough that they were worried about him, our wedding was a big event!"[2]

The couple served in Chunju for three more years, where their first two daughters, Lois and Bertha, were born, and they came to the United States on furlough in 1935. There they witnessed the events that led to the formation of the Orthodox Presbyterian Church. The Hunts left the Presbyterian Church (USA) and joined the new denomination at its First Assembly on June 11, 1936.

---

1 William Newton Blair and Bruce F. Hunt, *The Korean Pentecost and the Sufferings Which Followed* (Edinburgh: Banner of Truth, 1977).

2 Katharine Hunt, "Biographical Material—K.B.H." Unpublished manuscript, 1970. (Bruce F. Hunt archives, Montgomery Library, Westminster Theological Seminary). This appears to be an autobiographical summary that Kathy Hunt sent to churches in advance of visits by her and her husband.

This was not a decision lightly made. Kathy remembered that "this meant separating from our former work and the many relatives and friends with whom we had grown up in Korea," adding "there was great pressure for us to stay, and strong feeling about our leaving."[3]

Leaving the PCUSA required aligning with another mission field, and (what they could hardly anticipate at the time) serving in a dangerous part of the world. In the next year, the Hunts were sent by the Independent Board for Presbyterian Foreign Missions,[4] to Harbin, Manchuria, at that time controlled by the Japanese. They were joined in this mission work by Egbert Andrews, Heber McIlwaine, and the Coray and Byram families. In describing their assignment to Manchuria, Kathy wrote: "I must admit that going into a strange country with two little children and one on the way, made me feel like Abraham, or perhaps more like Sarah! But the Lord opened doors and in some ways it was one of the most fruitful periods of our missionary work."[5]

In Manchuria, Kathy gave birth to three more children, Katharine ("Connie") and a set of twins, David and Mary. The Hunts held Korean services in their home until the congregation grew big enough to rent a facility. Then followed a sustained period of trial and strain, because the Japanese-controlled government began to demand public worship of the emperor. The Hunts' church had to scatter because of its refusal to participate in this worship, and members frequently gathered secretly again in the Hunt home. Bruce continued his missionary work in the towns and villages, and Kathy "was never sure whether [her] husband would return when he went

---

3  Ibid.
4  J. Gresham Machen and others founded the Independent Board for Presbyterian Foreign Missions in 1933 in response to the liberalism that was infiltrating the mainline Presbyterian Board of Foreign Missions. This action led to Machen's ouster from the PCUSA and the founding of the OPC in 1936. Eventually the Hunts and other IBPFM missionaries would serve under the auspices of the OPC when it established its Committee on Foreign Missions.
5  Katharine Hunt, "Biographical Material."

to visit churches in other cities."[6]

On the morning of October 22, 1941, came that knock on the door as the family finished breakfast. Bruce was arrested and imprisoned for 45 days because of

The Hunt family in Manchuria shortly before the Japanese imprisoned Bruce

his stand against emperor worship. He was released on December 6, but with the bombing of Pearl Harbor the next day, he was re-arrested and sent to a concentration camp until his release the following summer. Manchurian winters are bitterly cold, and Bruce was deeply grateful for his wife's presence of mind in suggesting that he take his warm underwear. She was later able to send him more warm clothing and bedding.[7]

Though spared being sent to a concentration camp because of her children, Kathy was challenged with providing for their food and lodging in enemy territory. For much of this time, she had no idea where her husband was or whether he was alive or dead. "My immediate responsibility was caring for the children. And though we had no money coming in, it is wonderful how the Lord took care of us." She had been able to store some food in advance and was able to buy more by selling most of their furniture. In looking back, Kathy said, "I am still amazed at the peace of mind which the Lord gave throughout this time. I think it was because so many people were praying for us."[8]

6 Ibid.
7 The story of his imprisonment is told in his book, *For a Testimony: The Story of Bruce Hunt Imprisoned for the Gospel* (Philadelphia: Committee for the Historian of the OPC, 2000).
8  Katharine Hunt, "Biographical Material."

When Bruce's release finally came and they were able to return to America, Kathy could only say "it truly seemed like a miracle."[9] Returning to the States, the family settled first in Glenside, Pennsylvania, and later in National City, California, where Bruce served as a home missionary. These were "three happy, normal years of family life together." Yet the Manchuria experience was only the beginning of a recurring pattern that would challenge their marriage. As Kathy herself described it in looking back, "a characteristic of our life has been separation."[10]

While Bruce was traveling extensively to speak at churches about his imprisonment, Kathy wrote about the experience in the creative form of a children's story, from the point of view of her young children. It was published in the *Presbyterian Guardian*, and Bruce wrote to her that wherever he went, people were talking about her article: "Your *Guardian* article had been quite the sensation around here."[11] His letters also subjected his wife to his sense of humor as in the shocking beginning of a May 10, 1943, letter: "Dearest Kathy of mine, I find myself in a state institution again. Not for the same thing I was locked up in Manchuria for and yet indirectly that has something to do with it. Don't grieve for me, however, as I am being well taken care of and I have prospects of leaving here soon."[12] Eventually he revealed that he was staying in the guest quarters at the Nebraska Tuberculosis Sanitarium while visiting some friends.

Another season of separation occurred when Bruce returned to Korea in 1946, after permission was granted for missionary men to return. Because women and children were not allowed, Kathy and

9 Ibid.
10 Ibid.
11 Katharine B. Hunt, "For Jesus' Sake, Amen: A True Story for Children" *Presbyterian Guardian* 12 (May 10, 1943): 131–33, http://opc.org/cfh/guardian/Volume_12/1943-05-10.pdf.
12 BFH to KBH, May 10, 1943 (these and other letters cited are housed in the Bruce F. Hunt archives, Montgomery Library, Westminster Theological Seminary).

the five children stayed in Wildwood, New Jersey. The family was reunited when permission was granted for women and children to enter Korea.

As the OPC *Messenger* reported, Kathy kept busy. Beyond conducting weekly Bible classes and assisting Bruce in evangelistic work, "Mrs. Hunt is also the one teacher for three different schools (in the home) with four grades—Grammar, Junior High (two grades), and Senior High."[13] As early as 1949 the Hunts began regularly pleading for missionary candidates to join them in this desperately needy field. In 1948 Florence Handyside joined them as a missionary nurse. When she suddenly took ill, Kathy accompanied her from Pusan to Seoul for emergency medical treatment, and was by her side when she succumbed to death.

The work proved so strenuous that eventually it caught up with Bruce. With no colleagues on the field with whom to confer on important and sensitive matters, he suffered a breakdown, the result of nervous fatigue from overwork. In their return to the States, the *Messenger* called for prayers for his complete recovery and for "strength of body, mind, and spirit for Mrs. Hunt to bear her many responsibilities."[14] Those prayers were answered by Bruce's remarkable recovery of health that enabled his return to the field when conditions permitted in 1952. Once again, women and children were not permitted to accompany missionaries, and Kathy was reluctantly prepared to stay state-side with her children. But God provided another opportunity, which Kathy explained in a farewell letter before setting sail:

> It is with mixed feelings that we are getting ready to start again. We are thankful that the Lord has so definitely opened the way for us to go out. It did not seem wise for Mr. Hunt to go alone, and yet the need is so urgent that it hardly seemed right to stay away. Then quite unexpectedly we received a cable asking me

13 "Hunt Family Active," *Orthodox Presbyterian Messenger* 4, no. 4 (February 1949): 3.
14 "Bruce Hunt Ill," *Orthodox Presbyterian Messenger* 5, no. 9 (June 1950): 3.

to teach in Japan in a school for missionaries' children. This makes it possible for us to have a place from which Mr. Hunt can make trips to and from Korea.[15]

Kathy served as acting principal and fourth-grade teacher at the Christian Academy in Japan. She also endured health issues that required major surgery and a lengthy recuperation. All of this she managed in her husband's absence.

Mindful of her husband's re-exposure to loneliness and stress, Kathy wrote to him as frequently as four letters per week (a rate that prompted her to question whether she was wasting money on postage). Typically she would start her letters early in the day, continue her composition through the morning between household chores, and then finish quickly with a "dash to the postman."[16]

One letter demonstrates the long-distance encouragement she tried to provide:

> I wish I could be there to ease the load a little. But the Lord can do it much better! —That's silly! I know He does it anyway and we just try to be his instruments—never our own! Only in that place you surely need time for prayer and very often I don't think it would hurt at all, to have less time to spend talking to others (Don't you like my sermons!)[17]

A September letter encouraged Bruce during yet another time of difficulty on the mission field: "The fight is the Lord's not yours. So don't worry about it, beyond giving your counsel."[18] That these particular afflictions owed to conflict among Christians and not the suffering of persecution only intensified the pain of their separation.

Kathy had her own moments of discouragement. She often

---

15 "Missionaries' Farewells," *Presbyterian Guardian* 20 (December 15, 1951): 232, http://opc.org/cfh/guardian/Volume_20/1951-12-15.pdf.
16 KBH to BFH, undated, ca. 1952.
17 KBH to BFH, undated, ca. 1952.
18 KBH to BFH, September 7, 1952.

confided honestly about her struggles of managing the home without him. "I don't know when I'm ever going to get things done."[19] She frequently bemoaned her lack of patience with her children or a day that passed with much left unaccomplished.

One letter captured Kathy at her wit's end: "What a night! With the kids yelling at me—or me yelling at them! Sometimes I think the nights are worse than the days. Although, really neither is too bad—if I survive!"[20]

In another undated letter from this time, Kathy confesses: "I haven't been the comfort and help I should have been to you, honey—I sure am a fizzle as a wife.... I just pray that the Lord will forgive me and help me to be a better wife to you—and a better mother to my children." She complimented her children when they presented her with a hand-picked arrangement of flowers on Mother's Day. "They're really sweet—sometimes!"[21]

Perhaps her spirits were at their lowest when she wrote to her husband, "I feel like you that this just isn't living—we couldn't take it if it wasn't for Christ. What was it Rutherford said about the crabbed tree?"[22]

For Kathy, one of the most difficult problems of those "upset years" was seeing that her children were properly educated while functioning as a single parent. She remarked that "our oldest children did not spend more than two consecutive years in any school until they entered college." And yet, "God has taken care of our children and abundantly made up to them for anything we have

---

19  KBH to BFH, undated, ca. 1952.
20  KBH to BFH, March 1952 [exact date obscured].
21  KBH to BFH, May 11, 1952.
22  KBH to BFH, March 16, 1952. Her "Rutherford" reference is apparently to this letter from Samuel Rutherford to Lady Kemure, November 22, 1636: "God forgive them that raise an ill report upon the sweet cross of Christ. It is but our weak and dim eyes, and our looking only to the black side that makes us mistake. Those who can take that crabbed tree handsomely upon their back, and fasten it on cannily, shall find it such a burden as wings unto a bird, or sails to a ship."

had to sacrifice for them…. We are very thankful for the way [the Lord] has blessed them in spite of it."[23]

Relief came to the Hunts eventually. Kathy and daughter Connie were allowed to rejoin Bruce in Korea in 1953. Reinforcements came to the field when Theodore and Grace Hard arrived in 1954, allowing the Korean Mission of the Orthodox Presbyterian Church to be formally organized at long last. Within a year, the twins, David and Mary, were granted permission to come from their boarding school in Japan, and the Hunts helped organize a Christian boarding school that quickly saw an enrollment of over five hundred students. In 1960 Harvie and Dorothy Conn joined as the third family in the mission.

The Hunts retired from the mission field in 1976 (which they agreed to delay for two years to help the mission). Reflecting back on her years of service only prompted more humility from Kathy. She wrote, "Since the children have left, what have I done? Not as much as I might have wished. Because of unsettled conditions, I never did get to study the [Korean] language and am still not good at it."[24] She frequently asked the church to pray especially for missionary wives, that they might find time amid their many responsibilities to master the language.

Bruce Hunt died on July 26, 1992, and Kathy died on December 8, 1994. In addition to their five children, they were blessed with 21 grandchildren and 12 great-grandchildren. Kathy Hunt was called with her husband to suffer much hardship for the gospel. What stands out in their lives was their eagerness to cling tightly to Christ. This gave her strength to accomplish even the mundane tasks "with weakness and fear and much trembling" (1 Cor. 2:3). Once, when returning to the mission field, Kathy cited from Paul a passage that she told friends "I would like to take with us and leave with you." Perhaps more than any other words they sum up her life:

23  Katharine Hunt, "Biographical Material."
24  Ibid.

Though our outer self is wasting away, our inner self is being renewed day by day. For this light momentary affliction is preparing for us an eternal weight of glory beyond all comparison, as we look not to the things that are seen but to the things that are unseen. For the things that are sen are transient, but the things that are unseen are eternal. (2 Cor. 4:16–18)

**Kathryn P. Muether** *is the librarian at the Geneva School, a classical Christian school in Winter Park, Florida. She and her husband John are members of Reformation Orthodox Presbyterian Church in Oviedo, Florida. She has four children and two grandchildren.*

# 6

# Pauline Gaffin:
# Aunt Polly's Mission

## *Linda Finlayson*

Pauline Osborn Gaffin was a strong and intelligent woman, full of passion for her Lord and his call to mission work. Her steadfast purpose and self-discipline led to a life dedicated to serving God and his people, but it didn't turn out quite as she had planned.

Born in 1908 in the Presbyterian manse near Old Church, Virginia, two particular incidents had a profound effect on Polly early on. At just four years old she listened to the terrible tales of the sinking of the Titanic. Even at that young age, she faced her mortality and her need of a Savior. When she was nine years old, two missionary women came to her father's church with a slide show about their work in Africa. While the pictures fascinated her, she soon found the mission work itself had captured her heart. From that time, in typical Polly fashion, everything she did was toward her training for the African mission field.

Polly's mother died when she was 12. Even as Polly grieved, God sent Great Aunt Margaret Morton into her life. This prayer warrior carried on teaching Polly and her siblings the things of God, as their mother had done. Throughout Polly's teen years, she knew that Aunt Margaret was praying for her to remain strong in her commitment to be a missionary. Her father too encouraged her plans and sent her to Radford College in Virginia to study languages, history, and geography in preparation for mission work. Deciding to forgo marriage and children so she could give her whole attention to her calling, Polly was firmly convinced that after college she would go to Africa. However, God had other plans.

In her junior year of college, Polly travelled to a Student Volunteer Movement convention in Detroit. On the train she engaged in lively debates about social issues with other students from various colleges. Richard "Dick" Gaffin, also a delegate, overheard this passionate young woman and knew he had found his life's mate. They saw a great deal of each other at the convention and discovered their future plans were very similar. Polly thought little of it at the time, still committed to remaining single; but Dick was certain they should be together. For the next year and a half, they corresponded while they finished their college degrees. When he finally asked her to marry him, it was with the proviso that she would be as committed to missionary work as she would be to him. Polly accepted his proposal, surprised that God had provided such a like-minded man for her. Their families, however, were not so sure. The Great Depression had begun. Money was scarce. With youthful optimism that such "small" considerations didn't matter, Dick and Polly were married on June 17, 1931, by Polly's father in Lucketts, Virginia.

The following year Dick enrolled in Westminster Theological Seminary in Philadelphia in preparation for the mission field. Shortly after they arrived, Polly, missing the green hills of Virginia and her family, gave birth to their first child, Margaret. She later found much needed fellowship when she was able to join the Wives Club, formed by some of the professors' wives. She also was able to study church history with Dr. Paul Woolley in Dick's final year, fueling her life-long passion for history.

After Dick's graduation in 1935, they prepared to go to the mission field. Polly's excitement was dimmed when she had to let go of her long held plans to go to Africa. They were accepted by the Independent Board for Presbyterian Foreign Missions, which had been formed by Westminster professor J. Gresham Machen as an alternative to the missions board of the rapidly liberalizing Presbyterian Church (USA). The Independent Board was looking to send missionaries to China. After some inner wrestling, Polly acquiesced to God's will, asking him to give her a love for the Chinese people.

Arriving in China in October 1935, Dick and Polly were amazed at the number of people they saw everywhere they travelled. The Yellow River had overflowed its banks, making thousands homeless and starving. A compassion for the Chinese people began to grow in Polly as they travelled through many towns and cities until they reached Peking (Beijing). They had both a difficult and fascinating year, with the challenge of learning to speak Mandarin and learning about Chinese history and culture as they toured the many historic sites. Also during that year, Polly gave birth to their second child, Richard "Dick" Jr., in July 1936. During her pregnancy, Polly was cared for by a doctor whom she later credited with the good health of the entire family while they were in China. He explained how to avoid diseases prevalent in China and also advised Polly on food preparation, helping her let go of her American ways and learning how to eat well in their new country.

Pauline and Richard Gaffin with daughter Margaret and sons Harold, Richard Jr. and John

Near the end of 1936 the family moved south to the coastal city of Haichow (Lianyungang) to continue their language study and observe how mission work was already being done in the area by the Southern Presbyterian Station. They also joined the newly formed Orthodox Presbyterian Church under the auspices of the Committee on Foreign Missions. But troubling reports of growing Japanese militarism came in with unsettling regularity. In July 1937 war broke out when the Japanese invaded Shanghai. Air raid sirens went off almost daily as Japanese bombers flew overhead, causing everyone at the Station to flee to the basement. After weeks of fear and worry, the USS Pope arrived to evacuate them further north to Tsingtao (Qingdao). Many foreign nationals decided to leave China altogether, but Dick and Polly wanted to stay, along with other missionaries. So they settled into the seaside resort town where Dick began evangelistic work among the local fishermen.

During such an unsettling time, with many local people fleeing further north, the regional government disbanded and schools were closed. To help the families who remained, some missionaries started a primary school and asked Polly to help out. So each evening she would study to be able to teach a Bible story in Mandarin the next morning. She was also busy homeschooling five-year-old Margaret, until Polly was asked to become director of an English-speaking kindergarten that Margaret could attend. This was Polly's first taste of teaching, an area she had not thought she would pursue, but once again God's plans changed Polly's plans.

As the war escalated with the Japanese pushing north, goods were difficult to obtain. Polly decided to set up a knitting circle to make some much needed winter clothing. It was an opportunity to help local women and share the gospel at the same time. Pregnant with their third child, Polly's health was being affected, and for a frightening few weeks she lost the sight in one eye. Fortunately a local Japanese civilian doctor was able to treat her, and her sight eventually returned. Then in October 1939 Polly gave birth to Harold.

By June 1941 Dick and Polly realized they had to return home. The Gaffins had overstayed their term of five years, afraid that if they left they would be prevented from returning. But the Japanese were making steady inroads into China's interior, and American diplomats were urging all Americans to leave the country. Polly was surprised how much it hurt to leave a country in which she had had no interest just six years before.

Back in America, they settled near Philadelphia for a year, and in July 1942 Polly gave birth to John, their last child. Then it was off to Milwaukee, where Dick's father had arranged to have him called as pastor of Grace OPC, a home mission church. Meanwhile, with the bombing of Pearl Harbor, America joined World War II.

The Gaffin family spent a happy five years in Milwaukee building up the small congregation to the point where they were able to consider purchasing their own building. They also enjoyed time with Dick's parents. But the mission field, and in particular China, still called to their hearts. So they began to make plans to return to China, not realizing what lay ahead.

China was not a safe place. Although the war with Japan had ended, a new threat had emerged in the form of the Communist Party. While in 1947 they were not yet in power, the conflict with the Nationalist government was escalating. Still, Dick and Polly wanted to go back. However, only Dick could obtain a visa. Polly was refused one. Due to the dangerous conditions in China, mothers travelling with children were denied access. Now the decision was: should Dick go alone? They wrestled with the question until they finally decided that Dick should go, check out the conditions, and send for Polly and the children once it was deemed safe. Polly wasn't entirely happy with the decision, but knew they couldn't expose their children to danger; besides Margaret was beginning to think about her college education. Polly struggled once more with God's providence, trying not to be resentful. This was the very reason she had decided not to marry during her college days. But God, in his wisdom, had given her a husband and children, and she knew her first responsibility was to them. So with a heavy heart Polly accompanied Dick to San Francisco and waved farewell from the wharf.

The plan had been to be separated for only a year. Dick was sure the government would relent and let Polly and the children join him. So in 1948, Polly, with the help of Dick's parents, her sister and husband, and the small Milwaukee congregation, packed up all their belongings. She left out just enough for a quick visit to Virginia to see her family. However, the short visit turned into a long one. A longshoremen's strike prevented them from leaving for China, and the longer they waited the worse the Chinese situation became. Polly followed the southward movements of the Communists in the newspaper reports, worrying whether Dick was still safe in Shanghai. Letters took a long time to make their way to them and phone calls were scarce. When Dick was finally able to place a call, he told Polly and the children not to come. It was too dangerous.

Disappointed and worried, Polly knew she had to settle somewhere for the children's sake. They needed to get into school and have a stable home. Through providential circumstances, the family ended up settling in Wildwood, New Jersey. Polly longed for Dick to return to them, partly for his safety and partly for his strength and wisdom. Margaret, now 16, and Dick Jr., 12, found it difficult to settle, not having a place to call home, and Polly couldn't blame them. She felt the same way. She'd been prepared to call China home, and now it seemed to have been taken away from them. However, the Wildwood OP congregation took the family under their wing and cared for them. But it was not all one way. Polly also mentored some folks in the congregation. Slowly the family settled into as normal a routine as they could.

In May 1949 Shanghai fell to the Communists. Polly tried not to panic. There was no word from Dick for several months because the Communists stopped all mail. During that time Polly memorized Romans 8 to keep her mind and heart focused on God's sovereignty. When Dick was finally allowed a phone call, Polly was so overwhelmed she couldn't speak, but her heart sang to know he was alive and coming home.

In 1951 the Committee on Foreign Missions wanted to send

them to Formosa (Taiwan). Again, Dick and Polly faced a big decision. There was nothing obvious to prevent the entire family from
going, except that there were no schools available in the area they
would be serving. Margaret was away at college, but Polly knew she
couldn't homeschool Dick Jr., who was soon to begin his sophomore year of high school. After much discussion and prayer, both
Dick and Polly decided their covenant responsibilities to their children should come first. So for a second time, Polly said goodbye to
her husband as he left and she stayed behind.

This time the separation lasted three years, until Dick Jr. began his college studies. Polly and the children moved to Wyncote,
Pennsylvania, so she could take up the position of principal of a
Christian school, a necessary step because Polly no longer qualified for missionary support. Under the new circumstance, since
Polly could have lived on the mission field, the Committee on Foreign Missions would only pay for Dick's housing in Formosa. This
meant that she gave up the mission column she had been writing
since 1949 for the *Presbyterian Guardian*, a magazine focused on
OPC news. Only Polly's strong self-discipline allowed her to balance her job while caring for her children.

At last in 1954 Polly packed up her bags and sailed with Harold and John to join Dick in Formosa (Taiwan). They met Dick
in Taipei where he had been chaplain at the Interpreters' Training School and teacher at a theological seminary. Dick decided
to leave those positions, and they moved southwest to Taichung.
Once more Polly was setting up a new home, but this time with
more joy. She made their small two- bedroom house a comfortable
refuge for both her family and people in the community. Polly was
surprised and pleased to discover she could still converse with ease
in Mandarin. Harold and John were enrolled in the new school,
Morrison Academy, and soon Polly was also teaching there. A few
years later she was appointed principal, a job she threw herself into,
seldom sleeping more than six hours a night. Over three years she
introduced new subjects, found money to equip a laboratory and a
library, and spent time counseling parents and students.

While Polly was occupied with the school, Dick and OP missionary Egbert Andrews found a building to rent for the Reformed Gospel Bookroom. Here they were able to distribute Reformed literature and have opportunities to speak to people about the gospel. Eventually a small nucleus of believers formed and began meeting on Sundays for worship.

As their boys grew, they prepared to leave home. Harold returned to the States in 1957 to begin college. On Dick and Polly's furlough in 1958, they arranged with Dick Jr., newly married to Jean Young, to have John live with them. Then in 1959, Dick and Polly returned to Taichung to continue the work with the Bookroom and to work toward starting a conservative Presbyterian seminary. Polly was now able to be a full-time missionary with her husband. She also resumed writing for the *Presbyterian Guardian* as "Aunt Polly," educating children about mission work. Dick and Polly spent the next 21 years in Formosa (Taiwan), and were so much at home there it was difficult for them to retire in 1980. They moved to their home in Bridgeton, New Jersey, and later to Quarryville Presbyterian Retirement Home in Pennsylvania. Polly passed away in 1989, and Dick died in 1996.

God had brought Polly through some unexpected detours on her way to answering his call to the mission field. She came to realize that she had been doing God's mission work all along. While China was the obvious place to bring the gospel, she was also sharing the gospel with her children as they grew, the children she taught in schools, the many people who read her magazine columns, and those she met and spoke with in all the places she lived. Her Savior's love was never far from her thoughts or her lips.

**Linda Finlayson** *is a children's author and has eight published titles. She has written biographies and church history books for young readers and middle school children. She also works part time as administrative assistant at Cornerstone Presbyterian Church, OPC, in Ambler, Pennsylvania. She is married to Professor Sandy Finlayson, library director at Westminster Theological Seminary in Philadelphia.*

# 7

# Dorothea Duff:
# Missionary and Mother

*Margaret Graham Duff*

Dora Duff, the wife of Orthodox Presbyterian Church missionary Clarence Duff, was more than just a missionary wife in
Eritrea, East Africa. Born of German immigrant parents, she was
early in life the bread-winner for her family. By the time she met
Clarence, she already was an established missionary with the Sudan
Interior Mission in Ethiopia. Her enthusiasm for reaching the lost,
her capabilities in office and home management, and her timely intervention on behalf of the work in Eritrea are told here. It was my
privilege as her daughter-in-law to have known her in her retirement years, which she also managed with the same dignity, self-sacrifice, and determination she had shown throughout her life.

The eldest of four children, Dorothea Louisa Kuehner was born
to German immigrants, Louisa and Fredrick Kuehner, on April 16,
1907, in Philadelphia, Pennsylvania. Her father was reputed to be
an excellent machinist, but his health failed, compelling Dora to
leave school at age 14 and work to support the family.

In her application essay for admission to the Sudan Interior
Mission (SIM), she related that at an early age her mother took
her to Sunday school and taught her to pray. She was impressed
with the reality of God, and a deep sense of sin caused her to turn
to the Lord for salvation. When she was confirmed at age 14 at St.
Matthew's Evangelical Reformed Church on Erie Avenue in Philadelphia, it meant much to her. She recalled, "Pastor Sylvanus made

it very clear that this was not a means of salvation, but rather our testimony before God and the congregation that we had accepted the Lord Jesus as our personal Savior and would henceforth live for him."[1]

On leaving school after ninth grade, she completed high school by taking night classes for the next four years, focusing on bookkeeping and German since her parents spoke German. She also took a course in billing at Burrough's School. At Strawbridge and Clothier's Department Store, Dora worked her way up from messenger girl, to stock girl, then in sales as well as modeling in the women's department. Later she was a biller and bookkeeper for The North American Lace Company. Her early work prepared her to be a diligent employee in any task given and gave her poise for dealing with the public. Her bookkeeping experience was also used in her work as a missionary in both Ethiopia and Eritrea.

At 18, she and co-worker Mabel Eddowes, who later became a missionary to Nigeria, went to an evangelistic service where it was impressed on the young people the responsibility of giving the gospel to those who were lost. Soon she joined Mabel in attending Philadelphia School of the Bible in their night program, so that she could learn more about the Bible. It seemed whenever missionaries spoke in assemblies, they spoke directly to her, she said. In the summer of 1929 at the Mt. Gretna Bible conference, 24-year-old Dora heard about mission work in the Sudan and felt called to serve there. She prayed that the Lord would open the way for her to go.

Although she became very active in her church's Christian Endeavor Society, taught Sunday school, and spoke at meetings for several years, she felt constrained from going to Africa because she was her family's main support. However in 1932 on a Victorious Life hike, Mr. Rhoad, a SIM board member, was the speaker. She recalled, "He showed me the danger of trying to direct my life,

---

1 Source materials for this chapter are original letters saved by Clarence and Dora Duff, histories written by them when applying for mission service, and various *New Horizons* articles.

which I held in my hand, and what a power it could be if laid down for [God] and taken up again at his command. I came home and that night gave myself unreservedly to God for his service." After telling her family of her decision and knowing that her siblings by then all held jobs, she applied to the SIM.

At the beginning of 1934, she found herself at the SIM headquarters in Addis Ababa, Ethiopia, after an ocean voyage of six weeks traveling with a small group of missionaries. She proved to be a good traveler despite many storms, never missing a meal. With her bookkeeping experience, she was soon put in charge of the books. Dora met many people from other mission societies and world travelers and even attended the Ethiopian Emperor Haile Selassie's birthday party.

Soon after arriving, a young man named Clarence Duff came through Addis from his station in Southern Ethiopia. He was doing pioneer missionary work as a Presbyterian Church (USA) minister working for the SIM. A year later, when Clarence stayed at the headquarters while finishing Bible translation work, he and Dora got to know each other. He often spoke at mission prayer meetings where she played the organ or auto harp. They had to practice for duets. Evening walks in the moonlight were often mentioned in letters home. After trying to be just friends, Clarence finally proposed in February 1935. After a few days to think it through, Dora consented. Clarence had been in Ethiopia for over seven years without a furlough; so right after their engagement, he went back to the States alone. She was happy that her family could meet her intended. Due to the imminent threat of the invasion of Ethiopia by Italy, Clarence returned to Africa before his furlough was half over.

As he was boarding the ship in the rain in New York harbor, he learned that the trunk from Philadelphia with all Dora's wedding trousseau had not arrived. While the family said farewell, Dora's brother Fred hurried back to the mission house to find the trunk. Clarence's sister, Margaret, related, "Almost at the last minute before the plank was taken up Fred arrived with the lost trunk! Can you imagine the thrill? On it went and a little later he remembered the keys and sent them to Clarence with the purser. Fred called to Clarence, 'I broke every traffic law in New York to get here!' How he ever made it I can't see, for he didn't know the way and the time was so short. Dora would have been frightfully disappointed."

Upon return to Addis Ababa in September, Clarence was unable to resume his work in the south because of the threat of war, so they both were kept busy at headquarters. They decided to get married right away so that whatever eventualities the war caused, they would be sent together either to work or to the States. They sent home letters that told of the October wedding date, but since the war began mail was very slow. As the person working in the office, Dora got to know the many reporters hanging about in Addis to report on the war that started October 3, when Italy under Mussolini invaded Ethiopia. So it's not too surprising that late at night on October 10, 1935, her brother Fred heard knocking at the door of the Philadelphia home. He leaned out the window and was asked by a *Philadelphia Inquirer* reporter for information about Dora. Fred told him to return in the morning until the reporter went on to say that Dora had been married that day in Addis. So the surprised family got up and greeted the journalist. The following day, the wedding of a Philadelphia girl in Ethiopia during the war was on the front page! It was erroneously reported that the Emperor was present. Clarence's parents learned the news from friends all over their Western Pennsylvania neighborhood who had heard about the wedding on the radio and in newspapers. It was weeks before the actual letters from the happy couple arrived.

With Dr. Lambie, head of the mission, escorting Dora, the wedding took place at the headquarters building before a crowd of about 40 missionaries and officials of Addis Ababa. After a lunch, the bride and groom departed on their decorated horses to a camp tent set up about a half-day's journey south.

As the Italian-Ethiopian war escalated, missionaries came up to Addis from their stations and left the country. Clarence was put in charge of selling the mission property and closing the SIM work in Ethiopia. Dora continued with the bookkeeping. They were the last SIM missionaries to leave Ethiopia.

The Duffs sailed in August of 1938, five months after their first child, Donald, much-blessed by many visitors and officials, was born. From his years of study at Princeton, Clarence knew J. Gresham Machen, founder of the Orthodox Presbyterian Church. By the time they returned to the United States in 1938, he was convinced that he should leave the Presbyterian Church (USA) as well as the SIM and cast his lot with the recently formed OPC.

After visits to their homes in Philadelphia and Enon Valley, Pennsylvania, the Duffs set off in an old car pulling a small house trailer in search of a place to do missionary work for the OPC. After exploring needy areas in Texas and eastern Colorado, they accepted the offer of OP minister Ben Male to come to Denver to work in the mining town of Oak Creek in the Rocky Mountains. They put their trailer by a tiny two-room house and spent several years holding services, Sunday schools, and Bible schools.

During this time, Clarence's dad retired from active farm work, and sold the Duff farm in Enon Valley, Pennsylvania. The sale proceeds helped Clarence and Dora buy a house in Willow Grove, Pennsylvania, which later became the mission home for many missionaries on furlough. No sooner had they moved in, than Clarence in August 1943 sailed by ship to Ethiopia and tried to reenter with the war still on. His goal was to open a work for the OPC.

Dora's letters to Clarence tell of her life alone with the children, Donald then five and Dorothy, three. It was three months before she got a letter from Clarence. Over the next two years she lived under constant uncertainty about where he was, whether he would get into Ethiopia, and, when he was denied entry, where he could find a place to serve. When he found a place for missions in Eritrea, a northern province of Ethiopia, Dora was prevented from joining him because, with the ongoing war in Europe, ships would not take children.

During that time, she accomplished a great deal for her family and for the development of the Eritrean mission. Without a car, she managed to walk or use the train, trolley, or buses to get around.

Dora Duff with her children Don and Dorothy

She got herself and the children to church, to school, and to visit friends and relatives. Constantly in demand to speak at churches and missionary society meetings, she spoke in churches as far away as New Jersey and Maryland, sometimes taking the children with her. Dora's mother, now a widow, was able to live with her during those years. Although the children were too much for their grandmother to manage when they were awake, Dora could leave them in bed and go out to evening meetings.

Ever industrious, Dora sewed clothes for the children, often taking apart adult clothes and using the material to make the children's garments. She kept the coal stoves filled, and hauled out the ashes. She made necessary repairs to the house, put new screens on doors, rebuilt the back steps, and unclogged the plumbing. She related to Clarence about the toilet overflowing on a Sunday afternoon. "My! What a mess I had to mop up. I tried everything I could think of to fix it. I asked our neighbor if she had a plunger. It didn't take long after that until I got it working again. But I spent about two hours on Sunday afternoon trying to fix it. I surely did need you even as I have needed you so many times in the last year. However, I am thankful that always the Lord has given me wisdom to do things just when I needed that knowledge, even to being a plumber."

In February 1944 Clarence found the door closed to Ethiopia because the Ethiopian government refused to allow any new mission agencies to enter. But he could get into Eritrea. At this critical time when the OPC's Committee on Foreign Missions were wondering if they should even start a work in Eritrea, Dora spoke up boldly to present the needs of the African people and the possibilities for the mission. An early supporter of the OPC, Dr. Rian told her after church one evening that if he had been on the Missions Committee, he would have voted against sending Clarence out alone to Ethiopia. In a letter to Clarence she wrote, "I told him what I thought. I said the Committee was too slow and seemed to me to be lacking in faith. I thought we should do all we could to get people out as soon as we possibly can."

Rev. Robert Marsden, general secretary of the Committee on Foreign Missions as well as Home Missions, confided to Dora that when he got the news of the closure of Ethiopia from Clarence by cable, he couldn't sleep. He asked her, "Well, what do you suggest that we do?" So she proceeded to tell him all Clarence had written about Asmara, Eritrea. "I gave him the article on Eritrea in the National Geographic magazine and also *Light & Darkness in East Africa*. He was much interested in all I told him and seemed to feel very much better as a result of it," she wrote. Jim Rhorbach, a former SIM associate from their Addis Station who then lived in Philadelphia, told her, "Clarence can find a real work to do in Eritrea.... There is a real need up there."

When it looked like the war was nearing an end, Dora began preparations to leave—never certain on what day or what ship. She and the children made several trips by train to New York City where the government was giving yellow fever immunizations for the military. These shots caused pain for days, necessitating fortitude to return to complete the series. Once, they were packed and everything crated to go to the ship, the State Department refused permission for the tickets. They had to camp out in the house for over a month. By this time two other families also were heading to Eritrea, so Dora and her children traveled with Fern Stanton[2] and

2  At the time of their travel, missionary husband Charles Stanton already was in Eritrea.

her three little girls, and newly married Francis and Arlena Mahaffy. All of the delays in getting tickets ultimately made it possible for all three families to travel together. It must have been a great help to the new missionary families that Dora had sailing and mission field experience. My husband, Don, then seven years old, never forgot that as they sailed from the New York harbor and were passing the Statute of Liberty, the announcement came over the loudspeaker that the war was over!

In Eritrea, the three families settled in different areas, with the Duffs in Ghinda, In addition to language study, Dora had to care for the children and teach them using the Calvert School material, a precursor to home schooling programs. One day after a service in town, a woman came up to Dora, threw herself on the ground, and wrapped her arms around Dora's legs. She would not let go until Dora agreed to treat the sores on her legs. The Duffs used common sense first aid remedies which were so helpful that it wasn't long before many people came for help every day. Since they had no medical facilities, this demand lead to the construction of a small one-room clinic near their house and the arrival of nurses to help. Dora and Clarence never presumed to be able to handle medical work. However they felt obligated to treat simple matters that usually required careful cleaning and ointments after they saw within the local clinics temperatures taken with broken thermometers and people given injections with the same, un-cleaned needle, which resulted in ulcerated sores. Dora treated many people with horrible unsightly sores, including a child who had fallen in the fire, and had severe burns over most of his body. She would be called on to help with the delivery of babies when difficulties were expected. In 1965 the Compassion of Jesus Hospital was built. Eventually, the nurses took up much of that work and Dora helped, as family needs allowed, with the bookkeeping for the clinic and hospital.

Leaving family and friends was a personal sacrifice she was willing to make. In their years of service, there never were trips home for weddings or funerals of family members. She never saw her father again as he died a year after she went to Ethiopia. There were no phone calls and telegrams were rarely afforded. Undoubtedly the greatest sacrifice made concerned the children, Donald and Dorothy. Due to the isolated nature of their mission station in Ghinda, they finally felt that the children needed socialization in a school setting. Thus began two years with the children away for the school year at the SIM School for Missionary Children in Addis Ababa, a three-hour flight away, with letters their only communication. This served to undermine Dora's health. Her ulcers were aggravated, which ultimately led to emergency stomach surgery after Clarence died.

After a furlough home when the children were in sixth and seventh grades, SIM changed their rules and would not allow non-SIM children at the school. They spent the next two school years being taught again by Dora, who found higher math and sciences beyond her own education. Although the children on the mission field had the advantage of world travel and living in another culture, they only had a short-wave radio with no other access to enrichment—no library, TV, museums, concerts, or little league. The most difficult decision was made to send the children back to the States for their high school education. Donald, 15, and Dorothy, 14, were put on a freighter at Massawa, Eritrea, with $15 for the 45-day voyage to New York. Dora and Clarence did not see or talk to the children until their high school graduation.

As young adults, Don and Dorothy stayed in the loving home of the Rev. Leslie Sloat and family in Mount Airy, New Jersey. That became their home base during their college years. The Sloats even stood in as parents when Donald married me, Peggy Graham, in 1966 in Chula Vista, California. These were some of the sacrifices Dora and Clarence made.

The Duffs retired in 1971 after 27 years in Eritrea, plus five years as home missionaries in the US, and four years with SIM in Ethiopia for Dora and 11 years for Clarence. Clarence had suffered irreparable damage to his lungs from untreated bronchitis on long treks. In spite of working all their lives at sacrificial wages, because of their frugal ways, they were able to buy a small home in Ocoee,

Florida, a location favorable to his health. After writing two books about their Ethiopia and Eritrea experiences, Clarence died of cancer in 1982 at age 83. In 1990, when Dora's health began to fail, she made the wise but difficult decision to move to the Quarryville Presbyterian Retirement Community near Lancaster, Pennsylvania. She was able to fund her last days there. We observed, when our family visited her in Florida, one example of the constant frugality that made such a move possible: she folded the corner of her paper napkin at the end of the meal so that she could reuse it at the next meal.

One earthly reward for her years of service on the mission field was that when she went to Quarryville without knowing anyone, she was welcomed and made to feel at home by so many residents who knew her! She died of old age, at 93, on September 25, 2000.

Clarence and Dora labored faithfully in Eritrea seeing few conversions, but their letters give testimony to their tireless efforts to speak and witness to everyone they met in that land. A trip in any direction meant passing out tracts at every stop and speaking informally or Clarence preaching at every opportunity. The Eritreans heard the Good News. Dora was present on May 7, 1944, when Dr. John Skilton, a Westminster Theological Seminary professor, delivered the sermon at Francis Mahaffy's ordination service to become a missionary to Eritrea. Dora wrote to Clarence that Mr. Skilton pointed out that "the Gospel was not only to be preached so that people hearing it would be saved, but it was to be preached as a witness and even if none are saved yet a purpose of God is fulfilled in the preaching—that God is vindicated."

**Margaret Graham Duff** *is the wife of OP minister Donald J. Duff, the son of Dora and Clarence Duff. Peggy, born in Los Angeles to home missionary Robert Graham, grew up praying for Donald and his sister Dorothy in Eritrea. Donald, formerly the stated clerk of the OPC, and Peggy are retired and live near their children, both in Beaver Falls, Pennsylvania, and in Janesville, Wisconsin. She is a member of Immanuel OPC in Coraopolis, Pennsylvania.*

# 8

# Arlena Mahaffy:
# Living for Christ

## *Mary Arlena Bonner*

Among the troops boarding the Athos II on May 7, 1945, as it prepared to escort a convoy of merchant ships across the Atlantic Ocean were Arlena Mahaffy and her husband, Francis. With World War II endangering the waters, they were bound to secrecy as to their sailing date, forbidden to tell even family of their departure. They were also kept in the dark about the route they would take to reach their destination in East Africa. As they sailed out of New York harbor the following day, Arlena heard victory in Europe declared over the loudspeakers. Even so, the group sailed under complete blackout conditions. Years later, Arlena would recall coping with the uncertainty of that trip by following the Psalm 46:10 injunction: "Be still, and know that I am God." This journey launched her 22 years of missionary service, offering a foretaste of the steadfast faith and courage that would carry her through.

Born Arlena Catherine Cross on October 23, 1917, in Mishawaka, Indiana, Arlena never imagined she would end up sailing away to a foreign country, leaving friends and family behind. The daughter of a poor Baptist preacher and his wife, she aspired to become a teacher. In 1938, after obtaining a teaching certificate and eventually an education degree from Wheaton College, she started her teaching career in a one-room school house in Ashton, Illinois. She taught about 12 students in grades one through eight. Little did she know how God would use this experience to prepare her for teaching her own children and others on the mission field.

During her second teaching job in Zion, Illinois, Arlena took summer classes at Wheaton College. There, in 1941, she met Francis Mahaffy when she was assigned to help him in his job as a "dorm boy." Francis grew up in Minneapolis and had just graduated from Wheaton College when they met. He went from there to Westminster Theological Seminary in Philadelphia. It took persistence on Francis's part while at seminary to find an address for Arlena, but once he was successful they carried on a courtship mostly by postal mail. Their relationship blossomed as both were looking for a spouse with a strong commitment to the Lord. During their letter writing days, Arlena transitioned from being a Baptist to becoming a Presbyterian with a Reformed perspective, even as Francis moved from the conservative congregation of the Presbyterian Church (USA) that he grew up in to the Orthodox Presbyterian Church. They were married on June 22, 1944. Both of them had a growing desire to work in missions and were appointed to the mission field shortly after Francis's ordination in 1944 by the Orthodox Presbyterian Church. When the mission board asked her goals, Arlena said she wanted to serve God first by being a help meet to her husband, second by caring for any children God might bless her with, and third by assisting in mission work in any way she could.

They served two churches in Michigan while waiting close to a year for government permission to go overseas. Permission was finally granted in the spring of 1945. After a month-long journey that involved voyaging in the troop ship over the ocean, crossing Egypt by train, and the Red Sea in another vessel, the couple reached their destination: Eritrea, East Africa. Initially they served in a barren, predominantly Muslim area in the lowlands near the Red Sea, an extremely hot and humid area with temperatures often reaching 120 degrees in the shade. There Arlena worked diligently beside her husband to learn both the Saho language and Italian, which was still commonly spoken due to earlier colonization. As Francis put the Saho language into writing, Arlena made aids to help the people learn to read their own language.

During this time their first child, John, was born in an unsterile Italian hospital. Due to the poor conditions, Arlena developed a severe infection, and John failed to gain weight. They traveled on the deck of a water carrier across the Red Sea a few weeks after John's birth in search of better medical care. This trip only made matters worse, as John developed severe burns from the reflection of the sun on the water. After several weeks of treatment in an Italian hospital and then by an American military doctor, both recovered.

Back at their sweltering mission station, Arlena would hang wet sheets in the rooms in an attempt to cool the family off. At night they would often climb a rope ladder to the roof or sleep outside with their cots in a "V" around John to keep the hyenas away. They also were plagued with rats, snakes, many insects, and swarms of locusts. The latter, Arlena learned, were a delicacy when roasted.

Due to salt in the soil there was no way to grow vegetables in the lowlands. To feed her family nutritiously, Arlena had to wait on the monthly boat. Her vegetables always arrived in sad condition, having spent one day on the dock and another on the hot deck of the boat. She learned to make the best of it, soaking them in chlorinated water and cooking everything, stalks included. Government rationing made sugar and meat scarce, but she could buy fish and pasta locally. Goat milk to feed the children arrived sour and dirty after being milked with dirty hands into a dirty bowl and carried in filthy skins. All milk and water needed to be boiled before drinking, and eggs were often spoiled. When buying eggs, Arlena learned to duck under a blanket and shine a flashlight through each egg to see if it was cloudy—an indication that it was bad. Grain was bought dirty and had to be cleaned, washed, sun dried, and then ground before being cooked over a charcoal fire to make cereal.

Out of necessity, Arlena learned to provide a great deal of medical care while in the lowlands. This turned out to be not only a great work of compassion but a wonderful opportunity to share the gospel. Even when homeschooling her children, before classes began, she would often head out to the shed that served as a clinic and treat 50 to 60 people, giving medicine for malaria, anti-venom for deadly snake or scorpion bites, and treatment for horrible skin ulcers. One day a father begged her to come see his unconscious baby in a nearby hut. By the time Arlena arrived, the baby was flaccid and barely breathing. Noting the suddenness of the symptoms, she made an educated guess that the infant was suffering from pernicious malaria. Without any ability to test her hypothesis, she administered antimalarial medication, then sat with the child, praying that God would be merciful. Suddenly the infant became stiff, then relaxed and regained consciousness. That evening the thankful father returned to say the infant was back to normal! It was one of many answers to prayer.

Primarily during their time in the lowlands, Arlena and her family were confronted by bands of *shifta* (bandits from different tribes) fighting battles near their house where they would often hear the sounds of AR-15s close-by. Arlena and Francis would read Psalm 91 and, although fearful at times, trusted God to care for them. At one such time their Muslim worker saved their lives by bargaining with the bandits, who were demanding money of Francis. While the commotion continued outside, Arlena put the children to bed, assuring them of God's care. Then, thinking it might be better to turn off the propane lamp, she did so. This caused the bandits great fear, believing they were about to be attacked from the house. Only the quick thinking and intervention of the Mahaffys' Muslim helper kept the bandits from bursting into the house with guns blazing. Eventually, escalating threats from the *shifta* coupled with a worsening political situation caused the lowland mission station to be closed for a time.

In the early '50s the Mahaffys moved to the highlands, an area to which the people from the lowlands frequently migrated during the hottest season. Life was cooler and somewhat easier at this station, and for a time another missionary family worked in the same area. Periodically Francis would take month-long backcountry treks for which Arlena planned and packed food. The food had to survive a long journey, sometimes on camel back, with no refrigeration and only a fire for cooking.

At home, Arlena had a wood stove to cook on and the benefit of the town's generator that provided electricity for a few hours every evening. Here she grew a garden of fresh fruits and vegetables. Meat often involved skinning and cooking a goat or

The Mahaffy family in Eritrea

plucking a chicken. Frequently Arlena would go to the town's open-air market and haggle with the vendors to purchase food for the week. Although she never got used to the local tradition of cooking food in rancid butter, Arlena and the family grew to love the typical Eritrean diet, with its spicy sauces, spongy flatbread, and strong coffee. When invited to someone's hut for coffee, Arlena soon learned that accepting the invitation meant waiting for several hours while the coffee beans were cleaned, roasted, ground, and then boiled in a *jabina* over hot coals.

During their 22 years in Eritrea, Arlena bore seven children. Behind John came James, Paul, Samuel, Peter, Mary, and Elizabeth—all delivered in primitive conditions. She taught them through high school, except when on furlough, until they returned to the United States in 1966. Mary Bird, another OPC missionary wife, shared in some of the early teaching. Over the years, Arlena also taught several other missionary children, and developed curriculum for other families.

Arlena's days in Eritrea were filled with lesson plans, teaching, homemaking, and assisting Francis in language work. She was very encouraging of her husband's and sons' frequent pre-breakfast mountain climbs as well as her children's wide variety of pets, including a black stork, a klipspringer, and chameleons. Her home was always open for Bible studies and visitors. She took in a young child from another mission group for a couple of years, and for several months cared for a sickly Eritrean infant whose mother had died shortly after childbirth. Her days were full but, as she would say, "very fulfilling."

During their later furloughs, Arlena cared for both her mother and her mother-in-law. While on furlough in 1966, Arlena and Francis made the difficult decision to stay in the United States, both because of increased hostility to missionaries in Eritrea and to care for their mothers. In the summer of 1967, Francis returned to the field by himself for a year to help the local church function on its own. During this time he was accused of helping the *shifta* and placed under house arrest after providing clothes to refugees hiding out in caves. Arlena received cassette tapes with messages from Francis as he tried to make the best use of his time while hiding under a bed with bullets flying over the tin roof of the house! Though their tasks were very different, both Arlena and Francis had to rely on the Lord that year as they worked apart from each other.

Returning to the United States in 1968, Francis began establishing home mission churches in the greater Chicago area, with Arlena working faithfully by his side. Services were held in Winthrop Harbor, Illinois,[1] and in Kenosha, Wisconsin. Later he held studies in Janesville, Wisconsin.[2] In the early 1970s he also led a Bible study in Chicago. Although this work[3] disbanded after his death in 1980, it began again when Arlena opened her home to Bible studies in 1982.

1 Established as Hope Orthodox Presbyterian Church in Libertyville, Illinois, on October 7, 1979.
2 Established as Christ Presbyterian Church in Janesville, Wisconsin, in September 1975.
3 Trinity Chapel in Chicago, Illinois, organized as a church in 1987, continued until 1996, when it disbanded.

Arlena's life was no less busy in the United States than on the mission field. In addition to supporting her husband's work as a church planter, caring for their mothers, and being a homemaker, she began teaching at Christian Liberty Academy to supplement the family income. Her home was always open to visitors, and many were the meals she carried to a neighbor or friend in need. After Francis's battle with cancer and subsequent death in 1980, Arlena continued to support the work of the OPC and to teach in the Chicago area until 1985, when she moved to be with family in Tyler, Texas.

In Texas, Arlena joined Tyler OPC and began teaching at Good Shepherd Christian School. During this time she became an expert in motor skills and used that expertise to help many learning disabled students. Despite becoming legally blind in her later years, she continued teaching or tutoring until just a month before her death on April 30, 2015, at 97. She was fond of saying that God never intended us to stop the work he gives us to do until he calls us home.

There is no doubt that Arlena spent her life living for Christ. Hers was a life that involved many sacrifices, yet it was a life she loved. When relaying stories of her time on the mission field, Arlena begged Christian women to accept their responsibility for the lost in the world. To her, this meant giving their sons and daughters to the work, fervently praying, and giving sacrificially. "The faithful prayers and gifts of those here at home are the means used to maintain the missionaries abroad," she would say. "Let us act quickly for the night cometh!"

**Mary Arlena Bonner** *is the eldest daughter of the late Arlena and Francis Mahaffy. A member of Tyler Orthodox Presbyterian Church, she resides in Troup, Texas, with her family. She is a widow with five adult children and two granddaughters.*

# 9

# Hermima Davies:
# Helpmate in the Ministry

## *Trudy Bosman*

Hermima huddled close to John inside the umbrella tent they had pitched next to the public school in Neopit on the Menominee Indian Reservation. The wind howled, bending some of the tent poles. They prayed for God to keep them safe in the storm. When it was over, the winds of the tornado had blown out a window in the school door and blown down a barn a few miles away, but God had kept them safe. Not one tent peg had been pulled loose!

Hermima thought of all that had happened since she and John Davies were married on November 27, 1934. They had ministered in northwestern Wisconsin at Whitefish Chapel on the Lac Court du Oreilles Reservation, the land of the Chippewa, for two years. They then packed up and traveled two hundred miles to the Menominee Indian Reservation in northeastern Wisconsin where they began holding vacation Bible school and evening meetings in the public school. And now, after being there for only two weeks, John had been asked to lead out a group wanting to leave the John Sargeant Memorial Presbyterian Church because of the liberalism in the Presbyterian Church (USA).[1]

---

1 The Native Americans known as the Menominee Indians are original to northern Wisconsin and upper Michigan. Their name means "wild rice gathers," which was their main food crop. Some of their land was given to the Stockbridge-Munsee when they settled in Wisconsin.

The group became the Old Stockbridge Orthodox Presbyterian Church. Hermima, now expecting their first child, was quickly learning to pack, move, and set up housekeeping wherever the Lord led them.

Hermima busied herself with washing, ironing, cooking, and cleaning, as well as raising children, seven of them, John, Janice, Beth, Helen, David, Rachel, and Rebecca. She was also active helping with church work.

As a pastor's wife, Hermima, on Saturday packed up the portable organ and joined John in heading to the Menominee Reservation. They drove around town and down forest lanes to pick up children for Sunday school, which was held in the Roundhouse (typically used for ceremonial activities and dances) or outside in good weather. Hermima visited homes with her husband, especially on the Menominee Reservation where it was not considered proper for a man to visit a woman alone. Sunday mornings she rose early to get breakfast ready, made sure the kids were dressed and ready to go, attended morning worship, and helped to teach Sunday school at the Old Stockbridge Church. The noon meal was often stretched to feed guests her husband invited or visitors who came to the church. Tuesday nights were cottage prayer meetings with one of the Stockbridge families. Sometimes they would help with cornhuskings or in other ways, which was often more meaningful to the people than many visits.

On a quiet evening there might be a knock on the door. "Please help us! My wife needs to go to the hospital. She might need an

---

The Native Americans known as the Stockbridge-Munsee Indians originally lived on the East Coast. In 1735 it was agreed that a mission would be established in Stockbridge, Massachusetts. John Sergeant was ordained to serve as minister among the people, and did so until his death in 1749. Jonathan Edwards served the mission as well as an English congregation for seven years after that. In 1784 the tribe left the area. Many settled in Wisconsin.

For many years the two churches, Menominee Chapel and Old Stockbridge OPC, shared a missionary pastor. In the 1980s Menominee OPC became a separate congregation and called its first pastor, Ken Smith.

Hermima Davies (third from left) with the Ladies' Prayer Circle

operation. We don't have the $35 the hospital needs." Prayers were said and help given. On busy days John would have to watch the children while Hermima ministered to a sick mother, came home to eat a quick bite, and hurried off to meet with the Ladies' Prayer Circle. "This little dress will look so cute on Rose," Hermima might comment as she helped to pack up clothing that had been donated and set out with her husband to distribute it to those in need. In the summer many of the people left to do cherry picking. Hermima packed up children, food, and clothing, and joined her pastor husband for the long drive to minister to their people where they worked.

And the Christmas Programs! Hermima taught Christmas songs to the children and choirs. What joy to see the families come and hear the Christmas story; first at the Old Stockbridge Church, a second time on the Stockbridge Reservation, and a third time, often at a home, on the Menominee Reservation. Oh, and don't forget putting together and handing out candy bags for everyone.

It was a busy, busy life. God blessed their ministry. In an article that Hermima wrote entitled "And Yet There is Room," she explained how it also blessed her.

"Yet there is room," it means that there is room for the Indian as well as the black man, for the yellow and brown as well as the white man. That truth was brought home to me just a few Sundays ago. I felt as if I had a glimpse of what Heaven will be like. We were celebrating the Lord's Supper, and it was the first time in years when I could sit among the people, instead of being up at the piano or organ. I was moved beyond words. At one end of my pew sat a woman with a combination of Stockbridge and Oneida Indian blood. Beside me sat a Menominee Indian and in front of me sat those two Stockbridge Indian people who gave us a home when we had no other home to go to in this community except a tent, who shared all they had—and that was not much—of this world's goods so that we could eat.

The bread at this communion service was served by a Winnebago Indian man. My heart swelled with thanksgiving to God. Here were the people to whom we had been called to minister the Word, who loved the Lord and by God's grace were led to accept the Lord Jesus Christ as their Savior, all grouped around the Lord's table in remembrance of Him who gave to them eternal life; and God saw fit to allow me, lacking so much in the qualities a missionary should have, to participate in this great work. Truly, it was one of the "mountain peaks" in my life.[2]

Hermima left these people she had come to love, and moved to Wildwood, New Jersey, when her husband accepted a call to Calvary OPC. She took up a new ministry there until John retired in 1971. After a short two-year retirement they moved to Glenwood, Washington, and served there for three years in the OPC chapel. And in 1977 they returned to New Jersey where Pastor Davies served as interim pastor at Union Chapel in Wildwood for two years.

And then the work was done. The final move to a new and

---

2 Hermima Davies, "And Yet There Is Room, "*Presbyterian Guardian* 20 (May 15, 1951): 87, http://opc.org/cfh/guardian/Volume_20/1951-05-15. pdf.

glorious home for Hermima Davies was February 20, 1995. "Well done, good and faithful servant…. Enter thou into the joy of thy lord" (Matt. 25:23, KJV).

**Trudy Bosman,** *her husband, Steve, and their children moved from their home in Michigan in answer to a call in 1978 for people to come to help the Old Stockbridge Church and Menominee Chapel. They are members of Menominee OPC in Zoar, Wisconsin, and have come to know and love people from both churches. Trudy remembers coming with her parents to visit the Old Stockbridge Church once when she was young. She grew up attending Bethel Orthodox Presbyterian Church in Oostburg, Wisconsin, and relatives of the Davies family were her neighbors. They have seven children and 11 grandchildren.*

# 10

# Eleanor Kellogg:
# To the Harvest Fields of America

### Deborah Kellogg Kropp

Eleanor and Edward Kellogg shared a fairy-tale romance that survived the test of time, world conflicts, financial hardship, bicoastal ministry, and five children. Along the way, they played an instrumental role in the young Orthodox Presbyterian Church.

On February 7, 1913, a wintry day in Steele, North Dakota, Eleanor Hurd Peterman was warmly welcomed into the family of Rudolph and Ora Peterman. Eleanor was the firstborn of what would become a family with six children. In 1922, at the tender age of nine, Eleanor accepted Christ as her Savior and told her mother she wanted to become a missionary. This was an ambition she carried with her from 1926, when the family was uprooted and moved to a farm in Glenwood, Minnesota, to 1930, when Eleanor entered college in Wheaton, Illinois.

A well-used piano graced their farmhouse living rooms in North Dakota and Minnesota, filling the homes with delightful music and traditional hymns. Despite—or maybe because of—growing up in a Covenanter Church, where playing musical instruments was not allowed during worship, Eleanor eagerly embarked on a musical path that culminated in her becoming church organist and choir director for over 60 years. Eleanor was 90 when she retired from playing the organ or piano in worship services.

Eleanor's years at Wheaton College were some of her best, as she established lifelong friendships and met the love of her life,

Edward Louis Kellogg. When a job in the college library became available, Eleanor eagerly took the position. To be surrounded by the literary magic of library books was a delight to this English major. On trips to the library, Edward found himself checking out sweet Eleanor rather than books. Their ro-

Edward and Eleanor Kellogg

mantic courtship began and led them on canoe rides in the twilight hours, where Edward serenaded Eleanor with love songs.

Edward was born in Wheaton on June 25, 1912, one of five children. He was a great grandson of the founder of Wheaton College, Jonathan Blanchard. When Eleanor met Edward, this strikingly handsome young man aspired to use his mathematical gifts as an architect or engineer. However, both Eleanor and Edward were touched by chapel messages urging them to commit their lives to missionary service. Eleanor responded by consecrating herself to ministry overseas, but Edward felt that in a lucrative profession, like architecture or engineering, he could better serve Christ's kingdom by financially assisting a number of missionaries.

Then one day the words of Philippians 3:7 (KJV) caught Eleanor's attention. "But what things were gain to me, those I counted as loss for Christ." Eleanor and Edward pondered these words together and prayed for God's enlightenment as to what they might mean for them. After much prayer, Edward was led to make a career change, feeling called to become a missionary. As Eleanor said, they were both committed to go to the whitened harvest fields of John 4:35.

Wedding bells rang to celebrate their marriage on September 12, 1936. It was then two years after college graduation, and Edward was in the midst of his ministerial training at Westminster Theological Seminary in Philadelphia, Pennsylvania. Together Edward and Eleanor believed her life-long ambition to be a missionary would become a reality in India. But God had other plans for them.

The Kelloggs had booked passage to India through the Independent Board for Presbyterian Foreign Missions. J. Gresham Machen and others had established the board as a response to theological liberalism in the mainline church's foreign missions program.[1] Unfortunately, the board was in turmoil at this time. Some board members were less concerned with the board's Presbyterian identity than Machen was, and they ousted him as president and installed a minister from a nondenominational church. Eleanor and Edward's tickets to India were canceled, and they followed Machen into the fledgling Orthodox Presbyterian Church. After Edward's ordination in 1937, the Kelloggs began their life-long ministry, not in foreign lands as they had imagined, but coast-to-coast in the harvest fields of America.

Eleanor was excited when Edward received his first call to minister in a small mission church in Manhattan, New York City, but there were many challenges. The small congregation had limited means to provide financial support. A single cot was their bed in their small unit, and food was hard to come by. However, God always provided for them, whether with eggs or unlabeled cans of food left on their doorstep. What became a dinner meal was a daily surprise. Would the unlabeled cans yield peaches, tomatoes, beans, or corn?

They were encouraged at a speaking engagement in November

1 The Presbyterian Church (USA) interpreted the existence of the new board as a direct challenge to its denominational authority and brought members of the board, including Machen, to trial. In March 1935 Machen was found guilty and suspended from the ministry. This led to the 1936 founding of the Presbyterian Church of America, renamed the Orthodox Presbyterian Church in 1939. See D. G. Hart, *Defending the Faith: J. Gresham Machen and the Crisis of Conservative Protestantism in Modern America* (Grand Rapids: Baker, 1995), 147–54.

1937 when a congregation in Orange, New Jersey, held a benefit on their behalf. During a fun, playful scavenger hunt, 107 cans of food of all kinds were given to them. Eleanor wrote home of the wonderful blessing and quoted Isaiah 65:24 (KJV): "Before ye call, I will answer; and while ye are yet speaking, I will hear."

Tensions were mounting on the world scene when Eleanor and Edward headed to Middletown, Pennsylvania, where Edward ministered from 1938 to 1946 at Calvary OPC. An ocean away from rising conflicts in Europe, Eleanor was experiencing the painful blessing of childbirth. On a hot, humid summer day in July 1938, Gwendolyn Ruth entered the Kellogg family. She was followed by Susan Eleanor in December 1941, days after the bombing of Pearl Harbor. Edward Kimball arrived in May 1944, as the conflict of World War II continued. Most of the parenting was left to Eleanor, as Edward was consumed with pastoral outreach and long workdays.

Eleanor wrote home to her folks about the wonderful preacher Edward was. She proved to be a great encourager and support for her husband as he ministered. Eleanor did not show resentment that he had to labor for so many hours—as she had grown up during a time when working hard for survival was the way you lived. In conversation years later, Edward remarked that a 74-hour workweek was necessary to pastor a congregation.

After eight years in Middletown, Edward was called to minister at Immanuel OPC in West Collingswood, New Jersey. Following two heart-wrenching miscarriages, Eleanor spent most of her next pregnancy bedridden before Deborah Ellen was born in October 1950. It was fortunate that Eleanor's mother was able to live with them for a time to help with the other children and household chores. Less than two years later, in July 1952, Janice Margaret was welcomed into the family. The Kellogg household was lively and bustling in those days, with five energetic children spanning 14 years.

Hospitality was one of Eleanor's gifts that she enjoyed using throughout her life. The smell of pot roast and mashed potatoes after Sunday worship or an evening meal of lasagna and a homemade dessert, whet the appetites of many a guest from the various churches they served. They counted it a joy and blessing to meet and get to know so many people. Often overnight hospitality was offered as well.

Concerned about putting their children through public schools, Edward founded the Camden County Christian School in West Collingswood. Eleanor taught music and conducted a choir there for several years. A graduate of the school attributed Eleanor's gifted music leadership as the reason he and his sister pursued music careers, both recording songs with the London Symphony Orchestra.

Another eight years passed when in 1954 Edward was called to serve a small congregation being birthed on the opposite coast, in National City, California. Though the cross country drive was broken up by visits to relatives and sightseeing, it was a terribly long journey. The Kelloggs crammed their five children, ages two to 16, alongside them in the old two-seater Dodge. Singing hymns and Christian choruses together along the way helped to pass the time. It was comforting to Eleanor knowing that her aging parents as well as three of her siblings had relocated in Southern California. The Kelloggs would be welcomed by family they loved.

Several years after the Kelloggs' arrival, a church building project began in Paradise Hills, California, where the National City congregation would relocate. Edward oversaw the construction while continuing his pastoral responsibilities. It was an easier life now for Eleanor and the family than their time in West Collingswood when Edward was serving on 16 committees or boards for Immanuel OPC, the OPC denomination, Westminster Theological Seminary, and Camden County Christian School.

Years unfolded in Paradise Hills with Eleanor enthusiastically using her music and teaching gifts by conducting the church adult and youth choirs and teaching the high school Sunday school class. Eleanor also began working full time as a public school substitute teacher in 1956, followed by a fourth-grade teaching assignment. Although this was a heavy load to add to Eleanor's church duties, funds were needed if the Kellogg children were to attend Christian colleges.

With the weight of these many responsibilities, Eleanor considered it a necessity to have a daily walk with the Lord. When her children were small, Eleanor placed Bible verses over the kitchen sink to memorize. During her teaching years, Eleanor would have a prayer time as she commuted to and from school. According to Eleanor, nothing was too small and difficult to ask God.

Most significant was the practice of reading the Bible through every year. By the time of her death in 2009, there were a number of worn out Bibles in her possession, since she and Edward had read God's Word from cover-to-cover well over 60 times.

In addition to individual quiet times, having devotions together as a family was very important to Eleanor and Edward. Following the reading of Scripture around the evening dinner table, the family would gather at the piano and sing hymns. As Eleanor played, singing the alto part with daughter Janice, other family members chimed in singing soprano, tenor, and bass. Word spread that the Kellogg family sang together. When spontaneous requests were made to hear them at church conferences, they selected a hymn and figured out who would sing each part as they approached the stage.

On the home front, the room lit up when Edward wrapped his arms around Eleanor in a warm embrace and kissed her as she labored in the kitchen. Children present would all smile at the blushing couple, and sometimes wanted to get in on the hug. Eleanor often would turn and exclaim, "Isn't he handsome?"

"We never heard Mother say anything negative about Dad," says daughter Susan, wife of OP minister Roger Schmurr, former general secretary of Christian Education. This loving and committed marriage was a gift Eleanor and Edward gave to their children. If any conflict or hurt arose between Eleanor and Edward, they applied Ephesians 4:26 (KJV): "Let not the sun go down upon your wrath." "Sometimes at bedtime," daughter Deborah remembers, "Mother asked my forgiveness for something she said or did. I usually had not noticed anything amiss, but Mother's humility, respect, and love made an impression on me."

One day, while waiting in the grocery store checkout line, Eleanor observed a clerk having some tense interactions with a gentleman she was helping. Eleanor leaned down and whispered to Deborah and Janice, "Let's see if we can make her smile." The girls witnessed the change in the clerk's countenance as their mother graciously encouraged and engaged in small talk with the woman.

As a pastor's wife, Eleanor believed that she had to be careful to avoid favoritism towards select women in the church. In her view, a close friendship with another woman in the congregation would not be appropriate. Over the years, this friendship gap was filled by the wonderful relationship Eleanor developed with Kathleen Poundstone, who also was an OPC pastor's wife. Personal secrets and laughter buoyed their energetic conversations. In the late 1950s and early 1960s, they both enjoyed being the camp cooks at youth conferences. Working together was so much fun with a kindred spirit!

Moving in 1966 to a charming Spanish-style home in Point Loma, California, meant a longer commute to Eleanor's work as a remedial reading specialist. However, it was important that the Kelloggs live within the community they served. Eleanor and Edward's hospitable ways continued. Eleanor soon warmly welcomed her elderly mother, Ora Peterman, to live with them until her death in 1969. On weekends during the Vietnam War years, up to five off-duty US Marines from Camp Pendleton were graciously welcomed into the Kellogg home. They savored Eleanor's delicious meals and camped out on the living room and dining room floors. Sunday worship services recharged and blessed them for another week at the military camp or before some were shipped abroad. Eleanor and Edward also reached out to a recovered cocaine addict who had become a Christian while serving time in jail, and he lived with them for an extended time.

On a Sunday morning in the fall of 1976, Edward suffered a stroke while preaching. Though he recovered after several months, retirement was on the horizon. In 1977 Edward left full-time ministry, and he and Eleanor headed back across the country to lush, green Leesburg, Virginia. While Edward assisted his son-in-law Edwin Urban (Gwendolyn's husband) at Bethel OPC, Eleanor again used her skills at choral conducting and playing the organ and piano. As their lives unfolded in their retirement, Eleanor and Edward never stopped ministering to the sick and infirm or leading weekly Bible studies. These lifestyle habits were ingrained in them. Granddaughter Rebecca Schmurr would later write about seeing Grammie Kellogg share God's love with workers in various retirement and nursing homes. "With a loving smile, she asked them if they knew the Lord. She always wanted to point people to Jesus."

Eleanor was delighted to become a grandmother while serving in Paradise Hills, California. During the Point Loma years and on into retirement in Virginia, she welcomed more grandchildren and great grandchildren into the Kellogg Clan. Seven of these children were adopted from far-off countries, including Thailand, Korea, El Salvador, and Peru, ironically, bringing foreign missions at last to Eleanor's doorstep. Grandmother Eleanor loved her grandchildren and great grandchildren dearly and strove to pray daily for their salvation and well-being.

When the OP congregation in Bonita, California, was going through difficult times in 1990, they asked Edward Kellogg to temporarily fill in as pastor. Eleanor and Edward were warmly welcomed by this hurting congregation and served until a permanent pastor was found a year later. Their ministry experience and spiritual depth blessed the people in Bonita.

Eleanor was Edward's sweetheart, soul-mate, and companion for 65 years of marriage and ministry, until he entered heaven's gate in 2001. On February 6, 2009, Eleanor was ushered in to join her beloved Edward, hours before her 96th birthday.

**Deborah Kellogg Kropp** *is grateful and blessed to be one of Eleanor Kellogg's daughters. Having grown up in the Orthodox Presbyterian Church, she is presently a member of First Covenant Church in Oakland, California.*

# 11

# Florence Handyside:
# Count It All Joy

## Caroline Weerstra

Rains in the spring of 1945 poured down relentlessly on the little town of Mount Judea, Arkansas. The surrounding Ozark hills drained the floodwaters into swollen creeks that overflowed onto rough dirt roads. Every road into the remote farming village was closed, crisscrossed with deep, flowing water.

The local farmers and shopkeepers took little notice of these unpleasant events except to hope for the return of the mail truck once the torrent subsided. After all, poverty and gasoline rationing had conspired to leave few of them with the means of owning automobiles of any kind. Their lives were restricted to the collection of rambling shacks snuggled against the foot of Kent Mountain—the town they affectionately referred to as "Judy."

Young James Hefley and his friends sat on the porch of his parents' store and stared at the rain unhappily.[1] They always hated rainy days that trapped them indoors, but on this particular Monday evening, the rain meant something more—Florence Handyside and Helen Liese would not be able to hold their usual youth meeting. James did not like to admit that he would miss those two Yankee ladies. After all, he was an almost-grown young man of 14, and he considered himself far too old for hymns and Bible stories. He

---

1  James Hefley, "I Know Who I Am," in *Way Back in the Hills* (Garland, TX: Hannibal, 2008), 257–81.

even ran a gambling business
out of his parents' store, and
he had big dreams of being a
blackjack dealer in Las Vegas.
But, he grumbled silently to
himself, what else was there
to do around Judy? It was
sort of good fun to drop in on
the youth meeting, play some
mischief on the younger kids
and sing wildly off key while
Florence bravely plinked out
"The Old Rugged Cross" on
her accordion. Surely that was
all James Hefley and his wild
buddies were missing—the
fun of their Monday night
shenanigans.

Florence Handyside with the accordian
she played while sharing her faith in
small towns in Arkansas during the
mid-1940s

But the next Monday, as the flood waters receded enough for
a few large trucks to roll into Judy, James and his friends anxiously
lingered around the school where the meetings were held. Seven
o'clock came and went, and there was no sign of the old Model A.
Just as they were about to give up and head back home, they heard
it wheezing up the road. Sure enough, they caught a glimpse of the
freckled face of Florence in the driver seat as the car ground to a
halt in the school yard. Her missionary partner Helen stepped out
first, shaking her head at the close call they had at the last creek.
"The motor drowned out, but Florence got it started," she said.
They had barely escaped the high water.

The two young missionaries started their Monday meeting, apparently unperturbed by their brush with disaster. Florence and
Helen were used to rough living by now. Both grew up in middle
class homes and attended Moody Bible Institute with plans to be
missionaries in foreign countries. Florence wanted to serve in Korea, while Helen dreamed of India. For now, however, their plans

were on hold. Both locations were deemed too dangerous for single young ladies as the hostilities of World War II continued. Florence and Helen had been sent to the Ozarks for training.

Florence, who was born on November 9, 1918, would later remember the Ozarks as the least hospitable place she had ever lived. Her dwelling was a run-down shack with a roof so damaged that winter snow sifted through and settled in her hair. Summers were even more grueling—heat and mosquitoes and bumpy roads. Perhaps most discouraging of all, however, were the suspicion and hostility she encountered among many of those with whom she shared Christ in these insular, unchurched communities. Week after week, Florence and Helen ventured out through the Ozark hills to remote hamlets, holding meetings, singing songs, teaching Bible stories, and praying. And week after week, no one responded to their message. When the two missionaries gave up holding meetings in Judy, not a single person had been converted.

Florence Handyside refused to be discouraged. After all, she had seen at least one rather dramatic conversion in her own household—her mother. Florence grew up attending a Methodist church in Rochester, New York, at her father's insistence.[2] Her mother had little interest in religion. "I'm a good person," she always said. "I don't need Jesus." Florence's father, a truck driver with a conservative religious background, never took a confrontational approach to his wife, but he was deeply disturbed when the Methodist church removed their faithful minister and replaced him with a theological liberal. Frustrated at the apparent inability of their new minister even to declare with certainty the miracle of Christ's resurrection, Mr. Handyside began searching for a new church. He found a home at a small non-denominational congregation called Brighton Community Church.

By the time the Handysides left the Methodist church, Florence

---

2 The author thanks Rev. Kenneth Handyside (younger brother of Florence Handyside) for providing detailed background information, letters, and photos for this article.

was a teenager. Her father taught her to drive at an early age, and she took advantage of her new freedom to join a friend at Covenant Orthodox Presbyterian Church in Rochester. There, under the teaching of Rev. Peter Pascoe, she learned about the Reformed faith.

Florence's family never joined her at Covenant, but they were supportive of her new church home. Her brothers and sister had benefited from good teaching at Brighton, and they all (as her brother Kenneth later remembered) ganged up on their mother, insisting that she too must be saved.

Mrs. Handyside took little notice of her children's efforts for many months. Then one day, as she stood by a clothesline hanging up damp laundry, she noticed a small worm wriggling in the dust. She had nearly trod on it by mistake. She carefully stepped away from the small creature to avoid crushing it. "I suppose I am rather like that worm compared to God," she reflected. "He is so big and powerful, and I am so small. He could crush me at any time for refusing to obey him, but he is merciful just like I was merciful to the worm."

The worm in the dust proved to be an unlikely turning point for Mrs. Handyside. She was never the same from that moment. She threw herself into the service of the Lord, holding backyard Bible classes and teaching Sunday school. She even wished she could be a missionary, and was disappointed when a mission board told her she was too old.

When Florence one day informed her mother that she wanted to be a missionary, Mrs. Handyside was thrilled. She saw in her young daughter a chance to reach out to others with the gospel of Christ. Florence's home church was also supportive, and soon the adventurous young lady was on her way to Moody Bible Institute in Chicago for missionary training.

At first, Florence's missionary aspirations were modest. On her enrollment form at Moody, she indicated her intention of being a home missionary. A class project on missions in Korea soon changed her goals. She learned about the work of Presbyterian missions all across that distant peninsula, and the dramatic results over a few short decades—churches, hospitals, even colleges established. She also learned about shocking persecution by Japanese officials who seized control of Korea and northwest China—Christians put in prison, beaten, even executed. OPC missionary Bruce Hunt, who was working with ethnic Koreans in Manchukuo in northeast China, had even served time in a Japanese prison twice before he and all other foreign missionaries were expelled. Now a curtain of silence had fallen across the once vibrant Christian work in Korea. Nobody knew what had happened to the thousands of Korean Christians still laboring under ruthless Japanese oppression.

Florence began to pray for Korea. She made friends with a few Korean students at Moody. Soon she had changed her life's ambition: she now wanted to be a missionary to Korea. At the moment, however, this was utterly impossible. World War II was roaring to a bitter and dangerous end. American forces battled Japan from island to island across the Pacific, and submarines prowled the ocean.

With Korea decidedly out of reach, Florence joined Helen Liese on home missions to the Ozarks. She served with her usual energy and enthusiasm, but she never wavered from her ultimate goal. When World War II finally crashed to an end and Japan surrendered, Florence could only think of one thing: Korea would soon be open for missions.

Florence quickly came to Philadelphia and contacted OPC foreign missions. The news was initially discouraging. Korea was simply too dangerous, she was told. The withdrawal of the Japanese and the influx of the American army had proved a difficult transition. There were communist uprisings in the north and the southwest brought on by Koreans who had grown resentful of all foreign involvement. As the months wore on, some missionaries were able to return. Bruce Hunt found his way back and encountered a devastated but determined band of Korean Christians still carrying on amid burned and vandalized churches. He joined them in the slow process of rebuilding.

In 1948, 29-year-old Florence finally found a way into the

elusive nation. The US Army in Korea needed secretaries. Attempts to hire local Korean women to fill these jobs had proved frustrating. Language barriers made communication difficult, and cultural traditions discouraged cultivated Korean ladies from working among rough army men. Desperate for English-speaking typists to handle the endless paperwork involved in management of military bases, the US Army quickly recognized the necessity of importing secretaries from home. Florence had found her ticket to Korea.

With the blessing of the OPC and her family, Florence set sail across the Pacific on March 21, 1948. Friends who saw her off on her journey remembered her face "shining with happiness." The journey started unpleasantly. "I was seasick," Florence wrote home, "in spite of all my mental resolutions about it." Soon, however, she adjusted to the motion of the ship enough to befriend the chaplain, various servicemen, and several missionaries returning to work in Korea. She even took up language lessons while still aboard.

Her arrival in Seoul cheered her. The dire predictions of difficult conditions never materialized significantly to a woman who had spent months in rural Arkansas. The army provided housing and even a salary. Young, energetic, cheerful Florence acclimated well to the American community in Seoul. She was soon a regular at Youth for Christ meetings packed with young soldiers and missionaries. But American society in Seoul was insular. Florence shared a house with other American secretaries and spent the bulk of her time on the American military base. Army policies actively discouraged contact between employees and Koreans. Maintaining her focus on mission work among Koreans proved challenging. "Sunday I went to a Korean church again," she wrote to her family. "I had to go alone, however, because no one especially wants to learn Korean."

In early June a visit to the OPC mission work on the southern coast seemed to refocus her missionary ambition. Bruce Hunt welcomed the new prospective missionary warmly and gave her a tour of the seminary and a nearby leper colony. Florence took special note of a small country church, writing later to her friends:

It was a small Korean building but very clean with the floors polished until they actually shone. Outside the building was the church bell which the Koreans had made from a large bomb shell. The Japanese took away practically all the church bells. It seems significant to think that the Japanese took away the church bells and dropped bombs on the Koreans and yet the Lord has even used the bombs for his glory. That which man used to destroy the church God is now using to call people to the Church.

As Florence stared at the church bell on the first day of June in 1948, she had no way of knowing how her own life would reflect that same lesson. In fact, this would be the final summer of her young life.

The end of Florence's story began in January 1949. With the US military winding down operations in Korea, Florence was given the option of ending her contract early. She was transferred at her request to a missionary visa. The dream she had tenaciously held for years was finally taking shape. The OPC foreign missions board made her the first single woman missionary in the denomination, and she made plans to join Bruce Hunt at the mission in Pusan.

"I'm beginning to feel like a real missionary!" she declared in a letter to her family as she eagerly awaited the train that would carry her to her first foreign mission assignment.

Florence's transition into full-time mission work went smoothly. Bruce Hunt's wife, Kathy, later recalled, "After being with us two weeks,

Florence Handyside with Bruce Hunt
in Korea

Florence moved into her room in the same building with a Korean Christian family. She had already made a 'home' of it. I marveled at the way in which she fitted into a life which was so different. Although she lived her own life, the family also felt almost as if she belonged to them."

Without the responsibilities of full-time work and the distraction of military life, she could devote herself to serious language study, and she plunged in eagerly. In fact, it was on her way to language lessons one Monday afternoon on a bicycle in a brisk February wind that the first signs of trouble began. Florence felt unusually tired. Her legs were stiff and achy. She barely made it home, blaming the cold wind and demanding schedule for her exhaustion. By Wednesday, however, there was no denying her illness. She had a fever, and her legs were in terrible pain. When she awoke on Thursday, she could no longer get out of bed. Her legs were almost useless. Paralysis was slowly creeping up her body.

The trouble could not have come at a worse time. The mission's doctor was away in Seoul, and Bruce Hunt was holding classes out in the countryside. Kathy Hunt consulted local doctors, and all agreed that Florence ought to be taken to a medical facility in Seoul at once. But this recommendation was not easily carried out. Bad weather had set in; planes were grounded.

By Friday evening, when Florence could no longer move her body or speak clearly, Kathy made a difficult decision—Florence must be taken to Seoul by train. The missionaries did their best to make Florence comfortable for the long ride, carrying her aboard wrapped in snug blankets. Kathy later wrote to Florence's parents, "On the train she tried to speak to me when I did something for her. But it was such an effort, and so difficult to understand her that I tried not to encourage it…. I suggested that she rest, and she smiled at me and seemed glad to do it."

Only after Florence had been unusually quiet for a while did Kathy notice the strange pallor of her face. Without a word or sound, Florence had died. The paralysis had reached her heart. It was February 12, 1949. Doctors later speculated that she had contracted polio, a common affliction in that era. But the diagnosis was no comfort to the friends and family of Florence Handyside. She was buried in a small cemetery alongside many other missionaries who had perished on the field. Missionary Francis McKim played Florence's small accordion—the same with which she had led the Ozark boys in "The Old Rugged Cross"—while the gathering sang some of her favorite hymns.

The story of Florence Handyside could be a stark warning on the dangers of mission work—how everything that can go wrong may go wrong one day at the worst possible time, and plans may come to utter ruin. But Florence's friends and family never saw her story as a failure. Her life still rang out the good news of Jesus like the bell in the old country church—still calling to people even amid the destruction of her life. James Hefley, who had as a boy set himself to creating as much mischief as possible during Florence's youth meetings in Mount Judea, became a pastor and Christian publisher, crediting Florence Handyside and Helen Liese with teaching him about Jesus. Letters from dozens of Florence's army friends to her parents after her death told them how she encouraged them in faith. Florence's younger brother Kenneth, inspired by her steadfast example, dedicated himself to mission work in the Congo. He later recalled his mother, who had lost one child already on the mission field, standing on the deck of the boat that would take her son away to the jungles of Africa. "She gathered us together there and prayed for us. And then she gave the future to the hands of God." Kenneth and his wife served ten years in the heart of Africa before returning to work in children's ministry in New York.

In 1987—almost 40 years after Florence's death—Kenneth Handyside traveled to Korea to visit his sister's grave. He was the only one of his family ever able to make the trip. He found the small marker overshadowed by the tombstones of more well-known missionaries. Time had worn down her name. He called his brother about buying a new tombstone. "But we decided against the purchase," he said. "It doesn't matter to anyone now where she is buried. God knows where she is buried. A worn-down grave marker halfway around the world won't mean anything on the Day of Resurrection."

**Caroline Weerstra** *publishes Reformed curriculum for children through* Catechism for Kids. *She and her husband and children are members of Calvary Orthodox Presbyterian Church in Schenectady, New York.*

# Part Two

# Choosing to Build
# 1950s–1960s

# 12

# Mabel Danzeisen
# and JoAnn Vandenburg:
# From Strength to Strength
# in the Dakotas

*Rebecca R. D. Schnitzel*

When JoAnn Vandenburg was seven years old, she and her parents attended the worship service at Leith Orthodox Presbyterian Church in North Dakota, where Dr. J. Gresham Machen preached his last sermon on December 27, 1936. This infant denomination, which Machen helped to found, shook a small town in rural North Dakota and impacted the lives of two North Dakota women—Mabel Danzeisen and JoAnn Vandenburg. They, in turn, have influenced generations to come.

## Mabel Grayce Houchin Danzeisen

"My parents and your Aunt Lola spent their first North Dakota winter in a tent."

"Yeah, right, Mom…. Wait! You're not kidding … or are you?"

She insisted, and even led us to the spot just south and west of my home town of Carson where her parents and oldest sister had shivered through their first months after moving to North Dakota from Iowa. In 1910, Carson was just being built. There was nowhere to "stay."

Perhaps God used the ruggedness of her family to help my

mother stand up for her faith at an early age. It could also have been the resolve for change that she learned from being tethered to a clothesline while under the care of her older sisters, who called her "Punk." In reality, she was anything but a punk. In 1936, when the OPC emerged from the Presbyterian Church (USA), my mother, born on June 30, 1916, was 20 years old. It is remarkable that as a relatively young, single woman, and in such a remote corner of the kingdom, God raised up in her the conviction and courage to stand up and walk out of a church where she had first learned about, and had committed her life to, the Lord.

At the time, 33-year-old Rev. Sam Allen was the pastor of the PCUSA in Carson. He was a protégé of J. Gresham Machen and well aware of the events at Princeton Theological Seminary that had precipitated the founding of Westminster Theological Seminary in 1929. Among the issues for which Machen contended were the virgin birth, the inerrancy of Scripture, and the way in which foreign missions was being carried out by the PCUSA. When Rev. Allen brought these issues to the attention of his congregation, not everyone was convinced that they were of such urgent concern. However, standing in truth, and in solidarity with Machen and colleagues, Rev. Allen brought a fledgling group, including my mother and her two sisters, out of the PCUSA and into what would become the newly born Orthodox Presbyterian Church. At first, the group worshipped in the town's fire hall, two blocks away from the church they left. Eventually they occupied an abandoned Seventh Day Adventist church and moved the building onto property donated by my uncle and aunt, Ervin and Esther Erickson. This location was only half a block away from the PCUSA church they had left.

Now, in a town of 300 closely-knit people, how do you think that went? Small town, rural life on the plains was all about working and surviving together. Almost sacred are the bonds forged through such experiences as helping a neighbor harvest his wheat before a hail storm arrives, sharing your coal-heated home with those who lost power, plowing the road of someone who needs medical attention during a blizzard, sharing your hay during that blizzard so your neighbor's cattle do not starve, or sharing your tornado shelter with those without one. My mother had made the decision to separate from the "Big Presbyterian Church," as we called it, but she still loved those who had chosen to stay in it.

The strains felt by the folks left behind were not those of resentment, nor of ill will, but of bewilderment that church issues could actually trump real life! Those who were more sympathetic to the concerns did not want to disrupt the community. So, on Sunday mornings, the air was a little stiff when long-time friends opened their car doors a half block away and walked into separate buildings for "church." When all of this was being worked through, my mother was absent for months at a time because, during the school year, she attended Dickinson Teacher's College. When she came home, she noticed that the shock of the break was waning, but there was a "coolness" that squatted in the depths of their kinships that never went away. They learned to speak of everything but the split.

Enter Ernest James Danzeisen. He frequented Lark Hall to play basketball, and attended the socials that took place there, including when the Lawrence Welk Band often played. On one of those occasions, Ernie met Mabel. They enjoyed dancing, going to basketball games, and hunting rabbits at night in a car, with my mother driving and my father aiming his .22 through the passenger window. They were married on April 23, 1938, in my aunt and uncle's home.

Ernie farmed with his father until he and Mabel were able to move onto their own farm, nine miles north of Lark, and 18 miles from Carson. Even though the Carson church was a distance, they continued to attend there because it had a morning service. The Lark church had a 1 p.m. service because the pastor served three congregations, Carson, Lark, and Leith, and he could not fit in three morning services.

Even with three congregations to support the pastor, paying him was difficult. Each one had a large constituency of farmers, so if crops that year were good, all was well. Those were dust bowl and grasshopper years, however, and if the crops were meager or destroyed, the responsibility of paying a pastor was dismaying. On at least one occasion, the pastor gave the amount of his pay to the budget fund, essentially paying himself, in order to preserve the good name of the congregation.

In 1964 my parents suffered financial crisis, the result of three years of drought. That was the end of farming for my father. We moved to Carson, where he worked various jobs, and my mother was again faced with the strained friendships of 1936.

One of the vehicles God used to help her shore up these ties was as a member of the Community Homemaker's Club. In working shoulder to shoulder with those outside the church, Mother had opportunity to dispense compassion for the weak and needy, and to bolster the community. To her, these projects were always occasions where she could show integrity, and feet-to-the-ground faith. In fact, she spearheaded the startup of an elder-friend program, which provided companionship and help with light housework to the elderly who were still residing in their homes, a program from which she eventually benefited. Another way that she showed her concern for community life was in accepting the nomination to the North Dakota Silver-haired Legislature, an organization that for three decades educated senior citizens on the state legislative process. By attending their meetings in Bismarck, the state capitol, she could enrich her home town, apprising townspeople of current issues and practices.

By God's grace, my mother's hardy constitution and faith carried her through all of her responsibilities and endeavors, at the same time taking seriously her oath to be a faithful member of the OPC. She was the supportive wife of a founding elder of 42 years, readily extending hospitality, and pouring out herself as a spiritual offering to the Lord in the church family. Such service does not stem from human loyalties, but only from faith given by Christ, who gives freely to all as he builds his church.

In addition to caring for her home and family, my mother

worked full time outside the home, as a rural, one-room schoolhouse teacher, a public school secretary, a public school teacher, a legal secretary, and, in her later years, the town librarian. Providing for physical needs was always an upstream task, yet, one of my dearest memories of her is seeing her sit at her bedroom vanity, in her house coat and curlers, counting out the offering money. God's work came first, our needs second.

Mabel Danzeisen teaching school

Jobs needed to be done in church life too. So, in addition to her other employment, the Lord gave her the strength to be our congregation's Sunday school superintendent, and adult Sunday school teacher for over 30 years. She was always daunted by the responsibility of teaching, but her college training had prepared her, so she reluctantly agreed to fill the need. She also held every office of the missionary society time and again. Often this little group was unsure about how they could help since they were so far away from the OPC offices in Philadelphia and the missionaries themselves. Yet, they loved the new church God had given them, and were committed to its ministries.

Summer was the time for vacation Bible school. This was a joint venture among the churches in Lark, Carson, and Leith, and was held in Lark, the congregation that had the largest building and the most kids. Since it was more convenient for farm parents to bring children in the morning, and to pick them up at the end of the day, VBS was held Monday through Friday from 9 a.m. to 3 p.m. Those long days required extensive planning. My mother made plans and executed them alongside her consanguine and spiritual sisters during all of my growing up years.

Mabel G. H. Danzeisen was a stout-hearted handmaiden of

the Lord in the OPC. With my father, she raised my three older brothers and me. We are all married to believers, we are walking closely with the Lord, and we are serving him in his church. This, too, is part of her godly legacy. Hers was not a cushy life. In fact, it was even less so when my father suffered from mental illness. When I once asked my mother how she stayed the course, she responded, "I loved him." That kind of love comes only from the eternal source of love, and her reflection of that love was a source of strength to all the saints who were watching her.

As one of my brothers quoted from Psalm 84 on the way to the funeral home when she died, "She went from strength to strength." We all witnessed her steady growth in grace, and we praise God for the work that he accomplished in and through her. My father died on January 12, 1979, at the age of 63, making my mother a servant-widow for 20 years. She died on December 7, 1999, and was buried in the Carson Cemetery, nestled in the hill country outside of town, about two miles from where her family took up its chilly residence in North Dakota.

## JoAnn Vandenburg

"C'mon Judy, fold the clothes and clean up this room. Aunt Jenny needs a place to sleep tonight.

"C'mon, Genell and Linda, make some bread. I am going to pick up the Michelson kids cuz Lucille's car just broke down, and Monroe is in the field. Sandra and Perry, weed the garden while I'm gone... and pick the beans while you're out there. We'll need them for supper."

"C'mon, Alan! We have seven miles of country to cover with those cattle."

"C'mon, Barb, would you like to go with me to visit Elsie at the Care Center?"

I am sure that when JoAnn Vandenburg said, "C'mon," to folks, they braced themselves. Sometimes people dug-in their feet, but she had ways of persuading them. The day was never long enough to accomplish all the service in her head, but she was going to mobilize her family—and others—to do whatever they could.

JoAnn was always looking for ways to attract anyone to the Lord, and to his church. It didn't matter if you were the mop-haired kid with scruffy shoes, the bedraggled mom, the exhausted farmer, or anyone's family member from a distance. Everyone was important to God, so everyone was important to her.

JoAnn Vandenburg hugging Rebecca Schnitzel's daughter Allegra in 2000 as son Ted makes his presence known

As the youngest child by four years and the only girl in my family, I was always thrilled when my mom said I could "go play at Vandenburg's." With six kids born between 1952 and 1960, there was always something happening there. I was afraid of the older three kids, but the younger three were lots of fun! They lived nine hilly, gravel-road miles from our farm, north of Lark, North Dakota, and about 20 yards across the gravel "street" from the OPC in Lark (population 13, eight of whom were Vandenburgs). I was not the only one who knew that welcome always awaited me there. A shriek, a smile, the grab of a towel to brush off her hands from whatever task was being done, and a hug, was the eager reception. We visitors could stand by and visit, or we could join in the work. Either way was fine with me. I got to go there.

I always felt special with her. Everyone did. I still do. Her habit was to wrap her arm around me (and others) and say, "Precious!" How would one not feel loved and valued by her? She saw things in me that she could help to shape, and she gave me the gift of learning how to serve others sacrificially. She never had to spell out the needs that people had, some obvious, some not. She just loved those people in front of me.

She was not afraid to dirty her hands in service behind the

scenes either. She was the one the pastor phoned when he needed someone to go out to the farm of a sickly sister in the Lord to
do the unappealing work of cleaning and cooking in a less than
pleasant environment *for two years*. When that sister broke her hip,
JoAnn cared for her in her (JoAnn's) home for the next *five years*.
If you think that must have slowed her down, think again. She
continued her life style of hospitality to others, which included,
but was not limited to, driving many elderly saints to and from
doctor appointments nearby and in Bismarck, 65 miles away. That
is showing God's love in the church!

In 1964 when I was six years old and moved to "town" (Carson), my time with JoAnn was trimmed to Sunday evenings and
VBS in the summer. Her Sundays were always busy. She taught
Sunday school, played piano for worship when needed, cared for
her own (and other) young children, and often had someone over
for lunch. For at least eight years before evening worship, she led
the Girls' Ensemble, of which I was a member. Though she did
not see herself as a first-rate musician, she recognized that we were
a group of about ten girls who enjoyed singing, so she gave us the
opportunity to hone our talents and to bless others with the fruit of
our practice. After evening worship many a family enjoyed "coffee"
at their house, which usually included cake, and ice cream from the
Schwann truck. And, VBS was nearly JoAnn's last name—**Vandenburgs**! Of course, she had a lot of help, but the week would have
been so different without her welcoming way and energy. She led
the music (in the early days playing piano with two fingers), taught
a class, arranged for snacks, and planned the VBS family picnic on
Saturday. If you were new to the group, she brought you in. You
knew that at least one person was very happy to have you there.

JoAnn loved the youth in the church. When she was a youth,
she enjoyed being a member of the Machen League, which attracted kids from many surrounding farms. She also learned how to
provide similar fellowship for the generations that would follow.
In my day, she helped to lead the youth group. She had us picking
rocks out of farmers' fields, raking yards, painting, and holding

bake sales and rummage sales. We had the best parties, too, partly because we kids loved being together, and partly because she not only knew how to work, but how to play!

When we went to youth camp in the Dakota Presbytery, she was always in the convoy driving us there. At first, camp was in South Dakota, then in Nebraska, and eventually in Colorado, which was a 12-hour drive. Did she rest after we got there? Of course not! She was counselor and friend to many a teenage girl, talking them through the maze of growing up, often late into the night, aiding and encouraging kids on the volleyball court, and hugging them at camp fires. Over the years, she continued to be interested in the next generation, leading the youth group at Bethel OPC in Carson, North Dakota, into her late 70s, still doing "camping, rummage sales, and all"!

Adult ministry did not elude her either. JoAnn was the backbone of the Lark Missionary Society. That is where she came together with other women in the church to focus on missions. They made blankets and quilts to send to Korea. They collected stamps. They made flannel graph Bible stories for, and sent clothing to, Eritrea. They sent Catherine Vos Bible story books to mission fields to help with literacy, and made scrapbooks of the letters they received from missionaries so they could better know and pray for them.

Missionary societies were the foundations of presbyterials, the OPC's denominational women's ministry, which was designed to promote missionary and denominational interest. JoAnn was an eager participant of both, often holding office in them and loving to get to know and encourage other OPC women. While missionary society was a local commitment, a *long* day of travel was always necessary in order to attend the Dakota Presbyterial. (It could have been held anywhere from North Dakota to Texas!) When it was in Carson, she would host as many guests as her house would hold. She knew that it is too easy to relax into one's own world, so she fought that inclination by using these means given to her, in order to enlarge her heart for God's worldwide family.

The wedding of Willy and JoAnn, in 1952, was the first formal wedding at the Lark OPC. Sadly, Willy died of a heart attack in 1983 at the age of 58, so JoAnn was married for 31 years, and has been a widow for 33. For 13 years of my married life, whenever we would visit my mother in Carson, we would stay at Hotel JoAnn, since my mother lived in an apartment. Usually we arrived late at night, so she would leave her back door open for us. We would sneak down the steps and drop into several of the eight extra beds she had in her basement. After my mother died, we endured a 15-year "desert" of not seeing JoAnn, but were finally able to visit her in May of 2015. One of the stories she told was how she broke both hands when she slipped on ice while returning an elderly saint to her home after having taken her to a doctor appointment. I marveled that she has "seen it all!" to which she countered, "The Lord gives strength for the things he wants to teach us." When asked what God is teaching her now, she replied, "Patience and thankfulness." I know that she desires patience to quell her yearning to be of more service, but I also know God will give her grace to be thankful for his provision.

JoAnn, who was born on March 30, 1929, is now 87 years old and has faithfully served the church from early days when she saw Machen preach his last sermon in the pulpit. She resides with one of her daughters and son-in-law in Grand Rapids, Michigan, where they attend Harvest OPC. After morning worship, I picked up a brochure for their upcoming Family Camp. Guess whose name is listed as a member of the planning committee?

**Rebecca R. D. Schnitzel** *was born in Elgin, North Dakota. With a BA in French Education from the University of North Dakota, Rebecca taught French in Smithers, British Columbia, and Silver Spring, Maryland. She now lives in Roslyn, Pennsylvania, with her husband of 28 years and one of her three young adult children. She is a member of Calvary OPC in Glenside, Pennsylvania.*

# 13

# Harriet Teal:
# Self-Taught Saint

## Elizabeth Male Van Abbema and Mary Male Wynja

"I'm just an uneducated ignoramus." Not many would agree with that statement from Harriet Zarena Teal. The wonderful influence she had on so many lives will last a long time!

Harriet was born in Pennsylvania on November 15, 1884. Her mother died when she was only seven years old. Although she began school at age eight, she was taken out of her Quaker school at 16 to care for her father and two aunts, who had health problems. She was known as a "girl in the kitchen." Housekeeping in those days meant brooms and wash tubs. Nothing automatic.

Harriet became an avid reader. She read all of Dickens, the Waverly novels, Kipling's stories, and many others. One day she met a woman on a streetcar who told her she ought not to read just fiction but history, biographies, and travel books. Harriet followed her advice. She loved poetry and wrote many poems, one of which appears below. She had a dislike for rubbish.

Harriet would have benefited from being taught by a good teacher. She couldn't do rudimentary arithmetic. She didn't learn English as a subject, but was able to correct some educated people on how to use it because she read good literature and studied the King James Bible. Often she was asked where she went to college.

When her father and aunts passed away, Harriet had the opportunity to travel and teach children's Bible classes. At this time, she met Rev. W. Benson Male, who was the pastor of a dispensational church called the Bible Testimony Church of Norristown, Pennsylvania, where Harriet worshipped. He was just discovering the Reformed faith as a student at Westminster Theological Seminary and introduced it to her. In 1938 Ben Male graduated from Westminster, and he and his family moved back to his home state of Colorado. Through his ministry, Harriet learned of the Orthodox Presbyterian Church and wanted to join it.

During this time, Harriet conducted a vacation Bible school and later a Sunday school on the second floor of a car repair shop in an underprivileged area of Norristown. When she realized that she needed help, she called Westminster, and student Robert Nicholas responded. Nicholas, who would become an OPC minister, played the piano, led the singing, and taught a class. After he was married, his wife also helped.

The next summer Harriet followed in the Males' footsteps, moving to Denver, Colorado. This move must have been difficult for her. She loved Philadelphia and had family and deep roots there. However, her love for the Reformed faith and the Male family, along with the challenging opportunities there for children's Bible classes, convinced her to make Colorado her permanent home.

Harriet Teal with her VBS students at Park Hill OPC in Denver

Once settled in Denver, Harriet submerged herself in the needs of that diverse city. She immediately began teaching VBS in a black neighborhood, followed by weekday classes in Hispanic communities. Second Congregational Church, which later became Park Hill OPC, was pastored by Rev. Male and became the home base for Harriet's work. There she led VBS, Bible clubs, and Sunday school classes for women and children from a variety of social and ethnic backgrounds.

In addition to her teaching, Harriet lovingly babysat and helped the Males with their seven children, who called her Aunt Patsy. "She was a great babysitter," said one of the Male children. "How we loved her bedtime stories. I recall one night when she dozed off while telling a story, and we were sitting on the edge of our beds. 'Aunt Patsy, what happened?'"

During World War II, OPC missionary Clarence Duff and his family had to leave Ethiopia and return to the United States. The Duffs came to Colorado and brought the gospel to the mountain mining town of Oak Creek, in the northwest part of the state. Harriet joined them in conducting VBS and Sunday schools. Clarence Duff once wrote of her: "She uses flannel pictures on felt board to illustrate Bible truths. Children take to her. She is unassuming and plain, but very fine. She holds classes in homes."[1]

Rev. Male and others started a camp near these mountain towns, called Camp Chief Yahmonite. Young people from the mountains and from Denver came to hear speakers, like John Murray, Cornelius Van Til, E. J. Young, Rev. Duff, and others connected to the OPC. Harriet joined the camp staff and contributed articles to *The Presbyterian Guardian*[2] about the camp and the work in

1 Letter written from Oak Creek by Clarence Duff to his sister, Margaret Duff.
2 "The *Presbyterian Guardian* (1935–1979) was an important voice in the early years of the Orthodox Presbyterian Church in its vigorous opposition to modernism and its proclamation and defense of Reformed orthodoxy. Established on the eve of the founding of the denomination, it was closely associated with the OPC, although it remained an independent magazine,"

mining towns. She also wrote VBS materials, Sunday school lessons, and some children's stories. Some of these stories were published in a Lutheran school textbook and in a *Guardian* series called Stories for the Children's Hour, which included "Falling on a Banana Peel," "Kenny Learns the Fifth Commandment," and "The Gossip Snowball."[3]

When the Duff family returned to the mission field after the war, Harriet Teal continued the work in the mountain mining town as best she could. The OPC's Home Missions Committee approved of her efforts.[4] For the sake of the gospel, she put up with primitive living conditions, including mountain cabins with no plumbing. On Saturday nights she took the train overnight from Denver, a two-hundred-mile trip. Can you imagine in the winter, a woman under five feet tall trudging through snow and sub-zero temperatures early on Sunday morning to get to Sunday school? She held her classes, then returned home to Denver that night on the train. If the train was late, she had a nine-hour wait for a bus. After five years, she had to discontinue the mountain Sunday school for health reasons and settled on staying in Denver to help the Park Hill church.

Harriet's living conditions changed often, but she seemed to make adjustments quickly. She lived in apartments, the church basement, and in private homes. After Rev. Elmer Dortzbach became pastor of Park Hill OPC in 1956, she lived with the Dortzbachs several years and became very close to them.

Harriet was a prayer warrior. She spent many hours on her knees. She had a foam rubber prayer cushion that was well worn. She prayed faithfully for missionaries, ministers, and their families.

---

http://opc.org/guardian.html.

3 *Presbyterian Guardian* 13 (April 10, 1944): 112–13, http://opc.org/cfh/guardian/Volume_13/1944-04-10.pdf; 13 (October, 25, 1944): 303–5, http://opc.org/cfh/guardian/Volume_13/1944-10-25.pdf; 14 (May 25, 1945): 154–56, http://opc.org/cfh/guardian/Volume_14/1945-05-25.pdf.

4 "Today in OPC History—Harriet Teal, August 15," http://opc.org/today.html?history_id=463.

You could call Harriet Teal a "practical Christian." Some Saturday mornings she would show up at the minister's home in her work clothes with a pail and rags. "I came to help you get ready for Sunday." Mrs. Dee Male, Ben's wife, with her seven children and many duties, did need help.

Sabbath observance was very important to Harriet. She loved worship. Communion services were especially meaningful to her. Even though she was tone deaf, she found the hymns of the church especially dear. She loved the poetry in the Psalms and hymns. Her favorite songs to teach children were: "Come to the Savior," "There Is A City Bright," "All Things Bright and Beautiful," "When I Survey," "There Is A Green Hill Far Away," "The Twelve Disciples," and "John 3:16."

Sometimes when in the Male home, Harriet corrected or critiqued the minister's sermons. She was very concerned about the clear preaching of the Word. She was a best friend of the pastor and often accompanied him on pastoral calls. Even though she was a quiet and humble Christian, Harriet influenced many. William Culbertson, one of the young boys in her Bible classes, became the president of Moody Bible Institute, and remained a life-long friend of Harriet's. A mother of children whom Harriet visited and taught the catechism to on Saturday mornings still talks of the blessing that Harriet was to her family.

Harriet spent most of her last year on earth living with one of Ben and Dee Male's daughters, Elizabeth Male Van Abbema, and her husband, Chuck. Harriet lovingly encouraged Elizabeth through a difficult pregnancy due to German measles, often quoting Psalm 139 and constantly praying for a healthy baby. Those prayers were answered when Ardella was born. One highlight of Harriet's stay with Elizabeth and Chuck was a visit from Dr. Jay Adams. He wanted to meet this amazing woman of prayer he had heard about.

Harriet Teal passed away on August 15, 1968, at the age of 83. "Aunt Patsy" received her reward and is rejoicing in heaven with her Lord and Savior.

### Beside a River, *by Harriet Teal*

Beside a rippling river, I saw some children play,
And I thought how soon a river would bear their lives away.

And I listened to their laughing voices,
And this is what I heard,

Said one of them to another
"Look and listen to that bird"

And I thought how soon the darlings
Like birdlings so too should fly

And reach the golden gates
Beyond the starry sky.

Beside the rippling river, I walked another day,
And upon the silv'ry strand 'stead of children at their play,

I saw an old, old woman with
Tottering steps and slow

And her hair was whiter, whiter
Than the whitest of the snow,

And I knew her boat was stranded—
And think she soon would be

Beyond the Golden Gates
And in eternity.

**Elizabeth Male Van Abbema and Mary Male Wynja** *are daughters of the late Rev. Benson Male and grew up in Park Hill OPC in Denver, Colorado. Elizabeth and her husband, Chuck, live in Berthoud, Colorado, and have four children and 16 grandchildren. Their daughter Charlene Tipton is an OPC minister's wife and serves as the database administrator at the OPC offices. Mary Wynja is married to Dick Wynja, a retired OPC minister, and lives in Thornton, Colorado. They have five children and 13 grandchildren.*

# 14

# Margaret I. Duff:
# A Life of Sacrifice and Prayer

### *Margaret Graham Duff*

"Do you really mean you'll pray for me by name? Do you really think that you'll save me?" asked the worldly-minded young man living in her home.

"No, I'll not save you," Margaret Duff replied. "But it may be that the Lord will."

When Margaret wanted two of her Sunday school teens from un-churched homes to come to a special church service, she said, "I made it a special matter for prayer and then went the night before and invited both to go, saying I would pick them up. My faith was small." But the boys did come!

Margaret Isabelle Duff had a remarkable influence on young men over the years. These men, some seemingly beyond hope and others who were greatly interested in theology, were recipients of her prayer, active concern, and actions. She remained unmarried, an ordinary woman, plain, sometimes awkward, often overanxious about details and decisions. Yet she sacrificed her own desires for much of her life to help others, especially her family.[1]

Margaret's brother Clarence was known to many in the Orthodox Presbyterian Church as our missionary to Eritrea for 27 years.

---

1 The source of much of Margaret's story is gleaned from family correspondence covering several decades, and the memoirs of Clarence Duff, *Ordinary People, Used of God.*

Margaret I. Duff in the 1930s

His earlier work for the Sudan Interior Mission in Ethiopia and the OPC in Eritrea are told in two books he wrote.[2] But Margaret, though less well known, was just as tireless in her work for the Lord. Clarence, in his memoir entitled *Ordinary People Used of God*, wrote, "Margaret probably had a greater influence in my life and life-work than any other one person, except Father and Mother."

Born on March 19, 1897, Margaret was the second of four children, and the only daughter. They grew up on the family farm in northwestern Pennsylvania. As her brothers left home for their life's work, Margaret, since she was single, spent much of her life taking care of a succession of ailing relatives: her mother, Elizabeth Walker Duff, who suffered many strokes; her father, William Duff; an aunt Margaret Walker, who needed constant supervision; and her uncle and his sister.

The ordinary events of her life were overlaid and undergirded with prayer and her zeal for mission work. After graduating in 1919 from Westminster College in New Wilmington, Pennsylvania, and studying the Bible for a year at Tennent College in Philadelphia, Margaret worked as a home missionary for the Presbyterian Church (USA)'s Presbyterial from 1933 to 1935. In the Western Pennsylvania mining towns of Avella and Duquesne, she did neighborhood calling, taught Sunday school and Bible school, and always held prayer meetings! She even had to fill in one Sunday in the absence of the pastor.[3] When Clarence and his family left Africa during

2  Clarence Duff wrote *God's Higher Ways* in 1977 and *Cords of Love* in 1980.
3  Margaret shared with the congregation a review of a Christian missionary

World War II and started an OP church in Oak Creek, Colorado, Margaret made two trips to help with Bible school. "I'd have stayed the winter if not needed at home," she said.

With the advice of Clarence in Oak Creek and reading helpful books and articles, Margaret and her father were persuaded of the modernism of the PCUSA church of which they were members. By 1943 Margaret and her father had become members of Calvary OPC in Harrisville, Pennsylvania, although it was a difficult drive. That move was not an easy one since her father was a respected elder and their church held the Duff family pew for generations.

Margaret soon was asked by Pastor Ed Kellogg to help Calvary OPC in Middletown, Pennsylvania. For three years she did extensive neighborhood canvassing and taught Sunday school and summer vacation Bible schools. At one time Sunday schools were held in several parts of town. Margaret told Clarence about the importance of prayer: "My work there has been effective, too—the people keep praying for me." When I married Margaret's nephew Donald Duff in 1966, people from Middletown wrote to me such fine tributes of Margaret's work there.

Margaret also made shorter trips to help other churches, such as OP congregations in West Collingswood, New Jersey, and Wilmington, Delaware. At this time, she also produced the vacation Bible school primary department materials on *The Life of David* and *The Life of Christ* for the OPC Committee on Christian Education. Not only did she write the lessons, she also made the stencils to reproduce the lessons for the churches. In the late 1940s, the failing health of family members began to cut short her times of "missionary" work. Ever faithful, when the ailing family member died, she would return to her own mission endeavors until her father's death in 1948. At that time, Margaret became the managing head of the household at Maple Lane farm so she settled there. The Lord then used her zeal for him locally. Margaret remained on the farm until the mid-1970s when she moved to Florida to be near Clarence and

---

biography.

his wife, Dora, after they retired to Ocoee, Florida.

After the family moved to the Maple Lane farm near Pulaski in 1944, Margaret lived with aging Uncle Fred and his sister, May Walker. Since they were capable of caring for each other, Margaret was able to teach remedial reading and freshman English at nearby Westminster College for six years. After a year of selling encyclopedias and earning her masters in English lit, Margaret was given a salaried contract position at Thiel College in Greenville. When she was hired, Thiel's president told her, "Your experience and enthusiasm for the work will be of great benefit to the students, and we are pleased that your colleagues at Westminster College held your work in high respect. Your background in full-time Christian service is of the greatest interest to us."[4] She was diligent in her work with students, correcting hundreds of themes and research papers per term and holding up to one hundred student conferences before finals. She would not tolerate cheating or plagiarism.

Not only was she a full-time teacher, she continued handling all the same responsibilities that would typically fall to a farmer's wife. Seasonally she canned beans, corn, tomatoes, cherries, peaches, and meat; drove the tractor for haying; and did the spring cleaning, including washing the winter's accumulation of coal dust off the wall paper, taking the rugs out and beating them, and stretching washed curtains. She also quilted, painted the house inside and outside, painted the car; removed the ashes from the coal furnace, put chains on her car tires on snowy days, "dressed" the chickens, and coped with snakes in the kitchen, rats in the drains, and neighborhood hooligans who stole gas from their private tank. Alongside these duties were those obligations of living in a rural community: calling on friends and relatives; visiting the sick in the hospital; taking flowers to the family grave sites yearly; entertaining large groups for holiday meals; attending weddings, funerals, and church functions of all sorts; and playing piano and organ for many events.

---

4 An August 13, 1955, letter from Margaret to Clarence (Jack) Duff, who was in Ghinda, Eritrea.

Margaret and her brother Clarence had been very close as children, calling each other by the same name—Jack—all their lives. Margaret remarked to Clarence about their childhood happiness, "Children never know how much trouble and loving care and prayer other folks spend on them, do they? We were greatly blest." Margaret served as the "back home" correspondent for Clarence's missionary work. She copied his letters, made stencils of them, and ran them off on an old machine she acquired from the West Collingswood Church. Those letters she sent to family members, friends in rural Western Pennsylvania, and to many OP churches.

She also encouraged Clarence. After he had served in Eritrea for five years with few conversions, she wrote in March 1948: "Prayer is undoubtedly the greatest need; but prayer must be based on knowledge to be effective—knowledge of God; of the conditions of prayer; of the fields and people for whom we pray. What great things might be wrought in Eritrea *by the people here at home!*" To that end she kept the churches informed faithfully for more than two decades.

Over the years Margaret wrote Clarence two to three times a month about local happenings, reports of relatives, and local and denominational church news. Beyond the facts, she described the beauty of spring, the colors and smells of her flowers and garden produce, the joy of hearing great concerts, and all of her questions and concerns about the condition of the Presbyterian churches of which they had been a part. Reading and questioning helped Margaret learn about the liberalism of her former denomination. Once she understood, she was zealous in persuading others.

After her father's death, Margaret continued to find it difficult to get to the Harrisville OP church regularly. During the week she became involved at the closer New Bedford United Presbyterian Church where Auntie May had membership. She wished and prayed that she might have a part in teaching the youth with a systematic, well-planned Bible study and music program, which was being started in 1950 by a seminary student assigned to that church—Mr. G. I. Williamson. He wanted Margaret to teach one of the groups, but said she needed to become a member of the church or she would compromise her witness among the people of the community. "I tried to explain why I was in the OPC and why I preferred not to join the UP," she said.

G. I. Williamson, who later joined the OPC and wrote the widely used study guides for the Westminster Confession of Faith and Shorter Catechism, recalls the influence Margaret had on him. "In my study (at Pittsburgh-Xenia Theological Seminary) I was struggling with the effects of a lack of unity in doctrine among the professors. I'm sure this must have been evident because she bluntly asked me if I would mind if she gave me written criticism of my preaching. Somehow God enabled me to say 'sure, I'd appreciate it.' She evidently felt that I might have a promising future. She gave me a few books by Machen and other Westminster Seminary men. Those proved to be life-changing. I remember the visit of Rev. Clarence Duff. Meeting him added to my more and more favorable impression of the OPC."

Margaret wrestled with concerns about joining the United Presbyterian Church because they were not for or against the modernism which caused the OPC to leave the PCUSA denomination in 1936. Rather, they suffered from "indifferentism." She wrote to Clarence on August 6, 1950: "So long as I cannot live near an OPC, don't you think I ought, for the sake of my influence upon my neighbors and non-Christian people of the community, and especially upon the children whom I teach, to join the church here, so long as that church is not actively teaching unbelief?... It would be humiliating to me to have to leave; it will distress me; it will also distress me to sit back and have no part in any church, the mere fact of physical distance making it impossible for me to worship or to use my talents in my chosen church. My own feelings do not matter, however, nor the activities—the question will have to be decided according to the will of God, what will be for His glory, what is according to His Word."

After consulting with Clarence and Harrisville's pastor LeRoy Oliver, Margaret made the difficult decision to leave the OPC in order to help the New Bedford church. The Saturday Youth Club soon had over 50 youth attending.

As Margaret was used to guide G. I. Williamson toward his eventual membership in the OPC, her becoming a UP member also lead to the formation of the Nashua OP Church in her home-town of Pulaski. In 1956, when a merger between the United Pres-byterians and Presbyterians USA began to look certain, Margaret asked OP pastor LeRoy Oliver to set up an OPC informational meeting at the New Bedford UP church. Mr. Wendell Miller, a New Bedford elder, spoke at that meeting in 1957, saying that Mr. Williamson's preaching and teaching at New Bedford had shown him the importance of true biblical doctrines. Mr. Miller agreed to lead the movement to leave. Margaret said of Wendell Miller, "He doesn't want to cause any hard feelings in our church. He always tells the session what he is doing and invites them to come. We are astonished at his wisdom and courage." As Margaret wrote to Clar-ence, "I can always go back into the OPC myself, but I believe … a stand (should) be made in the UPC first with the idea of having a continuing church if possible."

This group strove to educate the New Bedford congregation about the perils of union with the UPUSA church. When the New Bedford congregation voted for the union, a group of about 50 from the surrounding area met April 24, 1958, to organize official-ly as the Nashua Bible Fellowship. The Nashua OP Church, which celebrated 50 years as a congregation in 2008, began in a small one-room schoolhouse. Margaret now was back in the OPC.

Margaret never ceased to encourage young men to ministry within the Reformed circle. While teaching at Westminster and Thiel Colleges, she singled out her pre-ministerial students and gave them good Reformed literature and endeavored to have her pastor or visiting OP ministers speak with them. She encouraged them to visit Westminster Theological Seminary and invited OP pastors, like Bob Atwell and Tom Tyson, to speak at chapel services.

She worked tirelessly to keep Westminster College as a Christ-honoring college when a new president began the move to modernize the theology. She used her mimeograph machine to send out large mailings to college alumni and community friends about the new theological trend at Westminster. Her support of faculty that were dismissed to make room for the president's favored people, ultimately led to her dismissal also. When the president fired the students who staffed the student newspaper, Margaret again used her mimeograph to help Westminster College student editor Norman Shepherd put out an underground newspaper.

What a busy life Margaret managed in spite of a life-long chronic colitis condition, yet by putting the Lord, her family, and others first all her life, as Clarence so aptly put it, "her influence for good on a multitude of others will be known only hereafter."

After suffering in her last few years much the same mental and physical decline as the family members for whom she had cared, Margaret Isabelle Duff received her heavenly reward on November 19, 1976.

**Margaret Graham Duff** *is the wife of OP minister Donald J. Duff, a nephew of Margaret I. Duff. A lifelong OPC member in California, Colorado, Illinois, and Pennsylvania, Peggy is the daughter of the late OPC pastor Robert Graham. Donald, formerly the stated clerk of the OPC, and Peggy are retired and live near their children both in Beaver Falls, Pennsylvania, and in Janesville, Wisconsin. She is a member of Immanuel OPC in Coraopolis, Pennsylvania.*

# 15

# Elizabeth "Betty" Wallace:
# Any Better, I Couldn't Stand It!

## *Barbara Cerha*

"Any better, I couldn't stand it!" Spoken in her Irish brogue, this was Betty Wallace's mantra. No matter what was going on, no matter the difficulties, through sickness and in health, her response was the same. Indeed some of her last words to me, her granddaughter, were, "Any better, I couldn't stand it!" This Irish farm girl who became a founding member of Franklin Square, OPC, in Long Island, New York, believed that living in God's will was the best place to be—anywhere else would be unbearable!

Granma, Elizabeth "Betty" Wallace (nee Brown), was born on May 8, 1903, in Drumach, Northern Ireland. As the first daughter after four sons, she quickly became responsible for her six siblings who followed her. Named after her grandmother, Elizabeth Brown, Betty spoke of her grandma as "a good woman who loved the Lord. I can still see her reading her Bible. I would tiptoe to her bedroom and hear her pray, and she did a lot of praying for all her grandchildren."[1] Betty's family all lived and worked on her grandmother's farm.

She attended Sunday school and morning and evening church services regularly. When an evangelist came to their church for revival meetings, Betty realized she was a sinner, and desired to ask

---

1 All quotes (except for one from Pastor Shishko) were taken from a letter Betty wrote to her children on April 5, 1984.

the Lord into her heart. After first asking her mom's permission, she responded to the invitation the following evening, along with her brother, cousin, and a few others she had already witnessed to. Upon returning home and reporting what she had done, her father responded, "That wee girl doesn't know what she is doing!" Betty's immediate response was to pray, read her Bible, and thank the Lord for his saving grace in her life.

Her two older brothers went to fight in World War I, while Archie, the third in line, worked at the railway station in Belfast. Betty's father died just after the war ended, leaving behind his wife with seven young ones. Archie came home every two weeks to give them money for food and clothing. Betty was always grateful for Archie's faithful support. Some years later, her mother sold the farm, moved the family to Ballymena, and started a tea room to make dinners for farmers coming to sell their goods. Betty was sent to a friend to learn dressmaking, since, as her mom said, "It will be good to know how to make things when you are married."

After the war, her older brothers immigrated to America, and Betty, who was 25, longed to do the same. She wrote to them, asking that they send for her. On March 24, 1928, she began her ten-day voyage by ship to America. Her brothers claimed her on April 4, and she moved in with them. Since they worked nights and slept during the day, Betty was lonely so before long she moved in with an Irish couple from church, Mr. and Mrs. Hurst. Betty got a job making sandwiches at Schrafts Restaurant and loved it. After a year, Schrafts told Betty they were sending her to a new store where she would have to work every other Sunday. Instead of accepting this position, Betty walked into Woolworths in search of a new job, knowing they were closed on Sundays. The following Monday, she began making sandwiches at Woolworths, and was so fast, they decreased their staff by half.

My grandfather, Bob Wallace, lived on a farm in Ireland. After his father passed away, life was very difficult for the family. A friend visiting from New York encouraged them to come to America. When they arrived, the friend had an apartment ready for them.

That was in November 1928, the same year my grandmother arrived. Bob, who was then 17, and Betty had not known each other in Ireland. Betty reminisced in a letter to her children:

> One night I came home to Mrs. Hurst after work and your father's mother, his two sisters, and he were sitting there visiting the Hursts. They had moved from Brooklyn to the same building I was in. Now what do you think of that? Who sent them there? The Lord, of course. Mrs. Hurst was taking mail out of her mail box one day and Mrs. Wallace, Bob's mother, was also getting her mail. She said, "Irish mail today," so she and Mrs. Hurst got talking and Mrs. Hurst told her she had an Irish girl living with her.
>
> Now who would you say arranged all that? The Lord, of course. And of course we were together a lot. We would all walk home from the evening service through Central Park. It was safe in those days. We didn't even hold hands. Could you believe it? Your father was such a wonderful young man. I thought a lot of him and later on he would call me and ask me if I wanted to go and hear the band in Central Park. Of course I did.

Bob and Betty were married on May 29, 1936, and traveled to Ireland for their honeymoon, meeting each other's families. Returning to New York, they lived in an apartment with Bob's sisters, one of whom married Betty's brother Bill a year later. After two and a half years, the Lord began blessing Bob and Betty with children: Jean Elizabeth, Ruth Ann, Mary Margaret, Betty Joan, and Robert James.

Since Bob's background was Presbyterian, he and Betty became part of an effort to start an Orthodox Presbyterian Church in New York City. The group first met in 1937 under the oversight of Minister Charles Woodbridge, followed by Ed Kellogg, Robert Brown, Bruce Coie, and aided by Professor John Murray of Westminster Theological Seminary. On January 29, 1939, regular worship services and Sunday school classes began in the American Legion Hall in Franklin Square. On October 19, 1939, the congregation was accepted as a particular church of the Presbytery of New York and New England. Bob Wallace was ordained and installed as a ruling elder on December 10, 1939, and the first baptism performed in the new church was of his own daughter Jean in 1940. Since then, Bob and Betty served under all of the pastors of Franklin Square OPC: Bruce Coie (1942–1945), Robert Vining (1945–1950), Elmer Dortzbach (1952–1956), John Hills (1957–1979), and William Shishko (1981–2016).[2]

During the late 1940s, Bob and Betty and their children began vacationing at the shore in Ocean Grove, New Jersey, a square-mile town set up as a Christian community by the Methodists. When their son, Robert, was about 12, he had a clear, plastic retainer, instead of braces, valued at about $125. (As a point of reference, their $99 mortgage was paid every three months.) Early that vacation while swimming in the ocean, he was knocked down by a wave, resulting in the loss of his retainer. Extremely upset and distraught, he reported back to his parents. While keeping cool, Betty replied, "We'll just pray about it."

Pray she did. Every day they went to lost and found to see if the retainer was turned in. Every day was a disappointment. On the last morning of their vacation, after they checked out of the bath house (a changing room they rented for the week, since no bathing suits were worn on the boardwalk), and still no retainer, the air raid siren sounded. They ran back into the bath house for shelter. When all was clear, they decided to check lost and found just one last time. Lo and behold, some kids had just turned it in, after finding it washed up on the beach! What an amazing answer to prayer!

Not only did Betty encourage prayer and gratitude, but she lived it. As a Sunday school teacher for the beginners, ages two to

---

2 See *The Orthodox Presbyterian Church, 1936-1986* (Philadelphia: Committee for the Historian of the OPC, 1986), 172–73; *Presbyterian Guardian* 5 (April 1938): 80, http://opc.org/cfh/guardian/Volume_5/1938-04.pdf; *Presbyterian Guardian* 5 (October 1938): 187, http://opc.org/cfh/guardian/Volume_5/1938-10.pdf.

Bob and Betty Wallace with their children (left to right): Ruth (Clouser),
Betty (Watson), Mary (Kolb), Robert Jr., and Jean (Denton)

five, the songs "Count your blessings, count them one by one" and
"I've got the joy, joy, joy, joy down in my heart" were often on her
lips. She co-taught with Dot Hartman and Anne Muether.[3] Parents
would often relay difficulties they were having with their children,
and she would incorporate them into the lesson. For instance, my

3 Anne Muether was the wife of Franklin Square OPC elder Herbert
Muether and mother of OPC historian John Muether, OPC pastor Chuck
Muether, and OPC elder Bill Muether.

sister, Susan, was terribly afraid of thunder storms. While pacing back and forth, quacking, and flailing her arms, Betty began:

> There were three little ducks splashing in the water, having a wonderful time, when all of a sudden, a great wind came up, and a loud crash of thunder! "Mama, mama" they cried! "What is that awful noise?! We're terribly afraid!"
>
> Their mama answered, "Now dear ones, remember what I've told you? What time I am afraid, I will put my trust in God."

To this day, that verse is embedded in us, comforting us in times of trial. When Betty struggled with debilitating illness, she faithfully left her cares at her Savior's feet through prayer and quoting Scripture, always responding, "Any better I couldn't stand it."

During the severe gas shortages of the 1970s, my family was unable to afford returning for the evening service since we lived 25 miles away. We solved that problem by staying every Sunday afternoon at my grandparent's house, a few blocks from church. Little did I realize the impact those days would have on me. We could count on chicken, mashed potatoes, corn, and another vegetable. We knew not to leave the table afterwards, for Pop Pop would lead devotions. Beginning with the Scripture reading suggested in the devotional, he and Granma then alternated reading the day's devotion and leading in prayer. It was a solemn occasion of coming before our Lord together. Listening to them pray emboldened my own prayer life. Nothing was too insignificant or great to bring before the Lord. Everyone from pastors, missionaries, world leaders, and grandchildren were prayed over by name.

Afterwards, my family retired to the finished attic for an afternoon nap. Before resting, Granma first wrote to the missionaries. Every week. I don't know what was in those letters, but they were appreciated! At that time, John F. Kennedy Airport in New York was the only international airport in the area, so our missionaries (and we knew *all* of them!) came through JFK. Franklin Square was blessed to regularly welcome our missionaries home, but *we* would have the privilege of sharing meals with them since Granma usually entertained them. In my younger days, I struggled with keeping them all straight—the Birds, the Duffs (I thought they were ducks), the Hards, the Andrews, the Dortzbachs, and more. Knowing those missionaries personally enabled us to be keenly aware of the need for the gospel, as well as the sacrifices these families made. How well I remember pleading with God for Debbie Dortzbach's release; we mourned the loss of Anna Strikwerda, and still reminisce with Dr. Rietkerk.[4]

After worship services, Granma always greeted the pastor and thanked him for the sermon. Even if he thought it wasn't the best, she assured him that God blessed us with his service. Anyone visiting was typically greeted first by my grandparents with a handshake and an Irish-brogued welcome. Dr. George Knight and Westminster Theological Seminary professors Dr. John Skilton, Rev. John Murray, Dr. Ned B. Stonehouse, Dr. Cornelius Van Til, and Dr. Paul Woolley were all nourished by Granma's home-cooked meals after preaching at Franklin Square OPC. When my mother, Jean, professed her faith, Rev. Leslie Sloat came since Elmer Dortzbach wasn't ordained as their pastor yet. Even during Granma's later years, confined to a wheelchair at the back of the sanctuary, many would be blessed by her presence. Pastor Shishko reminisced:

> Despite her illness and frailty, she always radiated the love and joy of Christ. She was, to all of us, an example of the grace of God that not only saves us but "keeps us ... through faith for the salvation ready to be revealed at the last day," cf. 1 Peter 1:4–5. (KJV). Betty modeled the keeping grace of God—keeping us in a state of heavenly-mindedness even as we suffer here on earth.

4  Anna Strikwerda and Debbie Dortzbach were kidnapped by rebels in 1974 while working at the Compassion of Jesus Hospital in Eritrea. Miss Strikwerda was killed, while Mrs. Dortzbach was released unharmed about a month later. Details of this account are recreated in the book *Kidnapped*, written by Karl and Debbie Dortzbach in 1975.

In May 1983 we received word that Granma had a stroke. Doctors tried to console us, indicating that they were keeping her as comfortable as possible. Our prayers were answered, when about a week later, Granma "woke up" and reported, "Any better, I couldn't stand it!" May God be praised!

Nevertheless, one of her biggest fears, being confined to a wheelchair, became a reality. She never complained as Pop Pop dutifully tended to her needs. During her last days, I attempted to feed her some applesauce and made small talk. Of course, when I asked Granma how she was, her reply remained, "Any better I couldn't stand it!" Granma entered into eternal rest on November 22, 1986.

Her legacy of faithful and joyful service to our Lord and Savior continues to ripple throughout her family. Her daughter and my mother, Jean Denton, played the organ for 64 years at Franklin Square OPC. She shows gracious hospitality as a resident at Quarryville Presbyterian Retirement Community. Another daughter, Betty, is the wife of Rev. Douglas Watson, who has pastored several OP churches in Delaware and New Jersey, and is the OPC accountant. Her granddaughters, Barbara Denton Cerha and Susan Denton Hagan, play the piano for their respective OP churches in Hamilton and Hackettstown, New Jersey.

**Barbara Cerha** *is Betty Wallace's granddaughter, and daughter of Jean Wallace Denton. She is a member of Grace OPC in Hamilton, New Jersey, and resides with her husband, Joe, a deacon at Grace. She has five children, ages 15 to 25.*

# 16

# Dorothy Anderson Barker: Devoted Educator and Wordsmith

## *Ann H. Hart*

Dorothy Anderson Barker recalled the first time she was contacted about working for the Orthodox Presbyterian Church. She was a recent college grad, teaching at a Christian school north of Boston. "I received a letter that began: 'You have been chosen ...' It had a nice Presbyterian ring to it," she added wryly.

The young teacher accepted the volunteer writing assignment, believing that she could draw on her own Christian education growing up in the church. Over time, her writing labors proved among the most widely read Sunday school materials in the OPC. At retirement in 1987, Dorothy had worked for 33 years for the OPC's Committee on Christian Education, and was curriculum project editor with Great Commission Publications—the joint initiative with the Presbyterian Church in America.

The daughter of Hillis and Florence Partington, Dorothy was born on April 27, 1927, and grew up with a sister in Westfield, New Jersey. This quaint town is located just 25 miles southwest of New York City. Church life and education dominated the Partington home, and Dorothy imbibed this atmosphere. Her father was the principal of Lincoln School in Westfield for 28 years. Although only 5′8″, he clearly had a larger-than-life influence on his daughter in the years to come.

Dorothy remembers hearing snippets of her parents' conversations about the family's church home. Mr. Partington served as an elder in the mainline Presbyterian church in Westfield. However, he and his wife grew increasingly dissatisfied with some of the denomination's decisions. Dorothy recalls they objected to the denomination's liberal tendencies and were disheartened by the direction of foreign missions and of Pearl Buck's writings on missions, in particular.

And so it was that Dorothy as an adolescent found herself helping her parents set up rows of folding chairs at the local Masonic Temple for a special evening event. Her parents and a small group of Presbyterians were eager to hear Professor J. Gresham Machen of Westminster Theological Seminary. Looking back on the event decades later, Dorothy found it ironic that she was exhausted that night and fell asleep on one of the back rows.

Her parents, however, were awake to Machen's message. The Partingtons were charter members of Grace OPC in Westfield, founded in 1936 after meeting in various homes. Grace was one of the earliest congregations in the denomination. As it happened, Dorothy grew up in the years paralleling the maturing of the young denomination in what has been called "The Christian Century." Providentially, the OPC was destined to be central to this pre-teen's life in ways she could not have imagined.

An early lover of reading, music, and chess, Dorothy often perused her parents' copy of *The Presbyterian Guardian*, the predecessor to *New Horizons*.[1] The *Guardian* was published from 1935–1979, and both of Dorothy's parents contributed either articles or letters to the magazine. Later, Dorothy would write on occasion for the *Guardian* as well.

In 1940 Rev. John Galbraith was called as pastor of Grace OPC. He remembered Dorothy fondly. "She was a smart young woman, serious about her studies and the things of the Lord. If the church was open, Dorothy was there," he recalled. The young people of the church, he recounted, were passionate about their

---

1 The *Presbyterian Guardian* was closely associated with the OPC, although it remained an independent magazine. See http://opc.org/guardian.html.

faith. "They would take the train up to New York City to serve at a mission in the Bowery," he said.

Rev. Galbraith also recalled that Dorothy was a gifted and competitive chess player and joined the chess club at Westfield High School. "She beat her father most of the time," Rev. Galbraith added with a laugh.

Dorothy excelled in school and entered Wheaton College in Illinois at age 15. After her freshman year, she moved home for two years and then transferred to Barnard College in New York City where she earned a BA in English. After college, she ventured up to New England to teach in a Christian school in Cambridge, Massachusetts. In her spare time, she also completed a master's in education at Harvard University. "The Harvard degree sounds more impressive than it was," she quipped later. However, she was glad to have more professional tools for her work in Christian education.

During the 1940s the *Presbyterian Guardian* contributors debated the role of Sunday school in the life of the church, among other issues. Should Christian education be conducted primarily for instructing covenant children or for evangelizing non-Christian children? OPC Pastor Edmund Clowney favored a mediating position. He believed that the primary responsibility of the church's teaching is to bring covenant youth to understand the covenant claims and blessings. However, he also contended that Sunday school teaching was a solemn obligation for evangelizing non-Christian children.

When Rev. Clowney was called as pastor at Grace OPC in Westfield in 1950, he recognized Dorothy, a daughter of the church, as a gifted writer and editor. Clowney then enlisted her to help him write Sunday school curriculum for the Committee on Christian Education. In 1954, under his supervision, she produced an impressive study of the Shorter Catechism for junior high school students. The original two-volume *Bible Doctrine: A Workbook based on the Westminster Shorter Catechism* of the Westminster Confession was compiled in a modest spiral-bound notebook, selling for $1.25 each. And yet the content was rich. The series divided the catechism into four parts: first God and man; second, Christ; third, the law, and fourth, the means of grace. Never forgetting her young teen audience, Dorothy skillfully translated complicated material into concepts that teenagers could begin to grasp. The first printing of *Bible Doctrine* quickly sold out. It was then republished in a more professional manner.

Undoubtedly, she drew on her skills as a teacher to communicate effectively. Consider her introduction to the workbook: "Nothing in life can be separated from God and His revelation of Himself." With this in mind, she married artwork from the Metropolitan Museum of Art, the Yale University Art Gallery, and the Philadelphia Museum of Art with her copy to express the creativity of God and the creative gifts he has bestowed on man.

She also was alert to teachers: "The danger in using workbooks is that the child will merely complete exercises in mechanical fashion and never see the lesson in its total message. The teacher's job is to keep the students from getting lost in the details."

In 1954 she also worked on a vacation Bible school course junior workbook called "Our Bible," with lesson titles like: Moses the Prophet, David the Psalmist, Isaiah and Immanuel, Jeremiah and Daniel. Moving to the New Testament, she wrote on the apostle Paul and Dr. Luke, Peter, and a survey of the New Testament books.

While Dorothy believed that some already published materials by evangelical presses were appropriate, she was especially motivated to write catechetical materials on the riches of the Reformed faith. If she had a question or needed to know more, she visited Dr. Clowney's office (by then he was a professor at Westminster) and listened to "an hour lecture on biblical theology," she recalled.

Outside of work, Dorothy met Robert W. Anderson, a graduate of both Wheaton College and Westminster. They shared many interests, as well as a love of the gospel. On October 1, 1955, the couple were married. Bob was ordained in the Presbytery of New York and New England on June 22, 1956. They soon were blessed with two sons, Jonathan and Peter.

Bob Anderson took several calls in OPC churches in New

England. Yet, after years of struggling with sermons, he left the ministry in 1968. The Anderson family moved back to the greater Philadelphia area where Bob took a job in business. He served faithfully as an elder at Trinity OPC in Hatboro, Pennsylvania, and Dorothy played the organ for worship services.

Linda Posthuma, a friend who taught the Anderson sons at Philadelphia-Montgomery Christian Academy recalls this period. "Bob Anderson was quiet and studious. The family lived in an older home in suburban Jenkintown. Dorothy was always a gracious hostess, a good cook, and a great conversationalist." Robert died suddenly on April 4, 1977, at age 49.

Dorothy once again immersed herself in the work of Christian Education. Linda Posthuma remembers Dorothy in those years as "immaculately dressed, often with pearls, with premature white hair and an abundance of energy." In fact, she formed a "dynamic duo" with her colleague and friend, Penny Pappas.

In August 1984 Dorothy remarried, coming full circle from

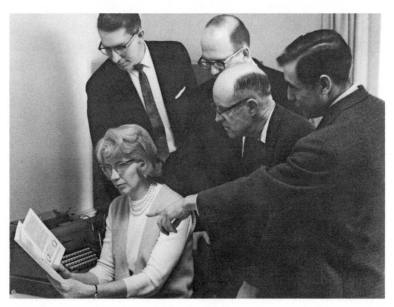

Dorothy Anderson Barker showing educational materials to Robert Nicholas (center, front), Robley Johnston (right) and two visitors

her youth in Westfield, New Jersey. Richard A. Barker, an electrical engineer and a widower, was the clerk of session at Grace OPC and also had served as stated clerk of the OPC's general assembly. He was no stranger to Dorothy. She had known Dick since their days as classmates at Westfield High School where they both were members of the chess club. Rev. Galbraith commented that "Dorothy's father and Richard's father were elders together on the Westfield session when I was pastor."

In 1991 the Barkers were interviewed together for a beautiful oral history. At the time, they were living in Westfield and still playing the occasional game of chess together. In that conversation, Dorothy spoke enthusiastically about the church's need to evangelize. With great affection, she described the OPC's evangelistic efforts at the Boardwalk Chapel on the New Jersey shore in Wildwood. She echoed the evangelistic impulse that took her to the Bowery as a teenager and caused her to pick up the teacher's chalk and the editor's pen throughout her career.

In 2009 the Barkers moved from Westfield, New Jersey, to near Lancaster, Pennsylvania, where they spent several happy years living at Quarryville Presbyterian Retirement Community. However, Dick died on March 1, 2012, at the age of 86, leaving Dorothy a widow for a second time.

Friends who remember Dorothy Barker as energetic, witty, and driven, say that when they visit Dorothy these days, she welcomes them warmly. Inevitably, she will need to put down a book to engage in conversation. Although clearly slowing down at age 89, and confined to a wheelchair, Dorothy still has a love of words and the Word, as well as an interest in others—qualities which have characterized her long, well-lived life.

**Ann H. Hart** *is managing editor of the* Journal of World Affairs *at the Foreign Policy Research Institute in Philadelphia. She has appreciated being a member of OP churches in Glenside, Pennsylvania; Escondido, California; and now Hillsdale, Michigan. She is married to elder Darryl G. Hart.*

# 17

# Helen "Penny" Pappas: Renaissance Woman

## *Amy Joy*

"This old dog will just have to learn new tricks," muttered Penny Pappas as she contemplated the challenge of teaching and leading the high school Sunday school class at Trinity Orthodox Presbyterian Church in Hatboro, Pennsylvania, in 1993. "Those unruly rascals were so gifted mentally, artistically, and spiritually. I was truly no match for them."[1] The fact that Penny was 70 at the time and that the young people requested and even begged her to take their class is proof of the influence she had on their lives and minds. "But God has never failed to equip me for the work he called me to do," she continued, "and those youngsters still bring joy to my heart as I remember their hearty response to God's Word." Penny became "Granny" to all of them, challenging their minds, teaching them to grow in their spiritual walk with the Lord, as well as taking them camping and on picnics with her husband.

Helen "Penny" Smith was born into a Lutheran family, in Kensington, Minnesota, population two hundred on June 10, 1922. Penny and her whole family accepted the Lord in an evangelistic service when she was 13. She had been playing the organ for the service, and came forward with her family; and thus began her service for the Lord. Penny lived life to the fullest, playing piano,

---

1 Quotes and recollections recorded here were gathered by the author in conversations and interviews with Penny Pappas and others.

organ, violin, clarinet, and recorder. She marched in the school band and even played piano for her own high school graduation. She went on to study at St. Olaf's College in Northfield, Minnesota, and graduated from Macalester College in Saint Paul, Minnesota, with a degree in primary education. She taught for several years in Madison, South Dakota.

During that time, Penny traveled to a teachers' conference. She was waiting in the lobby one evening to be picked up for a dinner date, when a dashing serviceman named John Pappas came by and invited her for a cup of coffee.... Her original date never saw a trace of her that evening! She and John married in December 24, 1942, and then he was shipped overseas.

Several years and one son later, they made their home in Willow Grove, Pennsylvania. Penny began teaching first grade at Willow Grove Christian School, now Philadelphia-Montgomery Christian Academy. Young people have always been the heart and soul of Penny's work, teaching them to love and honor the Lord in all things. She promptly painted the walls in the classroom blue, adding sheep and Bible verses. She taught with exuberance and love for the children, and she was soon asked to teach more classes. "I never turned out a bad reader," she said. She believed in teaching reading by phonetics, and had her first-grade class reading from the New Testament by the end of the year. She offered this advice to teachers: "A teacher has lives to mold, not only material to cover, and a teacher must set an example at all times to her pupils. Remember you are handling a person's child—you are handling their dearest possession." Penny loved keeping the children involved, and she would organize the school programs and arrange the music herself. Knowing that good habits start at home, she started a Mom's Club after school to encourage the mothers in everything from hygiene to nurturing their marriage and family relationships.

After teaching a few years, she took a year off to raise her first two children. The Christian Education Committee of the still young OPC, knowing that she exhibited great skills as a teacher and was now "available," asked her to develop a Sunday school teaching curriculum for the primary grades—which she proceeded to do with great gusto. Penny had come into the Reformed faith only recently and spent the summer reading the likes of Calvin, Berkhof, and Machen before starting on the material. The first Sunday school material was published in 1964. Penny continued to write material for the primary and junior grades over the next ten years, working with John Tolsma, Dorothy Anderson Barker, and John

Penny Pappas, a teacher of teachers

Mitchell, among others. She contributed to the senior high material as well.

Until then, Sunday school material for the OPC had simply been mimeographed sheets. The CCE wanted to create a curriculum that would be full of Bible content, Reformed in doctrinal outlook, attractively printed, and teachable. Quite an undertaking for this small, new denomination! The material soon became known as Great Commission Publications, and was being used by not only OPC churches, but other Reformed congregations and even some evangelical churches looking for attractive materials true to the Bible. Penny was influential in encouraging the OPC to break new ground by incorporating multi-racial pictures of children in the materials, something that had never been done up until that time. She said, "If we want our material to be welcomed by a wide spectrum of people across America, we have to depict these people." She exuded a multitude of talents, creating puzzles, poems, games, pictures, and other activities to keep these young minds involved in the materials. By 1973 there were 558 congregations using the material, of which 435 were non-OP churches. Penny was a pioneer in the true sense of the word when it comes to the education of our children in the Reformed faith. It is not an easy task, communicating ideas like total depravity and unconditional election to primary children in a way they can understand.

But she didn't stop there. Next she was asked by the CCE to conduct workshops in the northeast presbyteries. Penny and her husband, John, traveled up and down the East Coast helping Sunday school teachers learn to use the material and teach more effectively. She was full of ideas on how to motivate not only the children but their teachers as well. She would bring little grab bags to the teachers' workshops with items they could use to make their classes interesting. By this time, Penny was also the principal at Phil-Mont Christian Academy *and* teaching the first-grade Sunday school at her church *and* raising four children: Jon, Merrie, Stephanie, and Mark.

Although teaching and developing Sunday school materials were significant contributions, they were not the only things Penny was known for. She was also a wonderful caterer, preparing a magnificent spread for many a wedding, including the cake. Having married into a Greek family, she fell in love with the food, traditions, and culture. The house was often full of people for Sunday dinner with more food choices than a Chinese buffet. Her moussaka and baklava were to die for! She and John were well known for their grand Christmas parties. Penny loved to decorate for the holiday, with a tree in every room. She and her friends would cater weddings and events to help raise money for the Christian school. She remembers one wedding that took place just after Christmas. They asked for people's Christmas trees that were about to be thrown out and created a winter wonderland in the church for the wedding, complete with a seven-layer cake. She also remodeled the basement for the young people of Trinity OPC with her innovative decorating, using whatever materials she could find. Her family attests to the fact that wherever they lived, Penny would transform their home into a beautiful place, decorated with antique finds from Maine, seaside treasures, and her own creations.

Penny showed a great interest in anything she turned her mind to. With an inheritance from her father, she decided to buy a boarding house in Doylestown to take in and minister to troubled young people in the area. She ran it for four years, cooking, cleaning, and offering Christian counseling and Bible studies to the young people, making a positive impact on a number of these lives. At the boarding house, she dealt with a number of challenges, such as a young man she discovered was growing marijuana on the roof, and another young man who nearly burnt the place down from a cigarette in the bed. Never a dull moment!

Penny's counseling wasn't limited to the boarding house. In fact, many people sought her out for this over the years. They were drawn to her love for them and desire to help them in their relationships, marriages, and family situations.

After GCP moved its offices to the Atlanta, Georgia, area in 1990, Penny went into real estate. She helped a number of seminary students and professors find quality housing in the area. So, Penny added one more hat to the list of those she had worn—educator, writer, mentor, Sunday school teacher, principal, caterer, interior decorator, workshop leader, and now realtor. And she was always ready for one more challenge. It has been said that Penny exhibited every gift but preaching, and had to hold her tongue from doing that!

Penny said she was never bored. She always had a thirst for deeper knowledge of our faith, and avidly read books on theology and the defenders of our faith, as well as the Scriptures in Greek. She truly was a self-taught theologian.

After 57 years of marriage, Penny's husband, John, passed away on March 14, 2000. Penny moved to Liberty, Maine, to be close to her daughter Merrie and son-in-law John Bettler. She attended Lakeview OPC in Rockport, where she continued to shower the congregation with her wonderful baked goods on Sunday mornings. Penny went to be with the Lord on March 20, 2016, at the age of 93, leaving behind four children, 13 grandchildren, and

13 great-grandchildren. She truly embodied the spirit of a Titus 2 Woman: praying without ceasing for members of her church, friends, and family; encouraging young and old to put God first in all their relationships; and always seeking to learn more about the Lord.

**Amy Joy** *attends Lakeview OPC in Rockport, Maine. Her father, Thomas Eesley, spearheaded the formation of this church in the 1970s. She was a member of Covenant Players, an international repertory theater company, for 15 years, performing in the United States, Canada, the British Isles, France, and Mexico. Amy now works with clients doing in-home personal care.*

# 18

# Grace Hard:
# Determined to Serve

## *Diane L. Olinger*

In 1953 Grace and Theodore Hard were both appointed to go to Korea as missionaries of the Orthodox Presbyterian Church. Before departing for the East, they traveled cross-country toward the West Coast with their two children in tow, Sterling, five, and Rodney, about to turn four. Their station wagon was so full of all the items they would take with them to the Pacific that the poor boys had to sit atop the luggage, almost touching the car's roof. Along the way, they endured flat tires in the Dakotas and a sandstorm in Arizona that was so severe it took the paint off their car! But the trip gave them the opportunity to visit many OP churches along the way, an opportunity for which Grace was grateful, although she found it difficult.

Finally the day came for Grace and Ted and the boys to begin their journey by sea to Japan. From there they would seek permission to enter Korea, which was still recovering from the ravages of the just-ended Korean War. During the trip, Grace, who was then five-months pregnant, battled seasickness and had difficulty keeping food down. Her condition was certainly not aided by the battering their freighter took from a strong typhoon. Indeed the storm was so serious that the passengers had friction burns on their skin from sliding about as the freighter was tossed on the waves.

At last the Hards arrived in Japan, and from there Ted was able to enter Korea on January 19, 1954. But Grace and the boys had to wait another two months for permission to enter the war-torn country—*just three weeks* before Gwendolyn was born on April 9 in Pusan.

I was stunned when I first heard this story at a presbyterial meeting.[1] My husband was then the Ohio presbytery's regional home missionary, traveling from town-to-town ministering to OP mission works, while I stayed at home with three small children, about to have a fourth. I wondered, how did Grace do it? I struggled to make it to the grocery store and back with my children by my side; she traveled to the other side of the world with hers and lived alone with them for a time in a foreign land. I felt put-upon by the inconvenience of moving so frequently and having my children in different hospitals in different cities; Grace gave birth weeks after arriving in Korea. Her determination to serve the Lord made her an ideal complement to her husband in their work as OPC foreign missionaries. As Ted would later say, she was his "help meet—[his] appropriate help."[2] I was blessed to know Grace during her retirement years. She was an inspiration to me.

Born in New York on April 30, 1928, to Henry and Violet Vogel, Grace was nine years old when she began to feel that the Lord wanted her to be a missionary. Growing up on Long Island, her interest in missions was kindled by her Presbyterian Church (PCUSA) pastor, who was a former missionary to Africa. Though her parents were not Christians, Grace soon found that the church was the center of her life, attending missions rallies, vacation Bible school, and youth groups. Although this was the time period when theological liberalism was gaining a stronghold in the PCUSA (leading to the formation of the OPC in 1936), Grace's congregation was blessed with a series of ministers who preached the truth and were marked by evangelistic zeal.

1 Details about this trip, as well as other details about the Hards' lives and work, were gathered from newsletters, short autobiographies written for the Committee on Foreign Missions, and Ted's personal memoir, *Hopefully Faithful and Useful* (2005), in the OPC Archives.
2 Hard, *Hopefully Faithful and Useful*, 20.

In 1944 Grace entered Wheaton College in Illinois to prepare for missionary service, which she hoped would be in Tibet. Majoring in Koine Greek, she carried a heavy class load, while working 35 hours a week to pay the bills. At Wheaton, Grace met Ted, who described this meeting in his memoir:

> En route to New York on an all-night coach for Christmas vacation I found my seatmate to be a fellow Wheaton student I had not met before. She was tired, distracted, and not keen on conversation, even with my charming self! Fortunately (and perforce?) polite patter progressed to cordial and interested exchange, and we felt well acquainted by trip's end—and impressed with each other's spiritual pilgrimage and desire to serve on the foreign mission field.... This attractive, quiet, cool, self-possessed college junior, mature beyond her years, was bent on a foreign missionary life career, come married partner or not![3]

Among her books, Ted noticed a Tibetan grammar—written in French, because she couldn't find one in English. This was enough to convince him that Grace's interest in missions was no passing fancy, but a serious commitment. Although Ted had been planning on going to the Philippines for missions work, he soon became convinced that Grace would need some companionship and help in the lonely mountains of Tibet. While still at Wheaton, the Hards were married on June 26, 1947, and their first son, Sterling, arrived in April 1948. They were accepted as candidates for the Tibet mission of the Scandinavian Alliance Mission, after graduating together from Wheaton in 1949. But before they could begin preparations, Communist China invaded Tibet, cutting off most missionary access.

Grace and Ted pondered what to do next. While at Wheaton, they had been introduced to the Reformed faith through Sunday afternoon discussion groups led by Edmund Clowney, an OP

---

3 Hard, *Hopefully Faithful and Useful*, 10–11.

minister who was pastoring in the area and was later to become a professor and president of Westminster Theological Seminary in Philadelphia. So, in lieu of preparations for Tibet, Ted enrolled at Westminster in

Ted and Grace Hard

1949, the same year their son Rodney was born. In addition to her responsibilities at home with two children, Grace taught third and fourth grade at the Willow Grove Christian Day School (a precursor to Philadelphia-Montgomery Christian Academy). According to Ted, this time at Westminster was valuable for the Hards' spiritual life and theological anchoring and led them to join the OPC. Another important influence during the Westminster years was OP missionary Bruce Hunt, who visited the seminary while on furlough and made an impassioned plea for more missionaries in Korea. It was then that Grace and Ted began to consider Korea as a mission field.

In 1953 the Korean Armistice Agreement was signed, ending the Korean War and expanding missionary access, and Ted was ordained as an OP minister. Soon after, he and Grace and their children set off for Korea on the epic trip described above, with Grace giving birth to Gwendolyn shortly after arriving.

Pusan, Korea, was the city where the Hards lived and worked, along with their mentors, OP missionaries Bruce and Kathy Hunt. The Hunts and Hards were later joined in Korea by other missionary couples, the Spooners in Pusan; the Conns and Sons in Seoul; and the Englishes in Pusan, Seoul, and Kangneung.

Pusan is a seaport at the southern end of the Korean peninsula, where the Korea Theological Seminary was located. Ted's main work in Korea was as a librarian and faculty member of the seminary, though he also preached, taught in another seminary for lepers, wrote and published, started several seminary and church libraries, managed public Christian reading rooms, and did relief work. Ted's relief work included the typical distribution of food, clothing, and medical supplies. But it also included the design and production of several solar devices for cooking and water heating to combat the extreme shortage of fuel and its high cost for struggling Korean households. The residents of Pusan, many of whom were refugees from the north, had suffered from the Korean War, deep poverty, and a catastrophic local fire. The church situation was difficult as well, since the Presbyterian church with which the OP worked had 428 churches, but only 50 ministers. Having gone through their own battle with modernism, these churches, like many OP churches in the 1930s and 1940s, lost their buildings when they were forced to come out of the larger church body.

Despite their years of preparation, Ted and Grace had many adjustments to make as they began life in Korea in 1954. But, as Ted wrote in his memoir: "Any adjustments I had to make in settling in war-devastated wintry Pusan were dwarfed by Grace's taking care of the baby and the boys, soon setting up housekeeping, finding foodstuff and fuel" and hosting Koreans, missionaries, and American soldiers.[4] At this time Grace mainly focused on the home and the education of the children. This led to the organization of a school in Pusan, where she was principal and teacher for three years. Two more children were born, Nelson in 1956 and Gregory in 1958. How could Grace combine such heavy demands at home and school with missions service? Rather seamlessly, it would appear. According to one American soldier then stationed in Korea, "One day we soldiers were playing volleyball with [the Hards]. The next day Grace, having played volleyball with us, gave birth to a healthy baby."[5]

4  Hard, *Hopefully Faithful and Useful*, 14.
5  John Miller, *A Short Trekker* (Maitland, FL: Xulon, 2012), 38. I'm not sure which of the three Korean-born Hard children this relates to.

The Hards lived in a "run down, poorly constructed bungalow, surrounded by crowded houses on narrow streets and alleys, with open ditches," while "a stone's throw distant" there were small hotel-like buildings housing as many as a thousand prostitutes. Here the Hard children played and grew, rapidly outpacing their parents in learning Korean.[6]

Back on the home front, the OPC's Committee on Foreign Missions was making changes that would affect Grace. The committee reported to the 1960 General Assembly that under "ordinary circumstances" wives of missionaries would no longer be officially "appointed" as missionaries along with their husbands. The committee reasoned that wives of missionaries may

> perform many services on the foreign field, as on the home field, which directly contribute to missionary witness and to the furtherance of missionary work. But the necessity of bearing witness to the Christian faith, a necessity inherent in and arising from Christian faith and profession, constitutes no more reason why the wife of a missionary should be appointed a missionary than should every other Christian woman.... The wives of missionaries are not in a category different from other wives of Christian character, whose husbands are engaged in the work of the ministry.[7]

To some, this change may seem little more than semantics, since it didn't seek to limit the roles these women could have within the mission or outside it; but for Grace—who was trained for missionary service—it felt like a demotion.[8] Her service on the mission

---

6 Hard, *Hopefully Faithful and Useful*, 16.

7 Report of the Committee on Foreign Missions in Minutes of the 27th General Assembly of the OPC, 1960.

8 In one respect, being "appointed" as a missionary may not have been a matter of semantics, as it may have determined who was a voting member of the mission organization. Over time this matter has worked itself out so that the manual of the Committee on Foreign Missions now provides that the wife of a missionary is a member of the mission and may vote on matters put

field would still be welcome, but she would no longer be "appointed" along with Ted. Rev. John Galbraith, who was general secretary of the Committee on Foreign Missions at that time, acknowledged that this was very difficult for Grace to accept. But she was determined to serve—and went right on serving as she had before.

In Ted's memoir he writes glowingly of three Korean female co-workers and their Christian spirit for service and witness for the Lord. He praised them "not because they are women" but because they served faithfully even though they "were not on the ordination and official title climb."[9] I can't help wondering whether he had Grace in mind as well when he wrote those words.

On the mission field Grace found many ways to serve. She maintained the family home, supported Ted in his work, was a gracious hostess to many, was treasurer for the mission and served on a number of its operating committees, taught Bible studies and Sunday school classes, and, along with Ted, authored articles in the *Dictionary of Theology* published by the Korea Society for Reformed Faith and Action.

Grace also continued her teaching career, which changed over time as the needs of her family and the Korean mission changed. When the children were young, she either homeschooled or taught in Christian schools to defray the cost of their education. She later held teaching positions in schools operated by the US Department of Defense and by the Kori-Westinghouse nuclear energy company. On furlough in the United States, Grace taught first grade in Bristol, Pennsylvania, and completed her master's degree in education at Temple University. Finally, when the children were grown, she taught seminary courses in Korea on Christian education. In the 1980s the Hards' work expanded to seminaries in Dehra Dun, India, and the Philippines, with Grace teaching courses on Christian

---

before the organization, unless those matters are "ecclesiastical" or "theological," in which case, only missionaries ordained as teaching or ruling elders may vote. So, with respect to voting, the wife of a missionary is treated in the same way as a missionary deacon would be.
9 Hard, *Hopefully Faithful and Useful*, 38–39.

education, Bible study methods, English, and Greek.

In 1991 the Hards retired from active service as missionaries and moved to southwestern Pennsylvania, near the West Virginia border. Grace welcomed retirement and immersed herself in the activities of Reformation OPC in Morgantown, West Virginia. The transition to "normal" life was tougher for Ted. In part to ease this transition, the Hards retained adjunct missionary status, which allowed them to return to the East from time-to-time to visit the seminaries and churches where they had served, and to continue their book ministry, known as CLASP—Christian Literature Asia Service Program. Through CLASP the Hards were able to send out about two thousand books annually (collected and sorted in their basement) to foreign seminaries, colleges, and training programs in at least ten countries.

According to Rev. Larry Semel, the Hards' pastor at Reformation OPC, their faith was strong even in their years of declining health. Grace died at the age of 79 on June 14, 2007, and Ted died two years later. Visited by a session member just before her death, Grace said, "See you on the other side."

**Diane L. Olinger** *is a lawyer who serves as a copyeditor for* Ordained Servant Online. *She is a member of Calvary OPC in Glenside, Pennsylvania, and resides in Glenside with her husband, Danny Olinger, general secretary for the OPC's Committee on Christian Education. They have four children, ages 12 to 19.*

# 19

# Elizabeth "Betty" Andrews: Dedicated to God's Calling

## *Linda R. Posthuma*

As the freighter traveled east across the rough seas of the Pacific Ocean that wintry January in 1957, Elizabeth "Betty" Heerema—soon to be Andrews—had plenty of time to reflect on how she had come to this moment in her life. During the course of the journey—first to the Philippines, then on to Hong Kong, before finally arriving in Japan, where she was to be married—Betty made a conscious effort to ease her queasy stomach by getting to know fellow passengers. Her cabin mate, a veteran of overseas living, was also a Christian nurse, so she and Betty spent many hours sharing experiences, talking about their faith, and reading the Bible together. Betty also reflected on where the Lord had guided her and wondered what he had in store for her.

Betty was born on June 29, 1917, in Orange City, Iowa. When she was 16, her mother, Gerbina, told her about her difficult birth. After many hours in labor, she had almost given up in pain and exhaustion when she turned to God, crying out to him for help. "Instantly you were born," she told Betty.[1] The Heeremas already had two boys, Ed and Jack, and five years after Betty's birth, a third son, Nick, was born.

Albert and Gerbina Heerema had emigrated from the Nether-

---

1 Elizabeth Heerema Andrews, *Memoirs of Betty* (Quarryville, PA, 2004), 1.

lands to the United States, seeking a better life. Albert, a baker, continued that trade in Iowa. Gerbina, the eldest of 11 children, was raised on a farm in Holland. Although she loved going to school, she gave up her education to become a nanny in Groningen, where she met Albert at church. Only after they arrived in the United States did they marry.

The Heeremas brought their Christian heritage and strong Calvinistic beliefs with them to America. They were dedicated to raising their young family to love and worship God, encouraging them to study the Bible. Of her parents, Betty remembered, "Both Father and Mother were well read in the Bible and in doctrine. As children we often listened to discussions on doctrinal truths which would last the greater part of an evening. This faith, and the fact that my parents were willing to move and make sacrifices in order that we got a Christian education, are two factors which have influenced my life greatly."[2] Education and hard work were stressed in the Heerema home.

About the time Betty entered elementary school, she learned to play the piano, something that brought her great joy throughout her life. At 12, she began playing the piano for Sunday school and church services. She also sang in the school choir, developing a fine soprano voice.

After her high school graduation at 17, Betty and her family moved to Grand Rapids, Michigan, where her older brothers had attended Calvin College, the denominational college of the Christian Reformed Church.

Times were hard for the family. Betty had to work for two years before beginning her college studies. After her freshman year at Calvin, she left college to work for a telephone company so that she could assist her family financially. She longed to return to school and decided to pursue nursing instead of teaching, her first love, because the tuition costs were more manageable. It wasn't until she

2 Personal reflections taken from Betty's application for missionary service with the OPC's Committee on Foreign Missions, 1956.

was 25 that Betty graduated from Calvin and completed the nursing course at Blodgett Memorial Hospital in Grand Rapids. After graduation, she put her new skills into practice, serving as head nurse in the plastic surgery department for a year before attending the University of Chicago. After earning a bachelor of science degree in nursing education, Betty returned to Blodgett Hospital where she taught nursing students for three years and served as educational director for a fourth. During this time, she led the nursing students in a Bible study and organized and directed a small singing group—all helpful preparation for the mission field.

In 1947 Betty received a letter from the Foreign Missions Board of the Christian Reformed Church with an unexpected request: would she be willing to go to Shanghai, China, as a missionary nurse? Betty had never considered foreign missionary service, although her interest in missions had grown after friends encouraged her thinking in that direction. Now she was being asked to go to China to assist in restarting a medical work that had been disrupted by the Japanese in World War II. She didn't know what to do.

Betty shared the letter with her parents, pastor, and friends, all of whom began to pray. After months of indecision and soul-searching, Betty's mother counseled, "I don't think you will have any peace until you say 'yes.'"[3] So Betty finally did. Six months later, Betty was in Shanghai, China.

This was a time of turmoil in China. Insurgents were rising up against the government, but it was still thought that mission work could continue. Betty joined other new missionaries in Beijing for language study and realized for the first time that learning Chinese would be difficult. A letter from the US Consulate informed American citizens at the language school that the Chinese Communists were planning an offensive push to the south. They were urged to return to the United States unless it was absolutely necessary for them to remain.

Betty, however, returned to Shanghai and has never forgotten

3 Andrews, *Memoirs of Betty*, 28.

the atmosphere: danger, panic, hopelessness, death, and misery. This time when they were notified that a US naval vessel would take Americans home, the missionaries finally decided to leave China. On New Year's Eve 1948, Betty and her fellow missionaries boarded the last passenger ship sent by the US Navy. She had been in China for less than five months.

Betty's second missionary experience followed a year later. Upon her return from China, while setting up a teaching program back at Blodgett Hospital, she was approached by a missionary doctor from Pakistan who was looking for a teacher for nursing students at a Christian hospital in Lahore. Betty, now truly interested in missionary service, agreed to go for three years.

Long days teaching nursing students, working in the hospital wards and clinic, and taking on administrative responsibilities taxed Betty. Yet she made time for Bible studies and reaching out to share Christ with patients. Betty desired to bring the gospel to those with whom she came in contact, with the view toward building up Christ's church. There was some time for R&R in Betty's schedule, and one of her more memorable excursions was a trip to Kashmir, where she had tea one afternoon with a vacationing Indira Gandhi.

When Betty returned to the United States for furlough, she tendered her resignation, needing time to rest, to reconnect with family, and to move on. Little did she realize what the Lord had in store for her.

Once again back at Blodgett Hospital, Betty supervised the new post-operative intensive care unit. Soon she became a teacher and the dean of women at the Reformed Bible Institute, now known as Kuyper College.

During this year, Egbert Andrews, a missionary of the Orthodox Presbyterian Church—and a bachelor—reappeared in Betty's life. Egbert had been a classmate of her brother Ed's at Westminster Theological Seminary in Philadelphia, Pennsylvania. Betty had met him years before in her brother's home when Egbert was on leave from missionary service in China and in Grand Rapids on seminary business. After a short period of getting reacquainted, Egbert popped the question, and they were engaged.

When Betty had been in Pakistan, she had received several marriage proposals, but had turned them down. One of her suitors asked her, "If you don't want to marry any of us, who do you want to marry?" "I think I want to marry a minister and a missionary," she replied.[4] Now, in God's providence, her hope was becoming reality.

Now began a time of hurried preparations. A replacement for her job at RBI needed to be found. Applications for missionary service must be completed; medical exams scheduled; a trip to meet the Committee on Foreign Missions organized; and a new denomination embraced. And, of course, a wedding needed to be planned.

Betty Heerema seeing Egbert Andrews off for Taiwan just after their engagement in July 1956

Betty and Egbert decided to be married in Japan and from there go directly to Taiwan where Egbert served as an OP missionary in the capital city of Taipei. Shortly after their engagement, Egbert had returned to Taiwan. Betty was to meet him in Japan so she planned to sail from San Francisco in January 1957, and be married in Tokyo in early February. Betty found it difficult to leave her parents, realizing that they were older and knowing that it

4 Ibid., 61.

would be some time before she would see them again.[5]

When she finally arrived in Japan, Betty was greeted at the dock by Egbert, some college friends, and a number of OP missionaries. They shared a happy reunion, and then Betty was escorted to the mission guest house where she would stay. That night, after being instructed on how to turn off the gas heater in her room, Betty fell exhausted into bed. She woke around midnight with a terrible headache and feeling woozy. Although she was sure she had turned the gas heater off, she heard the hissing sound of escaping gas and discovered a spigot wide open. She closed the spigot, opened the windows, then fled to the bathroom to be sick. The next day, which was to have been her wedding day, she recuperated, feeling much better by evening. When Egbert visited her that afternoon, they decided to postpone the wedding by another day.

Three days after arriving in Japan, on a snowy February 7, 1957, Betty married Egbert Andrews in Tokyo, with OP missionaries Heber and Genie McIlwaine in attendance. She was 40 years old; he was 48.

When the newlyweds arrived in Taipei in early March, the winter school break was over, and Egbert resumed his busy life teaching at a local seminary and college. He also was involved with neighborhood evangelism, teaching evening classes, preaching Sundays, and overseeing a literature ministry.

Left alone for most of the day, Betty felt isolated:

"I had to go to church for years and not understand a word that I was listening to," said Betty. "I had to get my own spiritual food from my own Bible reading. We had that at breakfast and prayer in the evening also."

They depended on prayer. "We prayed together before going to bed. No matter how late, no matter what condition, we were going to pray together." When Egbert was out in the

---

5 Betty's father died while she was on the mission field. Her mother died at 95 after the Andrewses had retired and returned to the United States.

evening, she said, "I would often spend two hours in prayer."[6]

Betty faced other obstacles as she began to settle in. Their new house was large and minimally furnished. The kitchen, mainly the domain of a cook, was a dark, dingy room with a low ceiling, which tall Betty described as "torture to my back." Without any knowledge of Mandarin or the Taiwanese dialect spoken by people in the neighborhood, Betty could not communicate with the people around her. Although other OP missionary families, Richard and Polly Gaffin and John and Gertrude Johnston, also labored in Taiwan, they lived a considerable distance away. Betty needed help.

Most expatriate families employed a house helper, so the Andrewses chose the daughter of a local pastor to fill that role. The young woman was not happy with her new position, wanting to learn English instead and go to school. Working with disgruntled help added to Betty's challenges. As determined as the young woman was to be miserable in her labors, Betty was more determined to work with her, to learn to communicate with her in Taiwanese, and to be a witness to God's grace in all sorts of difficult situations. Betty did a lot of praying. The young woman finally resigned herself to her work and, after more than two years, moved on to a position more to her liking. Years later Betty learned that this woman had married a pastor and led a women's ministry. Other house helpers followed, proving less difficult for Betty to manage.

Betty next tackled learning Taiwanese. Egbert, who was born and raised in China, spoke fluent Mandarin. This was the language used for teaching and preaching in meetings of the Reformed Fellowship, a group he established because of the lack of a Reformed church to which converts embracing the Reformed faith could be sent. A young college student, Daniel Hung, taught Betty her first Taiwanese phrases. He later graduated from Westminster Theological Seminary and became a pastor in the Taiwanese church which grew out of the Reformed Fellowship. Betty slowly gained the ability

6 Patricia E. Clawson, "Betty Andrews: A Woman of Prayer," in *New Horizons* 32, no. 2 (February 2011), 8–9.

to make everyday conversation, but more structured instruction was needed. When her husband assisted in starting a language institute, her formal studies began there and continued with private tutors. Progress was slow and painful, but her persistence brought a measure of success. Betty felt that it was difficult to learn a new language after 40, especially when you lacked an aptitude for languages. She continued studying Taiwanese for most of her missionary career.

Betty and Egbert served together as OP missionaries to Taiwan for almost 22 years, first in Taipei and later in Kaohsiung. Their ministry was extensive and varied. Egbert concentrated on establishing congregations for the growing Reformed Fellowship, preaching and teaching, and spearheading evangelism efforts.

Laboring alongside her husband, Betty taught English classes, worked with college and high school students, and forged new areas of ministry as her language skills increased. She led church activities for women and children, taught Sunday school, and directed weekly prayer meetings for women. She taught nearly illiterate women how to read Taiwanese, conducted sewing classes, and visited homes in local neighborhoods. She also used her nursing skills to help the sick. In all of these activities, she shared her faith.

Sharing her musical gifts brought Betty particular joy. Over the years, she played the organ in a number of churches and organized church choirs and singing groups. One Christmas she was chosen to be the soprano soloist for the performance of the *Messiah* that a large chorus presented in Taipei annually. She also encouraged the musical talents of the young people in the church by giving organ, piano, and voice lessons.

While on furlough in the United States every fourth year, Betty and Egbert continued their busy life. During their 1973 furlough, they spoke in 78 OP churches, and a number of others. Betty spoke 45 times and Egbert 187 times.[7]

Over the years, the Andrewses chose to live in poorer neighbor-

7  Report of the Committee on Foreign Missions, in the Minutes of the 41st General Assembly of the OPC, 1974: 74.

hoods among the Taiwanese rather than in expatriate communities, recalls fellow OP missionary Lendall Smith. Helping neighbors was gratifying to Betty, knowing that they trusted her and would come to her with problems or concerns. Once a neighborhood family had a sick baby, who wouldn't eat and seemed to be dying. Not knowing what to do, the parents called Betty. She prayed all the way to their home, asking God for wisdom. She found a very sick baby, who had been lethargic for most of a day despite receiving medicine from a doctor. Betty went in search of the doctor for more medicine, again praying all the way. Would his office be open at night? Would the doctor give medicine to a stranger? He gave her one dose, which was accepted gratefully by the parents.

With the parents' permission, Betty prayed for their son, and then contacted a Taiwanese nurse she knew. By the time the nurse arrived, the baby had begun to take his bottle and had opened his eyes. His parents were overjoyed. "To this day," Betty said, "I don't know what was in the medicine the doctor gave them, but I was thankful for it and thankful to God for sparing the child."[8]

In 1979, after many years of committed and physically exhausting service, Betty and Egbert's missionary labors came to an end. Although the Andrewses were not scheduled for retirement until the mid-1980s, those plans changed when Egbert suffered a stroke while in Taipei on mission business on January 11, 1979. After receiving medical care and convalescing, Egbert suffered a second stroke. The Andrewses got their affairs in order and left Taiwan on May 4.

At the time of their retirement, the face of the OPC Taiwan Mission had changed: the Johnstons and the Gaffins had retired to the United States. Lendall and Sherrill Smith, Bob and Shirley Marshall, and Steve and Faye Hake had arrived in Taiwan with their families to study Taiwanese and take up the work. They were a huge support to Betty when Egbert fell ill, providing assistance and moral support during Egbert's illness and helping to prepare them

8 Andrews, *Memoirs of Betty*, 79–80.

for departure. Although the Andrewses were sad to leave, they were thankful to the Lord for providing a stable and true Taiwanese Reformed church and OPC stewards to nurture it.

Stateside, Egbert's health remained fragile, and the Andrewses moved to Quarryville Presbyterian Retirement Community near Lancaster, Pennsylvania. He passed away in May 1982 at the age of 71.

Not ready for retirement, Betty moved to Florida where she lived near her youngest brother, Nick, and his family. She became involved in the local church and wrote a biography of her husband's youth and her own autobiography, as well as assisted friends and fellow missionaries in writing their life stories. She corresponded with many and visited numerous relatives and friends.

In March 1991 Betty returned to Quarryville Presbyterian Retirement Community. She loved the music program and sang in the choir and played the organ until deteriorating eye sight prevented her participation. She is known for her diligence in visiting those who are sick or confined to their rooms and for her committed prayer life. While she was still able, Betty often walked at night through the halls at Quarryville with her note cards in hand, reading Scripture verses and praying for a long list of requests.

On June 29, 2016, Betty celebrated 99 years of life—a life that has been characterized by her love and service for others as an out-pouring of her love and service for her Lord.

**Linda R. Posthuma** is *the daughter of a Christian Reformed Church pastor and home missionary to the Navaho and Zuni Native Americans in New Mexico, where she got a taste of missionary life at a young age. Linda taught German and history at Philadelphia-Montgomery Christian Academy before becoming the administrative assistant of the OPC's Committee on Foreign Missions in 1986. Linda first met Betty—who was one of her mother's teachers at Blodgett Hospital—through her work with retired OP missionaries and enjoys their time together. Linda is a member of Trinity OPC in Hatboro, Pennsylvania.*

# 20

# Mary Cummings: Showing the Love of Christ

## *Gail Mininger*

Raised on the mission field with Korean cooks in the kitchen, she shed tears on her honeymoon at needing help to make oatmeal. Yet she became a marvelous hostess, feeding church folks, interns, neighbors, presbyters, and professors for six decades.

## Korea

Born in Korea on December 10, 1911, Mary Hunt Cummings was the youngest of five children of missionary parents, and sister of future Orthodox Presbyterian missionary Bruce Hunt. Living under Japanese rule, Mary remembered her mother slitting the wallpaper to hide Korean flags from Japanese inspectors.[1]

At nine, Mary was sent to a boarding school in Korea. "Too young," she rued at 80 years of age. "I needed my father's discipline. I think I learned a way of covering up. It's always easy for me to appear as better than I am. Still!"

Graduating from Korean high school at 16, she traveled to America, earned a degree in Bible and history at Wilson College in Chambersburg, Pennsylvania, then studied at Moody Bible Institute in Chicago. While at Wilson, Mary attended a League

---

1 Details are courtesy of letters, tributes, journals, emails, memorabilia, and interviews with family and friends; an interview of Mary by the late OPC Pastor Charles Dennison; and *New Horizons* and OPC archives.

of Evangelical Students convention in Pittsburgh, Pennsylvania, where she met Westminster Theological Seminary student Calvin Knox Cummings.

Cal and Mary began a four-year courtship by correspondence, meeting only five times before they married on September 6, 1935.

## Pittsburgh

Cal was denied ordination by the Presbyterian Church (USA) in 1935 for not pledging blind allegiance to their liberal boards. In 1936 he and Mary became constituting members of the Presbyterian Church of America, soon renamed the Orthodox Presbyterian Church. Cal was ordained at the OPC's First Assembly and called in 1937 as pastor to the newly established Covenant OPC in Pittsburgh.

Cal Cummings was known for his dogged door-to-door neighborhood calling, street meetings, tract distribution, large vacation Bible schools, and diligent instruction of new believers. He served the Pittsburgh congregation with Mary at his side for 37 years. He led his family in prayer and Bible reading three times a day and founded the Christian School of Wilkinsburg, later known as Trinity Christian School. A long-term member of the OPC Committee on Christian Education, he wrote *Confessing Christ*, still widely used in OPC membership classes. He also served 51 years on the Westminster Theological Seminary board.

"But the heart and soul of Cal's ministry was his wife Mary," claims Reformed Theological Seminary professor, John Frame, one of Cal's many interns and eventual son-in-law. "Her hospitality was legendary. During my internship, I had lunch with the family most every day, and there was a constant stream of people coming through their home." Her son David reminisces, "She could always rattle a few dishes and somehow come up with enough to feed all five children, a foster daughter, and one to ten more, on the corners, two on the piano bench, and another four in the hallway around a card table! Her laughter was infectious and she loved playing games with family and guests."

"Her goal was always to show the love of Christ," recalls Frame. "Mary would often take people aside to find out how they were doing, would always know just what to say to meet the person's spiritual need, had a wonderful memory of all who passed through her life, wrote meaningful notes to many, and carried on her constant prayer life."

Ruth Morton, wife of OPC pastor George Morton, reflects on the tearful day the Morton's sixth child was diagnosed with Down syndrome. After a dinner meeting that evening, Mary Cummings put her arms around Ruth, "You didn't eat any of your delicious meal. May I ask why?" As Ruth shared her news, they wept together, with Mary consoling, "Isn't it wonderful that our God loved you so much to entrust this special child in your care? You must meet my friend who has a Downs child." Mary followed up with a note of comfort, "Remember that God makes no mistakes."

Service-minded Mary taught numerous children in vacation Bible school with engaging stories, visual aids, and motion songs. Charter member Millie Quinette still pictures Mary often on her knees cleaning the church. "She was a woman of prayer, and she showed us by example how to submit to our husbands." Even before becoming a church member, Pat Lowry was asked by Mary to assist her in making baskets with tracts and snacks to welcome new neighbors. Mary encouraged fellowship and reached out to unsaved women.

### Tallahassee

Upon drawing retirement income, Cal sought to pastor a small congregation unable to provide a full salary. He and Mary began serving Calvary OPC in Tallahassee, Florida, in 1975.

I first met Mary when she and Cal traveled from Tallahassee to our Orlando, Florida, home so he could collaborate with my husband, Larry, pastor of Lake Sherwood OPC. Mary asked for a dishtowel, began drying silverware, then proceeded to seek *my* advice on Bible study materials, counseling, parenting, and recipes. I was amazed. Me, the fledgling pastor's wife, she, the 37-year veteran and more than twice my age! Wasn't she the expert? Yet her example freed me, the rookie pastor's wife, from the tyranny of unrealistic expectations of myself to be all-knowing.

When her husband signaled he was ready to depart, Mary joyfully bee-lined to the car—having trained herself not to keep Cal or the Lord's business waiting.

Ironically, by her seeking to learn from me rather than aiming to instruct, Mary Cummings taught me a priceless lesson—that I always have more to learn, from the veterans, from the rookies. At her death, behind my tears I wondered, did she ever know she was my mentor?

### Melbourne and Chicago

In 1981 Cal and Mary began a brief ministry to newly planted Christ OPC in Melbourne, Florida. Meanwhile their son David, while pastoring an OP church in the Chicago suburbs, was also helping a small congregation in Chicago with limited funds. Burdened by the great needs of Chicago, in 1983 Cal became the first full-time pastor of Trinity Presbyterian Chapel.

Then in her 70s, Mary continued mentoring younger women and spent a week in a cramped apartment helping a mother after a complicated birth.

While serving in Chicago, Cal developed cancer. Always cheering him on, Mary wrote to their children, "Keep praying for Dad. He's giving every ounce of strength he has to the work. Reminds me of the Korean Christians who called out to their loved ones in prison, 'To the end! To the end!' It's a privilege to live with Dad and pray with him. Really draws me close to the Lord."

### Philadelphia

With Cal's health waning, in 1987 the Cummings moved near their son Wilson, who was ministering at the OPC's Emmanuel Chapel in South Philadelphia. Later that year, Cal died.

"Jesus Christ is made to me all I need," was sung at Cal's memorial service. Mary wondered, "Could I serve alone, travel alone, make decisions alone? Could I still laugh?" Later she testified, "I have found that song to be true. Jesus Christ is all I need. This has not been the easiest year of my life. Yet it has been a wonderful year of experiencing again God's faithfulness in keeping his promises."

Friends who visited Mary in Philadelphia recoiled at her rough environment—trash on the street, a murder nearby the night before, drug dealers around the corner. Mary raved, "Oh, I love it here. There's three of us who want to bring this block to the Lord. Isn't that exciting?" Mary baked cookies for the neighborhood children, led them to pick up trash, and read Bible stories to them.

After a neighbor tried to compensate Mary for delivering her groceries, Mary reflected with tears, "I don't want her to pay me—I want her to know Jesus." Granddaughter Eunice recalls, "Grandma did not hide from the brokenness and effects of sin around her but met them with grace, love, and a deep desire to be part of God's redemption. I know Jesus better because of my grandmother."

When her son Wilson preached about heaven, Mary responded, "I want to go there now. As Jesus becomes dearer, I miss Cal more because I want to share with him what's going on. With his memorial gifts the Chapel had a face lift and has already attracted visitors. Some on drugs are now walking in the Light and bringing others to learn of him."

### Family

Mary considered raising her five children to be her greatest accomplishment. The Cummings children have served the Lord around the globe: Wilson as an OPC pastor, Cal Jr., as an OPC missionary to Japan, David as an OPC and PCA pastor, and Mary Grace Frame and the late Gwendolyn Weeks as teachers married to professors. At last count, grandchildren and great-grandchildren total 43, a number serving in ministry, education, and medicine.

Wilson cherishes his mother for "entering into my ideas and dreaming my dreams after listening to me. She had a good way of summarizing my thoughts—helping me see them from a biblical perspective, helping me to be free in Christ, turning me from dwelling on myself."

She would sing while doing her housework, "Give, said the little stream, for Jesus give, for God and others live." On Mary's own birthdays, she gave the children presents, quoting, "It is more blessed to give than to receive." There were Christmases, though, when

Cal and Mary Cummings and their children Cal Jr., Gwendolyn (Weeks), Mary (Frame), and Wilson (and David yet to be born)

she could not afford gifts. "I'd take an oatmeal box and try to make a doll bed out of it or something. But the children were perfectly happy."

Mary Grace remembers a time when her mother had only two dresses and two pairs of shoes in her closet, yet people provided the children with boxes of clothes and shoes. Her mother's sacrificial living for others seemed to provide for all of them.

Cal Jr.'s wife, Edie Cummings, a retired missionary to Japan, treasures how Mary so quickly "adopted" her into her family. Having no idea of what a Christian home or marriage looked like, Edie looked to Mary for advice in everything from missionary work to parenting.

Yet Mary Grace reveals that her mother "really believed everyone was so much better than she was. She thought she couldn't do what pastors' wives should do—she was not a secretary or a pianist. But God used her sense of inadequacy. She genuinely made people feel needed and loved." She parented an orphan girl for years and "gave her a sense of worth."

Grandson Colin Weeks adds, "Her love was not blind. When she saw us doing something wrong she gently but firmly showed us our sin. This above all showed her love. She desired that we know Christ and put our trust in him."

She also taught her children an attitude of service. If they complained when Cal was out doing ministry, Mary cautioned, "The fact that your dad is using this time to call on people who need the help of Jesus should tell you that we need to step up to the plate to help and support Dad." The Cummings children responded, providing rides for the elderly, mowing, playing piano, cleaning, typing, and serving in VBS.

As the children left home, Mary and Cal took turns writing each child every week, Mary's letters were eight or more pages.

### Heaven

"As she neared her 90th birthday, Mary chastised herself for not knocking on neighbors' doors and inviting them to church," remembers granddaughter Elizabeth Cummings. "She didn't consider her work for the Lord finished simply because her body had deteriorated and her husband no longer labored beside her. Grandma spent her time in prayer, keeping her eyes fixed on Jesus."

During her final hospital stay, despite severe pain, Mary continued to express her concerns for the family and the neighborhood. But her wit also surfaced, "Oh that Uncle Wilson, he's bringing all of the United States to see me!"

Granddaughter Elizabeth Cummings recalls Wilson explaining to the family, "There is one more procedure the doctors are willing to try, but if that doesn't work, then...."

"'Bye-bye,' Grandma chimed in, with her cheeriest voice, and her face wreathed in smiles. The rest of us, bawling our eyes out, suddenly had to laugh. Grandma was ready to meet her Savior."

On Mary's last day, February 28, 2002, her heartbeat fluctuating, family members read Scriptures, holding hands around her bed, singing "The Lord's My Shepherd."

During the Psalm's last line, "And in God's house forevermore my dwelling place shall be," the heart monitor dropped to zero. At age 90, Mary Cummings met her Jesus face to face.

**Gail Mininger** *lives in Orlando, Florida, with her husband, Larry G. Mininger, pastor of Lake Sherwood OPC, where she serves through music, Scripture memory, hospitality, and teaching. The Miningers have five adult children, one of whom, Abigail, worships with them in Orlando. Their son Marcus is an OPC minister and professor at Mid America Reformed Seminary. Their daughters April and Linda are married to PCA ministers and their son Lucas is a PCA member as well. As her nest emptied, Gail taught public high school piano classes, touring as the school's assistant choral director and pianist until her recent retirement.*

# 21

# Margaret Dunn:
# From Korea to the Jersey Shore

## *Holly Wilson*

Margaret Hunt Dunn was born on June 23, 1909, in a Presbyterian missionary compound in Chairyung, Korea. Her life would span more than a century and be characterized by zeal for the lost, bravery, and servanthood.

Margie was the daughter of William Brewster Hunt and his second wife, Anna Lloyd, who were Presbyterian Church (USA) missionaries to Korea. Many in the Orthodox Presbyterian Church are familiar with Margie's half-brother Bruce Hunt who served with his wife, Kathy, as an Orthodox Presbyterian Church missionary in China and Korea.

Anna Hunt taught Margie at home using Calvert School curriculum until she was old enough to attend a boarding school in Pyongyang. This was a town in the southern part of North Korea, very near the border of China. Margie graduated from high school there and went on to Wilson College in Chambersburg, Pennsylvania. It was here that she had a "vivid spiritual experience" and gave her life to Christ.[1] Upon graduation in 1931, she felt it was only natural that she should become a missionary, so she went to Moody Bible Institute for further training. Graduating in 1934, she was

---

1 Unless otherwise noted, all quotes and comments attributed to Margie or Les Dunn are from recollections of their daughter Dorothy "Dotty" Williams, who was interviewed by the author on June 12, 2015.

hired by the boarding school in Pyongyang as a dormitory matron and physical education teacher. She must have been well loved, since the students devoted their yearbook to her in 1939.

The Japanese had been occupying Korea since 1910. As the Second World War was heating up in the 1930s, they were tightening their grip on the country. In 1940 the Japanese took over the school in Pyongyang and shut it down. This led to Margie travelling through Japanese-held territory to Harbin, Manchuria, China, where Bruce and Kathy Hunt were stationed. There were photos of the Japanese emperor plastered all over the country, including the sides of trains. Margie would later tell her daughter, Dotty, that it was a strange feeling to be the only one standing when the Koreans at a train station would all bow down to these pictures. As her visit with Bruce and Kathy wore on, it became evident that war was looming. She left China on one of the last boats out before the country was effectively closed for the duration of the war. This would have taken courage for a young, single woman, like Margie.

Upon arriving in the States in 1941, Margie was hired as a secretary in the OPC offices. There she met Les Dunn who was the pastor of Wildwood OPC in Wildwood, New Jersey. He had been widowed and had a six-year-old daughter named Karin. In later years Margie said that she had not thought she would marry, but after Les Dunn kissed her, she changed her mind! They wed on May 11, 1946, and started serving together in Wildwood.

Les had a passion for evangelism that matched Margie's. He was instrumental in getting the Boardwalk Chapel in Wildwood up and running, serving as its executive director from 1941 to 1952. The chapel, which still operates today, is an effort to evangelize tourists in the area using nightly presentations of the gospel and making books and tracts available to passersby. Margie was not involved in the program of the chapel, but she found her way to the chapel kitchen where she served meals for those who were involved in the ministry. Early in their marriage she did not know much about cooking, but she worked hard to learn in order to better serve her husband, her growing family, and the many visitors who were brought home

Karin (Les's daughter by first marriage), Les, Dotty, Margie, and Richard Dunn in the early 1950s

from worship services.

The Dunns, having married later in their lives, adopted a daughter, Dorothy, as an infant, and shortly after that a son, Richard, at age seven. Les's daughter, Karin, was seven years older than Richard. Margie also often served as a "foster" mother for her nieces and nephews whose parents were on the mission field. When they came to the States for college, they knew the Dunn's home would be a place for them to spend holidays or to get help in organizing a wedding.

Margie and Les served a number of churches through the years. From Wildwood they went to Westfield, New Jersey; Portland, Maine; and Tinley Park, Illinois. While in Maine, Margie had an opportunity for a job, but Les felt it would send the message that the church was not paying him enough, so he asked her not to accept it. Margie played the piano for each of the churches they served, was very active in the choir, and attended prayer meetings. They worked shoulder to shoulder, serving those around them with meals and housing, teaching and ministering wherever there was need. For many years Margie also taught Machen League, a youth ministry for catechism and Bible study, telling stories with flannel graphs that were still in her possession when she died. Her favorite verse was Psalm 118:24, "This is the day that the Lord has made, let us rejoice and be glad in it." She fostered an attitude of gratitude for all that God provided through some very lean years.

As the wife of a pastor, Margie saw her role to be a supportive one, working behind the scenes to provide all that was needed wherever they were. She and Les enjoyed gardening together—Les overseeing the vegetables and Margie the flowers. After Les died in 2001, Margie started showing signs of dementia, and she moved to Wisconsin to live with her daughter, Dotty Williams. Dotty said, "What she taught me was grace, she spent her life not thinking about herself but giving to others, teaching. She made our home a happy, pleasant place. She just did it graciously. She lived her life for the Lord."[2] On February 14, 2015, Margie went to be with the Lord whom she had served for so long. She was 105 years old.

**Holly Wilson** *is the wife of Larry E. Wilson, pastor of Redeemer Orthodox Presbyterian Church in Airdrie, Alberta, Canada. They live on a beautiful farm just outside of town with one dog, two cats, four chickens, 32 calves, 34 cows, and an untold number of honey bees. She has four adult children and two grandchildren living far away in the United States.*

2  Bill Glauber, "Aging Gracefully," *Milwaukee Wisconsin Journal Sentinel*, September 11, 2010, http://www.jsonline.com/news/milwaukee/102705334.html.

# 22

# Norma Ellis:
# A Life of Excellence

## *Susan Dreger Perez*

"Recently we watched the mist hanging low in the lush Napa Valley in California. Now it veiled the hills. Now it was gone. God has swept away the sins of his people like a cloud, their sins like the morning mist. He has displayed his glory in them. He calls upon the heavens and the earth to bear testimony to this redemption and to sing for joy, and shout and burst into song."[1]

I was a young housewife with seven children and making room in my busy days for a quiet time was often difficult. One day browsing through our extensive library, I found this book that my husband had purchased years before from our church's book table. I gave it a try as a devotional, and God used that book in my life to show me himself through the book of Isaiah in ways that I had not encountered previously. All I knew at the time is a husband/wife team were the authors, and I as the reader was made to feel that I might be sitting at their kitchen table with them while they discussed the riches of Isaiah with me.

Norma Ellis, the wife half of that writing team, left a lifelong legacy pointing to her Savior not only through her writing, but as a mother, wife, pastor's wife, women's speaker, friend, and as organizer and leader of women's groups in the Orthodox Presbyterian

---

1 Charles and Norma Ellis, *The Wells of Salvation: Meditations on Isaiah* (Banner of Truth: Carlisle, Pennsylvania, 1985), 156.

Church. In fact, her son, Pastor Richard Ellis of Faith OPC in Elmer, New Jersey, described his mother as "hardworking, creative, artistic (in writing and painting); steadfast in her love for her husband; fascinated with creation (especially the beautiful coast of Maine); a woman of the Word; competent; and 'steadfast, unmovable, always abounding in the work of the Lord.'"[2]

Norma was born on February 18, 1915, in Germantown, Pennsylvania, an only child, and according to her son, "a rather pampered one." When Norma seemed a bit slow at picking up homemaking tasks, her mother decided to have her learn piano instead. When Norma started her own family, she had to learn housekeeping tasks on the job, Richard Ellis said. "After she tried to iron Dad's Sunday shirts, he quietly began taking them to the local cleaners—and on a minister's salary—and continued to do so until wash and wear shirts were invented."

As a child, Norma and her mother attended Memorial Baptist Church in Germantown where she was baptized as a young girl. There she learned Philippians 4:8, which became a favorite verse throughout her life. She later wrote in *Long, Long Thoughts* (a family history written in 1989), "God wanted me to think on the beauty of his world and the creatures he made and the media he had provided that this beauty may become tangible to me—the art, the music, and the literature, especially poetry."

In 1929 Norma's family moved to Haddonfield, New Jersey. Norma and her mother soon left the Baptist church they attended there to look for something more biblically sound. That took them to Collingswood Presbyterian Church (PCUSA) where Harold Laird was the pastor. It was there Norma became grounded in the Reformed faith. She was still a part of that church when a later pastor, Carl McIntire, led the church out of the mainline denomination.

After high school, Norma's love of the arts and her growing interest in writing prompted her to major in American and

2 December 2015 interview with Richard Ellis.

English literature at the University of Pennsylvania. Unable to find a teaching position after completing her undergraduate work, she continued in her education to earn a master's degree at Drexel Library School at the Drexel Institute of Technology. This was a rare accomplishment for a woman at that time.

In 1939 Norma moved with her family back to the Philadelphia area, where she began attending Calvary OPC in Willow Grove, Pennsylvania. There she became involved in a young people's committee of the Presbytery of Philadelphia, which was chaired by Westminster Theological Seminary Professor E. J. Young. The purpose of this group was to promote unity in the regional church by engaging the group in a project. Professor Young's idea for this project was a pageant on the history of the OPC. But Norma thought that topic would be "dry" and "difficult to dramatize." She suggested instead tracing the Bible through the centuries, dramatizing attempts to snuff out God's Word and featuring those whom God had used to rediscover and preserve Truth, concluding with the story of J. Gresham Machen founding the OPC. Professor Young's reaction to this idea was to name Norma as the pageant writer. Someone, however, was needed to provide her with more information on church history, so a young Westminster student was recruited for that purpose. That is how Norma met Charles Ellis. Working together at Norma's family home as they prepared the pageant, Charles commented to Norma, "I'm sure you know that it is not just this pageant that makes me come here."

"Till All Be Fulfilled," taken from Matthew 5:18, was the pageant's title which was performed in the central hallway of Machen Hall. Among the actors were Edmund Clowney, Richard Gaffin Sr., Edwin Rian, Arthur Kuschke, LeRoy Oliver, Edwards Elliott, Robert Eckardt, and Robert Strong, all from Westminster.

Norma and Charles Ellis were married at Calvary OPC on December 26, 1942. After Charles graduated from Westminster the following May, the young couple moved to Immanuel OPC in West Collingswood, New Jersey, where Charles would serve as pulpit supply for the next three years. Their oldest two children,

Raymond and Dorothy, were born in those years. Charles then took a pastorate in Cincinnati, Ohio, from 1946 to 1948 where Carol joined the family. In 1948 they returned to New Jersey where Charles pastored a church in East Orange until 1955. Their next three children, Elaine, Virginia, and Richard, were born there. In 1955 the family moved to Silver Spring, Maryland, where Charles served as pastor of Knox OPC until 1979. While there, John, their youngest child, completed their quiver of three sons and four daughters. Today the Ellis heritage includes 21 grandchildren and 20 great-grandchildren. Their final move in the pastorate was to Rockport, Maine, in 1979 where they remained until retirement in 1983.

Norma and Charles continued to write together as well. In addition to *The Wells of Salvation,* they also co-authored *Heirs Together of Life: Daily Bible Readings for Husbands and Wives*, which was published by Banner of Truth in 1980. Richard remembered that his mother directed a choir for young people, designed and developed the church library, taught Bible classes for young women, helped start a Christian day school (now Washington Christian Academy), and served on the school's board.

Norma and Charles Ellis leaving the church after their wedding on December 26, 1942

In addition, Norma wrote numerous columns for youth and women, book reviews, and stories for *The Presbyterian Guardian* and *New Horizons*. Norma and Trudi Rockey, another OPC pastor's wife in New England, together wrote a newsletter for pastors' wives in their presbytery. Norma often spoke at retreats and kept a personal journal from the time she was a teenager. "She seemed to process things better with pencil in hand," said Richard. "Even at the end of her life, following Dad's death and while she was suffering from Alzheimer's, she started a book she called *Woman Alone*. She had lost her capability to write coherent sentences, but she had to write, and was eager to tell us what she'd been doing each time we saw her."

Norma taught her children the importance of obedience: "obey promptly, thoroughly, and cheerfully." She told them that their speech should be: "kind, necessary, and true." Her children and even her grandchildren, still pass down these rules of conduct to their children and, as in the case of one granddaughter who teaches at a Christian school in Indonesia, to their students.

Even small things have been gleaned from Norma's influence. Joanie Doe, an OPC pastor's wife, remembers that at a retreat in 1983, she roomed with Trudi Rockey and Norma. "I was touched to see her [Norma], especially at her age get on her knees to pray before she crawled into bed."

Charles died on February 21, 2003, and Norma died on August 17, 2008 at the age of 93. Richard recalled that one of his mother's strongest passions throughout her life was her love for the Word of God. "When we were grumpy we probably heard a hundred times: *This is the day the Lord has made. Let us rejoice and be glad in it.*"

Indeed, this love for the Word was also expressed innumerable times through Norma's writing. "Do our children wonder what good it does to read the Bible?... The good in reading and studying God's Word lies in obeying the God who speaks in it. As we see the smudges we need to cleanse ourselves from them. We need to comb that disheveled hair. This is the lesson of James the teacher. 'Faith, if it hath not works, is dead' (James 2:17). His lesson is for us today and for our children."[3]

**Susan Dreger Perez** *is a member of Church of the Covenant OPC in Hackettstown, New Jersey. She is the executive director of Pregnancy Resource Center of the Poconos in Stroudsburg, Pennsylvania, where she resides. She also does editorial freelance work for Crossway Publishers in Wheaton, Illinois. Susan has seven grown children and 14 grandchildren.*

---

3  Norma Ellis and Charles Ellis, *Heirs Together of Life: Daily Bible Readings for Husbands and Wives* (Carlisle, PA: Banner of Truth, 1980), 264-65.

# 23

# Betty Atwell Armour: Found—A Capable Wife

## *Miriam G. Moran*

Morning worship at Calvary Orthodox Presbyterian Church in Glenside, Pennsylvania, had concluded. Greetings and handshakes were finished, and the pastor's wife hustled home to welcome the guests who would be joining her family for dinner. Taking her hat off with one hand, and turning up the burners with the other, Betty Atwell was in her element. Afterwards, her three young children would undertake to clear the table and untangle the jumble of dishes and cooking utensils in the sink.

She was born Mary Elizabeth Stuart on April 1, 1914, in Bellevue, Pennsylvania, a small borough west of Pittsburgh. As the only child of Reuben R. and Margaret M. Stuart, she stood with them as they struggled against the slide of their home church, Crafton United Presbyterian Church, into liberalism. As a student at Carnegie Institute of Technology (now Carnegie Mellon University), she was active in the League of Evangelical Students, a forerunner of InterVarsity Christian Fellowship. It was at a League conference that she noticed a young student from Westminster Theological Seminary—Robert "Bob" Lyttle Atwell— because "he was so good-looking."

Not one to talk about herself, even Betty's children knew little about their parents' courtship and marriage. Since Bob was about to leave the established Presbyterian Church (USA) to unite with the nascent OPC, he could offer no security, and little in the way of substance. But he found in Betty Stuart a young woman who shared his convictions, and was not afraid. She was personable and kind, she didn't mind being "paid in chickens" for the sake of the gospel, she loved meeting people, didn't mind moving, and when Bob Atwell asked her to be his wife, she said yes.

It all came together in June 1936: the OPC was established on June 11, Betty received a bachelor of science degree in home economics from Carnegie Tech on June 19,

Betty

and on June 24 she married Robert Lyttle Atwell, 13 days after he had become a founding member of the OPC.

The newlyweds set up housekeeping in the borough of Harrisville, Pennsylvania, where Bob was pastor of a dual PCUSA parish just coming into the new OPC: New Hope Church in Branchton and Faith Church in Harrisville. Three years later, the Atwells made the first of what would be eight moves around the country. Bob became pastor of First OPC in San Francisco, California, and Betty became a mother when they adopted six-week old Margaret "Margie" Elizabeth, born May 10, 1942.

From San Francisco the family moved to Grace OPC in Westfield, New Jersey, where they adopted two little boys: James Edwin, born March 25, 1944, and John Stuart, born November 21, 1944, who came as a surprise. Betty was one who "handled herself in crises with grace," her daughter observed, and so she did when the social worker called about John. However, if Betty herself had answered the phone instead of Bob, she might have demurred. The baby was already 18 months old, just eight months younger than James, and he came from a troubled background. But Bob's heart was touched, and Betty graciously rose to the occasion. She would need to do so again when, not long after, young John developed a mild case of rheumatic fever.

As the OPC expanded, Bob was in increasing demand around the country, and the work of parenting fell increasingly on Betty. She was industrious, creative, and fast in her homemaking tasks, but parenting—especially with an emotionally needy child—was an unwieldy endeavor. Margie was so obliging her brothers claimed she never did anything wrong! Like her mother, she went on to marry a pastor, and raised three children in the manse. But her brothers were a challenge.

Bob was not insensitive to Betty's work in the home and with the children. When a traveling salesman came to the door, Betty realized what a convenience his steam iron would be, but was nonplussed at Bob's indifference—until after the salesman left. Bob reached to the top of the refrigerator and brought down a gift that explained everything—a brand new steam iron.

"[Betty] taught by example and doing," recalled Ruth Morton, wife of retired OPC Pastor George Morton. Wherever they moved, Betty was an active member of the congregation, and of the women's missionary society. She taught VBS, and used her artistic skill as an outreach, offering classes in oil and tole painting. For 15 years (1948 to 1962) she was head cook at the two-week French Creek Bible Conference, which her husband had helped to found.

In Glenside, she augmented the family income by making phone sales of food for home freezers. By the time they moved to Westfield a second time (1967 to 1975), the children were grown, and Betty undertook to establish her own decorating firm, Studio House Interiors, for which she made and sold furniture covers.

They retired to Bob's parents' home in Grove City, Pennsylvania, where they attended Covenant OPC. They had the leisure to visit their children and grandchildren, but soon much of Betty's time was devoted to caring for Bob as he struggled with Parkinson's disease. After he died on October 31, 1988, their pastor, Rev. Daniel Osborne, commented, "Betty accepted Bob's death in faith and submission. She spoke and acted like a person who really knew God intimately and was well acquainted with his providence. She loved Bob sincerely, and she also loved God."

In time, Betty began keeping company with Arthur S. Armour, a charter member of the OPC and a widower since 1984. When they married July 1, 1990, Betty became the capable wife of a parishioner. As a pastor's wife, she and her first husband had made a good team in their service to the church, but they shared little in the way of outside interests. Bob enjoyed hunting and fishing, while Betty preferred to travel abroad, which she did with Bob's sister for company. Art Armour, on the other hand, was an artist in hammered aluminum. He and Betty took an art course together, entered contests, entertained frequently, and traveled. After they had been married awhile, Betty confided to him, "These years have been among the happiest of my life."

But they were to be few in number. Betty was under treatment for thyroid cancer when she suffered a heart attack and died on May 6, 1993. At her funeral, Pastor Osborne's meditation was aptly titled, "Faithful unto Death."

She is buried in Lisbon, Pennsylvania, beside her husband of 52 years, Robert Lyttle Atwell, and many have risen up to call her blessed.

**Miriam G. Moran** *is the author of* Someone to Be with Roxie, *a biography of her mother, a missionary in China. She is a member of Covenant OPC in Grove City, Pennsylvania, and the wife of retired OPC Pastor Allen P. Moran. They have one married daughter and three grandchildren.*

# 24

# Mildred "Millie" Quinette: Serving a Homespun Mission Field

## *Pat Lowry*

Ninety-year-old Mildred "Millie" Quinette is a charter member of the Orthodox Presbyterian Church, and she has lived, as well as witnessed, its history from her home in Western Pennsylvania. In her weakness, service, and perseverance we can see a reflection of the church she loves.

One moment two-year-old Millie was enjoying a ride on her daddy's shoulders, the next she was toppling to the ground. No broken bones—what a blessing! Several months later Millie's hands began to tremor, not due to the fall, but due to the chronic neurologic condition Saint Vitus Dance. These intrusive, uncoordinated, and jerky movements affected her hands and arms, and later her speech. Her parents were told that she would never drive a car and probably never marry. "I did both and much more by God's grace," she delights in saying.

Millie, born October 25, 1925, was the first child of Clair and Margaret Hartley Dyer, who lived on a small farm near Harrisville, Pennsylvania. She had two sisters, Louise and Dorothy, and a brother, Clair, all now deceased. She loved school and didn't mind walking nearly a mile every day to the little one-room school with a pot belly stove, an outhouse, and one teacher for all eight grades. At the beginning of her high school years, the doctor suspected a heart condition, and her formal schooling was ended. "I was disappointed because I had always hoped to become a missionary. But I wasn't discouraged because I knew the Lord was in control."

Granddaddy Hartley, who lived with the family, was a source of encouragement to Millie. He was a carpenter and a giant of a man; little Millie had been his shadow since she learned to walk. "As he walked to the barn singing 'Lead on O King Eternal' with his hands clasped behind his back, I was right behind him, my hands clasped just like his." The family attended New Hope Presbyterian Church in Branchton, Pennsylvania, where Granddaddy

Millie with Granddaddy Hartley

served many years as an elder. "I remember when I was ten years old being excited about a congregational meeting Pastor Robert Atwell called to discuss joining with those interested in forming the Orthodox Presbyterian Church." As a result of that meeting, Millie's family became charter members of the OPC in 1936, and she has faithfully served it ever since.

During her teenage years, Millie helped Pastor Atwell organize afterschool youth programs for children in the area, taught Bible school, served as a counselor at Seneca Hills Bible Camp, and attended Friday night youth groups. "I remember being a front seat passenger in Pastor Atwell's car and gathering up the teenagers. The car was packed; there were kids in the open trunk and riding on the fenders. I don't think we could do that today!"

Millie didn't allow her limitations to isolate her, and she especially enjoyed the extended fellowship of the newly formed OPC churches in the area. "We invited the young people of the other churches to a retreat and told them to dress for a day of hiking. The 'city girls' came in high-heeled shoes; we all had a good laugh, but they did finish the hike."

At a time when friends were graduating from high school, going to college, or getting married, Millie was at another crossroads. Not one to feel sorry for herself, she got busy cleaning house for those in need and waited patiently for the Lord to provide work suitable to her limitations. Answered prayers took her to a job working in the kitchen at Grove City College where she worked for about eight years, adding another layer of skills that God would use in her service to her family and the OPC community. Her love of learning led her to enroll in a Scripture Truth course at Moody Bible Institute. She received her course certificate in 1945.

Still living at home with family and her beloved Granddaddy Hartley, Millie was active in her church and gained many friends in other OPC congregations. She especially enjoyed attending Wednesday prayer meetings with her friend Art Armour at what is now Calvary OPC in Harrisville, Pennsylvania. It was then that the doctor's prediction that Millie would probably never marry unraveled. One week a handsome young man named Edward Quinette from Covenant OPC in Pittsburgh just happened to be at prayer meeting. They met, and it must have been love at first sight, because soon Millie received a letter asking if he could come to visit her. The perfect place for their first date was the young adult fellowship dinner at her church. At that time Ed was driving a school bus for Trinity Christian School, a school started by Rev. Calvin Cummings and other parents from Covenant OPC. On July 8, 1955, after a short courtship, they were married by Rev. Cummings at New Hope OPC.

Following a short stay in Middletown, Pennsylvania, the Quinettes made their home in Pittsburgh and

Millie and Edward Quinette on their wedding day

worshipped at Covenant OPC. For many years Ed operated a Sunoco gas station near their home. Having no children of their own, they became foster parents to a son, Richard, who was with them from age six until after his college days. He missed his parents, who lived in the area but could no longer care for him. At first he rejected Millie's desire to fill this void, and she had many struggles to overcome. But she had much love to give. The teachers at Trinity Christian School helped him to find contentment in his new home. Millie is still a member of Trinity Christian School Association, and at the school's 60th anniversary she was honored for her many years of service.

Ed and Millie had a Christ-centered marriage, faithfully serving the Lord, his church, and each other. The doors of their home were always open, and Millie was caregiver to both of her parents and two aunts, one of whom lived to be one hundred years old. When a summer intern at church needed housing, nine out of ten times he stayed with the Quinettes. Every year on the Fourth of July there was a celebration in the Quinettes' backyard, and the entire church was invited to share lots of good food, games, devotions, and singing. At least once a year the adults were invited for a living room hymn-sing and, of course, dessert. "Neither of us could carry a tune, but we enjoyed making a joyful noise." Millie's favorite hymn is 'He Leadeth Me, O Blessed Thought' from Psalm 73:23–24, "You hold me by my right hand. You guide me with your counsel." Indeed, the Lord has held Millie's tremoring right hand and counseled her throughout her life.

Millie served two terms as president of the Women's Auxiliary of the Presbytery of Ohio (now called Women's Presbyterial), and was speaker at various events, such as mother-daughter luncheons. At Covenant Church she was instrumental in starting the coffee break Bible studies, elected president of the women's auxiliary, served on the missions committee, and chaired the social committee for over 30 years. She also enjoyed going to a local nursing home for a monthly hymn-sing with the residents.

During the 1980s and 1990s, Ed's angina required many

hospital visits and eventually open-heart surgery. Millie was by his side with lots of tender, loving care. Soon it became necessary to give up their home of many years. The Lord provided a small apartment in the same neighborhood with easier access to shopping and church. On December 19, 2005, having just celebrated 50 wonderful years of marriage, the Lord called Ed home.

In 2007 Covenant Church was partially destroyed by fire, and the leaders of the church decided not to rebuild but to join with a local congregation of the Presbyterian Church in America. Millie and others who wanted to remain in the OPC came together and formed what became known as Redeemer OPC Mission in Pittsburgh.

Millie continued to live at the apartment, and the flow of Christian friends to attend her needs did not go unnoticed by neighbors. This gave opportunity to put her missionary focus into action again. Every Christmas she organized a caroling party for the residents of the apartment building, and her church friends supplied the cookies and hot chocolate.

In 2011, 86-year-old Millie, then using a walker, was asked to speak at the 75th anniversary celebration of the OPC in Maryland, a highlight experience for her. She recalled the early days of the church, using only a few notes. "Once I got started, the Lord gave me remembrance," she says.

Apartment living was becoming more difficult for Millie. Her tremors and decreased mobility put her at risk, especially while cooking and baking, which she loved to do and share with her guests. She made the difficult decision to leave the apartment she had shared with Ed, but the Lord provided a studio apartment at Seneca Hills Village, an independent living facility in the same neighborhood. "I have three good meals a day, housekeeping staff, and a ride to church every Lord's Day," she said.

An added blessing at this season of her life is that she shares a dining table with two other women who also were members of Covenant OPC and her friends of many years. They delight in sharing their stories about their OPC heritage, the pastors who served them, and the friendships they shared. All three are looking forward to that day when perfect love and friendship will reign through all eternity.

**Pat Lowry** *is a wife and homemaker who lives with her husband, Jerry, in Mount Pleasant, Pennsylvania. They have four adult children, nine grandchildren, and one great-grandson. They are members of Covenant OPC in Grove City, Pennsylvania.*

# 25

# Grace Haney, Winifred Holkeboer, Gladys Coie, and Mary Bird: Honoring Our Widows

### *Susan M. Felch*

Recently I was handed a small pamphlet, a simple church bulletin. On the cover was a tree in full leaf, standing tall above orderly rows of crops against a dramatic cloud-filled sky. The inscription read "Great is Thy faithfulness," followed by the chorus of this familiar hymn. When I opened the bulletin, I found the order of worship for the funeral service of Grace Haney on October 4, 2014.

> "Great is Thy faithfulness!" "Great is Thy faithfulness!"
> Morning by morning new mercies I see;
> All I have needed Thy hand hath provided—
> "Great is Thy faithfulness," Lord, unto me![1]

This refrain not only marked the life of Grace Haney, but also the lives of Winifred Holkeboer, Gladys Coie, and Mary Bird. Their confidence in God's faithfulness continues as their testimony and legacy to the church. Through difficult times—including the deaths of their husbands, which left them as widows—they knew that God's mercies were both new every morning and sufficient for every dark night. "Strength for today and bright hope for

---

1 Hymn 27, *Trinity Hymnal* (Philadelphia: Great Commission Publications, 1961).

tomorrow" might well have been their motto.

Grace Vanden Bosch Haney was born on February 21, 1928, to an Iowa farm family. She was the fulcrum of her family, with four older siblings and four younger ones. Life on the farm was challenging. Grace left school after the eighth grade to help her mother, but eventually completed high school and then left for Grand Rapids, Michigan, to attend Calvin College. After graduation, she became a schoolteacher in Pella, Iowa. One of her brothers introduced her to George Haney, who was already ordained in the Orthodox Presbyterian Church and serving as pastor of First OPC in nearby Waterloo, Iowa. They married on September 7, 1959.

Having lived most of her life in Iowa, Grace may have found it challenging at age 31 to become not just a pastor's wife, but also wife to a pastor who was asked to take on churches in Maine, Wisconsin, Pennsylvania, and Virginia. To a growing family of four children—Mary Anne, David, John, and Stephen—she added the responsibilities of an active church member. And she kept an open house: parishioners, visitors, students, her children's friends, all were welcomed around the table, in the living room, and out in the garden. In Bangor, Maine, the Haneys worked to re-establish a home mission work that had fallen on hard times. In addition to building up the core group, they drew in people from the community and from the nearby Air Force base. Grace offered hospitality to many young servicemen and their families.

Using their experience in Maine, the Haneys next moved to Menomonee Falls, Wisconsin, where they began a mission work. The core group was composed largely of young people from established rural OP churches who were now working in the Milwaukee area. Once again, Grace opened her home to this young congregation.

In 1974 Grace and George moved to the Philadelphia area so that George could assume the role of general secretary for the OPC's Committee on Home Missions and Church Extension. After a number of years in this role, George accepted a call to Grace Church in Vienna, Virginia, but, after some health difficulties, the

Haneys returned to Philadelphia to serve again with Home Missions. They settled into Trinity OPC in Hatboro where Grace became active in the women's groups and with many international students. After George's death on May 22, 1999, Grace continued her service and active participation at Trinity. If you asked her, "How are you?" the answers invariably turned first

Grace and George Haney

to her joy in her family and then to her busy, productive life at church.

George Vonhof, an elder at Trinity, remembers that Grace always sat near the front of church, greeted folks who were new, and often hosted a tableful of guests for Sunday dinner. Her pastor, George Cottenden, remembers that she regularly invited a mix of single people and couples of various ages to her home so as to build bonds across the congregation. She faithfully supported the worship services at a nearby nursing home and took a leadership role in Love and Stitches, a group for retired people at Trinity. She went out of her way to befriend international students and newly-arrived immigrants. Teaching folks to read English became an opportunity to read the Bible with them. She also extended her teaching ministry to the prisoners enrolled in the Crossroad Bible Institute: she would grade their coursework and write letters of encouragement to them. Guests were always welcome in her home, including OPC pastors who traveled to Philadelphia for committee meetings. She remained her cheerful self after her move to Quarryville Presbyterian Retirement Community where she died in 2014.

When Grace married George Haney in 1959 and moved to Waterloo, Iowa, she followed in the steps of a recent widow,

Winifred Holkeboer at Calvin College

Winifred Holkeboer, whose husband, Oscar, had previously pastored First OPC from 1947 until his sudden death in 1956. Winifred was born on May 3, 1910, in Grand Rapids, Michigan, where she attended Christian day schools. After graduating from Wheaton College, she taught at several high schools before her marriage. Oscar Holkeboer had been ordained and installed as pastor of First Presbyterian Church in Oostburg, Wisconsin, in 1932, but joined what later became the OPC in 1936. In 1933 he and Winifred, seven years his junior, married and their early years together found them navigating tumultuous times. The *Milwaukee Journal* of July 29, 1936, headlined an article on their church "Oostburg Congregation is in favor of Sticking to Fundamentalism," although it also quoted Rev. Holkeboer as saying that "I am interested in keeping my congregation here from breaking up. I will do anything—even submerge my own personal wishes—to accomplish that." Despite this irenic attitude, Oscar and Winifred helped to form a new congregation, Bethel Presbyterian Church, which later affiliated with the OPC. They moved in 1944 to Patterson, New Jersey, where Oscar taught Bible and Reformed doctrine before going in 1947 to Iowa, where Winifred was instrumental in establishing a women's presbyterial association.

After Oscar's death in 1956, Winifred returned to Grand Rapids, where she taught English at Calvin College from 1957 until her retirement in 1976. During this time she received her master's degree from the University of Northern Iowa and raised her five children: Bob, David, Jean, Cecelia, and Lois. Before there was an OP congregation in Grand Rapids, Winifred frequently hosted

Calvin College students from OPC backgrounds at her home and invited speakers to their regular fellowship times. Some of the students whom she mentored later became ministers in the OPC, including Chip Stonehouse, Dick Gaffin, Don Duff, Ivan DeMaster, and Michael Stingley. Other OPC students who enjoyed her hospitality included Connie Hunt, Jean Young, Fern Emma Stanton, Ruth Male, Gwen Cummings, David Clowney, George Elder, Suzanne Galbraith, George Marsh, and Grace Mullen. Winifred organized a group of students to travel to Evergreen Park in Illinois in 1963 to help OP Pastor Bruce Coie promote pre-Easter services in that community. She also spoke often about her own experiences during the early days of the OPC in the 1930s. Winifred continued to be a faithful teacher, mother, and mentor until she went to be with her Savior on February 18, 1986.

Another mother of the church, Gladys McCornack Coie, was born June 3, 1905, in North Dakota and later moved with her family to Eugene, Oregon. She married Glenn Coie, a charter member of the OPC. In the fall of 1936, he led a group out of the Presbyterian Church (USA) to form Westminster Church in Bend, Oregon. Later Gladys and Glenn, with their son Bob, moved to Knox OPC in Silver Spring, Maryland, and then to pastorates in Long Beach, California, and Hialeah, Florida. On March 5, 1966, Glenn died in a boating accident, after helping to save the lives of several young people who were sailing with him.

After Glenn's death, Gladys moved back to Long Beach where she remained active in the Garden Grove OPC congregation. The church so valued her experience and wisdom that the missions committee of the presbytery hired her in a part-time position. For years,

Gladys and Glenn Coie

according to Nancy Mehne whose father, Rev. Edwards E. Elliott, pastored the church, Gladys "did door-to-door calling and had the unique ability to reach women who were home during the day with an invitation to church.... She was theologically educated and spent her life in loving service to the OPC." Her physical life ended on July 23, 1996, but her legacy lives on. The inscription on her gravestone is taken from Proverbs 31:28 (KJV): "Her children arise up and call her blessed." That verse could well describe not just her physical descendants, but also all the spiritual children she nurtured throughout her life.

The same could be said of Mary Wolcott Bird, a long time OPC missionary to Eritrea with her husband, Herb. Herb and Mary Bird first arrived in Africa in 1952. They had been students together at Wheaton College in Illinois in the early 1940s, later rekindled their friendship and romance at the OPC church in Rochester, New York, and married on August 16, 1947. They had three children: David, Steven, and Ruth. Herb's first pastorate was at Faith OPC in Lincoln, Nebraska, but both Mary and Herb had desired for years to serve as missionaries.

Mary was born in upper New York State on December 10, 1919, an only child who came to faith in her early teens. She was captivated by stories told by an intern at her local church, who was a grandson of missionaries to Burma. After graduation from Wheaton, Mary taught at two Christian schools, an experience that served her well when she later homeschooled her own children in Eritrea. She also served actively as a women's teacher, and together she and Herb hosted young people's classes in their home in the evenings. Often she would teach sewing classes that included Bible verse memory work—a way of stitching God's word into the minds and hearts of young women while they worked needles with their hands. Mary also visited patients in the hospital and women in both Coptic and Muslim homes.

In a *Presbyterian Guardian* article published in 1959, Mary wrote about an ordinary morning in Senafe, Eritrea:

This morning … we got up, did the usual chores such as pumping bicycles, filling lamps, doing music lessons, etc. Then we had breakfast and devotions, and by 8:30 were ready to get on our bikes to go to the Mahaffy home for school…. I [also] have two Tigrinya women who are trying to learn to read. There are around 250 forms in their alphabet so the ground work is tedious. However, it is a phonetic language, and once they know the alphabet reading is easy…. Tuka [the Mahaffy's kitchen girl] says she cannot leave the customs of her religion (Coptic Christianity) until she learns to read and can search the Scriptures for herself. So for two months we have been concentrating on the first seven forms, with 243 yet to learn. Lately I started teaching her the 23rd Psalm, which along with the Catechism enters her mind a bit more readily. After the women I teach Kedani [a male worker] a little English and try to absorb a little Tigrinya myself while teaching him. We then tie a can containing two quarts of

Herb and Mary Bird on board ship for Eritrea with children David, Steven, and Ruth

milk on Ruthie's tricycle and the same on my bike, and we start for home—at that time of day (noon) ever grateful for our sun glasses.[2]

Mary Bird concluded her report with these words:

Always when we come towards our home at sunset the little Coptic church of our village, silhouetted against the fading colors in the sky, comes into view. It is ever a symbol to us of our mission in Eritrea. It is our mission, and it is your mission, to bring the living message of Christ's atonement to a people who long ago forgot that message, and who substitute their feasts and their fasts, their meats and their holy days, for the One who came to save them from their sins.[3]

After 19 years abroad, the Birds returned to the United States where Herb took over the editorship of Great Commission Publications. When Herb died on October 24, 1976, Mary continued to live in the Philadelphia area, remaining active at Trinity OPC in Hatboro. For many years she arranged the flowers each week to beautify the sanctuary on Sunday mornings. She maintained contact with and ministered to Eritrean families who had come to the United States, including those who joined Trinity. She extended hospitality to many people, but took especial care of the young singles that she met. Along with Grace Haney, she supported the worship services at the local nursing home, serving as pianist there for many years, and was a mainstay of the Love and Stitches group.

The Scriptures teach us to honor and care for widows. James says, "Religion that is pure and undefiled before God, the Father, is this: to visit orphans and widows in their affliction, and to keep oneself unstained from the world" (1:27). And when the Old Testament people of God gathered to celebrate the holy feast days they were enjoined to invite family, servants, and especially "the

2 *Presbyterian Guardian* 28 (April 10, 1959): 101, http://opc.org/cfh/guardian/Volume_28/1959-04-10.pdf.
3 Ibid., 102.

sojourner, the fatherless, and the widow who are within your towns … because the Lord your God will bless you in all your produce and in all the work of your hands, so that you will be altogether joyful" (Deut. 16:14–15).

While the widows of the OPC would certainly testify to God's provision for them through their churches, it is also certainly true that they have blessed the churches with their faithful presence and their joyful hospitality. It is we who have received their visits, it is we who have been taught by their exemplary lives, and it is we who have been welcomed into their homes and around their tables. "Great is Thy faithfulness, Lord, unto us."

**Susan M. Felch** *is professor of English at Calvin College and director of the Calvin Center for Christian Scholarship. She is married to Douglas Felch, a minister in the OPC, who served pastorates in North Carolina and Virginia and was professor of systematic theology at Kuyper College. Susan's most recent publications are* Teaching and Christian Imagination, *with David I. Smith (2016); and* The Cambridge Companion to Literature and Religion *(2016). The Felches live in Grand Rapids, Michigan, and attend nearby New City Fellowship, a church-plant of Harvest OPC in Wyoming, Michigan.*

# 26
# Trudi Rockey:
# Surrendering to Serve

## *Joanie Doe*

The year was 1938. A mother was looking for a good church when she came across a newspaper article about a new denomination that was starting a congregation in her city of Schenectady, New York. After a phone call, Mrs. Zuelow and her three children soon became part of this new work. One of those children—12-year-old Trudi Zuelow—learned much that expanded on what her Dutch Reformed mother had taught her. She stayed under the teaching of this church through many years. Trudi could not begin to imagine how this foundational teaching prepared her for future service in the Orthodox Presbyterian Church.

After graduation as a chemistry major from Cornell University in 1948, Trudi returned to Schenectady to work for General Electric until 1960. After a brief time at another electronics company, she moved to Boston where she worked for Aviation Company of America from 1961 until 1965. Although none of these jobs required Trudi's knowledge of chemistry, they did require her scientifically-trained mind. While living in Boston with five other women, Trudi also volunteered to mentor young women in InterVarsity Christian Fellowship.

Trudi's friend Grady Spires wanted her to meet a widowed friend of his. Wendell Rockey served as an OPC pastor in Hamilton, Massachusetts, while he cared for his three motherless children. Back in 1949 Wendell had married Joy, a student he had met at Gordon College. After college Wendell headed for seminary. Over the next nine years the Rockeys gave birth to two girls and a boy. While they were at Wendell's second church in Cranston, Rhode Island, the normal life of a pastor's family was disrupted. Joy was diagnosed with brain cancer. After surgery and other unsuccessful treatment, she died in 1962, leaving three children aged nine, seven, and four. What a difficult time this must have been for this young pastor.

Two years went by and the Rockey family was then at a church in Hamilton, Massachusetts, not too far from Trudi's home in Boston. Grady Spires, who was also Wendell's friend, took the first opportunity to introduce his friends to each other. In October 1964 they met at Grady's home supposedly to look at a kitten for the children. Thus began Trudi's and Wendell's short courtship.

In February of 1965 Wendell proposed. Much to his surprise Trudi said she needed time to think it over. Only after a skiing trip to Vermont was she ready to answer his question with a yes. Wendell was thrilled as they began to plan a wedding at her home church. How appropriate that the place where she had grown in her understanding of the Reformed faith would be where she would become the wife of a Reformed pastor. On June 5, 1965, at 39, she became Trudi Rockey.

At first Trudi did not go back to work, but after assessing their finances, she returned part time to her old job. This arrangement soon became too stressful, and Trudi decided to focus only on the home front while doing some volunteer work.

Trudi's world had changed dramatically in a short time. Before the wedding, she had a very responsible job with a good salary and a lot of respect. She was free to travel and able to replace her car every couple of years. After the wedding, just taking care of basic bills was often a challenge. Trudi and her stepchildren were working to adjust to their new roles. About one year after the wedding, Trudi and Wendell's son Mark was born.

Wendell, who now is 92, told me that he did not fully understand how great were the changes Trudi had made. Even when

Wendell and Trudi Rockey

things were tight financially she never mentioned to Wendell all that she had given up.

Trudi took what she had learned as a supervisor of engineers and other employees and rechanneled it, not as a boss, but as a sister in Christ. She often seemed to read body language and other cues that things weren't going right with people. When she knew someone was going through hard times, Trudi recognized that it was time to be alert in order to know how to serve.

At their church, Trudi began to lead Bible studies. She often used whatever study book had been chosen, but did not let the book determine what was talked about. Filling in the gaps of what the ladies did not know, Trudi had the unique ability to be thorough and concise at the same time. She had a wealth of good ideas about the ways the women could serve others.

Trudi and Wendell came to the conclusion that since hospitality and fellowship were more important than the menu, Trudi's lack of confidence about her cooking would not keep them from having others over. It was decided grilled cheese would always be on the menu on Sunday when company was there. Mark, their youngest, was used to the routine of attending church followed by grilled cheese sandwiches. When the church held a Thanksgiving Day service, Mark pulled the cheese whiz from the fridge before others told him that grilled cheese was not on the bill of fare.

The time came when Wendell decided to leave the Hamilton,

Massachusetts, church, now known as the First Presbyterian Church, North Shore, in Ipswich. He accepted a call to a new church plant—the OPC of Cape Cod—in 1975. A current member recalled visiting the church a number of times as they planned a move to the Cape. This woman was amazed that on the second visit Trudi remembered her name, the names of her family members, and other facts that she had shared during their first visit. This woman and her family joined the church. She is now known for her hospitality, quite possibly because of Trudi's thorough and loving greeting.

In 1977 Trudi received a diagnosis of chronic leukemia. Although it did not dramatically shorten her life, she needed medical treatment on a regular basis. It must have lessened her level of energy.

In 1983 a conference for pastors' wives, sponsored by the OPC, was held out of a concern for pastors' wives after two women had committed suicide. Trudi and her friend OP minister's wife Norma Ellis were asked to contribute ideas.

After the conference Trudi could not shake the idea that all women in the church would benefit from this opportunity, not just pastors' wives. Where else would they have a chance to build bonds that cross over the boundaries of the local church while they explore an issue from a biblical perspective? Slowly Trudi gained support for her ideas. When she realized that at her home church were two very important parts of the conference puzzle, she felt more certain that God would complete the work. Linda Whiting, who had amazing administrative and computer skills, offered to be part of the team. Lynn Rienstra, who was the pastor's wife at Cape Cod after the Rockeys moved on, agreed to be the main speaker. Trudi, with Wendell's help, found the site for the conference in Massachusetts.

The date was set for April 1995. Since this was the first time a women's conference was to be held and the Presbytery of New York and New England was so geographically large, Trudi was certain no more than 30 people would come. One hundred women registered. I was one of them, a young pastor's wife who felt out of place and lonely in my new church. When Trudi understood what was happening to me, she insisted that I attend and offered to pay my way.

Since that inaugural year, at least one hundred women annually have gathered to sing, pray, renew old friendships, and start new ones, all the while encouraging each other to live Christ-focused lives. Many have helped to make each retreat successful, but without Trudi the dream may not have survived.

Trudi's health was on the decline, and Wendell brought her to the retreat the last time she came. Trudi was known for her warm, enthusiastic way of greeting friend and stranger alike. This Trudi was quieter, more reserved. Later we discovered Trudi had been given a diagnosis of Alzheimer's. Trudi took the news calmly as another facet of the working of her loving, sovereign, heavenly father.

In 2008 the Rockeys moved to Quarryville Presbyterian Retirement Home in Quarryville, Pennsylvania. Trudi who had lived most of her life focused on Christ, left this life to be with her Lord on June 21, 2011.

As I spoke with Trudi's husband, stepdaughter, and friends a consistent pattern emerged. Trudi was known for not gossiping, known for praying and planning well, and known for always following through on what she started. She encouraged a number of women with her personal, handwritten notes. She was well read, especially in the Bible. Trudi would also dialogue well with women as she sought to hear their ideas and understand them better. If after reading this you are tempted to compare yourself to Trudi, remember this. I believe Trudi would say, "Don't focus on me, focus on Christ." As you center your life on the Lord, you will be following Trudi's example as you seek to glorify him.

**Joanie Doe** *experienced the encouragement of Trudi when she became a novice workshop leader for the first few years of the New York and New England Women's Retreat. Joanie was at the side of her husband, Steve, as they both experienced the ups and downs of being pastor and* *wife for four OP churches. Joanie writes a blog, and occasionally edits her husband's writing and devotionals. She is the mother of four children and eight grandchildren.*

# 27
# Roverta "Bobbi" Olinger:
# A Joyful Woman with a Heart
# for Missions

### Kathy Albright Erickson

"Why *me*?" The words flew out of Bobbi Olinger's mouth. "Partly because you were known as The Missionary Lady. And The Stamp Lady," I replied.

"Well," Bobbi said firmly, "be sure to tell them it wasn't *me*. It was *all* the Lord."

Roverta "Bobbi" Adella Johnson was born in the little town of Northville, South Dakota, on March 18, 1922. Growing up as an only child on a South Dakota farm, Bobbi experienced hardship early in life. Her mother's death when Bobbi was five was the first of many emotional losses. Afterward, she was shuttled between her father and grandparents. "Life on the farm was *hard*, and they just didn't have time to pay much attention to me," said Bobbi. But even as a youngster, she was resilient, learning to make the best of every situation, and never losing her delightful sense of humor. Learning was a joy to the little girl, who was an honor student from kindergarten through 12th grade. She was heartbroken when the Depression prevented her from attending college, where she had hoped to major in English and drama.

During the early years of World War II, Bobbi lived with a great-aunt and -uncle, whose peaceful home was a balm to her soul. Newly engaged, she got a job at Montgomery Ward and began making wedding plans. But after the engagement was broken, Bobbi jumped at the opportunity to move to Seattle and help the war effort by working for Boeing Aircraft.

Beautiful Seattle was a welcome change for Bobbi. She enjoyed both her day job at Boeing and a "night job" as a USO hostess. Though outwardly vivacious, inwardly Bobbi nursed her many hurts from the past and "hated everyone and everything." A friend's calm, quiet influence gradually helped Bobbi heal from those hurts and change her way of dealing with disappointments.

After the war, Bobbi moved to Southern California and in 1947 married Denny Olinger, whom she had met in Seattle. They made their home in Long Beach. One Sunday morning, Bobbi decided to visit a little church in their neighborhood, more out of curiosity than conviction. While she had been sent to Sunday school in various churches as a child, Bobbi had never understood the gospel and had no idea what the Christian life was. That changed at First Orthodox Presbyterian Church (now Faith OPC) under the ministry of Rev. Henry Coray. Bobbi and Denny soon joined the church and their faith grew and flourished.

In 1949 the Olingers moved to La Mirada, and in God's providence that move led to the formation there of Calvary Orthodox Presbyterian Church. A summary of the testimony given at that church's 40th anniversary in 1998 says that

> the church's roots grew out of a desire of the Olinger family … to worship closer to their home than Long Beach where they were faithful members of Faith OPC. In 1951 weekly Bible studies and prayer meetings led by the Rev. Henry Coray, pastor of the Long Beach church, and the Rev. James Moore, pastor of Westminster OPC, Los Angeles, were held in the Olinger home. Regarding the inaugural Bible study, Mr. Coray recalled, "According to Zechariah, we are not to despise the day of small things. It is always amazing to me the way tiny acorns grow to become sturdy oaks. Three people showed: a Mormon, a former Roman Catholic, and I've forgotten what

was the background of number three."

In 1958 the group became a particular congregation with Rev. Dwight Poundstone serving as pastor. By then, the Olingers' sons, Lynn and Ron, had joined the family.

Over time, Bobbi served in various capacities in both her home church and the presbytery, acting as both president and vice-president of women's presbyterial.[1] But her greatest contribution to Christ's kingdom was in missions.

Bobbi's first exposure to "missions" occurred while watching Frances Poundstone, sister of Pastor Poundstone, draw stick figures on a piece of butcher paper while teaching Sunday school children about the Bruce and Katharine Hunt family, then OPC missionaries in Korea. When Frances eventually moved away, she told Bobbi, "This is your job now."

Feeling like a fish out of water, Bobbi made good use of the OPC Foreign Missions Committee's resources. She compiled binders on each missionary family and rotated them among the Sunday school classrooms. She also gave weekly presentations during Sunday school and wrote skits about missionary families for the children to perform during VBS and other church functions.

Bobbi eventually became known outside her home church and gave missions talks in other churches and at presbyterial. Out of that grew a presbytery-wide monthly workshop for missions coordinators. Bobbi's energy, enthusiasm, and creativity were boundless, and when applied to the cause of OPC missions, these qualities sparked a contagious love for missions in countless others.

This work was not always easy for Bobbi, who was frequently sidelined by serious illness, including both throat cancer and

---

1 Of Bobbi, Carolyn Poundstone, wife of Rev. Donald Poundstone, said, "Bobbi was far and away the most energetic supporter of missions in the churches she attended," while Bobbi said of Carolyn, "She was great—a very good [presbyterial] president. We had so much fun they broke the rules and let us serve an extra term!"

Bobbi Olinger

breast cancer.[2] When widowed and left with two teenaged sons, Bobbi held on to God's promise, "For those who love God all things work together for good" (Rom. 8:28).

Mindful of her own pain and loss, Bobbi nevertheless concentrated on others' needs and continued to serve in the church without pause. Once asked to lead a workshop for the Northern California Presbyterial, Bobbi deferred, having just undergone radiation for throat cancer.

"If I 'pop' a hard candy, I can only talk for about ten minutes," she protested.

Undeterred, her petitioner insisted, "You can do it," and sent her a plane ticket!

"So," Bobbi said, "off I went. And after popping two hard candies, the Lord enabled me to give a 20-minute presentation!"

After some time, Bobbi admitted, "I got prideful. I stood up to tell everything I knew about missions and forgot what I was going to say! I left out a whole lot of information. And *that's* how the Lord got me to say what *he* wanted me to say."

Bobbi didn't just talk about missionaries; she talked *to* them, maintaining extensive correspondence with them and their children, encouraging others to do the same, and reminding them to save the stamps from letters they in turn received. The stamps would then be soaked and sent to 7401 Old York Road, former location of the OPC offices just outside Philadelphia, where they would be sold and the proceeds used for various foreign missions projects.

Bobbi also took great delight in hosting missionaries while they

---

2 Kathy Hunt, wife of OP missionary Bruce Hunt, once wrote Bobbi, "God must really love you to send you so much illness."

were on furlough. In fact, when there were only a dozen missionary families serving in the OPC, she hosted all but one, welcoming them into her home for several days to a week or more. She took equal delight in hosting international students, presbytery commissioners, and others who needed a place to stay, young and old alike. Her listening ear was always available, and those who asked for her advice appreciated her wisdom—which was always sprinkled with humor.

Children especially loved visiting Mrs. Olinger. Who else had a cardboard playhouse permanently set up in the living room? And who else knew exactly what their interests were, played with them, and treated them as peers?

Young adults also appreciated her godly influence and delightful personality. David Thibault, then an elder at Calvary OPC in La Mirada,[3] told my daughter Laura Gatlin, "There's someone in this church I want to be like when I get old."

Laura replied, "Don't tell me. I know: Bobbi Olinger."

Even in her 90s, Bobbi's cheerful optimism was still contagious, and she had a perspective she may have lacked when she was younger. Remembering her desire to attend college, go into drama, and write a book, she observed, "[Once] an anonymous donor paid my tuition for a week of writing classes at Biola College.[4] I ended up writing a bunch of skits, I went to college for a week, and I've even written a book![5] So the Lord gave me the desires of my heart, even if it wasn't the way I expected it to happen."

To this day, the mere mention of Bobbi's name brings a smile to my face, and the recollection of a good—and usually funny—story. Having known and admired Bobbi all my life, I asked her to be my girls' honorary grandmother. Bobbi said, "I'd love to. But

3  David is now pastor of Grace OPC in Costa Mesa, CA.
4  Now Biola University.
5  Bobbi has actually written two books: a self-published book for her family entitled *Footsteps Across This Threshold* and *What Did You Do in the War, Gram?* (San Diego: CSN Books, 2012). Somehow Boeing learned about the second book and flew then 91-year-old Bobbi up to Seattle for a book signing.

you'd better add 'ornery," to the title. So, she signed all her letters to us with the acronym HOG—honorary, ornery grandmother.

On Bobbi's part, her conversations always included grateful thanks to her heavenly Father for his faithfulness to her throughout her life ("He's been *so* good to me"), and she appeared totally unaware of the immense influence she had in others' lives.

One such person is OPC Short-Term Missions and Disaster Response Coordinator David Nakhla, who grew up in Calvary OPC in La Mirada. In a recent S.T.O.R.M. Report,[6] David wrote, "The greatest impact that Mrs. Olinger had on me was that she instilled in me a heart for missions.... May [the Lord] raise up many 'Mrs. Olingers' in his church to promote the important work of missions!"

Bobbi died at age 94 on May 20, 2016. Her family reported that in her final conversation with them she was "a calm, confident woman fully ready to meet her Lord Jesus Christ" and looking forward to her heavenly body.[7]

To God alone be the glory for raising up his faithful servant Bobbi Olinger.

**Kathy Albright Erickson** is the daughter of the late OPC pastor H. Wilson Albright and Jane Mullen Albright, and the wife of Carl E. Erickson, pastor of New Covenant OPC in South San Francisco, California, where Kathy is a member. The Ericksons have three married daughters, and ten grandchildren.

---

6  OPC S.T.O.R.M. Report, October 29, 2014.
7  E-mail from the Olinger family to Kathy Erickson on May 20, 2016.

# Part Three

# Choosing to Serve
# 1970s–1980s

# 28

# Louise Gilbert, Ada Galbraith, Betty Oliver, Ali Knudsen, Linda Posthuma, and Beverly Mariani: Faithful and Effective Service in the OPC Offices

### *Gabriela Reason*

Several women stand out in their faithful service to the denominational committees of the Orthodox Presbyterian Church from its inception. While mostly working behind the scenes as support staff, these women had a lasting impact on the operations of the committee offices and on the people they served.

### Louise Gilbert

Louise Gilbert was the first woman to work for the newly formed Orthodox Presbyterian Church. She was hired in the fall of 1936 as secretary of both the Committee on Foreign Missions and the Committee on Home Missions, serving under such notable men as J. Gresham Machen, Edwin Rian, Robert Marsden, LeRoy

Louise Gilbert

Oliver, and John Galbraith. Her tenure of over 25 years spanned several locations for the OPC administrative offices, starting in the Commonwealth building and then moving on to the Schaff building, both in downtown Philadelphia. She completed her service in the northern suburbs at 7401 Old York Road, working "efficiently, faithfully, and cheerfully."[1] At her retirement banquet, Mrs. Gilbert was surprised with a gift box containing more than five hundred silver dollars, contributed by a host of churches and individuals.

## Ada Galbraith

The move to 7401 Old York Road in 1961 was a vital step for the expanding work of the OPC. Rising costs of rental property downtown and the need for more space inspired the multi-year search for a new building. The solution came from an unexpected place—Ada Galbraith, wife of John Galbraith, then OPC general secretary for Home Missions and Foreign Missions. Ada's multi-faceted background and tenacious, persevering spirit made her uniquely qualified to serve the OPC in its building search. Before marrying OPC pastor John Galbraith in 1941 at the age of 29, she traveled daily from New Jersey to work as a secretary on Wall Street. The transition to a rural pastor's wife in Kirkwood, Pennsylvania, was a hard one, but Ada's whole-hearted commitment to serve God wherever she was called eventually led her to thrive in her new roles as pastor's wife, mother to two girls, and women's missionary society leader.

This same spirit of devotion and competence served Ada when John accepted the position as general secretary of the Committees on Foreign Missions and Home Missions in 1948. At home, she regularly hosted furloughed missionaries as well as large groups of seminary students for the Galbraiths' famous buffet hoagie and game nights. She provided an elegant table and enjoyed trying new recipes, although she had never cooked before getting married.

1 *Presbyterian Guardian* 31 (July-August 1962): 102, http://opc.org/cfh/guardian/Volume_31/1962-07_08.pdf.

Daughter Suzanne remembers her staying strong and cheerful in the long months when John would be visiting the various mission fields abroad. While she worried about little things, like daughters Priscilla and Suzanne walking too close to the edge of a sidewalk, she exhibited unwavering strength and faith in the big

Ada and John Galbraith

things, such as trusting God with her husband's safety while away.

A new opportunity presented itself when Ada's two girls attended grade school. An investment real estate firm offered her a temporary secretarial position. When the secretary didn't return to work, Ada took over the position. Forward thinking by nature, Ada realized that she could serve the firm even better if she became a licensed real estate agent. Ada's next step, a bold one for a woman in the late 1950s, was to become a broker and go into business for herself. Even in her business pursuits, she made the goal of serving her family and church preeminent. One of her aims in becoming a broker was to find a new location for the OPC offices. Her first task every week was to look through all the listings to see if anything suitable could be found. Finally, in 1960, she saw the listing for 7401 Old York Road and went to see it the next day. The OPC bought it the following day—before a sign was ever put out for the property. She didn't take a commission for the $49,500 sale. She also served many incoming Westminster Theological Seminary students by finding inexpensive housing, both for rental and purchase, with no charge to them.

Ada went on to have a successful career as a real estate broker. Her competitors were skeptical that she could succeed at first because of her pledge to honesty and her unwavering commitment not to do business on the Lord's Day, the "best day" for real estate. Instead, her trustworthy, faithful character drew clients and caused her to become a great light for Christ in the Jenkintown business community. Ada organized and became president of the first women's real estate association and was the first female broker in the area. Ever supportive of her accomplishments, John would accompany her to meet with clients in the evenings and washed the kitchen floor every Saturday night when she was baking for Sunday guests. Her steadfast character and strong faith even accompanied her decline into dementia that began in her mid-70s. Her husband marveled at her clear prayers uttered to God even when she could no longer recognize her family members. She was received into heaven on July 5, 1994, and John never considered remarrying. She was all he ever wanted.

## Betty Oliver

Like Ada Galbraith, Betty Oliver was first a pastor's wife and then the wife of the general secretary of Home Missions. Born in 1915, she married LeRoy Oliver in 1938, and they adopted two children, Jane and David. Betty and Roy, as he liked to be called, thrived in the ministry. From 1943 to 1961, Betty was a pastor's wife in OP churches in Middletown, Delaware; Harrisville, Pennsylvania; and Fairlawn, New Jersey. During Roy's tenure at the OPC offices from 1956 to 1974, Roy and Betty were very involved at Trinity OPC in Hatboro, Pennsylvania. Betty was a supreme hostess, generously opening her home to new and old friends every Sunday dinner. She extended her hospitality gifts outside the home as well, as she and her friend Penny Pappas organized lovely weddings and receptions for the members of Trinity OPC. As a support to Roy's work at the offices, she also frequently fed guests that visited on behalf of the work of Home Missions.

Starting in 1956, when Roy began his work at the OPC offices, Betty served as the Committee on Christian Education (CCE) office secretary until 1975. During the early years of her tenure, the CCE started the writing and publication of needed, high quality Reformed Sunday school materials. This was a bold venture for such a small denomination and involved a significant financial

Betty and LeRoy Oliver

commitment. Yet the risk paid off, and in 1975, the CCE's Great Commission Publications (GCP) became the joint ministry of the OPC and Presbyterian Church in America. At this point, Betty became the office manager and personal secretary to Tom Patete, the executive director of GCP, until her retirement in 1989.

Betty's strong faith was tested in 1977, when both of her children died suddenly at separate times that year. Tom Tyson, Betty's pastor at Trinity OPC at the time, remembers that "although it was a crushing situation, Betty was not crushed." She trusted God in the midst of these tragedies and coped by keeping her focus outward. Her friend and co-worker at GCP, Penny Pappas, recalled that when the Olivers' son, David, died, Betty was very sensitive to the needs of David's friends and reached out to them in their mourning. After her daughter, Jane, died a few months later, Betty and Roy were left with the challenging task of raising their grandson Van Allen. CCE General Secretary Roger Schmurr carpooled with Betty and recounts how she often on the way to work asked for prayer for her grandson and wisdom for how to raise him, as this was a daunting task to her and Roy.

Betty and Roy's faith was admired both in and out of the office. Penny Pappas stated that "in the history of all the churches I have been in, I have never known a pair as universally loved by all the people—the old people, the young people, ministers; everybody loved Betty and Roy Oliver." Similarly, Allen Curry, who was the director of educational services for GCP and good friends with Betty and Roy, said that "in my own life, I have not run across anyone that exemplified the Christian faith more than Betty and Roy. And they did that in the midst of horrendous personal difficulties." He remembered a time in Sunday school debating with a skeptic, Ralph, whom Betty and Roy had reached out to. Ralph stopped arguing when someone brought up the Olivers as examples of Christian character. He had to acknowledge that being a Christian made a huge, visible difference in their lives that he could not explain away.

Many attested to Betty's competence and warm character in the office. The late Tom Patete, former executive director of GCP, wrote, "Betty Oliver was one of those classic administrative assistants who performs more tasks than one can count and is the glue that keeps things together behind the scene."[2] Penny explained that if anybody needed something, someone would say, "Go ask Betty, she'll help you. She knows." Shortly before Betty's retirement, computers were introduced to the office. Lee Benner, the GCP business manager, deliberately put the first computer on Betty's desk since she was the oldest employee. She caught on so quickly that she shamed the rest of the office into transitioning quickly to computers.[3]

Not just her knowledge and hard work served the office, but her loving, cheerful manner. Penny remembered that "the office was a wonderful place to work because you worked with people who were so congenial, and so happy, and much of that has to do with Betty." Roger Schmurr also remembers her sacrificial spirit. When GCP had hard financial times in the mid-to-late '80s, Betty was of retirement age, but no one, including Betty, wanted her to

---

2 Thomas R. Patete, "By the Grace of God It Was Done! Reflections on Great Commission Publications," in *Confident of Better Things: Essays Commemorating Seventy-Five Years of the Orthodox Presbyterian Church*, ed. John R. Muether and Danny E. Olinger (Willow Grove: Committee for the Historian of the OPC, 2011), 297.

3  Roger W. Schmurr, "First—but Not the Last: The Orthodox Presbyterian Church over the Past Fifty Years," in *Confident of Better Things: Essays Commemorating Seventy-Five Years of the Orthodox Presbyterian Church*, ed. John R. Muether and Danny E. Olinger (Willow Grove: Committee for the Historian of the OPC, 2011), 64.

retire. So she worked without pay for a few years until GCP was able to repay her. When she finally retired in 1989, it took at least two people to replace her. She died in 2004, four years after Roy died.

## Ali Knudsen

The CCE was graced with the work of another notable woman, Ali Knudsen. Roger Schmurr, CCE general secretary from 1979 to 1988, was immediately struck by Ali's bold, confident manner. Although he was seriously considering hiring another applicant for the job of office secretary, the 50-year old Ali approached him in late 1979 and said she was convinced that it was time for her to begin work for the CCE. Ali's talents were immediately put to good use. When Ali was hired, Schmurr had just started the denominational magazine *New Horizons in the Orthodox Presbyterian Church*, in collaboration with GCP lead artist John Tolsma. This was an idea the OPC had contemplated for many years but wasn't sure how to execute. It was a huge undertaking, and Ali jumped right in. Ali handled lots of correspondence with writers, proofread articles before they went to the typesetter, and kept the mailing list up to date. She continued to handle all these responsibilities when Schmurr was on the road visiting churches. Without her holding down the fort, chaos could have invaded the office. As Schmurr explained: "Readers of *New Horizons* today probably have no idea of the significance of what was accomplished, and Ali was a significant part of

Ali Knudsen and Roger Schmurr

that effort."

Remarkably, although English wasn't her native language, Ali was a very precise proofreader for *New Horizons*. Born in 1931 and raised in the Netherlands, Ali met Robert Knudsen while he was pursuing doctoral work at the Free University of Amsterdam. They married in 1951, and he became an apologetics professor at Westminster Theological Seminary in Philadelphia. Ali and Robert raised four sons: Donald, Timothy, Richard, and Steven. Sadly, Timothy died of a brain tumor while in high school. While Ali was quite a private person at the office, Tom Tyson, her pastor at the time, remembered her trust and confidence in God's providence through this difficult trial.

Ali was no stranger to trials. She survived the Nazi occupation of Holland during World War II, and these traumatic experiences contributed to her being a very careful, forward-thinking person. While the administrative offices were still located at 7401 Old York Road, the CCE was located on the second floor. The floor had two exit stairs, but this was not enough for Ali. She kept a large, long rope in her office that she intended to use to escape out a window if there ever were a fire in the building. Her carefulness also translated into caring concern for others. "On a personal level, she assisted me in a quiet way," remembered Schmurr. As a Type 1 diabetic, Schmurr is prone to low blood sugar, which slows him down. "Ali was aware of that and kept a carton of orange juice in the refrigerator at 7401 in case I needed a quick fix."

Ali's carefulness tied together with her traditional Dutch strengths of precision and meticulousness. According to Tom Tyson, who took over as general secretary of the CCE in 1989, Ali hated to see anything wasted or thrown away, and sometimes to Tyson's amusement, she would stubbornly rescue boxes of documents that were meant to be thrown out and organize them for safe-keeping. In this way, documents were saved that could be used for historical reference later. She saved all the past issues of *New Horizons* on the top of the cabinets of her small office and had them arranged in stacks so that she could access any past issue immediately.

In editing, she could spot grammatical errors in copy that had already been checked by Schmurr. Although she retired from the position of office secretary in 1995, she continued her proofreading work until 2006.

Others who knew Ali more personally also admired her character. Gladys Kramm, administrative assistant to the Committee on Foreign Missions during the same time when Ali served the CCE, became good friends with Ali. They would often eat lunch together and walk laps around the 7401 building while sharing about their upbringing, work, and home. Ali's unique background and experiences gave Gladys a new perspective: "Ali was special. My family has been here since the Revolution, and having her as my friend brought me great lessons in life." Gladys respected how Ali overcame such a difficult past and her deep gratitude and love for her new home in America.

Ali approached challenges at work with wisdom and discretion. According to Gladys, "Ali was a praying woman. She would pray about her problems, and not get angry. She would also speak about them honestly, though she was always discreet, and never mentioned any names if there was conflict. She had deep respect for her husband as well and was quick to seek his advice when needed." Overall, Tom Tyson summarized her service to him—as his only full-time secretary—this way: "I cannot trace a single instance in which her work didn't demonstrate faithful service of her Lord and Savior." Bob died in 2000, and Ali lived for years in a retirement community in the Alzheimer's unit until her death on March 25, 2016.

### Linda Posthuma

Linda Posthuma, who has served the Committee on Foreign Missions (CFM) as administrative assistant for more than 30 years, also credits her Dutch heritage for some of her gifts. She thanks her background for her organizational skills, her strong work ethic, her thriftiness, and financial sense, which have helped her in administering the accounting facets of her work. Linda was born on

July 2, 1951, the daughter of a
Christian Reformed pastor and
a school teacher. She was raised
on the reservations of the Navaho and Zuni Native Americans
in New Mexico and in mission
churches throughout the western United States, where her interest in missions had its roots.

Linda Posthuma

After teaching for 13 years in line with her secondary education
degree, she began working for the CFM in 1986. Linda is one of
the few OPC staff who began work at the 7401 Old York Road office location, moved to a temporary site in Horsham in 1990, and
arrived in 1995 at the current location in Willow Grove.

According to Douglas Clawson, associate general secretary for
the CFM, Linda is meticulous and shows great attention to detail
her work. Over the years, Linda has worked with the committee's
finances and labored to meet the needs of the missionaries and their
families. Her responsibilities include assisting with financial matters, insurance and medical care, arranging logistics for getting missionaries to the mission field—including procuring visas and arranging for container shipments—scheduling furlough visits, and
being generally available if any need should arise. When Douglas
Clawson and general secretary Mark Bube are out of the country,
they know they can count on Linda to handle any administrative
complications—such as when a missionary traveling overseas was
stranded and needed assistance in the middle of the night. Linda especially enjoys getting to know people throughout the OPC
when speaking in churches and at conferences and women's meetings, while sharing with them the ministries of the committee and
its missionaries.

Besides her efficiency, thrift, and competence, one of Linda's
greatest strengths is her generosity towards others. One of her former assistants, Becki Whetsel, admires how Linda commits great
amounts of time and energy to a project or crisis. When new Haiti

missionary Matt Baugh died in a motorcycle accident in May 2006, Linda jumped into action handling all the details and spending many hours on the phone with his widow, Shannon, in caring compassion. Douglas Clawson observed: "When I think of Linda's care about the details of others' lives and knowing them so personally, I know that they're in good hands." Becki remembered the tender affection Linda showed Brian and Dorothy Wingard, the care she would give retired missionaries such as the Uomotos and Sons when they visited, and the laughs she shared with Grietje Rietkerk and other missionaries on and off the field.

One of the blessings of Linda's singleness is the flexibility it has afforded her to serve others. Jim Scott, managing editor of *New Horizons*, remarked that Linda would be the one to help when someone needed a ride to the airport at 3 a.m. What Linda has appreciated most about her work are the opportunities it has provided her to serve the Lord and his church and the way it shows her the big picture of God working all over the world in the global body of Christ. She reflected that, "when you see God orchestrating the details of difficult situations abroad, it strengthens your confidence he is at work in your life too, wherever you are, using you to further his kingdom."

### Beverly Mariani

In 1996 Beverly Mariani began her work for the OPC offices assisting Linda Posthuma as secretary for Foreign Missions. In 1998, she became administrative assistant to the Committee on Home Missions and Church Extension (CHMCE). Born December 22, 1935, to a Christian Science family, Beverly rejected the faith of her parents as a young adult. In 1953 after a long journey, Beverly joined Calvary OPC in Glenside, Pennsylvania. She is biblically divorced and has three children and three grandchildren. She earned a degree in sociology and worked mainly in secular environments but appreciated the opportunity to use her gifts for the church when she began work at the OPC offices.

Having grown up in the tradition of Old Philadelphia, Bev

brought grace and refinement
to the offices. No matter who
walked in the door, Bev had
tact and poise to handle them
with grace, remembered Becki
Whetsel, former secretary for
the CFM. Her work for Home
Missions general secretary Ross
Graham and associate general
secretary Dick Gerber involved
maintaining contact with well
over two hundred church plant-
ers, regional home missionaries,

Bev Mariani

and CHMCE members. This work required not only great organization and multi-tasking abilities, but also people skills. Bev loved
to learn new things and would easily encourage the many visitors
of the offices to share their thoughts and stories. Ross Graham recounts that Bev held many confidences on behalf of church plant-
ers and was always a woman of her word. For her co-workers, like
Becki Whetsel, Bev was not only a good listener, but also very good
at letting someone know when they weren't putting the Lord first.

Bev's gifts as an organized and skilled hostess also came into
play in the planning, design, and construction of the Home Missions workspace when it moved to its current location in Willow
Grove, Pennsylvania, in 1995. In honor of her retirement, an article by the CHMCE described her this way: "Suffering the frustra-
tions of three distinct computer replacements and the indignities
of stubborn software and uncooperative spreadsheets, she has kept
our offices focused on our service to God and the Orthodox Presbyterian Church with her organizational skills and her enthusiastic
spirit." [4]

For her part, Bev was inspired to see God building his church

---

[4] The resolution of appreciation for Bev Mariani was from the December 6,
2006, minutes of the Committee on Home Missions and Church Extension.

up close in a way she had never seen before. She saw the committee step out in faith time and time again, moving forward and outward with the Great Commission. Ross remembered a time when Bev recognized church-planting gifts in associate pastor David Harr, while he was preaching at the Boardwalk Chapel in New Jersey, and recommended him to the committee. The following year, David became the organizing pastor of a church in Medford, New Jersey, with Ross as part of the core group.

Although she retired from the offices in 2007, Bev has been busy serving the church in other ways. For instance, when her dear friend Grace Mullen, member of Faith OPC in Elmer, New Jersey, and long-time evening attender of Calvary OPC in Glenside, was failing during her last years of illness, Bev stepped in as primary caretaker. Bev was her friend, nurse, and power of attorney. The CHMCE's prayer for her in retirement is certainly coming true: "May God grant her many more years of faithful and effective labors for the Savior she loves."[5]

**Gabriela Reason** *is wife of Redeemer OPC pastor Roth Reason and mom of three children ages four, seven, and nine. She holds a master of religion from Westminster Theological Seminary and a master of social work from the University of Pennsylvania. Originally from Switzerland, she calls Danville, Pennsylvania, her home.*

---

5  "Bev Retires," *New Horizons* 28, no. 5 (May 2007): 11.

# 29

# Charlotte Kuschke:
# Singing to the Lord

## *Katharine Olinger*

For many years Charlotte Kuschke's melodic hellos greeted visitors and members of Calvary Orthodox Presbyterian Church in Glenside, Pennsylvania. In that warbling soprano I hear from my friend an echo of the Psalmist's words: "I will sing to the LORD as long as I live; I will sing praise to my God while I have being" (Ps. 104:33).

Charlotte's love of music is just one of the talents she uses to serve Christ's church. The 91-year-old is also a nurturer of God's good gifts to others, not surprising since she was a Christian school teacher for many years. My pastor's wife, Jenn Sallade, witnessed this firsthand:

> We often shared the pew with Charlotte during Sunday morning worship. My wiggly little girls could easily have been a bother and a distraction to her, but instead she considered them a delight. She praised them, engaged them, and perceived in them beauty that Christ is just beginning to work out.[1]

---

1 Some quotations and facts recorded in this chapter were gathered in conversations, interviews, and letters with Charlotte Kuschke and those who have worshipped and served with her; others were taken from articles available on the OPC's website, opc.org. See, e.g., "Today in OPC History—Charlotte Kuschke, March 8," http://opc.org/today.html?history_id=766; "Today in OPC History—Arthur and Charlotte Kuschke, June 30," http://opc.org/today.html?history_id=300.

Charlotte Kuschke and Peggy Porter
singing at son David Porter's wedding

Charlotte has sponsored music lessons for preschooler Rachel Sallade, who constantly taps and hums. Charlotte is "excited to nurture the buds of Rachel's talent, expectant that she will blossom," said Jenn.

In 1922 Charlotte's parents, Rudolph Milling and Catherine Könche Milling, emigrated from northern Germany to San Francisco, California. Rudolph was a cabinet maker, and Catherine worked as a domestic hand. Born on March 8, 1925, Charlotte didn't grow up in a Christian home, and yet, in God's providence, she began attending a local Presbyterian church at the invitation of neighbors. A young couple named the Fitches taught the teen Sunday school class and soon formed a bond with Charlotte and her classmates, only one of whom came from a Christian background. In 1939, at a time when more and more mainline churches were struggling with modernism, the Fitches realized that their minister was not preaching the gospel and began to look for a new church. They found a chapel just a few blocks away—which became First OPC in San Francisco in 1941, pastored by Rev. Robert Atwell. Like the tale of the Pied Piper, the young people followed the Fitches to First OPC. There was no looking back.

Charlotte recalled how Pastor Atwell dealt with this enthusiastic but "green" group. "He began by assuming we knew nothing, which was probably true, and teaching us what we needed to know, beginning with what the Bible is—God's Word." Atwell gave the youth passages to memorize about the inspiration of Scripture, like 2 Timothy 3:16–17. Eventually lessons turned to

TULIP, Calvinism, and the Pauline epistles. In her personal devotions, Charlotte read Loraine Boettner's *Reformed Doctrine of Predestination*, as recommended by the *Presbyterian Guardian*'s Christian book club. She was only 15 years old at the time: "I remember having a flashlight and reading under the bedcovers at night, because I was supposed to have the lights off at a certain time." Beginning a lifetime of service to the church, Charlotte played the piano at evening worship services at First OPC, putting her childhood lessons to use.

Charlotte graduated from Lowell High School in 1942 and then attended San Francisco State University to earn her teaching degree. She minored in music and took private voice and conducting lessons, enabling her to direct the choir at First OPC with skill.

Charlotte taught in California's public school system for a year and a half before deciding that she wanted to teach in an environment that integrated biblical instruction. Knowing this, Bob Atwell contacted Rev. John Galbraith, then the pastor of Kirkwood OPC near Lancaster, Pennsylvania. Charlotte left her home on the West Coast, moved to the East Coast, and became the sole teacher of Kirkwood Christian Day School, which met in the church basement. Her first year, Charlotte taught 12 students in four different grades. The second year, there were 25 students, and the school picked up another grade. Charlotte remained the only teacher.

During the summers, Charlotte helped at the newly formed Boardwalk Chapel, in Wildwood, New Jersey. She taught Bible study classes to children, accompanied the chapel singers on the piano, performed group numbers, and was a featured soloist.

While still teaching at Kirkwood, Charlotte was invited to Philadelphia for a weekend visit with Westminster Professor Ned Stonehouse and his wife, Winigrace. The Stonehouses lived just a mile from Westminster Theological Seminary, and Winigrace asked Charlotte if she wanted to walk to the seminary. She did. And there was Arthur Kuschke, working on Saturday to weed the seminary's tennis court. He loved to play tennis. Charlotte had seen him once before, on Valentine's Day at a Westminster alumni meeting that she attended with the Atwells. She remembers asking who a certain someone was, standing in the doorway right across the room, and the Atwells saying, "That's Arthur Kuschke." Charlotte's response? "Oh, I've read him in the *Guardian*."

Arthur and Charlotte started seeing each other, and Charlotte recalls fondly the Thanksgiving she spent with Arthur's family. The Kuschkes had invited Charlotte to join them on a trip to Atlantic City, New Jersey, when a nor'easter hit and put the Atlantic City roadways underwater. Plans were scattered and events thrown. Arthur drove Charlotte to a bus terminal in Philadelphia only to discover that it would be hours before the bus came. What do you do with that kind of time? Impromptu catechism quizzing. "Arthur started in and I kept answering, because I had been teaching it to the children at Kirkwood for three years. I got pretty far along before the bus came, and I really think that's what persuaded him. Gal knows something about theology."

Rev. Arthur Kuschke had been ordained as an evangelist for the Presbytery of Philadelphia in 1940, and served four years as the assistant to the field secretary of Westminster Theological Seminary. In 1945 he became the seminary's librarian. Charlotte and Arthur were married in 1951, raising three children, David, John, and Margaret.

When Margaret was two, she spent one day a week with her grandmother and another day with Doris Fikkert, wife of future OPC pastor Henry Fikkert; this way, Charlotte could teach elementary German and music at Willow Grove Christian Day School (later named Philadelphia-Montgomery Christian Academy) two afternoons a week. When all the children were enrolled, she was able to work two full days weekly. In time, she taught only music, believing it to be a more essential background for young children. "But the kids still talk about Frau Kuschke," Charlotte added. Charlotte was an enthusiastic supporter of Phil-Mont athletics, known for bringing a noisy cow bell to games and ringing it vigorously after good plays. She taught there for 30 years.

Today many of the students Charlotte Kuschke taught are still connected to Phil-Mont: as teachers, parents, or both, like Charlotte. She has always taken Christian education seriously. In 1948 Charlotte wrote an article for the *Presbyterian Guardian*, reviewing a book of curriculum for Christian school teachers. "It becomes the privilege of the Christian teacher to confront his pupils with their sins, with God's displeasure thereat, and to present to them the way of salvation, trusting that the Holy Spirit will accomplish His work in their hearts," she wrote.[2] Charlotte believes that Christian education is an opening up to God's sovereignty proclaimed in the Bible.

The Kuschkes were longtime members of Calvary OPC in Glenside, just across the street from Westminster and only a mile away from their home (the Kuschkes bought Westminster Professor R. B. Kuiper's house after his wife could no longer negotiate the steps). Their youngest child, Margaret, arrived in time to be baptized at Calvary Church by Pastor Bob Atwell, the same minister who had led Charlotte in her walk with the Lord so many years before at First OPC in San Francisco.

Charlotte's contributions to Calvary are numerous—but a good place to start is with music. You see, Charlotte is a singer. Charlotte is a *good* singer. Some who have heard her have commented that for such a talent to be devoted to such a seemingly insignificant cause is amazing. Charlotte delights in congregational singing, and, while attending Calvary even as a seasoned saint, kept us in tune with her strong, clear soprano voice. She also directed the Calvary choir for 25 years. Charlotte said that while one might think that "the choir is the place for prima donnas, this was a group who really loved the Lord, and to sing his praise and do it well." She recalls Westminster Professors E. J. Young on the cello and Meredith Kline on the violin participating at church music nights, and her own duets with Peggy Porter and Jean Clowney. During Charlotte's time with the choir, they produced a vinyl record titled

2 Charlotte Milling (Kuschke), "Course of Study at Christian Schools," *Presbyterian Guardian* 17 (January 10, 1948): 7, http://opc.org/cfh/guardian/Volume_17/1948-01-10.pdf.

*Festival of Sacred Music*—a copy of which now resides in the OPC archives at the OPC offices in Willow Grove, Pennsylvania. Charlotte continued to study music privately and was a soloist in local performances of *Messiah* and *Elijah*.

Charlotte even had a hand in the original *Trinity Hymnal.* For 14 years Arthur worked as the secretary of the OPC's hymnal committee, and the committee actually met in the Kuschkes' living room. "Two little babies locked up in a kitchen for four hours," Charlotte remembered, "I brought [the men] coffee and cake.... They went over everything with a fine-tooth comb. Robert Marsden [one of the men on the committee] would say, 'Arthur Kuschke's fine-tooth comb is finer than anyone else's'... and that was true. He was very much concerned that the truth of Scripture be clearly brought forth." Charlotte shares Arthur's view of hymnody. When asked what makes a good hymn, Charlotte responded "First of all, the words have to be true to Scripture. The second thing you have to consider is the music; that it be appropriate. How do you figure that out? The music should be reverent, but that doesn't mean it has to be long-faced or anything like that."

In 2010 Arthur Kuschke passed away, and Charlotte moved to a retirement community in Fort Washington, Pennsylvania. There Charlotte continues to seek opportunities to represent Christ. She is an active participant in community Bible studies—successfully inviting new members and reading Scripture at special events. Charlotte sings in the choir, participates in plays, and provides musical instruction to residents. Rev. Dr. Alfred Muli, chaplain at Fort Washington Estates, said, "Mrs. Kuschke has often sent me encouraging notes, commending a message I gave during a Sunday service or a memorial service. I have found in her someone I can go to when I need advice or encouragement. We have prayed together on many occasions."

When I was a ninth grader, Mrs. Kuschke asked me if I would work for her every other Saturday, 15 minutes away. She volunteered to drive me both ways. On our rides, Mrs. Kuschke would ask me about my German lessons at Phil-Mont, and how our bas-

ketball team was do-
ing. She would ask me
how my grandparents
were, if my siblings had
been busy, and whether
my dad was traveling.
I ended up cleaning
her apartment for four
years, and have been
given not only a beau-
tiful Christian exam-
ple to follow, but the
friendship of a funny and kind woman.

Charlotte Kuschke and Katharine Olinger

Mrs. Kuschke loves birds. She takes joy in music and is an art enthusiast. She loves her six grandchildren, and she's a Penn State fan. Through her words and actions, she inspires me to serve others and to uncover the beauty Christ is working out in them, and in me.

**Katharine Olinger**, *a graduate of Phil-Mont Christian Academy, is an English literature major at Geneva College in Beaver Falls, Pennsylvania. She is a member of Calvary OPC in Glenside, Pennsylvania.*

# 30

# Ruth Bacon:
# A Musical Legacy

*Giacomina Buzzelli Bacon, Janet Torongo Bacon,*
*Martha Sander Bacon, Ruth Squires Bacon,*
*and Martha Bacon Quinto*

Ruth Bacon was a long-time member of Westminster Ortho-dox Presbyterian Church in Hamden, Connecticut, where she served her Lord and the congregation through music. Her faithfulness to the OPC and her love of music have been passed on to her family and to many who worshipped with her there.

Her father, William Anderson, was a builder attached to the mission of the Southern Presbyterian Church in the Belgian Congo (now the Democratic Republic of the Congo). In 1920 in the Congo, William married Dorothy Hunt, the sister of OPC missionary Bruce Hunt, Margaret Dunn, and Mary Cummings,[1] and the young couple started to build their family. Two sons, one of whom died as a young child, were followed by a daughter, Ruth Anna. She was born on September 19, 1924, while the Andersons were home on furlough in St. Louis. The family returned to central Africa, where Ruth spent most of her childhood.

In 1945 Ruth graduated with a degree in Bible from Maryville College in Maryville, Tennessee, then moved to Philadelphia to

---

1 Bruce Hunt's wife, Katharine Hunt, is the subject of chapter 5 of this book. Mary Cummings and Margaret Dunn are the subjects of Chapters 20 and 21, respectively.

stay with her aunt while her parents were on the mission field. Ruth attended Mediator Chapel and soon caught the eye of Sergeant Henry Bacon, a Philadelphia native, who was in Army training. The following year, Henry was discharged from the Army and spent the next two years completing his college education.

Ruth and Henry were married at Mediator Chapel on June 19, 1948. Psalm 127:1 begins: "Unless the LORD builds the house, those who build it labor in vain." That was the theme of their marriage. From the beginning they established patterns of Christian living and service to the church that were passed down to their children. They raised six children in the church—five sons and a daughter. Three sons are ruling elders in OPC congregations, one is an OPC deacon, and another is a deacon in a PCA congregation. Their only daughter married an OPC deacon.

Dad moved the family to Connecticut in 1959 where we attended Westminster OPC in Hamden, then worshipping in a firehouse. Dad was ordained a ruling elder and served in that office for nearly 50 years. We lived 45 minutes from the church, but the

Flanking Ruth and Henry Bacon are their children: Bill, Dan, and Peter (on the left) and Martha (Quinto), Joel, and Karl (on the right)

family was rarely late for Sunday school and regularly attended both worship services and Wednesday evening prayer meetings. Dad led the family in evening devotions, and Mom took over when he was away on business.

In 1963 work began on a new church building. Dad's was one of six signatures affixed to the mortgage, guaranteeing payment. He had just purchased our house in Woodbury so it must have been daunting for Mom and Dad to entrust the family's financial security to the Lord's keeping. Their children knew little of this step of faith until many years later.

After the church was completed in 1964, a visiting Yale student, John Frame, formed a small choir.[2] When John's studies were completed, the job of director fell to Mom, who loved to sing. An avid fan of classical music, she played the piano and selected the music, conducted rehearsals, and directed the choir for many years. Under her guidance and occasional task-mastering, all of her children sing parts, read music, and are willing to use their musical gifts to praise the Lord in worship.

Mom played the organ for worship services, a humble act of worship for the glory of God. She practiced and practiced to improve her skill, but was willing to yield her place on the bench to another, then just as willing to resume playing when called upon. She continued to play the organ throughout several years of intense pain due to shingles. Her last service at the organ was Sunday, August 20, 2006, one month short of her 82nd birthday.

Praying for each member of her family, Mom's greatest concern was for each to know Christ and be known by him. Mom also loved the women her sons chose to marry. She considered them daughters, not daughters-in-law, and her son-in-law was as loved as her sons. "I'll never forget the first time I saw her after my mom died," said daughter-in-law Ruth Bacon. "I still remember the hug she gave me as we both cried together. I knew I still had a mother."

2 Dr. John Frame is a minister in the Presbyterian Church in America and professor at Reformed Theological Seminary in Orlando, Florida.

When grandchildren began to arrive, she didn't rush in with a lot of child-rearing advice, she waited to be asked. As much as the demands of the household and her health allowed, she attended many activities from Little League and Babe Ruth baseball games to 14 years of grandkids' band concerts to traveling for hours for Grandparents' Day at school.

Can a family with six children lead a quiet life? Perhaps not in decibel level, especially at the dinner table, but in terms of general order, discipline, peace, and contentment, YES! Perhaps the verses that best exemplified our household were 1 Timothy 6:6–8: "Now there is great gain in godliness with contentment, for we brought nothing into the world, and we cannot take anything out of the world. But if we have food and clothing, with these we will be content." We were mentored with a biblically-based work ethic that Mom demonstrated daily: Having just put dinner in the oven, Mom sat in her favorite chair, knitting—while reading a book, and watching a baseball game. An hour later, dinner was not burned, not a knitted stitch of the grandchild's sweater was wrong, 50 pages were read, and still she lamented that the Red Sox bullpen had blown another lead.

Mom and Dad had specific roles. There was no doubt that Dad was the somewhat autocratic covenant head of the house. Mom wouldn't openly question his initial reading on a situation or request, but she played a big behind-the-scenes role in mediating between Dad and his kids. Nevertheless, if Dad made a final decision on something, that was it. There was no playing Mom and Dad against each other. Sometimes she would fume quietly at what she perceived as Dad's unreasonable obstinacy, but not for long. Mom was Boss #2. If any of the kids questioned her authority, they would have Dad to answer to.

Until the end, Mom's love for her Lord was evident in everything she did or said. She was an example of a godly woman to all who knew her. On Monday, August 21, 2006, she received a diagnosis she had expected since mid-May, that the blood disease she had courageously fought for several years had morphed into acute myelogenous leukemia. "It's alright," she said. "I was prepared for that." She paused for a moment, then smiled. "I just pray the Lord doesn't draw it out and takes me quickly. I know where I'm going."

Nine days later Mom was granted her heart's desire.

"Make a joyful noise to the Lord, all the earth! Serve the Lord with gladness! Come into his presence with singing!" (Ps. 100:1–2).

Sing on, Mom. Sing on.

**Giacomina Buzzelli Bacon** *is married to Karl Bacon, a ruling elder at Westminster OPC in Hamden, Connecticut.* **Janet Torongo Bacon** *is married to Joel Bacon, a deacon at Trinity OPC in Hatboro, Pennsylvania.* **Martha Sander Bacon** *is married to Peter Bacon, a ruling elder at Merrimac Valley OPC in North Andover, Massachusetts.* **Ruth Squires Bacon** *is married to William Bacon, a ruling elder at Westminster OPC in Hamden, Connecticut.* **Martha Bacon Quinto** *is married to Jeffrey Quinto, a deacon at Westminster OPC in Hamden, Connecticut.*

# 31

# Doris Elliott, Julie Stone, and Jocilyn Warren: God's Gifts to Garden Grove

### *Susan Winslow and Kathleen Winslow*

Doris Elliott, Julie Stone, and Jocilyn Warren each served for many years at the Orthodox Presbyterian Church in Garden Grove, now located in Westminster, California. But their stories began elsewhere and have continued beyond the bounds of that congregation through the loving providence of their heavenly father. For decades these women have sung wholeheartedly *Whate'er My God Ordains Is Right,* and have lived purposefully as unto the Lord.

## Doris Elliott

For Doris, life changed in an instant on May 25, 1979. Before that day, she was the busy wife of a busy pastor. Even before that, she was Doris Harrison, raised in a Christian home, learning as a teenager during the Depression to be both frugal and generous. After college, she taught school. Then on September 4, 1944, she married Edwards Eugene Elliott; it was Labor Day, and Doris liked to quip, "I've been laboring ever since!" During their married life, Ed and Doris would serve in three OP churches.

From 1944 to 1950 they lived on the second floor of a Baltimore, Maryland, row house, and St. Andrews OPC met on the ground floor; Ned and Nancy were born there. In 1950 Ed was

Edwards and Doris Elliott on their 25th
wedding anniversary in 1969

called to First OPC in San Francisco, California, where Beth and Barbara were born, and Doris honed her skills as a mother—and as a hostess. In those days, OP missionaries to Asia and Chinese students in the United States would cross the Pacific by freighter. Many stayed at the Elliott home while awaiting transport.

Doris's children recall how often (and how long) overnight guests would stay at the manse. In one case, their father took a student to the dock for a scheduled departure. "No, the freighter won't leave for another week," they were told—week after week. When the freighter eventually departed, their unexpectedly long-term guest waved goodbye from the deck, yelling, "Tell Doris that she can finally wash the sheets!"

This tradition of hospitality continued when the Elliotts moved to Garden Grove OPC in Southern California in 1956. Doris never knew how many lunch invitations her husband would issue as he shook hands after morning worship. Like him, Doris invited folks to church and actively pursued one-time visitors so that they might return. Decades later, many aging members of Garden Grove OPC, now Westminster OPC, attest with thankfulness to the warm and generous open door policy at the Elliott home. With the manse next door to the church, Doris was diligently involved in the upkeep of both; she liked to paint walls and Sunday school chairs, and her family did much of the gardening. Both she and Ed sang in the church choir, trading puns with flair. She stayed busy, teaching in local public schools and taking graduate classes in the evenings.

Doris was born on May 16, 1917, so she was 62 on that day in 1979 when her life completely changed. A plane had crashed—and

Ed was on board, traveling home from an OPC general assembly. Doris was no longer a pastor's wife, but his widow. Through this trial, the faith she had lived so energetically for 62 years was tested and deepened so that many could testify, "That woman truly trusts the Lord."

The years after Ed's death were less busy, more reflective. Doris moved to Lookout Mountain, Georgia, to be near her children. There, she found ways to serve as a blessing to Covenant College students. She wrote of her experiences, dedicating one handwritten recollection, "for my children and grandchildren, so they might know the events of their father's and grandfather's Homecoming, and how the Lord so faithfully cared for me." In a notebook, she copied verses under the heading "Words of Great Comfort and Assurance and Praise from the Scriptures." Doris herself entered into glory on December 31, 2013, having lived for the Lord and waited upon him.

### Julie Stone

Richard Leslie Stone first met Julie Hicks at a Sunday evening movie. Ironically, Julie had told her mother that she was going to church that evening—and instead went to see *Julia Misbehaves*, starring Greer Garson! Dick and Julie met again at a dance the following week, and he offered to drive her home. Although Julie was a professing Christian at the time, she married Dick, an unbeliever, on July 13, 1949.

Julie had been born in Nebraska 18 years earlier on July 5, 1931, but shortly afterward her family moved to California where her parents had received job offers in the early years of the Depression. Although the family read each night from *Our Daily Bread*, sent to them by Julie's godly grandmother, theirs was not a particularly committed Christian home. Of her own volition, Julie was baptized and joined the liberal Methodist church the family attended when she was 12. By God's grace, she joined a Reformed church as a teenager, and that's where she and Dick were married.

Every Sunday, Julie walked to church, pushing baby Mike in

his stroller. Her faithfulness and knowledge of the Bible irritated her husband because, clearly, she knew something he knew nothing about. Dick began attending church to "make points" with Julie. Both of them were avid readers, and it was the personal reading of his Word that God used to bring Dick to saving faith.

Dick and Julie Stone in 1985

In 1963, by the time Mike, Tim, Matt, Jon, and Margaret were born, the Stones joined Garden Grove OPC. Dick eventually became a ruling elder, and Julie became known for her wise counsel and willing service. An older woman informed Julie that "elders' wives give devotions," so she began to teach—women's Bible studies, children's Sunday school classes, and devotions at wedding and baby showers. At Pastor Elliott's suggestion, she began writing for *The Presbyterian Guardian*,[1] despite wondering if a woman without a college education was qualified to do so.

Julie and Dick liked young people; neighbor kids and the church youth group were always welcome in Julie's kitchen. She was a mentor to younger women, including one whom she taught to make jam, while sharing godly wisdom about family relationships. As part of the church women's missionary society, both Julie and Doris Elliott were involved in monthly outreach at juvenile hall.

Julie liked older folks, too, and had a special heart for widows. She would do whatever they asked of her—scrub floors, take

---

1 For an example of her writings, see Julie Ann Stone, "Bride's Book or, 'Helpful Suggestions' for the Bride-to-Be from the Right Book," *Presbyterian Guardian* 43 (June/July 1974): 94–95, http://opc.org/cfh/guardian/Volume_43/1974-06_07.pdf.

them on errands, or simply visit. In 1993 Dick suffered a heart attack, and Julie became a widow herself. In God's good providence, she had previously heard Elisabeth Elliot speak on "The Gift of Widowhood." God had prepared her to give thanks even in this circumstance. In 1999 she moved to Washington to be near her children. There she joined Lynnwood OPC, where she remains a member today. Those of us privileged to know Julie and to be loved by her agree wholeheartedly with the thoughtful description penned by one of her younger friends. Julie is "a watchful listener, a wise counselor, a second mom who uncompromisingly scolds, warns, corrects, and supports with biblical guidance, humor, and steadfast love."

### Jocilyn Warren

"Are you wed to the OPC?" That was one of the less romantic questions William Eugene Warren asked Jocilyn Engbers during their whirlwind courtship. It was important nonetheless since Jocilyn was attending an OPC at the time. Bill, new to the Reformed faith, was about to graduate from Westminster Theological Seminary and was considering his future. Her response was an adamant "No!"

Jocilyn was born on September 27, 1937, and raised in Michigan, the youngest of eight in a family committed to Christian education and to the Christian Reformed Church. Her father was a school principal and a man of prayer; Jocilyn often found him kneeling at his bedside when she came to say goodnight.

Upon graduation from Calvin College, Jocilyn became a teacher. Only after moving to Pennsylvania did she realize how far Willow Grove Christian Day School was from the nearest CRC. So Jocilyn began attending Calvary OPC in Glenside. She and her housemates hosted a Sunday evening hymn-sing, which is where she met Bill. He showed up, a hungry seminarian, looking for the meal that followed the singing. They were married on June 22, 1963, exactly seven months after they met.

From 1964 to 1972 Bill pastored in four congregations of

various denominations. Kim was born in Bismarck, North Dakota, in the hospital where J. Gresham Machen died; Carla was delivered in Garner, Iowa; and Matt, in Hastings, Nebraska. In 1972 Bill was received into the OPC, serving first in Valdosta, Georgia, from 1972 to 1974, and then at Covenant OPC in San Jose, California, from 1974 to 1980.

Bill and Jocilyn Warren on their wedding day

When the children were young, the Warren family rarely missed a church event. When five-year-old Kim found out that her Catholic neighbors could pick which mass to attend from a list of service times, she said, "I'm glad we're not Catholic, because we'd go to all of them!" Yet despite their full participation in church life, Jocilyn recalled with gratitude that she was not pressured to fill a special role as "The Pastor's Wife." She didn't play the piano for church or teach a women's Bible study—though she has done both in recent years. Instead, she focused on being a biblical wife and mother for her husband and children; they were blessed by her faithfulness in personal Bible reading and prayer each morning at the kitchen table.

In 1980 Bill moved to Garden Grove OPC to fill the vacancy left by Ed Elliott's death. Both Bill and Jocilyn had taught in San Jose, so they helped to establish a Christian school for covenant children on the church property in Garden Grove. Jocilyn was principal and teacher of multiple grades for ten years, deeply loved and respected by each one who was privileged to sit in her classroom. A tall woman, she used her height and straight posture, along with a quiet voice and an unmistakable "look," to manage her students.

When discipline was necessary, she dealt with her students as their teacher, not as their peer. Her expectations were remarkably high, and she taught the importance of true obedience, "not by way of eye-service, as people-pleasers, but with sincerity of heart, fearing the Lord" (Colossians 3:22b). Teaching was a way of life for Jocilyn, and she continued to lead a weekly Bible study for women for many years. Her students, both young and old, flourished under her loving and faithful guidance.

Bill resigned his pastorate after suffering a serious stroke in 2001, a couple of years after Garden Grove OPC moved to Westminster and changed its name. He and Jocilyn turned their focus to his recovery. Their perseverance through this difficult providence bore fruit, and Bill has since served as regular pulpit supply for Orthodox Presbyterian churches in Pennsylvania, Arizona, and California. When asked what experience had the greatest effect on her own Christian walk, Jocilyn responded that it was observing her husband's enthusiasm for preaching the Reformed faith for more than 50 years—the majority of which they spent wed to the OPC! On September 21, 2016, Jocilyn entered Glory.

**Susan Winslow** *and her daughter* **Kathleen Winslow** *are members of Westminster OPC in Westminster, California. Susan and her husband, David, are active in encouraging the next generation to grow in their service to the Lord and his church through short-term missions and the Timothy Conference. Doing her best to follow in Jocilyn Warren's footsteps, Kathleen taught for several years in the same school in which she was taught by Jocilyn. Kathleen is currently serving as a missionary associate of the OPC in the Czech Republic.*

# 32

# Anna Marie Ediger:
# Onion Pie Mentorship

## *Holly Wilson*

On our way to Westminster Theological Seminary in 1975, where my husband, Larry, was to begin his studies, we stopped in Middletown, Pennsylvania, to attend Calvary Orthodox Presbyterian Church. After worship we were invited to the pastor's home for dinner and thus began a relationship with Abe and Anna Marie Ediger that continues to influence our lives as we serve in OP churches today.

Anna Marie was born on December 8, 1926, the youngest of three children of Dr. Charles and Mrs. Mable Eavey. Dr. Eavey was a professor and chair of the Department of Education and Psychology at Wheaton College near Chicago.[1] Anna Marie attended Wheaton and graduated with a degree in organ performance in 1947. About this time, Abe Ediger joined a choir that sang for the Back to the Bible Broadcast. The organist for the show left, and the director, a Wheaton graduate, hired Anna Marie.[2] Shortly after this, the bass singer in the male quartet also left, and Abe was asked to join the quartet. Not knowing all of the songs yet, he needed to put in some extra practice with the organist … and love quickly grew. Abe and Anna Marie were married on June 17, 1950. Abe went

---

1 Robert F. Lay, biography of Charles B. Eavey, http://www.talbot.edu/ce20/educators/protestant/charles_eavey/.
2 Abe Ediger, personal correspondence, 2007.

on to Gordon Divinity School, graduating in 1952.

Abe was ordained by Wheaton Bible Church in 1953. The early churches the Edigers served were in very small towns in the Midwest, a big change from the city of Chicago. The first was a community church in the tiny hamlet of Formoso, Kansas (1953–57). The city girl was grateful to have married a farm boy when one of the parishioners came to the door to present her with something for

Abe and Anna Marie Ediger

her soup pot—a chicken that was still very much alive![3]

Abe was drawn into the OPC through a close friendship with OP Pastor Don Stanton, whom he met when they were both students at the University of Nebraska. So after their time in Kansas, the Edigers moved on to Trinity OPC in Bridgewater, South Dakota (1958–61), then to Winner OPC in Winner, South Dakota (1961–67). Anna Marie organized social activities for the churches, taught Sunday school, organized vacation Bible schools, and accompanied the worship services on the piano—all of which was done well and enthusiastically with several young boys in tow.

From her very early years as a pastor's wife, Anna Marie was led to gather people around the table from all walks of life and feed them, find out what they were like, where they were going, and what made them tick, and last but not least encourage them. She was a wonderful cook and talented at engaging folks in conversation around the table. She did this effortlessly, it seemed, even though she had four active sons, a full-time job as a secretary, and served the church as pianist and Sunday school teacher.

3  Steve Ediger, personal interview, August 21, 2015.

When my husband served as Abe's pastoral intern in 1979, I had the opportunity to observe Anna Marie in action. She prepared a large Sunday meal on Saturday so she would be ready for guests. She adapted many of her recipes so that meals could be put on the table easily on Sunday. Her freezer was always well stocked with baked goods that could be pulled out for company. Over the years I have incorporated many of these methods for my own use. And I treasure the many encouragements she gave to me as a new mother and a future pastor's wife.

Anna Marie served as the pianist or organist in every church Abe pastored, occasionally she was even forced to use an accordion![4] Her pitch was perfect and her timing precise. Using the keyboard of a piano or organ, she could lead a congregation in hymns like a pro. It's not easy to leave four boys alone in the pew in order to play for a congregation, but Anna Marie never complained. Her son Craig admitted, "We got into some of our best mischief and fights while being accompanied by the great hymns of the faith."[5]

After leaving Winner, South Dakota, Abe was called to Immanuel OPC (1967–72) in Thornton, Colorado, and then Calvary OPC (1972–82) in Middletown, Pennsylvania.

When the Edigers lived in Thornton, Colorado, Anna Marie got a job as a secretary for a dermatologist's office. When they moved to Middletown, Pennsylvania, she became an assistant to the provost at a branch campus of Penn State University. She was well suited to this work because she was very organized and worked quickly. She could type and carry on a conversation at the same time. Her refrigerator was peppered with lists of all kinds to help keep her home organized. Her office skills were often used to make brochures for the churches they served. Many times these brochure ideas would spill over into her annual Christmas letter. Making double use of these was a great time saver.

The Edigers left Middletown in 1982 to serve Community

4 Steve Ediger, personal interview, August 21, 2015.
5 Craig Ediger, personal interview, August 23, 2015.

OPC (1982–88), a church plant in Kalamazoo, Michigan. My husband and I joined them there during a difficult time in our service to the church. For six months Anna Marie and Abe encouraged us and helped to recharge our batteries. Our children were the only two kids in the church, and Anna Marie took the opportunity to start up a Sunday school class for them. She was still organizing activities, and of course playing the piano every week as well.

In 1988 Abe and Anna Marie started driving two hours to Lansing, Michigan, every week so Abe could fill the pulpit at Grace OPC for a year. The church there was recovering from a difficult time, and the encouragement the Edigers brought is still remembered fondly.[6] Even as they entered retirement, Anna Marie's energy seemed never to flag. When I requested her onion pie recipe, she told me she had served it recently to company.

Anna Marie went to be with the Lord very suddenly on August 12, 2005, at 78 years of age. A few months later we brought Abe to our place for a visit. I fed him onion pie, and he ate it with great relish. It was our turn to encourage and minister to him, and it gave us great joy to do so.

### Anna Marie's Onion Pie Recipe

Crush 30 saltines. Mix with ½ cup melted butter. Sauté 3 cups thinly sliced onions in ¼ cup butter until brown. Put on top of crackers in shallow casserole dish. Sprinkle with ½ lb. grated sharp cheese. (You can do this all the day before if necessary.) Add ½ cup scalded milk to 3 beaten eggs, ½ tsp salt, and ½ tsp pepper. Pour over pie. Bake at 350° for 30 minutes until custard sets.

**Holly Wilson** *is the wife of Larry E. Wilson, pastor of Redeemer Orthodox Presbyterian Church in Airdrie, Alberta, Canada. She has four adult children and two grandchildren living in the United States.*

6  Stephen Pribble, personal correspondence, 2015.

# 33

# Marian Gilmore:
# The Ripple Effect

## *Virginia Graham Dennison*

Marian Lynd Gilmore's contact with the Orthodox Presbyterian Church was almost exclusively in one location, Grace OPC in Sewickley, Pennsylvania, a lovely tree-shaded community of large old homes on the Ohio River about ten miles from Pittsburgh. She was not involved in women's presbyterial or other denominational activities, but the impact she made from that one place had a ripple effect that was felt throughout the denomination.

Marian was born on May 30, 1913, in Washington, Pennsylvania, about an hour southwest of Pittsburgh. A year later the family moved to Cadiz, Ohio, where her father pastored the United Presbyterian Church in that small town for the next 20 years. She was blessed with loving parents who taught her godly living with a solid biblical knowledge. The family would always kneel to pray during family devotions, and this became a lifelong habit for Marian and her sister.[1]

Marian was a good student, but the only "A" she received her first year of college was in public speaking. As a student at Geneva College, she enjoyed languages and drama more than any other subjects. After her commencement in 1934, she taught high school in Bloomingdale, Ohio, and in Woodbury, New Jersey. She also earned her master's degree in speech pathology from Northwestern

---

1  Marian's sister was my mother-in-law, Elizabeth Gilmore Dennison.

University in Chicago, over the course of five summers.

In the years to come she used her many gifts in speech therapy, public speaking, and leadership. She served in the American Red Cross during World War II; became coordinator of speech and hearing services for the Delaware State Board of Health (pioneering much of this work); taught at what is now Case Western Reserve University; and became a speech consultant to the cerebral palsy unit of the Cleveland Clinic and also to the cleft palate team at Mt. Sinai Hospital,

Marian Gilmore serving in the Red Cross during World War II

Cleveland. In the healthcare arena Marian advocated for the patient as a person, rather than as a research target or a number. When she felt her voice was not being heard there, she accepted a position at Geneva College in 1961 to teach speech, speech pathology, and therapy. She also reluctantly accepted the position of dean of women a year later; her first love was teaching, and she didn't relish the added stress of being dean. She served the college with distinction and honors until her retirement in 1978.

It was during her years at Geneva that Marian's contact with the OPC began. In her beloved United Presbyterian Church, Marian was distressed by doctrinal issues, including the infamous Confession of 1967, which authorized the use of multiple creeds, Reformed and otherwise. OP minister Cal Cummings had recently assembled a group of interested families from the area northwest of Pittsburgh for worship Sunday mornings at the Sewickley Holiday Inn. In 1970 they called Rev. Don Poundstone to be the pastor of Grace OPC. Marian soon became a part of this group. She was the first of her family to make this difficult decision to leave the UP church. Her nephew (and my late husband) Rev. Charles Dennison followed her into the OPC, and his brothers, Bill and Jim, eventually were ordained in the OPC as well.

In joining the OPC in Sewickley, Marian now had a 45-minute commute to church. Geneva students started attending Grace OPC also, and soon Marian had her car packed full. Some were already from OP churches, while others came because they were invited by these students. They included Debbie Georgian, Lesesne Elder, and six young men who would become OP ministers: David Kiester, Mark Brown, Larry Wilson, and the Bobs—Bob Y. Eckardt, Bob Tanzie, and Bob Harting. Marian thoroughly enjoyed these rides with the students. Bob Harting remembered that she always had some story or insight to share. Bob Eckardt recalled her "faithfulness and kindness. She was unfailingly cheerful and always there." That was "a support for their pattern of faithful attendance." Marian took these two Bobs out for a farewell lunch before they graduated.

With an open pulpit at Grace OPC, in 1976 Marian suggested to the pulpit committee that they pursue Charles Dennison as a candidate. He pastored the church for the next 23 years. During these years, many more students and recent graduates came from Geneva and other colleges to Grace. Some of the men who came entered the ministry in the OPC: Doug Clawson, Woody Lauer, Bob Tarullo, Chad Bond, Zach Keele, Rob Broline, and Danny Olinger. A number of them became summer or yearlong interns, and Marian offered her expertise in speech writing and public speaking to give help where it was needed. Doug remembered her advice to smile when speaking on the radio, because the voice would sound warm to the listener. Danny went to her home every month for three years, and Marian would drill him in speech exercises to help him use his voice better ... and to talk about Rush Limbaugh! She would critique Danny's sermon delivery, while Charlie would critique his theology. Danny described Marian as honest, loyal, and theologically astute, with integrity "off the charts." These things couldn't help but affect the young men she helped to train.

Charlie was not immune from Marian's "instruction" either. In his first year at Sewickley, he preached from an outline, but tended to wander at the end of the sermon. Marian finally took him aside after church and said, "God's good creation has order and so should your sermons." He preached from a manuscript thereafter.

After Marian moved to a retirement home, she still had a long drive to church, but she was faithful in attendance. She continued to teach the junior high Sunday school class for many more years. During these years she also tutored a Vietnamese woman in English, and this woman (who called Marian "Mom") attended church occasionally with her husband.

Marian led a full and productive life. To my knowledge, she was completely accepting and satisfied with her status as a single, professional woman. However, when she was 82 years old, she surprised her family and friends when she married for the first time. Frank W. Harris III was a colonel in the Marine Corps, and they had been an "item" before he left to fight in the Korean War. When his first wife died, he started courting Marian, and they were soon married, moving to his home in Manassas, Virginia, near the Marine base in Quantico. Her life became considerably more active, with trips to various Marine functions across the country, and I know she was always happy to be headed home again.

As one who became her niece by marriage, I am particularly thankful for the life of Marian Gilmore. The OPC has also benefitted from this godly woman who used her many talents to serve others and who loved to serve her church.

**Virginia Graham Dennison** *was born to an OP home missionary, baptized in a tent, and moved three times before the age of ten. She also married an OP minister who pastored the Sewickley, Pennsylvania, congregation for 23 years, until his death. Virginia then taught for 13 years and recently retired to North Carolina, where she joined Redeemer Presbyterian Church, an OP church in Charlotte, North Carolina.*

# 34
# Mary Shaw:
# Planting Churches as a Way of Life

## *Anne Copeland Shaw*

Mary, a small brunette with large brown eyes, pushed her over-flowing grocery cart through piles of slush, grim determination etched on her weary face. Twin boys, no more than two years old, sat squished together in the cart, chubby fists gripping the same bar she wrestled. She reached her car, a wood-paneled station wagon, lifted the rear door, and sighed. The trunk was full; there was no space for groceries.

Weeks ago, she and her husband, Bill, had volunteered to transport the hymnals and keyboard to and from the small bank building where a church plant of the Orthodox Presbyterian Church was meeting. Nothing could be left there during the week, and there was no one else to volunteer, except perhaps the pastor, but he travelled an hour to and from worship each Lord's Day and needed no more tasks.

And so Mary, undaunted, buckled the twins into their car seats, fit the groceries on the floor and between seats, and drove home.

The woman in this apocryphal story is my mother-in-law, Mary Lou LeMahieu Shaw, and one of those chubby-fisted twins is my husband, Rev. John Shaw, general secretary of Home Missions and Church Extension in the OPC. Perhaps a lack of space in the trunk doesn't count as a great sacrifice for the cause of Christ, but Mary's perseverance in circumstances like this—and in some of far greater weight—has made an impact on the OPC. She and her husband, Elder Bill Shaw, have worshipped and served in five OP mission works. Their example has encouraged many involved in church planting, including John and me. This is Mary's story:

Mary Lou LeMahieu was born on April 11, 1938, the first child born to Lewis LeMahieu and Lenore Van Ess LeMahieu. Mary grew up in Oostburg, a tiny town in eastern Wisconsin, where nearly everyone she knew was either related to her, or went to church with her, or both. Her town had four churches, all Reformed or Presbyterian, full of the direct descendants of the Dutch Reformed and Huguenot pioneers who had settled the area generations before.

Mary's mother, grandparents, and nine aunts and uncles, were charter members of Bethel OPC in Oostburg. Her father, Lewis LeMahieu, grew up in the Reformed Church of America, but joined the OPC when he married Lenore. Mary and her six siblings were baptized at Bethel OPC, each tiny LeMahieu taking on the sign and seal of the covenant.

Mary grew up attending church services, prayer meetings, and Sunday school, went to a Christian elementary school, and was part of a Bible study taught by local pastors in the public high school. In Bethel's high school Sunday school class, she memorized the Westminster Shorter Catechism twice—once through ninth and tenth grades, and again through 11th and 12th grades. Before graduation, she and her classmates each went before the session and answered any of the 107 catechism questions they were asked!

In 1958 Mary's horizons broadened when she married her sweetheart, Bill Shaw. Bill had been a superstar trumpet player and athlete from a rival high school, so Mary had known of him for years. When they played together in the Kohler Company Band— he on trumpet and she on clarinet—they got acquainted and fell in love.

As Bill pursued his romance with Mary, he began attending church with her family. Under the weekly preaching and personal tutelage of Rev. John Verhage, Bill embraced the Reformed faith. At Mary's mother's insistence, Bill joined Bethel OPC before the couple was allowed to marry.

The newlyweds moved to Madison for Bill to finish his bachelor's and master's degrees in metallurgical engineering at the University of Wisconsin. This was the first time Mary had lived away from her family, but they were close enough to visit often.

That changed after Bill's graduation in January 1960 when he took a job in San Diego, California, far from their families. The move was a little less lonely, though, after the young couple was welcomed by Paradise Hills OPC. Elder Hiram Bellis and his wife, Edna, showed much-needed hospitality, and even allowed them to share their home for a time after the Shaws' lease ran out.

Within the year, the Shaws moved to La Habra, California, where they were welcomed by a church plant, which eventually became Hacienda Heights OPC. Pastor Wilson Albright and his wife, Jane, opened their home to care for Mary after the caesarean section birth of her first child, David, in January 1961.

When David was ten months old, the Shaws moved to Muskegon, Michigan, for a year and a half, and then—oh, happy day!—Bill's work took them back to Oostburg, Wisconsin. Mary quickly became active in the church of her youth. She taught ladies' Bible studies and helped to organize hospitality for a presbytery meeting. A second son, Jeffrey, was born during that time.

Happily ensconced in her home town, her home church, and close to her large extended family, Mary had no

Mary and Bill Shaw on their wedding day

desire to move away. Yet, in the spring of 1967, Bill's work once again necessitated a move, this time to Chicago. The Shaws quickly became involved in a mission work, pastored by Rev. Donald Parker, which would become Forest View OPC in Tinley Park, Illinois. The work met in a small room at Trinity Christian College, providing a challenge for the young mother with two wiggly little boys!

The Shaws moved four years later to Dayton, Ohio, where Rev. Lawrence Eyres pastored a church plant, now Redeemer OPC in Beavercreek. Rev. Eyres's wife, Geraldine, was, as Mary remembers well, an invaluable asset to her husband and to the church at large. She was hospitable, intelligent, an excellent teacher, and she did everything with love: she never had a negative thing to say about anyone. Mary learned much from Mrs. Eyres.

Not long after the birth of twin boys in 1972, the Shaws moved to Columbus, Ohio, where they found a need for a faithful, Reformed church. With years of church-planting under their belts and a Bible study already started in their home, they approached the session of Redeemer OPC and Rev. Eyres with the idea of starting a mission work. The session agreed to share their pastor's time, and, even while approaching the traditional age for retirement, Rev. and Mrs. Eyres were willing to expend their time and energy on an endeavor that daunts many younger people.

Pastor Eyres travelled to Columbus for weekly Bible studies until the core group called an organizing pastor, Rev. Robert Y. Eckardt. During this time, the Shaws traveled back to Dayton every Sunday, enjoying the hospitality of different church families between morning and evening services. The congregation in Columbus met for a time in a bank building—Sunday school classes happened in stairwells, chairs needed to be set up and torn down weekly, hymnals and a keyboard were stored at the Shaws' and transported to and from services. The Shaws shouldered as much of the burden as they could, employing their four young sons to carry hymnals, set up chairs, greet visitors, and show hospitality in their own home. Christmas parties and fellowship meals happened in the Shaw home and the homes of other core members. In the

Lord's good providence, Grace OPC was established and grew.

But Bill and Mary were not through with church planting. Or, rather, the Lord was not through using them to help plant his church. Well into their retirement years, Bill and Mary drove 45 minutes across Columbus to Providence OPC in Pickerington, providing invaluable wisdom and encouragement through the ups and downs of church planting.

In 2014 the Shaws moved to Green Bay, Wisconsin, where they worship at New Hope OPC. Mary was happy to retire from her duties as worship accompanist, but she and Bill continue to encourage and build up the church as they always have.

Mary Shaw knows well the difficulties of church planting: the discouragement of core families leaving or moving away, the frustration of expending large amounts of energy for seemingly small results, the worry of wondering who would come to church in a bank building or a smoke-filled bar, the exhaustion and expense of finding outside venues for special events because the worship rental space won't accommodate them, the loneliness of being the only people in your age group, the anxiety of seeing your children lonely because no other families will attend when there is no youth group. She knows well the sacrifices required of those who accept the challenge of church planting.

And yet, she knows the joy of being a part of a pilgrim people; of knowing fellow believers so deeply they become as close as family; of taking on jobs and challenges one might never have considered except for an immediate, pressing need; of enjoying friendships with believers all over the country; and of looking back over the years and seeing the Lord's hand at work in individuals, congregations, and communities.

Mary is known as a leader, most often leading by example: in hospitality and hard work, being willing to take on whatever tasks need to be done (including drawing on two years of piano lessons to accompany countless worship services), maintaining a positive attitude, and resting in God's good providence to provide anything lacking.

Karen Eckardt, wife of Rev. Bob Eckardt, recalled Mary's kindness to her as a young pastor's wife. "She led by her quiet steadiness and godly example." Another daughter in the Lord wrote, "People from her church, her extended family, those from the neighborhood, students from the school where her children attended, and the international community were treated to home cooked meals and warm fellowship." One of Mary's sons remembered her willingness to play even a Wurlitzer organ more suited to a jazz set than a worship service, and making it fit the service.

Mary Lou LeMahieu Shaw was trained early in the nurture and admonition of the Lord, was called into his glorious light, and was led to serve the Lord in ways she never anticipated, not in dramatic or drastic ways, perhaps, but in steady, kingdom-building ways. From state to state, home to home, congregation to core group to church plant, Mary has used whatever talents and abilities the Lord has given her for the good of the church, for the good of the OPC, and for his glory.

*With a master's in English Education,* **Anne Copeland Shaw** *has taught English and humanities in Christian schools, home school co-ops, and colleges at various times, but her main job for the last 18 years has been raising five children. Her husband, John, is the general secretary of the OPC's Committee on Home Missions and Church Extension.*

# 35

# Doris Fikkert and Helen Veldhorst: Leaders and Servants

## *Mary Jane Gruett*

Lake Michigan waves gently lap the Wisconsin shores on a summer day. In the mid-1800s immigrants from Europe, seeking religious freedom and a better life, landed on these shores. Many Dutch settlers chose to settle near Lake Michigan in Sheboygan County. Two small Dutch villages, an hour's drive north of Milwaukee, sprung up just four miles apart, Cedar Grove and Oostburg. Visiting these villages with populations below three thousand is somewhat like stepping back into the 1950s. Most still attend church on Sundays where they are joined by parents, grandparents, cousins, aunts, and uncles. Though some things are changing, (some businesses are open on Sundays), one is still surprised when hearing the sound of a lawn mower on the Lord's Day.

Calvary Orthodox Presbyterian Church in Cedar Grove and Bethel OPC in Oostburg are prominent churches in both communities. Both were formed in the late 1930s when they broke away from the Presbyterian Church (USA). The relationship between the members of Calvary and Bethel solidified as each congregation worked through obstacles: finding a place to meet for worship, setting up educational programs, and raising money to construct a new building. That strong relationship, forged in the struggle to preserve sound doctrine, continued as Calvary and Bethel worked together to plant two daughter churches, one in Menomonee Falls, a northwest suburb of Milwaukee, and the other in Green Bay.

Among the many who served in these churches, two women stand out—Doris Fikkert and Helen Veldhorst.

## Doris Estelle Guldenschuh Fikkert

"Mom had one dream," Marcia Vander Pol, Doris Fikkert's daughter, said. "Sometimes I thought she really hoped it might come true." Doris dreamed of opening a tearoom where she could serve fancy teas, sweets, and finger sandwiches on fine china. "Mom hadn't mentioned it," Marcia said, "but I'm sure if that dream had come true, tearoom Bible studies would have followed soon after."[1]

That dream offers a small glimpse into the life of this remarkable woman. She was born on June 15, 1923, in Buffalo, New York. Doris's parents and grandparents were colonels in the Salvation Army, all involved with the daily operations of the mission. "That's all my mom knew; that was her life," said Doris's son, Steve. Doris, the oldest of five sisters, was responsible for the younger ones. She graduated high school, attended college, and then went to New York City.

While Doris was working in New York City as secretary to Dr. Fant, president of the American Bible Society, six-foot-six-inch Henry Fikkert came into the office to be interviewed for a job as a shipping clerk. "I'm sure Dr. Fant was impressed with more than Dad's height," Marcia recalled, "but when he came out of the office after the interview, Dr. Fant said to six-foot-two-inch Doris, 'Now I've hired him. The rest is up to you.'" Doris and Henry were a perfect match. Their first date was in December 1947, and they were married a year later, on November 23, 1948.

After they married, the Fikkerts moved to Kansas where Henry graduated from Sterling College in 1951. Robert Atwell, an OPC pastor and member of the board of trustees for Westminster Theological Seminary in Philadelphia, went to Kansas to encourage

---

1 Response to an e-mail questionnaire by Marcia Vander Pol in May 2015. Other sources are Steve Fikkert, Helen Veldhorst, Elizabeth De Troye, and Brian and Kathy Gesch.

the Fikkerts to come to the seminary, Henry as student, and Doris as cook. The couple moved to Philadelphia, where Doris cooked for the students for three years. Steve remembers stories of students and faculty raving about her cooking. Henry graduated in 1955.

The couple was not immune to hardships and difficulties. The first problem they faced was Henry's heart health. The doctors didn't expect him to live a long time. Doris and Henry realized that they might

Doris and Henry Fikkert on their wedding day

have just a few years together. Yet God always provided the medical advances that helped Henry just when he needed them.

Four children were born to Doris and Henry: Steve, Alison, who died when she was 18 months old, Marcia, and Brian. The late OP minister George Haney was at Alison's funeral and described how the Fikkerts ministered to others:

My dear friends, Henry and Doris Fikkert, were at seminary at the time and had a little daughter who was diagnosed with a brain tumor and at about one year of age radical surgery seemed to give some relief, but the prognosis was not good. Eventually she died and I went to the funeral service conducted by the late Robert Atwell. Doris and Henry greeted us all as we entered the funeral parlor and, admidst their sorrow and tears, told us how thankful they were that they knew where little Alison was and that some day they would go to join her. I was totally unprepared for that kind of reception by the parents and was then struck with the message based upon Psalm 30:5, "weeping may endure for a night, but joy cometh in the morning."[2]

The loss of her daughter sparked a deep compassion in Doris for those who lost a child. Marcia doubts that her mom let herself grieve the way people today would be encouraged to grieve. Instead, Doris relied on Christ to make her content in any circumstance. She didn't look for a way out of difficult situations, but trusted God to help her through them.

In 1966 Henry accepted a call to Calvary OPC in Cedar Grove, Wisconsin. Steve was 15, Marcia, eight, and Brian, two. Being a pastor's wife was a 24/7 occupation, and Doris served alongside Henry for 25 years at Calvary. When Henry would visit shut-ins, Doris often accompanied him, taking a fresh-from-the-oven treat. Doris was a gracious hostess, and often there were guests around the table, especially at Sunday dinner. Henry and Doris had a way of making everyone feel at home.

Known for her robust laugh, Doris worked fun into educational programs. The Olympic Games provided the spark which grew into the Olympia/OPC, a program Doris planned as a motivator for catechism memorization. Students participated in Bible class opening ceremonies: the Olympic flame was lit and the games began with a pistol shot. One participant remembers chariot races: the older students attempting to ride tricycles around the church parking lot, and then racing to say the memory work as they earned points. For hurdles, the kids leapfrogged over their dads; water balloons were used for the shot put. Medals were awarded at a banquet at year's end.

Doris's talents ranged from planning and writing materials for all age groups to teaching all age groups. In 1969 Sheboygan County Christian High School began with students housed in a room at Oostburg Christian School. Doris taught every subject except math and science, and provided many extracurricular activities. She expected much from her students, such as outlining chapters

2  "Today in OPC History—George Haney, February 28," 2016, http://opc. org/today.html?history_id=856.

of the Bible and reciting memory work word perfect.

Doris launched an ambitious outreach project in 1975 called "To Tell the Truth." In conjunction with the study, Doris published a book with Great Commission Publications by the same title. The objective was to present Jesus Christ to women outside the context of regular church activities. This program was also intended to involve Christian women in the work of evangelism, whatever their abilities may be.

The program included child care, a snack, and a craft that matched the theme. Fifty minutes were spent in concentrated Bible study. The other 40 minutes of the program encouraged friendships between visitors and volunteers. Nursery workers, children's teachers, drivers, food preparers, greeters, and discussion leaders—a variety of gifts were needed for this program. Records show that about 40 women were involved every time the program was presented, a total of 14 times from 1975 to 1980. Doris wrote, "There is no woman who does not have *some* gift that can be used for the spread of the Gospel." [3]

The outreach program was planned for two larger surrounding communities, Port Washington and Sheboygan. Doris recruited women from Calvary and Bethel to help carry out the program. "You didn't say no to Doris," Helen Veldhorst said. "You made advertising posters, worked through the lesson with her, and canvassed neighborhoods." [4]

Pat Clawson's husband, Doug, served as a summer intern in 1984 at Calvary OPC with Pastor Fikkert. Pat remembers the float that Doris helped Calvary Church to build for the local Holland Festival parade. "Doris was a tremendous example to me of what a pastor's wife should be," Pat recalled. "She was positive, enthusiastic, and handled everything with a certain grace." [5]

---

3 Doris Fikkert, *To Tell the Truth* (Philadelphia: Great Commission Publications, 1975), 11.
4 An interview with Helen Veldhorst in May 2015.
5 A phone conversation with Pat Clawson in May 2015.

After Henry retired from Calvary OPC in Cedar Grove in 1991, the Fikkerts moved to Oostburg and joined Bethel OPC. Here Doris began a monthly program called Senior Saints. It usually involved a speaker or a singing group, and a nourishing lunch. One friend characterized Doris as compassionate and giving, demonstrating Christ in everything she did. Doris had the ability to get everyone to work together in a very nice way, another friend said. In her 70s, Doris joined the technology revolution by seeking advice and then purchasing a computer which she used for formatting and printing programs for Senior Saints.

Doris's three children and their spouses are serving the Lord in various capacities. Steve has been an administrator of Christian schools and now teaches high school Bible classes. Marcia, a professor's wife, home schools her son, tutors students, and teaches piano. Brian is a professor at Covenant College and president and founder of the Chalmers Center. Doris went home to be with her Lord, September 12, 1999, leaving a faithful legacy which includes ten grandchildren.

A day before Doris was scheduled to have delicate brain surgery, a friend and her daughter visited her. Later they received a note from Doris. She thanked them for the visit and concluded with words that demonstrated her strong faith in God: Maybe the Lord would grant her more time on earth, but if he didn't, she was ready to meet him. Whatever God's will was, she would accept it.

### Helen Joann Holle Veldhorst

"It's not my cup of tea," Helen Veldhorst said recently when this writer saw her at the grocery store. Helen prefers to teach older children, but someone was needed to teach preschool children on Wednesday night, during prayer meeting. No younger person had volunteered. She noted that when a baby is baptized at Bethel, the pastor faces the congregation and asks: "Are you willing to help these parents raise this child? Then please rise."

"I always stand," Helen said. "I figured I'd better do something about it."[6]

"Doing something about it" has characterized Helen Veldhorst's life. Although she taught sixth-grade catechism for 20 years, at 76 Helen is now teaching the three- to five-year-olds. The "Kids for Jesus" class recently numbered about 20 children at Bethel OPC in Oostburg, where Helen has been a member all her life.

Helen Joann Holle was born July 15, 1940, to Audley and Marie Holle. She had a pleasant childhood, enjoying the playhouse her father built for her, going for walks with her dad and their cocker spaniel, and going on picnics with her parents. Her dad had a very positive attitude, and Helen tried to be like him more and more. He always gave good advice: never date anyone you wouldn't consider marrying.

Though the family lived in rural Cedar Grove, her parents were charter members of Bethel OPC in Oostburg. Her parents were fine Christians. Her dad was an elder, Sunday school teacher, and Sunday school superintendent—busy all the time, or at least it seemed so to Helen. Her mother played the organ, and Helen sat with her dad and the elders in the front pew, giving her no chance to be naughty![7]

At an evening campfire at Calvin Bible Camp when she was 14, Helen publicly announced that Jesus was her Savior, and made profession of faith at Bethel as a senior. During high school, Helen was given the opportunity to teach fourth-grade Sunday school at Bethel. A former student was excited to be in her class because Helen

6 Response to a questionnaire, phone conversations, and in-person conversations with Helen Veldhorst in June 2015.

7 The custom of elders sitting in the front pew at every worship service may have been carried over from the Netherlands. Wilbert Nyenhuis, 94, remembers his father and other elders occupying the front pew in the Presbyterian Church (USA) in the early 1930s. The elders were to ensure that solid doctrine was being preached. If something said was wrong, the elders had the responsibility of discussing it with the pastor in the next monthly meeting. This practice was discontinued at Bethel OPC in the late 1980s. Information gleaned through phone conversations with Jack DeTroye on March 11, 2016, and Wilbert Nyenhuis on March 12, 2016.

used a wide variety of visual aids to keep the students interested. That's when Helen realized she loved teaching. After graduating from Cedar Grove High School, she studied to become a teacher.

Helen often joined her high school friends at Calvary OPC for Sunday evening worship. One of those friends, Howard Veldhorst, became her husband. Howard was home after serving two years in the army and Helen was in college when they had their first date in Cedar Grove; they married on August 11, 1961. Helen characterized Howard as loving the Lord, his family, and being kind, generous, and ambitious, with lots of friends. "Our children, David, Brenda, and Sandra, and the grandchildren adored him and so did I," she said.

When asked about problems she may have faced when raising their children she replied that the biggest hardship was Howard's work schedule; a salesman, he traveled nationally and internationally about 130 days a year. When he was home, he made time for his family. When he wasn't home, it was difficult to squeeze the kids' activities, parent-teacher conferences, and church meetings into his busy schedule.

Helen's life has not been free from sorrow. At 16 she found herself in Sheboygan's St. Nicholas Hospital with a Sister, who shook her finger in Helen's face, and told her that to get over this she had to cry. It seemed like a strong reprimand for a teenager who was in the hospital with the same symptoms her father had experienced, when he, just a month before, had died of a blood clot. Helen, an only child, was trying to "be strong" for her mother by not crying. "Losing my dad, my best friend, when I was a junior in high school was the biggest trauma of my life," Helen said. "God called him home at age 50. The next few years were rough, because my mom totally fell apart."

Helen has had other losses in her life. She has three grandsons in heaven, triplets, who were born early and couldn't live on their own. They are rejoicing with Howard, who died in August of 2010. Losing Howard one year short of their 50th wedding anniversary was a huge disappointment to her. She feels that her life circumstances, such as being an only child, helped prepare her for life alone.

Someone has said that when you use your God-given gifts faithfully, he bestows other gifts. Helen is an example of that; her gifts are wide-ranging. She has the gifts of hospitality, teaching, encouragement, and service, among others. Helen and Howard often opened their home to pastors and missionaries,

Howard and Helen Veldhorst

but also to those who needed a longer stay. Bethel's former pastor, Jim Bosgraf, and wife, Judy, characterized Helen as organized and enegetic. "She has extreme gifts; she is both leader and servant. The Veldhorst's were always looking out for the outsider, wanting to draw them into the fellowship," Bosgraf said.[8]

She has little sympathy for folks who, upon retirement, say they can't find anything to do. Helen said emphatically, "They aren't looking!" She keeps working for the Lord, reading to children in a Head Start program, volunteering weekly at Oostburg Christian School library, and organizing and cooking soup for the special suppers that help fund the OCS tuition assistance program.

For 25 years Helen has been head of the funeral committee and oversees the kitchen for VBS snacks. She is pianist for weekly hymn-sings at a retirement home, and volunteers at two resale shops that support local ministries. As a clerk at a Christian bookstore, one of her achievements was to turn a critical co-worker into a friend. Whenever the co-worker routinely criticized her work, she asked the co-worker to teach her how to do the job "better." Armed

8 An interview with Jim and Judy Bosgraf on March 28, 2015.

with humility and God's wisdom, Helen won over the co-worker.

"Mugs and Muffins Bible Study—Bring a Mug and a Bible," the flyers say. "Muffins provided." In 2015 Helen took on hosting and teaching a monthly summer Bible study for ladies, who filled her living room and spilled into the dining area. A young mom was happy to see many other young moms with their chikdren at the study. The children were well-cared for by three of Helen's 13 grandchildren.

Her son, David, sent on a short-term mission trip to Taiwan, later took his young family to the mission field in Japan, and most recently to Bangkok, Thailand, where he served as head of the Mission to the World team. David now is associate pastor at Bethel OPC. Both daughters, Brenda and Sandra, have done short term mission trips; they and their husbands are involved in the work of the church and Christian schools.

Looking back over the years, Helen said that she had a wonderful childhood, teaching career, marriage, and family that includes great spouses for her children and super grandchildren. "God has been and still is gracious. Thanks be to God for strength to do these things (at this season of her life). As long as God supplies me strength, I will be available."

*After* **Mary Jane Gruett** *joined Bethel OPC in 1985, she became friends with Helen and Doris. A retired elementary teacher, she has written Sunday school curriculum for various Christian publishing houses. She now keeps busy teaching the Bible lessons in the GEMS (Girls Everywhere Meeting the Savior) program, and first-grade catechism at Bethel. She is married to Glen and they have a son, a daughter-in-law, and two grandchildren. Her historical novel,* Shadow of the Phoenix, *tells the tragic story of fire aboard the* Phoenix, *a Great Lakes steamer bringing Dutch immigrants to Sheboygan County in 1847.*

# 36

# Anna Strikwerda
# and Debbie Dortzbach:
# Martyrdom and Kidnapping in Eritrea

### *Liz Tolsma*

May 27, 1974, started out as any other Monday in the dusty crossroads village of Ghinda, Eritrea Province, Ethiopia. The sun baked the parched land, and the temperature soon rose to over 100 degrees. Though it was Memorial Day in the States, life continued without interruption at the Mihireta Yesus (Compassion of Jesus) Hospital and clinic, run by the Orthodox Presbyterian Church. Young seminarian Karl Dortzbach and experienced pastor Art Steltzer left the mountain town that morning for the city of Asmara, the provincial capital, to conduct their weekly Bible class.[1]

Karl's wife, Debbie, a public health nurse now four-months pregnant with the couple's first child, made rounds with the physicians. Along with Dr. Grietje "Greet" Rietkerk, from Holland, Debbie ministered to the many cholera patients in the ward and was pleased to see improvement in most of them. Debbie and surgeon Gil den Hartog then checked on patients recovering from polio correction operations.

Even at nine o'clock in the morning, almost one hundred patients crowded the clinic's halls, waiting to be seen for a variety of

---

1 Background material for this chapter was gleaned from: Karl and Debbie Dortzbach, *Kidnapped* (New York: Harper and Row), 1975.

common regional illnesses. The staff dispersed and got to work. Surgery began. Across the H-shaped building, the clinic opened, and patients received medical care from Greet and Debbie, as well as the word of the gospel. Always, Scripture and medicine went hand in hand.

Nurse anesthetist Anna Strikwerda labored with Dr. den Hartog in the operating room. Her steps led her from the Netherlands to Tasmania, Australia, England, the United States, and finally to Eritrea where she gave her heart to the poor people of the region almost 11 years before. But she was far more than a nurse. She also loved to write, paint, and draw.

And yet another chapter of her life beckoned to her. A house she rented in Ghinda waited for her, her all-but-adopted son, Omer, and the orphans she planned to rescue, nurture, and instruct in the Lord. Growing up in the Netherlands as the sixth of 14 children, she had a great deal of experience overseeing a large brood. Funds flooded in from all over the world for her to turn her vision into reality.

She and Omer shared a special bond. Every night, he came to the apartment she shared with student nurse Sandy ten Haken. Anna read to him, and they played together. She took him to visit her family in Holland the year before. For now, though, Anna's hospital work called to her.

The morning progressed, the pace frenetic. Greet had many patients waiting. Even though, as a young girl, her family's financial circumstances forced her to leave school after the ninth grade, she worked

Anna Strikwerda and Omer

hard in the evenings to finish high school and get a scholarship to medical school. Inspired by Dr. Francis Schaeffer in Switzerland, she settled on mission work and arrived on the field in 1969.

In those five years, Greet delivered babies, treated illnesses, and endeared herself to the people in the surrounding countryside. The local people considered no distance too great to travel to be seen by the much-beloved doctor.

As she made her way through the clinic, Greet spotted movement. A man with a gun stood in front of her. An extremist from the Eritrean Liberation Front (ELF), the group that fought to win the Eritrean province's freedom from Ethiopia. They had kidnapped men from Tenneco Oil earlier in the year. Tensions in the area ran high. She knew what this guerilla had in mind.

He motioned for her to come with him.

Greet planted her feet. "Absolutely not."

Her boldness must have stunned the man. He moved on through the clinic, toward the surgery, searching for Dr. den Hartog.

As surgery wrapped up in the operating room, Anna headed from the hospital wing of the building toward the clinic to work. Along the way, she encountered a group of guerillas. They seized her.

She didn't fight them, didn't resist them. "I'll go. I'm not afraid." Her steadfast faith, the hallmark of her life, sustained her.

The men marched her outside.

Back in the clinic, Debbie returned to duty after morning tea. She first stopped at the supply closet to retrieve some thermometers and medicines. As she locked the closet, a hush fell over the crowd in the waiting area. How strange. Usually, a buzz filled the hall as people waited with anxious expectation.

And then, she discovered the reason for the hold-your-breath quiet that permeated the room.

A masked man with a gun.

She dropped her supplies and dashed to hide in an x-ray room. But how silly of her to be afraid of him. All he wanted was bandages, perhaps a few medicines. If she gave him what he wanted, he would leave. The day could resume.

With her heart beating a rhythm that would make any drummer jealous, she opened the door.

And stared straight into the dark eyes of the masked man.

He snatched her by the arm and pulled her after him. They traced their way down the clinic hall and through the gathered crowd that parted like the Red Sea. But the door at the front entrance was locked. Debbie didn't have the key, so he hustled her back through the waiting patients.

"Greet!" Perhaps the doctor was around. Perhaps she would be able to reason with this crazy man.

Debbie's cry went unanswered. Maybe Greet hid in another part of the hospital.

The soldier shoved Debbie out the back door and into the glaring sun.

There stood Anna, still in her surgical scrubs, a stethoscope around her neck. "Don't be afraid, Debbie. The Lord is with us."

That truth soothed Debbie as their ordeal began.

Five ELF guerillas herded the women from the compound. Blows from the masked men's walking sticks rained down on them. The women clutched hands and ran from Ghinda, toward the arid northern mountains, stumbling as they went.

"Oh Lord, help us!" Anna pleaded with God.

Debbie echoed her prayer. "Help us, Lord." She held on to Anna. "At least we're together." She wouldn't have to survive this ordeal alone. Anna's tremendous faith strengthened her.

"Go, go!" Their captors screamed the orders. The liberation fighters higher in the mountains returned their shouts.

The men drove them to a dry, rocky riverbed surrounded by thorny brush. Both had on wooden-soled, clog-like sandals, designed for the hot Ghinda climate, not for a run in this terrain. Blood soon soaked their feet.

"Oh, my sandals, I can't keep my sandals on." Anguish laced Anna's voice.

"Try to run on the sand." Debbie knew they couldn't stop. If they paused, the beatings increased. They had to keep going.

One of the fighters tore the nurses apart. Debbie received more blows from the sticks and continued her flight. They left the river-bed and climbed into the jagged, rocky mountains. The clinic now lay far below them in the hot, dusty valley.

Debbie glanced over her shoulder. Anna crouched down, trying to put her sandal back on.

"Go!" The kidnappers didn't let up their relentless beatings. She resumed her run.

A muffled gunshot filled the air.

Debbie turned.

Anna fell backward.

Shot in the head.

How could Debbie go on alone now? And when would they kill her? For days, she'd been dealing with phlebitis, the veins in one leg inflamed, leaving it swollen and painful. How long would she be able to run?

A helicopter flew overhead. Would the pilot see her? Report her position for a possible rescue? It disappeared from sight.

Thirst burned her throat. Perspiration soaked her white uniform. She motioned to the kidnappers that she was pregnant, so they would give her a break. But they refused to let her rest.

Two hours after the soldiers captured her, two hours after this nightmare began, the group arrived at a helicopter. The same helicopter that flew overhead a short time before. A white man greeted her.

One of the Tenneco Oil employees taken a few months before.

He was alive and bore no signs of beatings or torture. At least she knew they treated some of their prisoners well. That brought her a measure of comfort. Still, the threat of death hung over her. How could they have murdered Anna, the woman who cared so much for their people?

Though the Tenneco employee who piloted the helicopter objected to the large number of passengers that crowded into the bubble compartment, the guerillas demanded he fly. Little by little, they lifted into the sky.

Down below, the Ethiopian army learned of the kidnapping and went searching for the women. OP handymen George Wright and Jim Miner had gone from the mission hospital to Asmara for supplies earlier in the day. Turmoil ruled the compound as they returned. The words they heard were almost unbelievable. Though civil war raged in the country, and you always had to be careful what you said because you never knew whom you were talking to, they never dreamed life would come to this.

"Anna and Debbie have been taken. We don't know where they are."

And then came the request from the Ethiopian army. "We need an ambulance or some sort of transport."

George volunteered to drive their new mobile clinic to the location. Greet had raised the money for it. Whom would he find there? And in what condition?

When he arrived at the spot, he saw Anna on the ground, not far from the main road. She lay in the center of the ravine, at the bottom. He didn't have to go to her, didn't have to ask the soldiers who stood around her body what was wrong.

He knew she was dead.

He brought her home.

Within hours, the staff packed up and evacuated the hospital. Only six of them, those without children, stayed to finish the final details and keep watch over the patients too weak to be discharged.

The doors were closed and locked.

Debbie's husband, Karl, was among those left at the compound, waiting for word on his wife's whereabouts and well-being. Before he left Asmara after the Bible study, he received a phone call from Ghinda with the unimaginable news. He and Art Steltzer had informed the US Embassy of the situation. The Ethiopian army continued their search. He couldn't do anything other than pray and wait.

And so he did.

Debbie spent that first night on a cot in a hut in the middle of a small village high in the mountains. The native women welcomed her. The ELF soldier assigned to her was kind, bringing her tea to drink and food to eat. He assured her she would be taken care of. Yet, fears assailed her. She wasn't free to go where she wanted. She was alone. And she didn't know what would happen.

Karl and the few missionaries remaining in Ghinda rose early the next morning for Anna's funeral. Villagers from every walk of life packed the hospital courtyard. Some were Ethiopian Orthodox Christians, others were Muslim. No matter what their beliefs, Anna touched their lives, and they came to pay their respects. Missionary Art Steltzer preached the sermon.

Would Debbie's funeral be next?

Karl watched Omer, the hot, Eritrean sun beating down on him as he stood alone over the fresh grave. A woman from the local village came and stood next to him. "Why aren't you crying? Aren't you sad your mother died?"

Omer turned his attention to the woman. His eyes remained tear-free, calm, peaceful. "Yes, I am sad, but don't cry. Today is my mother's festival. She is rejoicing in heaven."

Debbie spent her long days watching her captors, resting in her hut, and writing in a notebook she had in her pocket at the time of her capture. She gathered wildflowers and sketched them.

Each morning, she met with God in prayer, asking only that he would help her through the day ahead. Early on in her captivity, she took a muslin bandage from a first aid kit, borrowed a needle, and begged thread from her captor. With this, she embroidered a verse from Psalm 34 (KJV): *I sought the Lord, and he heard me, and delivered me from all my fears.*

The women she met accepted her and were kind to her. Though language was a barrier, they managed to communicate with each other. Still, it was not her home. She longed to be with her husband. To be free of the constant worry, the fear that was never far removed.

The correspondence between the ELF and the mission moved

with frustrating slowness. It took days for the letters to pass from Debbie and her captors to Karl and the mission. What word he received from her brought him comfort, knowing she was well and hoping in the Lord. One of the missives requested supplies. She didn't have much clean water to drink, and the food made her sick.

It wasn't until June 10th that a detailed ransom note arrived. The demands included a request for $5,000 worth of cholera medicine, $5,000 worth of malaria medicine, typewriters, duplicators, microphones, and $75,000 in cash. ELF expressed remorse over Anna's death and concern about the large outbreak of cholera in the villages.

The OPC didn't have that kind of money. Even if they had the funds, they wouldn't pay the ransom. Doing so would embolden ELF and make such kidnappings more common.

Even Karl understood that.

In his reply to ELF, he mentioned how, because of the kidnapping, all the medical missions in the country were closed, no longer able to help the sick. Greet and the nurses, however, planned to give medicine and injections on their usual Thursday clinic in the countryside that week.

ELF responded by stating they did not believe the mission had any intention of helping the cholera patients. They decreased their request for cash to $62,500. The other demands stayed the same.

Again, the mission refused.

Debbie continued to stitch verses: *Is there anything too hard for thy God?* (Jeremiah 32:27). And the words of Psalm 121 (KJV), which sustained her during that fearful flight into the mountains: *I will lift up mine eyes unto the hills, from whence cometh my help. My help cometh from the LORD, which made heaven and earth.*

And then, without warning, on Tuesday, June 18th, ELF sent a letter to the mission. In it, they freed Debbie. They made no further demands.

Noise in the camp that same night awakened Debbie. A messenger brought the word that she was no longer a captive.

The men, once Debbie's captors, now led her through the dry, rugged mountains, toward freedom. Days into the arduous journey, Debbie arrived in the Red Sea city of Massawa, where she contacted the mission. On Saturday, June 22nd, after 21 days apart, Karl and Debbie were reunited.

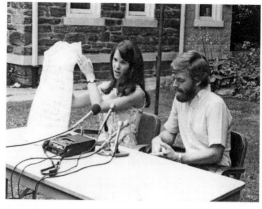

Debbie and Karl Dortzbach speaking with the press after her kidnapping in Eritrea was over

A week later, they flew home to the United States, and she gave birth to a healthy baby boy, Joshua, in October. During their time in the States, Karl planted Hope OPC in Libertyville, Illinois. Two more children were born to them. They returned to Africa with another mission in 1981, but not to Eritrea. Karl planted churches and Bible schools in Kenya, while Debbie continued her nursing work among the native people, treating AIDS victims.

The OPC mission reopened later in 1974 and continued to serve the Eritrean people for another two years, until a local man who worked with them was murdered. The clinic closed once again and remained shuttered for 19 years, until 1995. In that year, with much joy and anticipation, many workers set about repairing and refurbishing the hospital. The celebration was short-lived. The clinic and hospital closed for good in 1997. In its third time in Eritrea, the OPC established a theological college. Those missionaries returned home in 2007 when the school was forced to close.

Greet continued her medical work, laboring for a year in an Eritrean refugee camp in Sudan and for a year in Pakistan. In 1979 she and nurse Corrie van Galen opened Tei wa Yesu Family Care Center in Kenya, ministering to show Christ's compassion to the people of the area. They were the only medical facility in a

60-square-mile area with one hundred thousand citizens. She returned to Eritrea when the clinic reopened in 1995 and, after it shut down once again, finished her career in Kenya. She is now retired and living in the Netherlands.

In 1996 Omer was married and awaiting the arrival of his first child. His mother, Anna Strikwerda, was the OPC's first martyr.

The indigenous church continues in Eritrea, though under great persecution.

Greet best summarized the OPC's goal with its medical missions. "It has been our prayer that in all we do, people will clearly see the compassion Jesus has for lost sinners."

Anna, Debbie, and Greet each fulfilled this commission in her own way, but all with amazing stamina of faith and trust in God. As nurse Sandy ten Haken Wright said, "Through it all, the Lord never let us down."

**Liz Tolsma** *is a life-long member of the OPC and the daughter of Pastor Emeritus Neil Tolsma. She, her husband, son, and two daughters are members of Falls OPC in Menomonee Falls, Wisconsin. Their son is a US Marine. Her debut novella,* Under His Wings, *appeared in the* New York Times *bestselling collection,* A Log Cabin Christmas. *Her novel,* Snow on the Tulips, *was a 2014 Selah Award finalist, a 2014 Carol Award finalist, and the first in a series of inspirational historical fiction. She is a popular speaker, and an editor and the owner of* The Write Direction Editing.

# 37

# Addie Alcorn, Jeannette McKenzie, and Esther Porter: Three Elect Ladies of Albuquerque

## *Kathie Jerrell*

Threes are everywhere! Consider these threes: three strikes and you're out, the "Three Little Pigs," par 3 golf, three wishes, the rule of threes in decorating and landscaping, and of course, triangles. Here's another three: the Albuquerque Orthodox Presbyterian Church had its roots with three elect ladies who prayed and supported its beginnings.

The city of Albuquerque, New Mexico, sits with the Bernalillo Mountains as a background. In the 1970s a Christian Reformed Church and its mission were the only Reformed witness in this city of nearly 400,000 people. But God had long before begun his work in establishing an OP church in Albuquerque. In New Jersey, Pennsylvania, and Illinois he was raising up three ladies who would have a heart for a Reformed work in the "Land of Enchantment." We know them by their married names: Addie Alcorn, Jeannette McKenzie, and Esther Porter.

The background for Albuquerque OPC started in the 1930s. The Presbyterian Church was in conflict and Westminster Theological Seminary had begun its work. Addie Poinsett [Alcorn] was attending the Columbus Presbyterian Church in New Jersey—just miles from Princeton. During this time Les Dunn and students from Westminster were keeping the congregation informed about the growing storm. Addie soaked up biblical teaching as she followed the conflict. She knew OPC founding pastors Reginald Voorhees and Bob Atwell and had Henry Coray as her minister. Addie heard R. B. Kuiper, Cornelius Van Til, and sat in on some of John Murray's classes; she said that if you could "teach me anything, you were a good teacher."[1]

Then came J. Gresham Machen's trial. Addie intently followed the conflict and even attended part of Machen's trial. "It was plain to see that the things they were finding fault with in Machen were things about [what] Scripture teaches." She marveled at Machen's humility as he calmly answered from Scripture the accusations against him. She watched the downfall of many churches and knew that you "can't go against the Lord's will and expect to prosper." Addie, along with her sister Rebecca, who eventually became the wife of OP pastor Bruce Coie, prayed and voted to support the fledgling denomination.

In 1936 Addie took the opportunity to go to a Navajo mission school in Tse Bonito, New Mexico. She worked as a Presbyterian missionary, serving with the Rev. Howard Clark. She loved the Native Americans and even brought one of her students back to New Jersey to help introduce the work with the Navajo. During Addie's time at the mission, Rev. Clark received a letter from the PCUSA saying that there was a "heretic in the mission—a Machenite"! Mr. Clark was pressured to do something about it.[2]

In 1942 Addie enlisted in the US Navy—going as she said, "from the sublime to the ridiculous." Addie's love for the new little church never died though. She began praying that an Orthodox Presbyterian Church would be raised up in Albuquerque, the largest city near her beloved mission. Upon finishing her Navy service in 1946, she settled in Albuquerque as the now married Addie

---

1 Some of the information about Addie Alcorn is taken from a recorded interview with her by Charles Dennison on January 17, 1984.

2 Addie stayed until November 1941 when she returned East for a doctor's visit. The mission eventually became independent and continued in Window Rock, New Mexico.

Alcorn. She asked her brother-in-law, Bruce Coie, about how to start an OP church in Albuquerque.

Meanwhile near Pittsburgh, Pennsylvania, Jeannette Mitchell [McKenzie] had grown into a young lady. In 1938 she was in northeast Arizona as an office assistant at the Ganado Mission on the Navajo reservation. Ganado Mission grew to become the largest domestic mission of the Presbyterian Church and the largest Indian mission in the United States. Jeannette worked there for five years and then returned to Pennsylvania. In 1942 she married Harry W. R. McKenzie, a widower with two children. They planned to return to the Navajo mission; however, after just five years of marriage, Harry fell ill and died of complications from his asthma. Jeannette returned to the Arizona mission.[3]

In addition to Addie and Jeannette, the Lord was preparing a third lady for service in Albuquerque. In the early 1930s Esther Carter [Porter] was attending Moody Bible Institute in Illinois. She was an accomplished pianist and could play any instrument. Her family recollects that she was active in her college as her class secretary. After graduating *summa cum laude* in 1935, she worked as a missionary among the poor in the Appalachian Mountains of Kentucky. In 1939 she married her sweetheart, Guy W. Porter. The newlyweds were in Arkansas in 1940 where Guy was a missionary at a Bible school for the poor. They also worked in developing the Fayetteville Bible Mission church in Arkansas. There they had two daughters. However, within ten years of their marriage, Esther's husband got sick, so they resettled in Albuquerque. Guy died in 1950, leaving Esther with two girls to raise.[4]

Now back to Addie. Since there was no OPC in Albuquerque, Addie joined Chelwood Christian Reformed Church. Jeannette had written a similar church assessment, "The only Church I have found where the Word is preached at all is the Christian

---

3 It is unclear whether the children went with Jeannette or if they were older children who stayed with relatives in Pennsylvania.
4 From obituary in the *Albuquerque Journal*, 2012.

Reformed."[5] At that time Chelwood CRC transported up to 150 Native Americans from the Albuquerque Indian School for services each week. In 1970 Chelwood started a chapel, Valley CRC, located right across from the school. In 1974 Addie transferred to the Val-

Ginny Wisdom (pastor's wife) and her son Thomas with Addie Alcorn, Esther Porter, and Jeanette McKenzie

ley Church. Most likely, the appeal for Addie was that she could again be with Native Americans in Bible study.

In Albuquerque, Esther landed at Valley CRC where she led a Bible study with Native American women and played piano for Sunday services. Addie attended these Bible studies. There is a great possibility that Jeannette may have worshiped with Addie and Esther even though she still had her membership with the PCUSA. It is amazing that all three ladies converged in Albuquerque from three points east but all with a missionary spirit and a love for God's Word!

So how do these ladies fit into the beginnings of the Albuquerque OPC? On November 27, 1978, Jeannette McKenzie wrote a letter to Glenn Jerrell, pastor in Roswell, New Mexico, saying, "Simply stated, my request is that I might become a member … of the Orthodox Presbyterian Church of which you are Pastor.[6] I have been a Presbyterian all my life, but I can no longer be a part of the Presbyterian Church USA…. I care for a 95-year-old friend[7] of missionary days who makes her home with me. We are both eager to be affiliated with a true Church. We both served as missionaries

5  Letter of introduction to Glenn Jerrell, November 27, 1978.

6  Ibid. Roswell OPC was "only" 200 miles away.

7  Ibid. The older woman was Miss Jenny Lind, an art teacher at the Ganado Mission School. Interestingly, one of her many talented students was the widely known Navajo artist R. C. Gorman. Rev. Ben Male, an OP minister, conducted Jenny's funeral in 1980.

at Ganado [Arizona] on the Navajo Reservation.... I might add that through the years I have been greatly interested in Westminster Seminary."[8]

From this inquiry a Bible study began in June 1979 in the Albuquerque area. Once a month, six to seven ladies would travel to Jeannette's home in Cedar Crest for a monthly Bible study. Among those attending were Addie Alcorn and Esther Porter. Jeannette, especially, delighted in devouring books solid in Reformed thinking. She borrowed Kuiper's work on the Holy Spirit, delighted in Witherow's *The Apostolic Church: Which Is It?* and suggested Murray's *Christian Baptism* for a new family.

In February 1980, OP Missionary-at-Large Glenn Black visited Albuquerque with Pastor Jerrell to help assess the potential of an OPC work there. He wrote, "[Addie and Jeannette] give evidence they will do everything in their power to get a work started. They not only want a Reformed work, they want it to be an OP work. The older women are very well acquainted with the OPC and the Reformed faith and are very much committed to (this).... [Esther] ... has been doing missionary work among the Indians for many years, with financial support from a church in Chicago.... [She is] committed to the Reformed faith but uncertain relative to baptism."[9] Addie spoke very happily of the Black's visit; she was glad she had them in her home.

Westminster graduate Chris Wisdom and his family moved to Albuquerque by July 1980. On August 17, 1980, 13 people met to worship together in the Wisdom's home. Chris Wisdom wrote a letter to friends and neighbors, "There were younger people, older people, a doctor, an artist, a missionary to the Indians, a secretary, a bookkeeper, all there to worship the living and the true God in spirit and in truth."[10] He further mentioned that Jeannette would

8  Ibid.
9  Letter from Glenn Black, Home Missions Committee, Presbytery of the Dakotas, February 18, 1980.
10  Letter from Chris Wisdom to "Brothers and Sisters in the Lord," August 20, 1980.

be helping with some of the typing duties, and Addie would be assisting with local bookkeeping.

Two months later Mr. Wisdom noted in his monthly report that existing members were taking on greater responsibilities, and "[b]eginning this week, Jeannette and Addie will be preparing Sunday School lessons for six-seven year olds and eight-ten year olds respectively." And Esther would occasionally play the piano. What an example! Here are ladies 70 years old who were still working in the life of the church. Hadn't they already "done their time?"

What occasions and conversations did these ladies have after meeting each other? How they must have thrilled to share similar mission experiences. We don't know the conversations, but we can be sure that the Lord worked a love of the Reformed faith in three women that drew them together in Bible study and prayer for a Reformed witness in Albuquerque. Today there are two congregations worshiping in the Albuquerque metro area. God answered the faithful prayer of three elect ladies in New Mexico.

**Kathie Jerrell** *met the OPC and her husband, Glenn, at the Boardwalk Chapel in Wildwood, New Jersey. She supported him in his pastoral work while in Winner, South Dakota; Roswell, New Mexico; Walkerton, Indiana; and as regional home missionary for the Presbytery of Michigan/Ontario. The Jerrells retired to Knoxville, Tennessee.*

# 38

# Rosemarie Malroy and Carol Santo: The Lord's Ladies in the Northwest

## *Carolyn Poundstone*

### Rosemarie Wedge Malroy—Church Planting

If in 1936 you had looked at US population centers, you wouldn't have thought of the Pacific Northwest as promising for church planting. But God had other plans, and they included Rosemarie Wedge Malroy.

Rosemarie Wedge was born in 1940 and came to faith at First Orthodox Presbyterian Church near her home in Portland, Oregon. She often attended alone because her father lacked interest and her mother, a nurse, frequently had to work Sundays.

She met Fred Malroy while in college. They fell in love and were married in 1961. Fred pursued a forestry career with the US Department of Indian Affairs, a job that kept him on the move across the West, beginning in Washington State. Rosemarie sought out churches near their home that provided sound biblical preaching, but came up empty. On a visit to the town of Glenwood she met another couple, Juanita and Leonard Rolph. Juanita shared Rosemarie's desire for sound doctrine and worship. Together they invited community women to the Rolph home for Bible study. Leonard, though not yet a believer, supported the plan.

Women came to study—and returned! God blessed the effort to start a church in Glenwood and, with the encouragement and help of First OPC Pastor Al Edwards, a mission work began there in 1969.

Two years later Fred received a promotion and reassignment, and they moved to Ronan, Montana. By now the Malroy clan included three sons, Jason, Eric, and Sean. It didn't take long for Rosemarie to discover the church situation in Ronan was no better than in Glenwood. She shared her disappointment with Pastor Edwards who offered sound advice: "Stop com-

Rosemarie Malroy

plaining and begin praying!" She prayed, and God answered far beyond her expectations. Fred suggested they invite another couple, Richard and Pat Russell, to their home for dessert, since Pat felt homesick for Louisiana. When the two wives got acquainted they learned they shared the same concerns about church. The Russells had two sons who became friends with the Malroy boys.

Rosemarie and Pat met weekly for prayer. They also decided to listen to many good sermons on audio tape, not just for themselves but with others too. They asked friends and neighbors to join in listening to the tapes, and some showed enthusiasm for a church with such preaching.

In 1974 Rev. Russell Piper, though planning to retire, agreed to leave an OP pastorate in Nebraska and with his wife, Lucille, to start a church in Ronan. Shortly thereafter, Mr. Edwards reported that two OP families had just moved to Polson, a town north of Ronan. The Stukeys and the Hippmans joined the Ronan story.

Answered prayers don't always bring easy times. One of the challenges in Montana is winter blizzards. When Mr. Piper had to drive south through snow to Kalispell to visit families there, Rosemarie and her sons rode along to keep him awake, and also calm the heart of his wife.

In 1980 Fred received a new assignment, this time in Billings, Montana, where Rosemarie helped to plant another OP congregation.

Rosemarie once wrote of her role in promoting vacation Bible school. She asked, "Should your church have a vacation Bible school? The answer shouldn't be determined by how many difficulties you have to overcome. Difficulties can sometimes be in your favor to help you set aside ineffective means and depend more on God."[1] This advice sounds like an echo of the counsel she had received from Pastor Edwards years before. By faith, Rosemarie Malroy followed this advice, and God used her faithful service to bless the Northwest.

Because of the employment of Rosemarie Malroy's husband, the family moved often. During those years, Rosemarie discovered that solid churches and sound biblical preaching were not something she and her family could count on. But God, knowing the zeal in Rosemarie's heart and the gifts he had given her, began his work. With each change, God's Spirit moved Rosemarie to pray, and he faithfully answered her prayers. Several faithful churches—at least four—were started in the Northwest between 1970 and 1985.

### Carol Reno Santo—Personal Evangelism

In Northern California, God used the gifts of a lady whose circumstances were very different from those of Rosemarie. Carol Reno never moved out of the San Francisco Bay Area. But God used the gifts he gave Carol to encourage many individuals who had never before heard the gospel or who had rejected Christ. Many others received comfort or relief by her warm witness and Christian hospitality.

Carol Reno was born in San Francisco in 1937 and spent all her life in the Bay Area. Her family did not attend church regularly, but one Sunday in the early 1950s Carol and her sister decided to visit First OPC where Rev. Edwards E. Elliott was pastor. Carol continued to attend, and one Sunday she invited her neighbor Ella

---

1 Rosemarie Malroy, "The Burden We Had," *New Horizons* 5, no. 2 (February 1984): 15.

Miller to Sunday school. In time Ella professed her faith, much to the dismay of her brother Jack, who had no sympathy for Christianity. Jack made an appointment with Pastor Elliott to debate the claims of Christ—and this appointment resulted in Jack's conversion. Jack Miller went on to study and later teach at Westminster Theological Seminary in Philadelphia. He was ordained as a minister in the OPC and later served in the Presbyterian Church in America. One never knows where a simple invitation to church, like Carol's, may lead.

Another minister, Rev. Carl Erickson, recounted how God used Carol in his life. He was Carol's pastor for many years at what is now called New Covenant OPC in South San Francisco:

> One day, when I was a student at San Francisco State College, I searched the Yellow Pages for churches in the area. Taken by the listing for the Orthodox Presbyterian Church, I decided to visit. While I was on the bus I noticed a young woman with a Bible getting off at the same stop. I followed her. The church was meeting at a house and had a neon cross on display. That caused some suspicions; I turned away and took a bus home.
>
> Some years later, after I had completed seminary, I received a call to be a summer intern at First OPC in San Francisco. Carol Reno was there and told me the church had been praying for me for several years. I recognized her! She was the young woman I had seen on the bus with the Bible.

Carol married Robert Santo in May 1956. Bob was saved under the ministry of OP Navy Chaplain Lynne Wade on the island of Guam. He and Carol had seven children and many grandchildren.

Bob and Carol shared a deep love for the Lord and a desire to serve him and others. Sabbath keeping was essential for the family. At times when pressures became difficult, Carol would sit at the piano and sing "Rock of Ages." That song calmed her soul and those of her family.

On a lighter side, Carol had certain things she thoroughly enjoyed: the color purple, a pair of butterfly earrings, shopping at

Carol and Bob Santo in 1963

Cost Plus and Goodwill for children's clothing, and garage sales. Carol loved her children "unsparingly" and prayed that they would "be in church and be saved," said Bob. Their children recalled that she genuinely cared for their souls, talked to them about Jesus, and sang songs with them.

In 2002, after a short battle with cancer, Carol went home to be with her Savior.

Carol Santo's story isn't a flashy one—no heroics on the mission field, no ceremonies in her honor. But her story, simple though it may be, shows us how one woman's faithfulness can be used by the Lord to draw his people to himself.

**Carolyn Poundstone** *is a homemaker and resides in Portland, Oregon, where she is a member of First OPC. She and her husband, Donald Poundstone, a retired OP minister and former missionary to Cyprus, have four married children and nine grandchildren.*

# 39

# Sandy Heemstra:
# Trading a Dream Home for an RV

## *Gail Mininger*

### Her Husband Applauds Her

"God gave me a sweet Proverbs 31 woman," cheered Jim Heemstra, who radiated gratitude for his wife, Sandy. For two and a half decades she accompanied his travels, supporting his work as Regional Home Missionary (RHM) for the Orthodox Presbyterian Church's Presbytery of the South. "She was willing to sacrifice her home, belongings, and friends for years, to pioneer with me to extend the OPC. She could talk with women. We could reach families together. She made cookies and offered hospitality, even in the small trailer."

Born on February 25, 1945, Sandy married Jim Heemstra on October 20, 1962. In 1973, Jim was in his thirties when he, along with Sandy, and their two young daughters, left his plumbing job in Fort Lauderdale, Florida, as well as his eldership at Coral Ridge Presbyterian Church, to establish his own Christian plumbing business in Tallahassee, Florida. The Heemstras soon discovered that churches in Tallahassee were moving in disheartening directions. While worshipping with those congregations on Sunday mornings, they opened their home Sunday evenings for meetings with two other transplanted families. Larry Mininger, the OPC pastor in Orlando, preached for them, encouraged them to join the OPC, and connected them with Calvin Cummings Sr., who was ready to

retire from his extended Pittsburgh
pastorate. Calvary OPC in Tallahassee emerged, with Jim as ruling
elder and Cal Cummings as pastor.

Sometimes folks from other locations would ask Jim how to start
a church, and he enjoyed helping
them. His passion for evangelism
fostered a goal to "do something in
missions" in retirement.

But "retirement" came early
when chronic back pain forced Jim
to forsake his plumbing business at
age 50 while their two daughters

Jim and Sandy Heemstra

were at college in Mississippi. In 1987 he volunteered to become
the OPC's RHM for the Presbytery of the South. The Heemstras
sold their home and bought a "fifth wheel" travel trailer to haul
behind a truck. Sandy was "willing to fold up the tents and hit the
road with me," recalled Jim. "She gave up some nice things. She
was a tremendous blessing and a full support."

And "hit the road," they did. "From Dallas to Virginia and
Kentucky to Key West," Jim summarized his RHM role, "trying to
extend the kingdom of God through church planting." Responding to inquiries from the denomination or presbytery, he "never
had to initiate a place to go. We went to help a lot of people who
were in great need because they didn't have a good church home."

Because Jim was unable to meet all requests, Sandy, in her quiet
way, assisted in evaluating the feasibility of a work. Jim met with
those hoping to organize a new church and Sandy asked the women
some important questions: "'How do you feel about helping plant
a church or using your home for meetings?' For a mission to succeed, these ladies would have to offer their homes," Jim said. "We
might be moving to their area to invest two years of our lives. We
needed to determine if this was a great opportunity for the OPC."
Sandy's discernment was vital to Jim in determining whether the

families, not just the men, were involved and enthusiastic, not just agreeable. Occasionally as many as four different groups at a time asked the Heemstras to come. Jim and Sandy devoted themselves to the one best suited to establishing a church plant, but sometimes they served as many as three locations at once.

Seven churches comprised the Presbytery of the South when they began traveling. As the presbytery expanded, their ministry contributed to the Presbyteries of the Mid-Atlantic and the South, giving birth to the Presbytery of the Southeast. Jim planted churches in both regions but also assisted other works, sometimes as far away as Texas and Washington state. Overall they helped 33 churches get started!

Not all church plants survived however. Some lasted a year, some didn't make it, some prospered. "When, after two years with a group, it doesn't work out, it's disheartening," Jim lamented. "It's an emotional ride with people in churches. But Sandy was willing to go along. I can't say enough about that." Later they would visit and encourage churches they had helped to establish.

Sandy accompanied Jim's RHM travels for over 25 years. She and Jim "did mostly everything together," including side trips to visit their two daughters, both in college in Mississippi, and later when they were married with children and living in Florida and Texas respectively. Sandy taught children's classes, served guests, attended presbytery meetings, and helped to organize ladies' Bible studies, but was quick to clarify that she was not the teacher. While the small travel trailer was not large enough for meetings, Jim recounted, "Sandy was willing to have people for dinner to teach that hospitality is biblical."

Sandy's self-description? "I don't think I'm very

The Heemstras ready to hit the road

interesting," she understated. "I mostly went along to cook, clean, and care for Jim." Was it difficult to leave her home? "No, it was exciting to go to a new area, make friends in all these places, have people over, see something grow from nothing." She described the camper they inhabited for more than six years as "small, not much to care for, and at night when we closed the curtains, we were home." Later they lived in apartments, fixer-upper houses, and a mobile home. From 1995 to 2000 they moved back to Tallahassee, helping the Bradenton, Florida, church from a distance. But they sold that house and moved to Bradenton because, "we knew we needed to be there." Eventually, in his 70s, Jim retired from full-time RHM ministry, while still serving in Bradenton.

*New Horizons'* archives reveal glimpses of their efforts to start churches in many locations, including throughout the Presbytery of the South and Presbytery of the Southeast: Birmingham, Huntsville, Mobile, and Montgomery, Alabama; Little Rock, Arkansas; Bradenton, Fort Lauderdale, Gainesville, Homestead, Key West, Lake Worth, and Pensacola, Florida; La Grange, Georgia; London and Neon, Kentucky; Pineville, Louisiana; Chattanooga and Maryville, Tennessee; and Dallas, Texas.

Relocating wasn't easy. Before cell phones, their college daughters couldn't call home until telephones were installed at their new locales. Phone booth searches and monthly mail deliveries were challenging, as was wedding planning without a solid home base. College breaks meant parents visiting kids, not vice versa. But the repeated struggle for Sandy was leaving a new congregation once their work concluded and a pastor arrived.

Retired now in Ada, Michigan, and worshipping at Redeemer OPC, the Heemstras volunteer "mercy and cheerfulness" at Sandy's parents' retirement home. Sandy is the front desk greeter, with Jim and his three piece band singing hymns with the residents. The Heemstras winter with the Bradenton congregation they nurtured, reconnecting along the way with believers they served in other towns. "It's just wonderful," Sandy rejoiced. "You start with three families, and 30 years later, you return to people, pastors, buildings.

What more could you ask for?"

## An Example to Others

Tallahassee pastor's wife Mimi Hobbs recounted, "In grad school I was unable to go home for Thanksgiving, so Jim and Sandy had me over, the first of many meals around their table. Sandy is not only a wonderful cook, decorator, and seamstress, but she takes the time to do all the small things that make a house a home. Besides hospitable, I also think of Sandy as adaptable. It takes a special person to trade a dream home for an RV and go where you are needed to plant churches. She is truly one who is content in all circumstances. Since I became the wife of a pastor, her wisdom, gained from years of experience in all sorts of church settings, has been invaluable."

Beth Folkert, of the Bradenton congregation, recalled, "She was always there with a smile and a listening ear, an encourager who wanted to know about the children and what they were doing. Jim told us about the OPC and said he would give encouragement from afar. He was trying to stay back in Tallahassee and not move his wife again. But they came, and she was not complaining. She was always an example of a wife caring for her husband like it says in Proverbs 31:12, 'She does him good and not harm all the days of her life.' When Jim, with his bad back, gave the signal, she would politely and willingly excuse herself, saying, 'Jim needs to get home, see you later.'"

Bradenton's Brenda Wilson commended, "She is an example of the Proverbs 31 woman—an excellent manager of her household. She practices hospitality, she is a diligent and strong woman, a truly godly woman. Besides those highly commendable characteristics, the main thing is, she is my friend. I think there are many women across the country who could say that. She has a kindness about her that is unusual. She always seems to be interested in what concerns me, and she is very understanding."

## Fabulous Faithfulness

Sandy's daughter, Teri Hernandez of Dallas, reflected, "You find that a family is not a house. Mom did lots of waiting and being available because Dad was doing the work. It was hard and admirable that she was able to adjust. She was always crocheting, sewing, quilting things for us—a different way of keeping the family together. She showed us photos of the people. I don't remember Jami or me having complaints. When you're doing something important, it's more important than the inconvenience. She was always committed to being alongside of Dad. I'm glad they're retired and she's playing tennis again!"

Fort Lauderdale daughter, Jami Calatozzo, reminisced, "I have tremendous respect for her—she sold everything and took off. We women are so about nesting and the home. Wherever she went, they just loved her. She is soft-spoken, not a big limelight person. God clearly created her for this position. I just know she touched lives in a way only a woman can. I never, never heard a complaint. It's such a blessing to have that role model. She's a hard worker, but gracious. She created a real sense of family in each church, then had to leave it behind to start another. We never felt deprived. What they were doing was fabulous."

**Gail Mininger** *lives in Orlando, Florida, with her husband, Larry G. Mininger, pastor of Lake Sherwood OPC, where she serves through music, Scripture memory, hospitality, and teaching. The Miningers have five adult children, one of whom, Abigail, worships with them in Orlando. Their son Marcus is an OPC minister and professor at Mid America Reformed Seminary. Their daughters April and Linda are married to PCA ministers and their son Lucas is a PCA member as well. As her nest emptied, Gail taught public high school piano classes, touring as the school's assistant choral director and pianist until her recent retirement.*

# 40

# Donna McIlhenny:
# Be Careful What You Pray For

### *Donna McIlhenny*

Flames roared through the quarter-inch glass of our second-story bedroom window, licking up the curtains as it spread. So quickly it spread! So fast and furious! In the terror of the moment, our first thought was for the children in their rooms. It seemed such a long way down that hall to grab the kids from their beds. In seconds that seemed like an eternity, the children were lined up on the sidewalk in front of the house like three little soldiers. By now, the flames were spreading around the corner of the house into the ground floor of the church. They finally did it! Radical activists finally followed through with their threats to try to kill us—even as the children slept in their beds. [1]

## Three-Pronged Prayer

Seventeen years earlier, in 1966, while a student at Moody Bible Institute, I was exposed to a lifestyle that was an eye-opener to me. Moody was then situated in the transvestite district of Chicago. It was my first encounter with this homosexual lifestyle. With the same spiritually-arrogant attitude of the Pharisee in Luke 18, I was repelled by "those" people. "God, I thank you that I'm not like those people." Little did I know that the Lord would bring me to

---

1 Chuck and Donna McIlhenny, with Frank York, *When the Wicked Seize a City* (Lafayette, LA: Huntington House, 1993).

my spiritual knees; that like the publican, it would be me crying out, "God, have mercy on me, a sinner"; that I would suffer humiliations and near-death experiences of my own making; but that ultimately the Lord would provide a sweet and powerful deliverance beyond my understanding. No longer would I be overwhelmed by my sin, but by God's grace.

Donna McIlhenny

At Moody, I was going through that crisis of faith so many college students go through. In youthful arrogance I questioned: "Is Christianity for real? Does the church thing have any real substance to it—other than being a place to socialize? How about the Bible? Is it relevant for today? Is it relevant for me?" I was so much smarter than God back then! Yet in his gracious providence, God was about to take me through experiences in my life when all I had was him—and all I needed was him. Step by step, the Lord taught me in most powerful ways what life in Christ really means.

My faith journey began with a three-pronged prayer:

"Lord, please don't make me deal with 'those people';

"If you have a man for me, make him a committed man; and

"If Christianity is real, make it real to me."

God does have a sense of humor. For me, the answer to all three parts of my prayer came in the form of Charles McIlhenny. Be careful what you pray for!

Chuck and I met at Moody. We married in 1969, and moved to San Francisco in 1973, where Chuck would pastor First Orthodox Presbyterian Church. The first five years of that pastorate were rather uneventful and discouraging. There was no growth—in numbers or, to our eyes, in spirit; so Chuck called for a week of prayer. We met in individual homes; and every night Chuck ended the meeting with, "Lord, make us an impact in San Francisco." Be careful what you pray for.

### "Lord, don't make me deal with 'those people'!"

The dear old lady who tried to play the organ for worship meant well, but her playing was so bad that one was hard pressed to figure out what key to begin singing in, and it was anyone's guess what key we might actually end up in! We needed a new organist. A possible replacement was suggested to Chuck, and Kevin Walker was introduced into our worship service. What a wonderful talent! But eventually we discovered that Kevin was a practicing homosexual. Kevin came from a fundamentalist, Bible-believing home, and had clearly testified to his faith in Christ. He and Chuck discussed what the Bible said about homosexuality; however, Kevin refused to see that his homosexuality conflicted with his profession of faith, and thus saw no need of repentance. Chuck invited Kevin to keep coming to church, but had to remove him from playing the organ. In June 1979 Kevin sued Chuck, First OPC, and our presbytery. We won, but when the story came out in the press, we were attacked by radical activists from the gay community.[2] Be careful what you pray for!

### "Lord, if you have a man for me— make him a committed man!"

There were daily death threats, de-facing of our home and church, hate mail, windows broken out both in the church and home, demonstrators inside and outside the worship service. They firebombed the house and church in the middle of the night. If they had set the fire on the other end of the house, our son would not have survived. Things like this went on for over ten years. By far the worst for me were the threats against the kids. Anonymous callers would threaten the children by name, physical description,

2 Ibid.

where they went to school, and what sexually-deviant behavior they were going to perform on them before they killed them. Still Chuck held firm. Be careful what you pray for.

Living day after day, year after year, under the oppression of constant fear was a lonely place to be. As a mother, I just wanted someone to help bear the burden; to share the fear and take away some of the pain that kept my stomach in knots most of the time. "Someone ... anyone ... please ask me how I feel! Ask me about my children! Please care about my children's safety!" I know now that there were many who cared ... but I didn't know that then. I felt so alone trying to protect my three young children. Emotionally I felt like I was over the side of a cliff hanging on by only my fingertips. If I let go, I'd lose my mind altogether—so I just kept holding on ... but not without help.

### "Lord, if Christianity is real, make it real to me."

The night they firebombed our house on June 1, 1983, at 12:30 a.m., a neighbor took the children and me in while the fire was being put out. It had been so cold huddling together with the kids against the night wind before he took us in. My hands were shaking so hard, I could barely hold the glass he handed me. I drank this vile-tasting liquid ... but it was warm going down. Besides warming my insides, that drink helped calm my shaking hands, at least enough so I could keep the kids from seeing how scared I was. I needed something to take away my fears; to give me peace, calm, patience, courage—and hope. It worked immediately. I'd found my "miracle!"—something that not only made my life tolerable, but possible.

Alcohol worked great for me for a long time. Whenever we were attacked, I calmed myself with alcohol. Soon I found that alcohol worked well for the daily death-threat phone calls, inciting headlines, and hate mail too. The more relentless the attacks, the more I relied on alcohol. I don't know exactly when I "sold my soul" to it—I just know that I did. I knew why I started, but I didn't know why I couldn't stop; and by that time, peace had become chaos, calm had become anxiety, patience became uncontrollable anger, hope became despair. The fear that at first I drank to get rid of, in the end became overwhelming. I don't know when alcohol stopped working for me—I just know that it did. I prayed and prayed for God to deliver me from it, but he just didn't seem to hear me anymore ... or did he?

In 2005, after 32 years in that San Francisco pastorate, Chuck resigned and moved us to Southern California, where he became a healthcare chaplain.

My alcohol path led to hospital stays, ER visits, counselors, rehab, and finally (after a DUI) to my second rehab. A whole lot of misery. And in the midst of despair is where God most powerfully answered that third and most important prayer from so many years earlier: "If Christianity is real, make it real to me." One night I lay in my bunk in that second rehab, completely demoralized and thinking life was just over for me. I just couldn't do life anymore ... and I prayed: I asked God just to let me go ... to release me from my Christianity. I just couldn't live like this ... the guilt of my sin was too great ... and the fear and emotional pain were just too much. In that most desperate moment it was as if I heard the Lord say, "No, you belong to me. I'm not letting you go," and I had the most profound sense of the presence of the Lord and his care for me. A powerful assurance that I belonged to him overwhelmed me. God wasn't done with me yet.

I knew I had to face the consequences of my addiction; but the Lord was there, and I didn't want to die anymore. I "shook it out" (inside and out) for eight long weeks— because that's what alcoholics do when they detox. I shook and shook, but I was done no matter what. It was so hard, but I never lost that confidence that the Lord was with me walking "through the valley of the shadow of death."

Christianity was indeed made real to me in a most profound way that night in that rehab from hell! A peace I'd never known overwhelmed me. I only hoped for some minimal existence in my sober life ahead ... just living and not much else; but God has given me so much more. All has been restored … and better than it was. God has blessed me with the opportunity to do things I could never have imagined doing before, and the privilege of ministering to those still struggling in the sin of alcoholism. Now I can tell them that they don't have to live like that anymore; that there is sure hope for life—now and for eternity.

### Afterword

In the mid-1990s, I found out that Kevin, the organist who sued us, contracted AIDS, and had gone home to his family in Michigan to die. I spoke to his pastor to see if Kevin had gotten things right with the Lord before he passed away. The pastor assured me that he had. Kevin had repented of his sin and come back to the Lord. The pastor was able to minister the love of Christ to Kevin and the family throughout Kevin's death. Chuck and I rejoiced to hear it.

While we were still at First OPC in San Francisco, one of the callers who threatened us over the phone for so many years started coming to church. Jeffrey was in crisis after having difficulties with the gay community. To him, becoming a Christian meant being heterosexual—and he was adamant that Chuck was not going to "convert" him. But Jeffrey kept coming to church. The day we left San Francisco, Jeffrey came to say good-bye and begged Chuck not to leave. To our knowledge, Jeffrey did not make a profession of faith, but he certainly heard the gospel.

**Donna McIlhenny** *lives in La Mirada, California, with her husband, Rev. Dr. Charles McIlhenny. She is a member of Calvary OPC in La Mirada, and works as an affiliate (un-ordained) healthcare chaplain and substance abuse counselor. She has three children and 14 grandchildren and enjoys singing with The Gary Bonner Singers. Donna and Chuck, with Frank York, are the authors of* When the Wicked Seize a City *(1993).*

# 41

# Joan Savoy:
# Talking the Walk

### *Anita Klumpers*

Christians are often told we tend to "talk the talk" but don't "walk the walk." We are encouraged to display our faith not so much with words, but with our actions. Then there are the people so overflowing with joy in the Lord, they refuse to keep silent in case the rocks cry out. For decades now, Reading, Pennsylvania, resident Joan Savoy along with her husband, Rich, have spoken of God's faithful love and salvation to practically anyone who will listen. God has used Joan to bring many people to Covenant Orthodox Presbyterian Church in Sinking Spring (near Reading), where she and Rich are members.

Joan came to know Jesus while pursuing a degree in physical therapy at the University of Pittsburgh. Born October 25, 1962, in Wilkes Barre, Pennsylvania, and raised a Catholic, she spent her early college years in a zealous pursuit of worldly pleasures and physical excellence followed by an attempt at works-righteousness. Everything left her empty. A Christian acquaintance invited her to an event sponsored by the campus ministry of Coalition for Christian Outreach (CCO). At the casual bring-a-friend meal, Joan met and interacted with believers. She recognized something different about these people—they knew they were loved and their guilt was paid for. Joan wanted to be like them. Soon after, she attended a Jubilee Conference, also organized by CCO, where the speaker introduced a concept new to her. God created us to be in relationship with him, and only through Christ could the relationship we'd rebelled against be restored. At an altar call on February 27, 1983, she stood up, acknowledged her desire for that relationship, and her life has never been the same.

Friendship-building as a means of witnessing and modeling God's desire for a relationship with his people captivated Joan. Possessed of almost boundless energy and enthusiasm (she became a cheerleader in high school so she would have an excuse to jump around and yell), once Joan committed her life to Christ she set her face to minister actively in his name to others. Joan graduated from the University of Pittsburgh in 1984 and moved to Reading, where she worked at a local hospital as a physical therapist. She joined Young Life Ministries at nearby Wilson High School, and visited a few Reading churches. One of them was Covenant, and it was there, she knew, she would be challenged to pursue God.

In Reading, she became friends with Rich Savoy, an IBM salesperson who'd become active in Campus Crusade for Christ (now known as CRU) at Albright College. In 1986 Rich realized he loved this woman who loved the Lord. They started dating and Joan shifted to CRU to work with Rich and see if they could serve well as a team. He also began attending Covenant. David O'Leary, pastor at the time, encouraged and mentored them in their faith, and on September 10, 1988, officiated at their marriage. The couple continued their work volunteering in CRU, issuing invitations door to door on campus, and leading students through the basics of the faith. Joan and Rich taught the daily disciplines of prayer, Scripture study, and decision making with God's lordship in mind, and rejoiced to see many conversions. They picked up students from Albright for Sunday services at Covenant, led small group Bible studies, trained CRU members to do the same, and all the while worked full time in their careers.

Not until their second son, Nate, was born in 1993 did they begin to ease back from campus ministry. Joan knew the gospel was not only a treasure to be savored but also a gift to be shared, and had been interacting with coworkers and sharing her daily life with a godly perspective. Seldom at a loss for words, her outgoing interest in others had always, even before her conversion, been an invaluable asset to nurture friendships. Now God was using her delight in relationships and conversation to introduce unbelievers to the gospel.

Some coworkers, knowing Joan was a church-goer, began attending Covenant. When her friend Judy heard Joan clearly articulate the gospel and stress the importance of making a

Joan and Rich Savoy and their sons

decision, Judy visited Covenant, confessed Christ, and joined the church. So did Joan's brother Mark, after he saw the difference in her and she explained that this was what a life defined by grace looked like. Beth, also a physical therapist, told Joan she was already a believer. When she shared that she was dating a non-Christian and was unconnected with any body of believers, Joan challenged her not only to begin walking like a follower of Christ, but to get herself to church. At Joan's invitation, Beth began attending Covenant. Encouraged by Joan's concern and conviction and the preaching and teaching of the Word, Beth recommitted her life to Christ and was emboldened to invite family and friends to church. Although some people who heard the good news from Joan didn't profess Christ, she never pressured them or made them feel there were strings attached to their friendship.

This type of personal evangelism based on friendships and shared life experiences, along with intentional church training programs and street evangelism, contributed to an exciting period of growth at Covenant. By 1993 Pastor O'Leary could point to about 30 adults who had come to Covenant and traced their participation in some form back to Joan.[1] Many of these believers strengthened their marriages and families by challenging, mentoring, and encouraging each other. They witnessed in the nearby government housing projects as well as the middle class neighborhood right around Covenant. Not everyone this enthusiastic group witnessed to came to saving faith; not everyone who came to Covenant stayed at Covenant, but the Savoys and their friends continued offering the gospel to their neighbors—neighbors as defined by Christ in the story of the Good Samaritan (Luke 10:25–37).

God proves his faithfulness to his people in various ways, and the Savoys have faced some challenges. When Rich was diagnosed with a brain tumor, God's Word encouraged them to meet the trial as Daniel's friends did. Facing the flames of the furnace, they testified that God was able to deliver them, and if he didn't, they would still serve him. God did deliver Rich, and when Joan learned the tumor was benign and successfully removed, she danced around the waiting room singing, "The tumor's all gone! The tumor's all

Joan (middle row at far left) with her extended network of friends and relatives at Covenant Church

1  David J. O'Leary, "Evangelizing Friends and Relatives," *New Horizons* 14 (June/July 1993): 7.

gone!" God used even this frightening time to bring glory to himself. Their middle son's swim team at Penn State witnessed the faith of the Savoys and God's response. A magazine dedicated to the world of swimming shared their story,[2] and many unbelievers read of God's amazing work there and on the Savoy's Caring Bridge website.

One of their sons chose to follow a god-figure different than the true God of his parents, and Pastor O'Leary, their spiritual mentor even after leaving Covenant, reminded them to meet this challenge not with panic, but with faith. Believing friends prayed with them. And, since verbal communication is Joan's favorite method, they let her talk about the trials. Now she tells friends going through similar struggles what true victory looks like. It is not raising children who serve the Lord, but being faithful to him and doing what he commands.

Even a positive, enthusiastic person can experience self-doubt. Usually the most bubbly, energetic person in a room, Joan frets lest the very characteristics that attract others—talkativeness and vitality—might lead her to say too much and not listen enough. Her prayer is that God will give her the discernment to speak only when needed, and know when to keep silent. In typical Joan fashion, she deals with even this concern by talking about it—to friends, her husband, her God.

There are plenty of Orthodox Presbyterians who love Christ and his Word and appreciate pure doctrine and Reformed theology, but find it difficult to be bold and strong for the gospel, go into the world, and make disciples. Many want to be like Joan, but might not be naturally bubbly, energetic, and talkative. Perhaps we don't draw people by our natural charisma. God obviously equipped Joan and Rich Savoy to witness for him, but what about the rest of us—the timid and the tongue-tied? The Savoys don't

2 Michael J. Stott, "Rough Crossing: The Spiritual Journey of Nate Savoy's Family," *Swimming World* (March 2015), http://www.swimmingworldmagazine.com.

see their outgoing natures as necessary to evangelism. Instead, they view everyone they meet as a divine appointment to further draw that person to Christ. Joan has a gift for asking perfect questions of unbelieving friends to get them to talk openly about spiritual matters, but even imperfect questions asked with genuine interest and concern can spark a response in listeners.

These days Joan and Rich teach an English as a Second Language class at Covenant. While it isn't meant as a springboard to get people to church, students from every hemisphere are learning English and about God through Bible stories and testimonies of great Christians. In the summer of 2015, Joan accompanied Rich to Ukraine in support of missionaries they met at Albright who are working with a church in Kiev. At home, Rich concentrates on mentoring men while Joan meets with women. They took advantage of their son's swim meets to enjoy each other's company (when they weren't cheering on Nate and the team), and they bike and ski.

Joan does nothing halfway, but lives life to its fullest and glorifies God as she does. Without speaking a word, she can demonstrate that God, while wholly "other" than his creation, is gracious and concerned about those made in his image and invites them into relationship.

But true to her nature, Joan Savoy doesn't remain silent for long. When asked what message she wants her life to shout, she thinks for a moment and then answers, quite simply,

"God can be trusted."

**Anita Klumpers** *is an author, blogger, skit-writer, and drama instructor. She has two books published by Prism Book Group,* Winter Watch *and* Hounded. *A member of Providence OPC in Madison, Wisconsin, she lives in Cottage Grove with her husband, Byron, a contractor. The Klumpers have three grown sons, two daughters-in-law, and four grandsons.*

# 42

# Fumi Uomoto, Joan English, Dorothy Wingard, and "Sue Johnson": He Who Promised Is Faithful

## *Connie Keller*

My family and I have always loved having missionaries visit our home when they are on furlough. Together, we've enjoyed playing games, sharing a meal, and hearing about their work. Usually, the stories they tell in a friend's home are more personal than those they share in church presentations, full of struggle, heartache, and joy. These stories are the ones I have remembered over the years because they testify to God's grace in the missionaries' personal lives.

When I was asked to write profiles of missionary wives, I was delighted. I wanted to share their experiences so others could get to know them better—it's easier to pray for a friend than a stranger. But even more, as I heard story after story of unexpected trials, I wanted to share how God tenderly provided for them in the midst of testing.

Some of the trials the missionary wives faced were prosaic. *How shall I educate our children?* Others were dire, *How do I react when armed, renegade soldiers break into our home?* Yet in each of these tests, God blessed these women, strengthened them, and taught them that he will provide.

It is my hope that the stories will remind us in our struggles to "hold fast the confession of our hope without wavering, for he who promised is faithful" (Heb. 10:23).

### Seek First the Kingdom of God, *Fumi Onoda Uomoto*

When World War II began and the US government interned
Fumi Onoda and other Japanese-Americans, first in renovat-
ed horse stables at the Puyallup County Fairgrounds and later in
Camp Minidoka, Fumi began to understand that the life she had
imagined for herself was not one that God had planned. Yet, God
was not abandoning her. Instead, Miss Gladys Kaiser, who had dis-
cipled Fumi and other Japanese-American young adults when they
lived in Seattle, took a post at Camp Minidoka as a nutritionist so
she could continue to nurture and teach these young people. Years
later, Miss Kaiser's example of self-sacrifice would influence Fumi's
decision to give up the person she loved in order to serve the Lord.

At Camp Minidoka in Hunt, Idaho, the director, a conscien-
tious Quaker, urged the youth to attend college or graduate school,
which would allow them to leave the camp. This was permitted as
long as they attended institutions that weren't in the western half of
Pacific Coast states. Fumi took the opportunity to study nursing at
Whitworth College in Spokane while her fiancé and fellow camp
resident George Uomoto decided to attend Dallas Seminary.

Fumi was studying nursing when the war ended and General
Douglas MacArthur issued a call for missionaries to go to war-rav-
aged Japan. The lost souls of Japan, her parents' homeland, burdened Fumi, and she felt the Lord calling her to share the gospel
with them. Yet, her heart was torn when she thought of George
and the life they had planned together. She loved George, but she
remembered the sacrifice of Miss Kaiser, the need of the lost, and
the Lord's promise to "seek first the kingdom of God and his righteousness, and all these things will be added to you" (Matt. 6:33).

Faced with a difficult decision, Fumi followed in the footsteps
of Abraham and sacrificed the person she loved most in the world.
She wrote George a letter, explaining that the Lord had called her
to be a missionary in Japan and that George was free to break their
engagement. With an anxious heart, Fumi sent the letter. Then,

she waited for George's response, trusting in the Lord's will and knowing that "[w]hoever loves father or mother [or fiancé] more than me is not worthy of me" (Matt. 10:37).

What Fumi didn't know, was that George, too, had heard the Lord's call to go to Japan and evangelize the lost. And he had also mailed a letter, telling Fumi that she was free to break their engagement.

When Fumi received George's letter, she was overjoyed. Just as the Lord had given Isaac back to Abraham, so he'd given George back to her. God had proved in a marvelous way, "But seek first the kingdom of God and his righteousness, and all these things will be added to you" (Matt. 6:33).

Not long afterwards, George and Fumi were married and served the Lord as missionaries in Japan for 40 years.

[*Born September 17, 1924, Fumi Onoda married George Uomoto on September 27, 1946. They served as missionaries in Japan from 1951–1991. The Lord blessed them with eight daughters and three sons, one of whom, Murray, serves in his parents' footsteps in Japan. Fumi went home to be with the Lord on May 4, 2015.*]

The Uomoto family arriving at the Philadelphia airport in 1963 (Fumi in upper left)

## God Will Provide, *Joan Grotenhuis English*

I can't remember when I first met Joan English. It must have been when she and her husband Ralph were on furlough from Korea or Suriname. Or maybe it was on the pages of *New Horizons*. But after my husband became their pastor and I got to know Joan and Ralph, I was struck by the can-do spirit that they embodied. When the church fellowship hall needed a new floor, Ralph milled wood from his property for the planks. Joan filled in the gaps of service by printing the bulletin, sending out e-mails, and teaching a women's Bible study. Both of the Englishes did what needed doing. Their attitude has always been if God wants it done, he'll provide a way. Though I didn't know it then, I came to realize that they'd learned this lesson from their years on the mission field.

In 1975 when Joan and Ralph were planning to return to their mission work in Korea after their furlough, they discovered that the army-based elementary school their four sons attended had radically increased tuition. They wrestled with this burden in prayer, wondering whether it was right to pay so much for a secular education, especially when the quality of teachers varied from year to year. The more Joan prayed, the more she became convinced it wasn't good stewardship, that the Lord's answer was a resounding no!

But this answer didn't solve the boys' education problem. Though Joan had been a high school math teacher, she knew nothing about teaching first and second grade—algebra and geometry are not phonics and penmanship. Joan wondered if the Lord wanted them to find a missionary teacher, someone who would live with them and teach the boys.

Joan searched for a missionary teacher who could join them in Pusan. She asked in church after church and spread the word about their need. But through the Lord's providence, he again said, "No, Joan."

Before long, their furlough would draw to an end, and they'd be returning to Pusan without a teacher, without any plans for the boys' schooling. Clearly, the Lord wanted the boys to be educated.

But why hadn't he provided a teacher?

Though Joan didn't know it, the Lord had already given them a teacher, just not the person she had expected. But soon, the Lord made it clear. Joan felt as if the Lord was saying,

Joan and Ralph English in Suriname

"Joan, I have provided a teacher for the boys. Look in the mirror!"

While homeschooling is a respected education option now, in the mid-1970s it was nearly unheard of. Crazy.

However, the Lord's power is made perfect in weakness. So, with fear, trepidation, constant prayer, and requests for prayer from every church Joan and Ralph visited, Joan bought, packed, and shipped the schoolbooks to Korea.

Like many unexpected answers to prayer, the Lord would use homeschooling to bless the English family far beyond the academic instruction they'd prayed for. When the schoolbooks arrived late (October), Joan hurriedly wrote lesson plans and organized her small classroom and students to make up for lost time. During school hours, Joan shifted from mom to teacher. She rang the bell and the boys sat at their desks, quietly doing schoolwork under her steely eye.

Three months into their homeschooling experiment, Joan had an epiphany. When it came to discipline, she was a better teacher than mother. In school, she didn't allow the boys to whine or argue. Now Joan was reaping the fruit of this obedience as it spilled over into their home life.

In the end, the Lord knew better than Joan what she really needed. A problem became a blessing. And when the Lord wants something done, he'll provide the means. Truly, " 'I know the plans

I have for you,' declares the Lord, 'plans for welfare and not for evil, to give you a future and a hope' " (Jer. 29:11).

[*Joan English, daughter of OP minister Lewis Grotenhuis, was born on September 1, 1936. She married Ralph English on March 23, 1964. They served in South Korea from 1969–1987 and Suriname from 1987–1996. Later, Ralph pastored churches in Bridgewater, South Dakota; Abilene, Texas; and Roseburg, Oregon. They retired in 2002, moved to northern Georgia, and are members of Cornerstone OPC in Chattanooga, Tennessee.*]

## Walking through the Valley of the Shadow of Death, *Dorothy Brower Wingard*

When Dorothy Brower married Brian Wingard and left her job as a biochemistry lab assistant to go to Kenya in 1994, she had no idea that missionary life would lead her through the valley of the shadow of death.

Not long after they arrived in Kenya, Dorothy had her first brush with violence. One evening, she glanced out the window and said to Brian, "Look, there's a bonfire over there!" Brian paled and rushed out to investigate. It wasn't a bonfire. Instead, tribal tensions had boiled over and a home had been set ablaze. Thankfully, the family who lived there was uninjured, but later Dorothy found out that a guard had been killed.

Violence found Dorothy and Brian a few years later in 2001 after they'd moved to Mbale, Uganda. A noise woke them during the middle of an October night, the sound of someone inside their home. Disoriented by sleep, they assumed it was another missionary. Then, they remembered the heavy metal bars covering their windows and the locks securing their doors. A friend

Brian and Dorothy Wingard

wasn't wandering through their house. It was someone who'd broken through their locks or bars.

Moments later, three soldiers burst into Dorothy and Brian's bedroom and said, "We have come to kill you because you are Americans."[1]

Dorothy and Brian had no reason to doubt these threats. An Italian neighbor had recently been beaten by thieves. And soon after Dorothy and Brian's experience, an American neighbor, who resisted intruders, was beaten and killed.

As the soldiers paraded Dorothy and Brian through the house, ransacking it for things of value, Dorothy mistook the soldiers' guns for knives because she'd forgotten to put on her glasses. But her vision went from blurry to black when the lights suddenly went out. Was it one of the frequent power outages? Or had the soldiers cut the power lines? When the soldiers began using matches for light, Dorothy wondered how she and Brian would die. It would be so simple for the soldiers to set the house on fire and leave her and Brian tied up inside.

While Dorothy didn't fear death, knowing she would be with her Savior, she was terrified of the way she would die. She wanted death to be quick and painless. But if the soldiers had knives, that wasn't likely. Dorothy worried, wondering if she'd die by a knife to the heart. Or would death be by fire, like the thatched hut they'd seen burn in Kenya?

Dorothy hoped and prayed the soldiers would kill her quickly and get it over with. Instead, the ordeal dragged on, a long journey through the valley of the shadow of death. But she wasn't alone. The Lord was with her and Brian, his staff protecting and comforting them in the physical and emotional darkness.

After the soldiers had taken what they wanted, they tied Brian with a necktie and put him on the floor. They tied Dorothy, wearing only a thin, cotton nightgown, and put her on the bed. They

1 Anti-American hostilities were stirred up by US actions in Afghanistan after September 11, 2001.

gagged both of them with socks, but only after asking, "Are these socks clean?"

Finally, the soldiers announced they were leaving, but would return to kill Dorothy and Brian. Left alone, blackness surrounded them. And, they waited to die.

After some time, Dorothy was able to free her hands and untie Brian. In the emotional turmoil that followed, they considered escaping but believed that the soldiers were outside the house, planning to kill them. So, Dorothy and Brian huddled together on the bed and prayed, asking the Lord for their safety and for the salvation of the soldiers.

When daylight arrived, Dorothy and Brian discovered their landline phone was still working so they called OP missionaries Jonathan and Margaret Falk, who helped them in the aftermath.

Later that night, American doctor Ben Warf and his family were scheduled to come to the Wingards' home for dinner. Dorothy considered calling it off, thinking, "It's too much." The trial had left them anxious and exhausted. But as the Lord had protected them through the break-in, he had planned this meal for them as a providential gift. Instead of re-playing the terror of the darkness, Dorothy and Brian spent the evening laughing and playing games—God's merciful design to help them through the repercussions of the trauma.

Though it would take time for Dorothy and Brian to come to terms with the impact of the ordeal, it continues to be a testimony that as we walk through the valley of the shadow of death, we fear no evil for God is with us.

[*Born December 27, 1948, Dorothy Brower married Brian Wingard on December 11, 1993. They served in Kenya (1994–1997), Uganda (1998–2001), Eritrea (2002–2006), Uganda (2007–2010), and South Africa (2010–2016).*]

## Lean Not on Your Own Understanding, *"Sue Johnson"*

(*For the safety of this missionary family and those with whom they work, their names have been changed, and the names of the countries where they serve have been omitted.*)

Not long after Sue Johnson became a Christian, she felt God was leading her to be a missionary. But having grown up in a sheltered environment, she knew she needed exposure to cultural differences. So she laid aside her English degree and applied for a job as a flight attendant to gain cross-cultural experience. When the interviewer asked where she wanted to work, she jokingly told him the name of a country, a country which is closed to the gospel. A country where God would later call Sue and her husband, Nathan, to share the gospel.

Before going to this dark country, God first called Sue and Nathan to serve in another country hostile to the gospel, where proselytizing by foreigners is illegal. Not long after they had settled into their apartment, Nathan was teaching the book of John to three young adults. They were studying at a low table near the front door, Bibles spread open before them. A knock sounded on the door. It was late at night. Sue went to the door, opening it widely without thinking who might be on the other side.

Standing in the doorway was a uniformed police officer. And he had an unobstructed view of the Bibles. In his hands, he held official paperwork. Everything Sue and her husband had worked for was in danger—they were breaking the law in front of a government official. Immediately, her training kicked in. "Stay faithful, tell the truth, and respect the government authority who is questioning you." She began praying for God's protection. With one word from the policeman, they could be interrogated, fined, and expelled from the country. And the young adults who were studying God's word …

In the midst of Sue's prayers, the Lord brought to mind Proverbs 3:5–6, "Trust in the Lord with all your heart, and do not lean on your own understanding. In all your ways, acknowledge him, and he will make straight your paths."

Sue waited, trusting God and knowing, as never before, their lives were in God's hands. Instead of confronting them about the Bibles, the police officer said, "I'm here to check your foreigner registration. How many people are living here? What are their names, ages? What are you doing in [our country]?" Sue and Nathan answered the questions while the policeman collected information, checked passports, and wrote notes. Finally, he turned to Nathan. This was the moment when everything could fall apart. The policeman could demand to know why Nathan was teaching the Bible. The officer could write them up and cause no end of trouble. But he didn't. Instead, he said, "Are you teaching these students? Teach them well."

With those words, Sue and Nathan knew they were safe. God had answered their prayers. The police officer left. Nathan led in prayer, praising and thanking God for his mercy and protection. Afterwards, the young adults listened intently to the rest of the Bible study.

Later, Sue found out that the police were looking for people disturbing the peace with religious activity. Only, they weren't looking for Christians. They were scouting for cult missionaries who were burning incense and making noise. God used the incident to teach Sue and Nathan not to lean on their own understanding. What had seemed like a dire situation was really the Lord rooting out false teaching. And now, as Sue and Nathan have gone on to minister in a country so dark and hostile that Sue had once joked about going there, she knows that what might seem like trouble is really the Lord directing their path.

[*Sue and Nathan Johnson have been OPC missionaries for over 20 years. They covet your prayers for safety because the situation in which they serve is as difficult and tenuous as it was years ago.*]

**Connie Keller** *is the wife of Rev. Calvin Keller, pastor of Cornerstone OPC in Chattanooga, Tennessee. They have four grown children. Connie is also a novelist, copy editor, and book reviewer for* Crown Publishing/Publishers Weekly's *"Blogging for Books."*

# 43

# Patricia Hill:
# North to Alaska

## *Wanda Long*

"North to Alaska." What tune do you hum or what words come to mind when you hear people say the name of the 49th state—Alaska? Perhaps you have heard the terms—The Last Frontier, largest state in the union, land of the midnight sun, home of the frozen chosen—just to name a few. We who live in the northern most state all have reasons and stories about how we came to live here. Some come for job opportunities, some for the great wilderness adventures of hiking, hunting, and fishing. Some are running far from their problems and hoping for a fresh start. The great earthquake of 1964 brought my family here from Arizona for the numerous plumbing jobs available to my dad.[1] The varied reasons why people are here make Alaska unique and diverse.

In 2001 Patricia Hill, a 77-year-old widow, came to Alaska from the Akron-Canton area of Ohio, to be with her daughter who lived here and to help out the newly developing Grace Orthodox Presbyterian Church in Wasilla.

Over the years, Pat had often called Linda Posthuma, adminis-

---

1 Author's note: While composing this, Alaska experienced the largest earthquake since 1964. Quakes are always unnerving when objects come crashing to the floor but are powerful reminders that God is in control of our universe. "Therefore we will not fear though the earth gives way, though the mountains be moved into the heart of the sea" (Psalm 46:2).

Pat Hill relaxing with the Wasilla congregation

trative assistant for the OPC's Committee on Foreign Missions, to ask for ideas on how a mature woman on her own could best serve the church. In 1997, when she was 73, Pat taught at the OPC's Missionary Training Institute in South Korea. She also corresponded with missionaries as a way to encourage them. One day Linda recalled being shocked when Pat called to tell her she had decided to head to Wasilla to help their fledgling OP congregation. The Lord indeed had given to her two good reasons to head North—to be near her daughter Jennie and to help the OP church.

Pat found a cute two-bedroom apartment overlooking the magnificent Matanuska Valley near Knik Glacier in a town called Palmer, 15 miles outside Wasilla. She was introduced to our congregation as a widow wanting to serve and to help in Reformed churches that were in various stages of development. It didn't take her long to become a shining light in the land of the midnight sun.

A member of our church body, she proved in three short years to be a "workman approved by God." She never hesitated to befriend younger women and teach them the joys of doing God's work. It became known that her doors were always "open." Her little lime green car was constantly on the go, giving rides or picking up anyone who needed transportation. Ice, snow, or moose on the roads did not deter Pat from getting out and about, even when temperatures dropped below zero or when we had an occasional earthquake. Whenever she drove you to your destination, she would ask, "How can I pray for you this week?"

You always felt you could share with her any need, and she would work hard to find a solution. Her hours spent counseling clients as a volunteer at the Crisis Pregnancy Center and on their 24-hour emergency call line, no doubt persuaded many a young woman to reconsider the life of her unborn child.

Pat easily became a "family member" and some children probably called her "gamma." In our outlying villages the indigenous people call the older people in the villages their elders and show great respect to them and their opinions. Alaska is a young state, and because the winters are long, dark, and cold, a lot of our seniors become "snowbirds" and find more pleasant winter living conditions in the "lower 48." Our churches and community miss the wisdom and lifelong experiences of the elderly so it was a welcomed gift to have Pat in our fellowship.

Her devotion for doing kingdom work didn't stop with our local church. Pat had a passion to help our church family get connected with the missionaries the OPC supported. For a mini-missionary conference she hosted, Pat enlisted young people from our church to help make posters, collect information about our missionaries, and even to cook and eat the foods from their countries. Her enthusiasm also was contagious in the Sunday school classes she taught. Many years later, children reported their fond memories of having her as their teacher.

In her spare time, Pat corrected Bible studies mailed to her from prisoners in local and "stateside" prisons and inspired many others in our church to take on this same outreach ministry.

She demonstrated hospitality by inviting everyone who attended a Sunday evening service to her small but comfortable apartment that had a fabulous view of Pioneer Peak. She also hosted many Saturday prayer breakfasts featuring caribou or moose sausage and Sourdough pancakes with birch syrup.

At these prayer meetings, if you were shy about praying, she gently instructed you in the elements of prayer and made you feel comfortable about praying. I can still hear her saying, "God hears every prayer." If the elders forgot to pray for our nation, our leaders, and those in authority, she would meekly, but firmly, quote the appropriate verses. One verse she often quoted was John 10:10: "I came that they may have life and have it abundantly."

Pat lived an abundant life in our church and community. Often you would hear her giving thanks to God for every situation she found herself in and remind others to do the same. Mother of four adult children, Pat now lives in a retirement home in Sebring, Ohio. The people of the "great land" miss her and would welcome a return visit.

**Wanda Long** *is the wife of Bruce Long, one of the founding elders of Grace OPC in Wasilla, Alaska, and mother of their four adult children. When Patricia Hill attended our church we were meeting in our eighth location. Five more meeting locations and ten years later, by God's providence, we are now meeting in our own building on Bogard Road.*

# Part Four

# Choosing to Live for Christ
# 1990s–2000s

# 44

# Grace Mullen:
# Grace upon Grace

## *Patricia E. Clawson*

Although Grace Elizabeth Mullen looked as if she could be blown away by a strong wind, she was formidable in her love for her Savior and his church. As the first archivist of the Orthodox Presbyterian Church, she strove to preserve its history for generations to come. As God shed his grace upon Grace, he shed his grace through her upon many others.

"I have never known a more godly person than Grace," said Dr. Richard "Dick" Gaffin Jr., emeritus professor at Westminster Theological Seminary.[1] "By God's grace, every fruit of the Spirit I see her as exemplifying."

"Grace was a faithful Christian whose example is without equal to women, young women, and girls," said Kevin Parks, elder at Faith Orthodox Presbyterian Church in Elmer, New Jersey.[2] "Her quiet spirit and gentle personality were second to none, though she never wanted any praise or attention."

Born on March 7, 1943, Grace grew up in southern New Jersey along the waters of the Atlantic and loved every inch of it. Her grandfather I. T. Mullen was a founding ruling elder of Covenant OPC in Vineland, New Jersey.[3] Her uncle Tommy Mullen played

1  Richard B. Gaffin Jr., interview, August 10, 2015.
2  Kevin Parks, email to Patricia Clawson, July 21, 2014.
3  Danny E. Olinger, "Grace Mullen: A Life in the Shadows," *Ordained Servant* 23 (2014): 6, *Ordained Servant Online*, December 2014, http://opc.org/

the organ and had a 28-year streak of perfect attendance at Covenant. It was at Covenant OPC that Grace's father, Hopwood Mullen, met her mother, Rebecca Brandriff, who had grown up in a baptist church in nearby Newfield. They married in 1939 and had two daughters, Rebecca, known as "Becky," and Grace.

In 1946, Grace's parents moved to Wildwood, New Jersey, where Hopwood owned a Ford dealership. It was there, under the preaching of Leslie Dunn, pastor of Calvary OPC in Wildwood, that her mother developed a deep love for the Reformed faith. Sadly, over time Rebecca realized her husband wasn't a believer and struggled with being unequally yoked. Hopwood eventually left the church and lived on his own, yet continued to support his family until his death in 1987. Rebecca, Becky, and Grace became members of Calvary OPC in Wildwood. Grace would remain a member for 31 years.

When Grace was six, OP missionary Polly Gaffin and her children remained behind in Wildwood while Polly's husband, Richard Gaffin Sr., labored as a missionary in Shanghai during the Communist push to control China. "My mom was very helpful in counseling and helping Mrs. Mullen through a very difficult period," recalls Dick Gaffin. Grace, who was a believer since her earliest memory, looked at "Aunt Polly" as her lifelong mentor.

Rebecca instilled in Grace a great love for the church. "The natural affinity of the mother and daughter intensified because they were both strong believers and both committed to the OPC," said Dick.[4]

When Rebecca later moved back to Newfield, New Jersey, she and Grace became members of Faith OPC in Elmer on April 7, 1974. Grace's membership remained at Faith for four decades. By this time, Becky lived in Maryland with her husband and three children. Each summer Grace and Rebecca returned to their Wildwood

---

os.html?article_id=452&issue_id=100. This article provided background for this chapter.

4  Richard B. Gaffin Jr., interview, August 10, 2015.

home and worshipped with the Wildwood congregation.

Grace was educated in Wildwood and became involved with the Boardwalk Chapel, an OPC evangelistic outreach that had opened on the Wildwood boardwalk when Grace was a toddler. She also spent part of her summers at the French Creek Bible Conference in eastern Pennsylvania where her mother was the chief cook for two decades. Over the years as a camper, counselor, lifeguard, and kitchen helper, Grace grew close to many in the OPC, especially with the Lewis Grotenhuis family, whose son John helped to start Middle East Reformed Fellowship and whose daughter Joan and her husband, Ralph English, were OPC missionaries.

When Grace later became the executive secretary for the French Creek board of trustees, she worried on her first night at camp about having responsibility for one hundred children, any-one of whom could have an accident, an illness, food poisoning, or drown, and have great spiritual struggles with Satan, who wanted the hearts and minds of those children. "The week ahead seemed frightening and overwhelming," wrote Grace.[5] "Then I remem-bered how people from New England to Virginia in the churches were praying for French Creek, and I remembered what men of prayer started the conferences and how faithful our God has been over the years. There never has been a drowning or a terrible acci-dent. God has been gracious to us giving us physical protection, but more comforting is that he has blessed and answered prayer. Young people have learned to glorify and enjoy God, the church has been built up, and our young people have been encouraged to love and serve their Lord."

For 15 years, Grace joined Dick and Jean Gaffin and Mary Laubach as cooks for the senior high camp. In the evening when the staff played a dictionary game, Grace fooled other players by cleverly masking the definitions of words by making up new mean-ings, yet often correctly guessing when others did the same thing.

---

5 Grace E. Mullen, speech written at the time of the 40th anniversary of French Creek Bible Conference, 1989.

French Creek's founders, OPC pastors Lewis Grotenhuis, Robert Atwell, and Glenn Coie, insisted on having a co-ed camp to encourage the young people to meet one another, which yielded dozens of marriages. Grace, however, remained single although she corresponded for years with close male friends whom she had known from French Creek and college. Grace never appeared unhappy or missing out on life because she wasn't married, Dick said.

A quiet person with a sharp wit and keen mind, Grace studied English and history at Calvin College in Grand Rapids, Michigan. Her exceptional witness was recognized even in college when she was concerned to "do what's right."[6] One student wrote a friend about why he was dropping off his church rolls: "I don't think I ever want to be a Christian unless it is the kind of Christian Grace Mullen is."[7]

She loved everything outdoors and often rode bikes, climbed trees, and walked through cemeteries in the wee hours with fellow Calvin students. Grace studied abroad in 1963, spending time in Naples, Italy, and the Near East School of Archeology in Jerusalem.

After graduating from Calvin in 1965, Grace's adventurous spirit led her to teach in Christian schools in Charlotte (1965), Philadelphia (1966–1968), San Jose (1969–1970), and even in Shiraz, Iran (1972–1973).

John Kent, a member of Westminster OPC in Westminster, California, first met the 23-year-old Grace when she was his eighth-grade homeroom and English teacher at Philadelphia-Montgomery Christian Academy in 1966. He recalled, "Her combination of an unwavering stand for truth, clever insight into our sinful, junior high behavior, and heart-crushingly stern or heart-meltingly sweet delivery were very helpful, if then not fully appreciated, by an eighth-grade boy."[8]

Grace had earned her master's in English and education from

---

6  Grace E. Mullen, college notebooks.
7  Ibid.
8  John Kent, letter to Danny Olinger, January 11, 2015.

the University of Pennsylvania in 1971 before heading to Iran. In the mid-1970s, she returned to the Philadelphia area where she became an assistant records researcher at the Presbyterian Historical Society.

Her love of libraries, research, and preserving history coalesced in 1975 when she began her 38-year career as archivist and assistant librarian at Westminster Theological Seminary in Glenside, Pennsylvania. Grace diligently worked to help professors, seminarians, and many throughout the world with their research needs. Sandy Finlayson, WTS director of library services, called Grace "the heart of the library's operations."[9] The importance of her work may be best reflected in the number of times her name has been mentioned with thanks in dissertations and books published throughout the world.

Dr. D. Clair Davis dedicated *The Significance of Westminster Theological Seminary Today* to Grace. "I dedicate this with enthusiasm to Grace Mullen, WTS archivist and keeper and lover of the heritage…. I thank you, Grace, for working so hard at keeping our flame."

Calling Grace "an honorable colleague," Dr. James T. Dennison Jr. penned a letter to her on January 1, 1993, recognizing her help on the Francis Turretin book he edited, *Institutes of Elenctic Theology:* "Our Lord Himself knows how much of this is due to your 'Sherlockian' assistance."

Grace became a leading expert on the history of J. Gresham Machen, Bruce Hunt, and Cornelius Van Til. Dr. Van Til became so close to Grace that he bequeathed to her his *Bible* and *Calvin's Institutes,* both of which included his invaluable handwritten notes scribbled on the pages. Grace served as acting library director four times. A month before she died, she was granted honorary membership in the American Theological Library Association for her

9 Sandy Finlayson wrote this in a memorial for the Westminster Theological Seminary website, July 20, 2014, www.wts.edu/stayinformed/view.html?id=1814.

exemplary work.

Although Grace lived with Dick and Jean Gaffin while teaching at Phil-Mont, she grew especially close with Dick during her years at the library. A professor emeritus of biblical and systematic theology at WTS, Dick appreciated her professional competence, theological astuteness, and much more. "We saw things both ecclesiologically and theologically the same way," he said.[10] "In all my years at Westminster, I don't value any relationship more highly than that I had with Grace."

At her funeral, Dick noted Grace's gift of contentment, the very thing that drew Westminster student Ayla Higgins, a widow, to ask Grace how she obtained it. "Without hesitation she said to me, 'Ayla, if I have any contentment in me, it is a gift received from the Lord.'"[11]

Grace had a special devotion to the international students at Westminster, especially for those from Africa. Her interest in Philip Tachin went back to the student days of his father-in-law, the Rev. Anjov Ahenakan. After Philip arrived on the WTS campus from Nigeria in 2002, she often invited him for dinner. Over the months, Philip terribly missed his wife and children but couldn't afford to go to his Nigerian home to see them during school breaks, so he prayed. At one meal, Grace asked if he was going home for Christmas. He said no. The following day Grace told him she was buying him a ticket and would drive him to the airport. She only asked when he returned to bring her his family's photo. That picture was displayed in her living room.

In gratitude, Philip regularly cleaned her home both inside and out, then read the Bible, gave a brief exhortation, and prayed with her. After he graduated with his doctorate, Grace prayed for him and supported his ministry back in Nigeria, the Reformed Outreach Initiative. He has since been appointed as executive chairman of Nigeria's State Universal Basic Education Board. Her name

10  Gaffin interview.
11  Ayla Higgins, email to Patricia Clawson, January 25, 2016.

has been imprinted on many Bibles and on two boreholes drilled for water in Nigeria. "I think of her as a mother and a selfless believer who denied herself of all affluence in order to help others with her hard earned money," he said.[12]

Grace Mullen at the Westminster Theological Seminary graduation of Dr. Philip Tachin

Later on when Grace's cancer was getting the upper hand, Philip often called from Nigeria to encourage her to remain strong in her faith during that last difficult trial. "She showed that her priorities were not on earthly things, though important they were to her, but on heavenly realities. I've tried to emulate her life here in Nigeria," said Philip.

Grace's care for international students as well as her support of the OPC's work of foreign missions may well have stemmed from her mother, Rebecca. Her mother was involved with her church's Women's Missionary Society and contributed Bibles for worldwide distribution.

Every weekend Grace left WTS and drove more than an hour to South Jersey to spend time with her mother. Grace and Rebecca were very hospitable and both were heavenly minded. Neither cared too much for the trappings of this world. They wouldn't buy something new if they could strap together what they had and make do.[13] Independent, strong willed, and faithful to the end, Rebecca lived by herself until she was 99. She died on December 10, 2012, three months after turning 100. A year and a half later,

12  Philip Tachin, email to Patricia Clawson, April 2015.
13  Beverly Mariani in an interview with Patricia Clawson in May 2015.

Grace went to be with the Lord at the age of 71. Older sister Becky died the following year on November 10, 2015.

Grace's impact on the OPC grew after close friend Charles "Charlie" Dennison, an OP pastor, became our denomination's historian in 1981. At the time, the entire OPC archives fit into a shoebox. Grace diligently worked with Charlie to transform that shoe box into what today is housed in a large room on the second floor of the OPC offices. Before the collection moved there, Grace first stored them in her home and then for 20 years in the basement of WTS. Even while battling cancer, after a busy day at the library she often worked on the archives with Danny Olinger, president of the Historian's Committee. His deep friendship with Grace prompted him to buy a house down the block from her home when he became general secretary for the Committee on Christian Education. At the door to the archives hangs a plaque naming the place the *Grace Mullen Archives Room*. This recognition she didn't want but accepted only after Danny showed her the already engraved plaque. He knew she wouldn't want to waste the Committee for the Historian's money.

Charlie and Grace respected each other on many levels. Until his death in 1999, she listened to Charlie's cassette-taped sermons, which were mailed to her weekly from Pittsburgh. He often sent his poems to her for input. In 1994 he wrote: "Thank you for your help and encouragement over the last year. You do not know your value to the ministry here."

Grace also was of kindred mind with Lane Tipton, WTS professor, whom she asked to teach a study on the writings of theologian Geerhardus Vos. Lane led the monthly Vos Group in her home for 15 years.

Twenty-four years after I first met Grace when my husband studied at Westminster, we moved back to Philly and shared a pew with her during evening worship at Calvary OPC. After spending each weekend in New Jersey with her mother, Grace rarely missed an evening service back in Glenside, even after being diagnosed with Leimyosarcoma during surgery in 2003. Finding out how

Grace was doing as she battled this difficult-to-treat cancer was a challenge since she never liked to talk about herself. Gradually I learned that she had a malignancy of the smooth muscle tissue which resulted in tumors growing in many parts of her body.

Over her decade of fighting this disease, Grace had tumors develop in so many places I lost count. She had radiation at least seven times, chemotherapy a minimum of six times, half a dozen surgeries, and numerous hospitalizations. She continued working through her chemo and radiation treatments. When she finally went on disability ten years after her diagnosis, she still had 100 unused sick days.

If you asked Grace how she was, she would say OK. But as the cancer advanced, if you asked about her pain level, more and more often she would say in a quiet voice, "Not so good." Many of us didn't realize the toll the cancer was taking, but sitting next to her in the pew, I learned that if Grace sat down during a hymn she was in a lot of pain. Out of necessity she began to rely on others, which was difficult for someone so independent.

When her right hand started trembling, I offered to hold the hymnal. She would have none of that. She simply sang from memory. When driving after dark became troublesome, her frustration turned to blessing as I gave her rides to and from church. We became more than pew buddies. We became friends.

On January 2, 2014, I took Grace to an appointment with Dr. Joseph Mambu, her primary physician for many years. While Grace sat on the examination table, he explained that in the last two weeks, her tumors had doubled. He told her no more chemo, something she had already decided. But he thought radiation might help shrink the tumors. A tall man with thick white hair, he placed his hands gently on Grace's thin shoulders and put his face close to hers. "You could have radiation or you could let the cancer take over you. It would be the end of you."

Grace serenely looked up at him. "Physically it might take me over, but there's more than this life. To be absent in body is to be present with the Lord."

"You certainly are an inspiration," he said.

"I pray I'll be faithful. He is faithful to us." When the doctor asked if she was anxious about what was to come, she assured him she wasn't.

"Your faith has a lot to do with it," the doctor replied.

"It has everything to do with it," Grace assured him. "I am satisfied with what is happening."

"You are a shining example of faith," Mambu said, then added that if she was a nun she would have qualified for sainthood.

He didn't understand that she had been gifted with sainthood a long time before.

Just two weeks past her 71st birthday, Grace moved into a skilled care facility. In the providence of God, one of the first people she met was a tall young man who greeted her, "Hello Grace!" He was the nursing home's chaplain and a former seminarian whom she had often helped in the library.

In her room, she slept much of the time and became so skinny her flesh barely covered her wrist bones. Often she was too exhausted to open her eyes and spoke in a whisper, yet always asked about the other person. Grace was afraid that as her memory slipped, her faith also might fade so she asked friends to write down the Scripture passages they had read to her so she could remember them. What struck me was her response every time I asked what I could pray for. Help for her pain? Healing? Wisdom for the doctors? She only answered, "That I would be faithful."

In June 2014, the 81st General Assembly in Grand Rapids, Michigan, gave her a resolution of thanks "for the many ways your gentle, quiet, and faithful service has enriched the life of our denomination."

The last time Dick and Jean Gaffin saw Grace, she was very weak and couldn't get out of bed. He read from Romans 8, then prayed. Grace wasn't the huggy type, but Dick took her hand. "She gripped my hand when I took it, strongly affirming the truth of that which I read and prayed."

Her earthly service ended at 7:40 p.m. on Sunday, July 20,

2014. Her dearest friend Beverly Mariani and Danny Olinger listened as Lane Tipton read Romans 8. She momentarily opened her eyes and looked at Bev, who told Grace that she loved her and was happy she was going Home. A few verses later, Bev quietly said, "I think she's not breathing."

What a marvelous, quiet, peaceful way to go to your Heavenly Father. That night I wrote in my journal. "The lessons I learned from Grace—Don't complain. Care more about the other person. Listen and remember. Be content. Don't let your suffering and pain be a burden to others—please help me to cultivate those qualities in my life to reflect you."

Grace embodied the essence of 1 Peter 3:4: "Let your adorning be the hidden person of the heart with the imperishable beauty of a gentle and quiet spirit, which in God's sight is very precious."

**Patricia E. Clawson** *is the editorial assistant for* New Horizons *in the OPC and office secretary for the OPC's Committee on Christian Education. Pat was a reporter for three newspapers, including nearly a decade as a freelance reporter for the* Chicago Tribune. *A member of Calvary OPC in Glenside, Pennsylvania, she is married to Douglas Clawson, associate general secretary for the Committee on Foreign Missions. They have three daughters, two sons-in-law, two grandsons, and two step-granddaughters.*

# 45
# Juliet "Judy" Griffin and Carolyn Sackett: Lasting Fruit from VBS

## Susan Hollister

Vacation Bible schools have provided gospel opportunities for the Orthodox Presbyterian Church since our denomination began in 1936. VBS programs aim at the very center of Christ's call to his people to announce the good news of the gospel, with OPC women involved in every aspect.

Articles in *The Presbyterian Guardian* (published from 1935 to 1979)[1] describe the historic efforts of women with respect to VBS. At times the program's director was a woman,[2] such as Eleanor Shaw, wife of Pastor Lyle Shaw of Trinity OPC in Newport, Kentucky. She directed an evening VBS with 506 children in 1938.[3] That same year, Emily Gray, wife of Pastor Richard Gray of Covenant OPC of Orange, New Jersey, assisted in preparing curriculum for their two-week program, which included illustrations

---

1 *The Presbyterian Guardian* was closely associated with the OPC, although it remained an independent magazine. See http://opc.org/guardian.html.
2 Winifred A. Clelland, "Vacation Opportunity: The Summer Bible School," *Presbyterian Guardian* 19 (April 1950): 65, http://opc.org/cfh/guardian/Volume_19/1950-04.pdf.
3 "Daily Vacation Bible Schools of the Presbyterian Church of America," *Presbyterian Guardian* 5 (September 1938): 170, http://opc.org/cfh/guardian/Volume_5/1938-09.pdf.

of the daily lessons for 71 students.[4] Harriet Teal, Margaret Duff, Norma Ellis, Ruth Hamilton, and Ruth Schauffele are all appreciatively mentioned in OPC historical literature for their VBS involvement.[5] In 1948 the OPC's Committee on Christian Education hired Betty Colburn as office secretary and writer for the beginner department of the VBS program for the denomination.[6] In 1954 Dorothy Anderson Barker wrote a VBS workbook for juniors called "Our Bible." It was at this time that the OPC began to publish VBS and other educational materials under the name Great Commission Publications.[7]

Once denominational materials were available in the 1950s, the number of VBS programs increased substantially.[8] Often ministry to VBS attendees extended beyond the classes as teachers were encouraged to visit every student's home to share Christ's work with parents and to help families obtain Bible materials.[9] VBS remains one of the most visible and popular programs for educating covenant children, as well as interacting with the wider community.

Among the many women who have directed, taught, and written materials for VBS programs in the OPC are Judy Griffin and Carolyn Sackett, two women who have made unique contributions.

### Judy Griffin

Juliet "Judy" Ann Griffin was born on January 13, 1920, in

---

4 Ibid.

5 D. G. Hart, *Between the Times: The Orthodox Presbyterian Church in Transition, 1945–1990* (Willow Grove, PA: Committee for the Historian of the OPC, 2011), 169.

6 Charles G. Dennison, ed., *The Orthodox Presbyterian Church 1936–1986* (Philadelphia, PA: Committee for the Historian of the OPC, 1986), 37.

7 In the 1970s Great Commission Publications became a joint venture of the OPC and the Presbyterian Church in America. Dorothy Anderson Barker and Penny Pappas are among those who wrote children's educational materials for GCP.

8 Robley J. Johnston, "DVBS Materials," *Presbyterian Guardian* 27 (April 1958): 50, http://opc.org/cfh/guardian/Volume_27/1958-04.pdf.

9 Hart, *Between the Times*, 176.

Schenectady, New York.[10] She gained an appreciation for sharing the gospel in part by observing the evangelistic efforts of her parents as they hosted weekly Bible studies in their home. Following their example, Judy served in many capacities, one of which was developing an excellent thematic VBS curriculum.

When Judy was nine her family moved to Maplewood, New Jersey, where her father was a high school teacher. At 17, Judy graduated from high school and won a scholarship to Wilson College in Chambersburg, Pennsylvania. Although she majored in economics, the scholarship required that Judy study Greek, Latin, and Hebrew. After graduating in 1941, she was hired at Jersey Bell Telephone Company. Judy became involved with the OPC and the Machen League of New Jersey.[11] As president of the Machen League, Judy worked closely with young adults, and wrote and distributed a newsletter entitled *The Machen Leaguer*.[12] It was during this time that Judy developed a deep interest in studying theology. This interest led to a regular correspondence with Professor Cornelius Van Til of Westminster Theological Seminary, as Judy studied his lectures and syllabi on systematic theology and apologetics.[13]

Working at New Jersey Bell, Judy was promoted to business office supervisor. Frederick John Griffin Jr., trained her and won her heart. They were married in 1950. Four years later, Judy, Fred, and their two young children, Nancy and Glen, moved to Westfield, New Jersey, and joined Grace OPC, pastored by Rev. Leslie A. Dunn.

Although Judy was no longer employed outside the home, she labored diligently, using her executive abilities in many ways.

10 Nancy Anderson, email to Susan Hollister, July 8, 2015.

11 "Young People Hold Rally of Philadelphia Presbytery," *Presbyterian Guardian* 19 (July 1958): 139, http://opc.org/cfh/guardian/Volume_19/1958-07.pdf. Machen League was an organization for OPC youth, first established by the Presbytery of Philadelphia.

12 Nancy Anderson, email to Susan Hollister, July 8, 2015. *The Machen Leaguer* was later renamed *League Talk*.

13 Judy Griffin, correspondence with a friend, July 2007.

By 1956 Judy was the superintendent of the Sunday school at Grace OPC. She also organized many events, such as mother-daughter dinners, prayer retreats, and adult fellowship programs. In 1968 she was in charge of the registration for the general assembly, which met at Grace OPC that year. Judy liked to utilize the giftedness of others. Once she established a program, such as one for

Judy and Fred Griffin

the junior and senior high Sunday school, she wrote guides, and then helped others to take leadership of the program themselves.

During the late 1950s to the early 1970s, Judy authored and directed the VBS programs for the families and neighborhood children of Grace Church. OPC minister and Kuyper College Professor Douglas Felch was one of Judy Griffin's students in the late 1960s and early 1970s. "Judy is one of the brightest people I have ever known," Felch said. "The material Judy wrote was truly innovative. She was ahead of her time."

Each year, Judy took a simple idea, such as an airplane, a castle, a ship, or an Indian reservation, and transformed the entire church with special decorations to correlate with that idea. The various programs were named after the street address of Grace Church, such as "Midvale Castle" or "The SS Midvale." All the lessons, skits, music, crafts, activities, and rewards coordinated with the annual theme. "The kids absolutely loved it," said Felch, who described (with great enthusiasm!) the console he was in charge of building for the airplane-themed VBS program so many years ago. During Professor Felch's seminary years, he told his colleagues about the program, and subsequently sent them the material Judy wrote so they could use it in their own VBS programs.

Although small framed and not too strong, Judy exerted a tremendous amount of energy for the Lord. Unfortunately while her children were still young, Judy suffered a "state of collapse and was confined to bed for many months."[14] The diagnosis was unclear. The doctors felt that she had worn herself out, working constantly and striving for perfection. This, too, was used for God's glory as Judy shared with those around her the lessons God had for her in this time of weakness.

Not only was Judy involved in VBS, in the 1970s, she and other women of Grace OPC began a ministry called "Meet Us at the Coffee Pot." It drew many women from outside the church to share refreshments and listen to a gospel presentation. For the next 30 years, Judy studied Scripture and wrote weekly Bible studies for women. She also corresponded with missionaries and friends for decades. In 2007 there were still 96 people on her correspondence list.[15] In 2015 Judy, at 95, was still talking on the phone and receiving visitors who sat under her teaching at VBS.

Rev. Steven Miller is one of the many who have benefitted from Judy's service for Christ. Miller was an OPC minister from 1977 to 2014 and recently retired as pastor of First Reformed Presbyterian Church of North America in Beaver Falls, Pennsylvania. Miller knew Judy when he was a child in Westfield, New Jersey. "She loved children, and worked extremely hard," he recalled. On many occasions when young people were at her house, Judy would sit down with every one of them and press the claims of Christ. Once, Miller and "Mrs. Griffin," as he respectfully called her, were sitting on the front steps. By his own admission, he was a "rowdy little kid." At one point in the conversation, Judy asked him, "Steve, are you really happy?" The Lord used times like these to draw Steve, and ultimately they served to guide him into ministry.

14  Nancy Anderson, email to Susan Hollister, July 8, 2015.
15  Judy Griffin, correspondence with a friend, July 2007.

In 2014, during his last visit with Judy, who was 94 at the time, she said that she didn't feel that she had done all she could do for the Lord. At this point in my phone interview with Pastor Miller, his voice began to crack and he paused a moment before continuing the conversation. Then with deep respect for this woman whom God used so powerfully in his own life, as well as in the lives of many youth, he said he began to remind her how the Lord revived Grace OPC, in part from her efforts. He reminded her of the areas of service in which he and so many others have labored. "This too," he said to her, "is part of your fruit."

## Carolyn Sackett

With a heart for evangelism, Carolyn Sackett also uniquely contributed to the VBS outreach programs of OP churches. Carolyn was born in Moline, Illinois, on May 20, 1939, and grew up in Waverly, Iowa. Carolyn's love of nature developed there as she explored the woods near her home and participated in Girl Scouts. When she came to Christ at age 12, Carolyn discovered the joy of sharing the truths of God's Word with her friends. After graduating from Iowa State University in 1961, Carolyn married Dick Sackett, and moved to the Wheaton/ Winfield area in Illinois, where she and her husband raised four children.[16]

During the 1980s and 1990s, in addition to serving in Pioneer Clubs in her church, Bethel OPC in Wheaton, Illinois, Carolyn worked as a volunteer naturalist at Fullersburg Woods Nature Education Center and as a scout leader. After a difficult split at Bethel Church reduced its numbers by more than half in 1989, the congregation was concerned about how they would be able to provide a VBS for their children and those of the neighborhood with so few to teach and organize the VBS. Carolyn came up with the idea of combining her love of nature and her desire to share the gospel by developing the *Nature Camp Discovery Series*, a summer Bible school curriculum. The program worked wonderfully for

16  Carolyn Sackett, email to Susan Hollister, September 2, 2015.

Carolyn Sackett

the church since it was designed to utilize just a few leaders—a Bible teacher, a nature teacher, and several small-group leaders—perfect for a small church with many students.

Part of the beauty of Nature Camp is that it relates the natural fascination children have in the world around them to the majesty of the God of creation, the sinful condition of man, and what God has done through Jesus Christ to save sinners.

"This camp is unique," said Jim Megchelsen, pastor of Covenant of Grace OPC in Sugar Grove, Illinois. "It is not just a boxed camp theme or a gimmick. The kids really love it." This enthusiastic response has been repeated in other churches and locations. "From a church planter's perspective," said Pastor Megchelsen, "Nature Camp has made an impact on our community. It became a calling card for us, a helpful way to get the word out about our church."

Karin Potoshnick has taught the nature class portion of the Nature Camp at Bethel OPC in Wheaton for 25 years. Several years ago during the *Incredible Insects Nature Camp*, Mrs. Potoshnick brought Madagascar walking sticks to class. These creatures, when mature, have exquisite pink wings. While the class listened to her explain the nature of a walking stick, one of these creatures was hidden on a milkweed pod. As Mrs. Potoshnick taught about how God protected these creatures through camouflage, one took flight, and to the delight of the class, landed on one of the student's heads displaying the beauty of its delicate design! Mrs. Potoshnick had the students' attention and encouraged them to trust God who has created such marvelous creatures. Today at least 24 churches in 13 states, and several mission works in various countries have used the *Nature Camp Discovery Series* summer Bible school curriculum.[17]

17  Carolyn Sackett, phone interview, September 3, 2015.

Carolyn's heart for evangelism has extended beyond writing VBS materials. Since 1970 she has been involved in neighborhood Bible studies, sharing God's Word with women of all faiths. Since 2000 she has shared concepts of nature and the works of Christian authors with adults as a facilitator at a local chapter of the Lifelong Learning Institute. She uses this opportunity to teach Christian classics, such as *Mere Christianity*, *A Grief Observed*, and *The Four Loves* by C. S. Lewis, to bring Christian themes into discussion. In 2010 she began tutoring in the adult literacy and English as a Second Language programs of Waubonsee Community College.

God has blessed the spread of the gospel through VBS programs in the OPC. From the service of Judy Griffin and Carolyn Sackett, and many others like them, we have enjoyed remarkable, lasting fruit.

**Susan Hollister** *lives in Homer Glen, Illinois, with her husband, Rev. Bruce Hollister. They have four children and two grandchildren. She is a member of New Covenant Community Church of Joliet, Illinois, where Bruce is pastor. Sue has a master's degree in education and has taught in public and private schools, including home school.*

# 46

# Diana Coppes, Greta Entingh, Virginia Dennison, and Susan Winslow: Snapshots of Hospitality

## *Tricia Ann Stevenson*

Throughout the history of the Orthodox Presbyterian Church, hospitality has been crucial to its growth, both spiritually and numerically. I was assigned the privilege of interviewing some of the women in our denomination who are known for their hospitality. Since I love photography and capturing everyday moments in the life of the church and at home, I will present "snapshots" of four godly women, with stories spanning the past 40 years, from four different regions of the country. Each of these women has the same goal—hospitality. The hallmark of their service is grace and gratitude. These ladies know how to make a meal stretch and serve what is on hand. They know how to adjust the kind of hospitality shown according to their circumstances. When in God's providence they experienced times of loss or difficulties with their health, they benefited from the care of others, then passed on this care in thankfulness. These women followed the encouragement of the apostle Paul, who said, "Blessed be the God and Father of our Lord Jesus Christ, the Father of mercies and God of all comfort, who comforts us in all our affliction, so that we may be able to comfort those who are in any affliction, with the comfort with which we ourselves are comforted by God" (2 Cor. 1:3–4). They continued to open their doors willingly. Why? It's simple really. They love the Lord, and they love people.

"Cut it small and serve it all!" rang the voice of Diana Coppes, wife of Rev. Leonard Coppes, a retired OPC pastor who served three congregations. Now living in Colorado, Diana and Leonard are still eager to fellowship with others who come through the doors of Providence OPC in Denver.

Diana knows you can show hospitality over tuna casserole or macaroni and cheese. Her dishes are simple and good. It amused her when a guest asked for a recipe for a dish Diana had just "invented" with what she had on hand. Diana knows that people need to be "familied." "That's a verb, you know," she explains sweetly. People need to feel special, and what better way than around a table with food.

Hospitality isn't always easy. Leonard recalls when a guest broke furniture that then had to be replaced and when someone countered their offer of a meal with a request to go to a restaurant. Sometimes people were just looking for money or a handout, but Diana and Leonard offered them hospitality anyway.

Diana told me of her lonely days when her husband attended Westminster Theological Seminary in Philadelphia and worked at the library there. Her remedy to her loneliness was encouraging her husband to invite to dinner any young men who happened to be in the library that day while he was working. Diana would take the

train home from her job in Princeton and serve a dinner that evening to whoever showed up using whatever was in the pantry. Some of these men, like OP minister Larry Wilson and elder Edward Tress, became lifelong

Leonard and Diana Coppes

friends of the Coppeses. When someone comes to your home, it gives you a great way to develop a relationship.

Diana reflects that hospitality is more than food. It is sitting quietly with someone. It is being there. It is giving them the time they need, when they need it, and being flexible.

"Hospitality is a passion of mine," says Greta Entingh. Greta is a charter member of Redeemer OPC in Ada, Michigan. Her heart for visitors is evident in her consistent weekly effort. Greta wants first-time visitors who walk through the church doors to feel welcome. She keeps a card in her Bible on which to write the names of visitors and then invites them for a meal the following week. This helps to assure their return. She hosts them with another regular attending family in order to make connections. If there are children, she will endeavor to connect them to activities, like youth group. Greta wants people to feel "enfolded and welcomed," and she does that in her home with food.

Greta loves people of all ages. As a nurse, she makes her "rounds" of the older people in her congregation to see how they are doing. She notes that a card or phone call could make a difference in someone's day. She remembers with gratitude times when others showed they cared for her while she was on bed rest or busy with young children at home. According to Greta, hospitality doesn't have to be difficult—it can be accomplished with a trip to the store on the way to a

Greta Entingh chatting after church

visit. A loaf of bread with some soup, or a rotisserie chicken and a bagged salad can easily be obtained for a family in need. "Not only is this helpful," she says, "but you are touching their lives by letting them know that someone was thinking of them that day."

Greta remembers when her children were young how fun it was for them to be involved with hospitality. Everyone enjoyed the food and fellowship. It was part of the routine at home. Her quieter husband preferred fellowship at home around the table. The goal was to help connect people with others and to make them feel comfortable and welcomed.

"Keep your eyes out for new people and have something prepared to serve extra," advises Virginia "Ginger" Dennison. The daughter of Rev. Robert Graham, one of the original OP pastors from 1936, Ginger has enjoyed the benefit of getting to know others through food and fellowship throughout her life. Her mother, Ruth Graham, served a formal dinner each year for the elders and deacons of the church, with fresh flowers on the table and a rib roast. When Ginger married OP minister Charles Dennison, she continued this annual tradition. She also systematically worked her way through the church directory, hosting others in the church with a less formal meal during the week. When they moved to Grace OPC in Sewickley, Pennsylvania, they had people from all over coming to worship with them. This gave them an opportunity to connect others around their table.

Despite having a busy household with four boys, Ginger persisted in hospitality, knowing that it benefited the church when the pastor's family and others were being hospitable to new people. In fact, you could say that Ginger's hospitality was "contagious," as many families in the church invited guests to Sunday dinner. Ginger knew that any visitor who came through the door would be invited to someone's home. It was an effective way to get to know each other, give people an opportunity to ask questions about the church, and develop friendships.

When the OPC's general assembly was held at Geneva College, not far from Sewickley, many of the commissioners worshipped at

Grace Church on Sunday. Ginger's husband, Charlie, invited to their home for dinner as many commissioners as would fit around the table. "Charlie was the life of the party," she recalls. These were wonderful times of fellowship that lingered all afternoon.

Sunday evenings were an opportunity to host college students for a time of food and good discussion. OP folks who needed to fly out of Pittsburgh often stayed with Charlie and Ginger. The Dennisons had a hide-away bed in the living room with clean sheets on hand.

During those years in Sewickley, Ginger was known in her family for her "fab five" dishes. These were the five fallback meals that she knew were good, that people liked, and that she didn't have to think about how to prepare. Among these "fab five" were beef roast with a wine and tomato sauce and marinated chicken. She also had at-the-ready a homemade chocolate sauce with sherry. It could easily be heated up and served over vanilla ice cream. "The recipe made a large quantity, and it could keep in the refrigerator for a month," she says.

Ginger and Charlie Dennison (left) showing hospitality to Susan and David Winslow and their two daughters

After Charlie died, Ginger's opportunities for hospitality changed. She could still serve and carry on a conversation, but age and circumstances, along with a move to a new congregation, created a different atmosphere for her. Yet even in this new place and situation, she often opens her home to a visiting minister or someone in need.

"The goal is to make people refreshed and comfortable," says Susan Winslow, wife of David Winslow, an elder at Westminster OPC in Westminster, California. Since 1980, the Winslows have organized the Presbytery of Southern California's backpacking expedition in the Sierra Mountains for high school and college-age young people in the church. Despite what Susan described as a "colorful" childbearing career with miscarriage, bed rest, and little ones, she helped to organize these annual trips for the benefit of others. Some years she hiked with the group, although a heart attack in 2010 now precludes her hiking in high altitudes.

"It was the love of the people that drew me into the church," Susan recalls as she describes her first experience, at age 14, of hospitality in a Reformed church. "People were welcoming, they were nice to each other, and I was comfortable, happy, and content. I asked questions, and from there I came to faith."

David and Susan open their home out of a heart of gratitude, knowing that the Lord blesses such service. Susan doesn't want to miss out on opportunities to serve others, even when those opportunities happen on the spur of the moment and the only thing available is popcorn and drinks. "Do your best as unto the Lord using the means he has given you providentially at that time. You may need to serve canned soup or have to host while you have a sick child. This is all in his providence, and it is your best at that time whatever the circumstances." She adds, "I learned pretty early on that it's best if the hostess doesn't apologize for things that are not sin! Don't apologize—or call attention to—the dust, the clutter, the scant provisions, the crying baby, the poor lighting, the last minute invitation, the paper plates, or the fact that you forgot the mustard for the hot dog feast. If you need to say something, do it with a

laugh and a cheer-
ful "oops! forgot the
mustard!" and then
move on. Everyone
is more relaxed and
comfortable if they
don't sense that the
hostess is anxious."

Susan knows
you can make
guests comfortable
by showing them
where the glass-
es are and telling

David and Susan Winslow

them to help themselves to drinks while they visit. She recalls times
when she was hosted in homes that were neatly vacuumed and
gussied up and in homes where everyone pitched in over PB&J. It
didn't matter to her; she just loved it.

A can of paint is how former guests remember the Winslows'
place. They had a tradition of asking their guests to add their painted handprints to a special wall. The now covered-over wall was a
testimony of the many people the Winslows blessed over the years
by opening their home. It was also a testimony of how God blessed
the Winslows through their fellowship with those guests.

So, what can we learn from these snapshots of hospitality? One
of the things I have gleaned from these ladies was the benefit of
gratitude in our lives when serving one another. As we chatted, I recalled times when those in my circles modeled Christian hospitality
in their homes. The stories we shared pressed me to remember that
the Lord knows our weaknesses and our needs, and he gives us
the strength to serve. Even when we feel lonely we can reach out
to others who are in need. A cup of tea or a simple meal, a phone
call, a card, or a time of fellowship can be a benefit to those in the
church. All of these things show hospitality. When we serve with
a sincere and willing spirit, we show Christ. Our homes and our

tables can be welcoming, comfortable, loving places where we model for future hostesses the reality of what it means to practice Christian hospitality. The apostle Paul tells all of us, "Contribute to the needs of the saints and seek to show hospitality" (Romans 12:13).

**Tricia Ann Stevenson** *is married to Pastor Jim G. Stevenson who serves at Providence OPC in Tulsa, Oklahoma. She is the mother of four children: Rachel, Bethany, Jacob, and Joshua, known in OPC circles as "Calvinist Kids in the Kitchen." She and her daughter Rachel have volunteered during general assembly as photographers for* New Horizons.

# 47

# Barbara Needham, Shelly Weaver, and Ginny Wisdom: Chaplains' Wives Preserving the Home Front

## *Lindsey M. Roberts*

He gets up early and runs alongside a soldier to help her pass a physical training run test. Without changing out of PTs (physical training uniform), he keeps running, literally, to make an appointment with a married couple intent upon divorce and counsels them to save their marriage. Then comes what's called the "ministry of presence"—where he spends time with soldiers while they do their work—and the admin: he documents the hospital visits, funerals, counseling sessions. The last part of the day is spent comforting a sergeant major and his kids, who are mourning the recent passing of their wife and mother. This is all in a typical day's work for a military chaplain, and all before he goes home to shepherd his own family.

What about his wife's day? Where is the *she* behind this *he*? As one US Army bumper sticker states: "Army Wife: Toughest job in Army." In a normal day, a military chaplain's wife must be ready to stop her own labors long enough to listen to her husband talk about his grief over that sergeant who lost his wife at 40. To listen to how her husband prayed over the woman while she was in a coma before she died. Ultimately, the military chaplain's wife is the counselor's counselor. And in a *not*-normal day, she must be at all times prepared to have her husband come home and tell her that he's going to be deployed. She has to be ready, at a moment's notice, to pick up the full responsibility of the decision-making, the bills, the house repairs, the schooling, the discipline, the heart-to-hearts with teenage sons.

The Orthodox Presbyterian Church has a long history of caring for those who serve as soldiers and chaplains in the US military. In 1944, only a few years after the OPC's founding in 1936, 20 Westminster Theological Seminary graduates served as chaplains in the armed forces, eight of whom belonged to the OPC. Some of these men helped to care for the bodies and souls of wounded on the battlefields of World War II, sharing the comfort of Jesus Christ, which was their comfort, too.[1] In 1978 the OPC and the Presbyterian Church in America formed the Presbyterian and Reformed Commission on Chaplains and Military Personnel,[2] before the OPC formed its own standing committee on chaplains in 1997.[3]

Many of these chaplains have wives who walk beside them during their military journey. Some women know that they are saying yes to military life as well as yes to their husbands when they marry. Some women don't, as their husbands feel God's call to go into chaplain work later. Carmen Black wasn't a chaplain's wife, but when she married Glenn Black, a World War II pilot,[4] in 1942, she knew she would face similar responsibilities and fears. In 1944 Glenn was injured in North Africa. His life spared, he came home and became an OPC pastor and later a regional home missionary. What Carmen wrote in the March 1983 issue of *New Horizons*,

1 "Today in OPC History—Chaplains in WWII, February 10," http://opc.org/today.html?history_id=83.
2 James C. Pakala, "History of the PRCC," http://pcamna.org/chaplain-ministries/about-the-prcc/prcchistory.
3 Robert B. Needham, "The OPC's Chaplaincy Ministry," *New Horizons* 28 (July 2007): 10, http://opc.org/nh.html?article_id=516.
4 "Today in OPC History—Chaplains in WWII, February 10," http://opc.org/today.html?history_id=83.

remains true for chaplains' wives: "As a pastor's wife, I feel my responsibility is to try to keep my home in good order so that my husband is free to carry out his God-given responsibilities as pastor of the flock, to love him, to encourage him, and to

Barbara and Bob Needham with daughter Bethel

share his problems.... Nowhere in Scripture do I find any special orders for pastors' wives only." Nor are there any special orders for military chaplains' wives.[5]

Barbara Needham, born in Connecticut in 1941, is one whose husband felt the call after marriage. Robert "Bob" Needham, born in Chicago in 1936, went into the Navy Reserves after seminary and ordination, and was shortly after called into active duty. Barbara learned how to be a mom in her own mom's house in Provincetown, Massachusetts, while Bob was gone. After Bob returned, they moved to San Diego, where they had another daughter, and where Barbara got the kids to church by herself each Sunday while Bob conducted services on up to five ships. Their third daughter was born in California, and their fourth in Charlestown, South Carolina.

Like many military wives, Barbara has had her share of hardships: learning to be a mom without her husband; moving across the country while pregnant; enduring three deployments. And like most military wives, Barbara is a humble servant who doesn't think she's a hero any more than Bob thinks he is. They both just did

5 "Today in OPC History—Glenn and Carmen Black, December 31," http://opc.org/today.html?history_id=266.

what God asked them to. "God puts you in different situations at different times," she says. "And your obligation is to bloom where he plants you. Work for God wherever you are."[6]

Shelly Weaver has been a chaplain's wife almost her entire marriage.[7] It was certainly her prayers over the years that helped hold Shelly, her husband, Navy Capt. Bryan "Battle Chaps" Weaver, and their three sons together and allowed Bryan the freedom to serve wholeheartedly. Bryan, born in 1955,[8] ministered to sailors and marines, starting in 1986, spending 19 years of his 29 years of service with the Marines. He is celebrated for many brave moments, including disarming an enemy combatant with a homemade knife in Kosovo in 2003.[9] Once, "[h]e crawled under fire from fighting hole to fighting hole encouraging Marines in Combat," said Robert Coie, an OPC elder and secretary of the OPC Committee on Chaplains and Military Personnel. Bryan is believed to be the most decorated Navy chaplain at the time of his death in April 2016, receiving the John H. Craven Servant Leadership Award from the US Navy in 2014[10] and the Reformed Presbyterian Theological Seminary Alumni Faithful Servant Award in 2015.[11]

Military chaplains' wives fear that harm may come to their husbands when deployed (chaplains aren't allowed to carry guns, so they depend on the protection of their soldiers). Yet they carry on with their own responsibilities, which include tasks normally passed on to husbands—taking out the trash, mowing the lawn, shoveling the snow, getting up on ladders to change light bulbs. Shelly

6  Email correspondence with Barbara Needham and her daughter, Bethel.
7  "Captain Bryan J. 'Battle Chaps' Weaver," obituary, *Island Packet*, April 9, 2016, http://www.legacy.com/obituaries/islandpacket/obituary.aspx-?n=Bryan-J-Weaver-BattleChaps&pid=179562751.
8  Ibid.
9  Email correspondence with Robert Coie.
10  "Chaplain Weaver Honored," August 12, 2014, http://www.opc.org/news.html?news_id=213.
11  "A Plea for Prayer," December 2015, no. 155, http://www.opc.org/chaplain/PrayPlea155.pdf.

did all this, and she was Bryan's faithful helpmate every step of the way. When Bryan wanted the OPC to send supplies overseas during one of his deployments, the

Shelly and Bryan Weaver and their three sons

denomination contacted Shelly to figure out how to get about $30,000 worth of goods to him. Included were some two tons of beef jerky, phone cards, sewing kits, and more, from 31 churches. Within five minutes, she had given instructions for shipping supplies securely.[12] As her husband faced his last battle, one with brain cancer, Shelly's verse of comfort was Romans 12:12: "Rejoice in hope, be patient in tribulation, be constant in prayer." Indeed, Bryan's last words were: "Jesus, Jesus."

With a husband working irregular hours, and sometimes deployed for months at a time, there is often no choice but to lean upon the Lord and pray that he would help in extraordinary ways to provide someone to watch the kids while Mom goes grocery shopping or to help clean the house. Robert Coie is the organizer of the OPC's Plea for Prayer, a list of prayers for military personnel within the denomination.[13] He explains, "The wife takes on the role of explaining why Daddy isn't there, of being Daddy and Mom, of disciplining kids when there's no backup around, and then all of the household responsibilities." In many ways, military chaplains' wives must balance two extremes: becoming more

12  Information from Robert Coie.
13  "A Plea for Prayer," January 2016, no. 156, http://opc.org/chaplain/ PrayPlea156.pdf.

Chris and Ginny Wisdom

independent and self-sufficient and yet more dependent upon the Lord and the church body for help.

While their husbands serve in grand ways, the wives often feel helpless behind the scenes. Yet they are not without help, as they often see what English author John Flavel called "the mystery of providence."[14] And they often get more opportunities to see God's faithfulness. A wife may be talking to her deployed husband when explosives go off in the background, and yet her husband survives. She may need to move the family from one house to another while the husband is working and find someone to help drive the truck. Chaplains' wives always find that God is right there with them in the details.

In 1991 Ginny Wisdom, wife of OPC Battalion Chaplain Christopher H. Wisdom, heard that her husband was safe after the cease fire in Kuwait. She subsequently asked her pastor to have the congregation sing, "Call Jehovah Thy Salvation" only to find that the bulletin for that Sunday had already been written. And her requested hymn was already on it. God is the helper of the soldier, and he is the helper of his wife.

"Our chaplains minister wherever warriors serve, behind and beyond the wire, in fighting holes, on flight lines, and on ship's decks and holds," Coie said to the 82nd General Assembly. "They have been sent to minister to those who serve us—to the saints and to proclaim redemption in Christ Jesus to the lost and perishing, and have done so since colonial days. This has been done in

14 John Flavel, *The Mystery of Providence* (1678).

realization that they serve where pastors cannot go. They go proclaiming the claims of Christ, a lamb without blemish in a much blemished world, calling sinners to repentance and faith in Christ in obedience to Christ's Great Commission."[15]

Our chaplains fight for the souls of our soldiers, who fight for their country, their homes. Our soldiers' and chaplains' wives fight to make sure there is a home to come back to.

**Lindsey M. Roberts** *is the wife of Stephen Roberts, an evangelist of Falls OPC in Menomonee Falls, Wisconsin, and a chaplain in the US Army Reserves. They have a son, Seth, and a daughter, Tabitha. Lindsey is a freelance writer and editor, covering topics of parenting, faith, and interior design for the* Washington Post, Haven Ministries, Gray *magazine, and more.*

---

15  Robert Coie, remarks to the 82nd General Assembly.

# 48

# Bertha Kinnaird:
# Giving John a Rich and Full Life

## *Bertha Hunt Kinnaird*

I have generally defined or introduced myself by the men in my life: Bruce Hunt's daughter, John Orr Kinnaird's wife, John Hunt Kinnaird's mother. I don't say this to imply I personally am insignificant; I don't feel that way at all. But what I did as I lived these 80 years of my life was generally constrained by those three, plus my four other children, Malissa, Deb, Malcolm, and David.

John Hunt, our first child, was born severely handicapped. This fact impacted every decision and action my husband and I made for the 45 years of John Hunt's life.

I think one of the biggest influences on parenting John, was seeing the way my mother, Kathy Hunt, lived out her life with all its traumas, responsibilities, and loneliness. She and my father, Rev. Bruce Hunt, were Orthodox Presbyterian missionaries to Manchuria and Korea. She accepted "single parenting" for a good portion of her life while raising five children and while my Dad concentrated on being a missionary. She did what God (and my father) asked of her and did it with grace. She raised us while he was in prison in Manchuria and when he spent every week preaching in the Korean countryside. Dad also left us behind in America when he went back to Korea for several periods of two or more years.

I think the acceptance of John's disabilities and the resultant efforts I made were partly from watching her and partly from my husband's attitude. When John was born, we knew that there were real problems physically and probably mentally from the brain damage he suffered at birth. John didn't have a sucking reflex—one of the most basic of instincts—so we fed him drop by drop of milk. As a nurse I knew too much not to be terrified. Would he ever even know us? The doctors at Children's Hospital in Pittsburgh couldn't give us any guesses, only that he was very badly injured. My husband and I tried to get him the best care he could have.

One of our first choices: Should we have more children or concentrate on caring for John? We decided it wasn't an "either/or" but a "let's do a bit of each." We cut back our plans for many children to a few, so that he would have siblings who loved him, and we would have more time to care for him. The best gifts God ever gave John through us were two sisters and two brothers. Malissa was just a year younger so even before he could communicate with us, we were able to predicate his interests and intelligence based on what interested her and what she understood. Was it time for her to be interested in Disney movies? He must be too. And he was.

About age two, John had learned to communicate "yes" by looking up and "no" by a VERY small shake of his head. In all of his years of life, John's speech depended on moving his eyes up or down or his head to one side or the other. This was a huge joy and help—talking at two! We could judge his intelligence (very high) and find out what he needed, and amazingly so could anyone else.

My husband continued to supply what John needed: a wooden cart made from an old baby carriage frame with two upholstered plywood seats so John could be propped up in the front seat and the current baby could first lie, then sit, in the second seat. We were mobile!

We tried everything that looked like it had any possibilities of helping. For three years we "patterned" him with the help of neighbors, friends, volunteers, and people from our church—one person was at his head and two more moved his arms and legs in a crawling pattern. Except for the side effects of many people interacting with him five times a day and keeping him flexible, this was not useful.

Even though he, and we, hated it, we sent him to a boarding

school for two years. This school worked to move severely handicapped young children forward in their area of greatest need. With John it was his tremendous frustration when trying to communicate. They developed a tray for his wheelchair with six grids on it, each with rows of colors and columns of numbers. John could communicate by looking at the grids and referencing the verbs, nouns, numbers, and the alphabet on the grid on his tray. This was his primary means of communication until he moved to Good Shepherd Home in Allentown.

My sister Margie decided he should take up writing as a means of venting both his frustration and expressing his thoughts. He did so using his board with me as his scribe. Finding out what he wanted to say in *his* words and not hurrying the process by trying to guess what he wanted to say, taught me patience

There was so much we couldn't know about the future, but God continued to supply joy and blessing in our lives. One big concern my husband and I had was John's future when we were gone. It was never our plan that one of the other children would have John live with them. God had given him to *us*. So we bought a farm in the country an hour's drive from my husband's work but near Bethany OPC where he served as an elder for 35 years. The farm was intended as a financial investment that we trusted would grow in value over the years to provide money for John to live on after we were gone. We knew how important it was to be part of a community, for ourselves, John, and the other children. Since John wasn't able to go out freely, we brought the world to him.

Again I benefitted from my mother's example. She entertained constantly and easily. My dad would bring home American soldiers he saw on the streets of Pusan—she fed them. Likewise Sunday dinners in California during the war years usually saw us with extra dinner guests. My mother made it seem so easy, and so it became.

Guided by my mother's example of hospitality, we used our home to create a community for John. Over our almost 50 years of living in this place, it has become "The Farm" to hundreds of people. Almost every weekend or summer holiday, family, friends, and various church groups picnic or camp out—traditions that started at least partly for John and through my mother's example. The children brought their friends. The uncles, aunts, and cousins spent holidays here, swimming, fishing in the pond, and playing marathon volleyball games, with John as much in the middle of things as he was able.

Everyone learned to use his board to talk with him. It could be very slow and frustrating, but John wouldn't let you go until you understood what he had to say—politics, God, jokes, and complaints. When it came time for his generation to marry, one criteria of evaluation—not just for his siblings but also for all the cousins—was how the prospective spouses reacted to John.

When John was 25 and all his brothers and sisters had left home, he decided it was time to leave also. My husband had already done a great deal of research. We had visited a number of places while John decided what he wanted to do and when. We found the best place for someone severely physically handicapped but mental-ly very bright was The Good Shepherd Home in Allentown, Pennsylvania. It was close enough for John to come home frequently, and on the cutting edge of research for augmentative communication devices. What a comfort to know that even when his father died, as we expected would happen first, he would have the

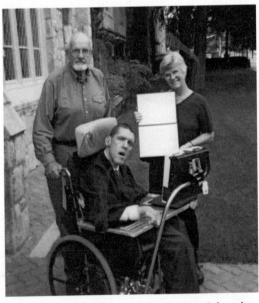

John and Bertha Kinnaird with their son John when he completed a course at Temple University

best help there was.

John lived there for 20 years, continuing to be frustrated by all he could not do. But he always pushed to find ways to make a contribution. He was a founding and active member of Living Hope OPC in Allentown. He helped to develop communication devices with his therapist. John spoke to the Allentown Chamber of Commerce and persuaded them to block off the streets around Good Shepherd so all the electric wheelchairs could move safely.

But most particularly, he wanted to witness to God. He did this with his writing but also by going with a friend to various high schools in the area and speaking about acceptance of the handicapped and against sex outside the bounds of marriage and abortion. No one seeing John could ignore his words: "Though I sometimes would rather not be here, I am made in the image of God, as is every baby. We may not destroy that image."

John went to be with God nine years ago, on March 27, 2007, with much relief and joy. He had often spoken of his desire to leave his broken body and be with Christ. As his sister said after he died, "John has accomplished all God had for him to do and much more than most people; it was time."

We miss him! But in God's great wisdom he took him home just at the time that we began to find that our caring for him was almost impossible.

I began by saying I defined myself by the men in my life. But these men, as well as my mother, drew me closer to the One who was with me each step of the way.

**Bertha Hunt Kinnaird** *is the wife of John Kinnaird, who served for 35 years as an elder at Bethany OPC in Oxford, Pennsylvania. The daughter of OP missionaries Bruce and Kathy Hunt, she was six months old when she attended the First Assembly of what would become the Orthodox Presbyterian Church in 1936. The Kinnairds, who have five children and seven grandchildren, live in Nottingham, Pennsylvania.*

# 49

# Eleanor Meeker, Jean Gaffin, Mary Eckardt, and Judy Bosgraf: Sisterhood of Grief

## *Rebecca Sodergren*

At the 75th General Assembly in 2008, three women with long ties to the OPC—Bertha Kinnaird, Jean Gaffin, and Judy Bosgraf—stood chatting together when they realized they had all lost adult children. The ensuing hugs, tears, and memories transcended the usual bonds between Christian women. In their "sisterhood of grief," they shared a faith that has deepened through darkness.

This sisterhood is made up of many Orthodox Presbyterian women, but each of their stories is unique. The Kinnairds' son, John, endured profound disability until he died at age 45, as Bertha recounts in the previous chapter. Eleanor Meeker experienced several miscarriages and had to bury her only living child, who died at age eight. Jean's journey has mirrored Mary Eckardt's in that they grieved their own losses and also witnessed the grief of their young grandchildren. Judy now battles cancer, the same disease that took her youngest child.

But grief did not sideline these women. They have developed a gritty, practical trust in Christ that helps them serve and encourage the church. Faithful in suffering, these sisters live out the biblical truth that God transforms weakness into strength.

## Eleanor Meeker

In the first hours after her eight-year-old son died, Eleanor Meeker spent the evening comforting someone else.

Apart from the lens of faith, Robert Meeker's death might have felt like bitter irony. Robert's uncle drowned while swimming in Lake Michigan, and Robert inherited his uncle's bike. He was riding that bike when he was struck by a car. He languished in the hospital for a week before he died.

Robert's cousin Janet Gregson, office manager in the OPC's administrative offices, was 13 when Robert died in the mid 1960s. A year earlier, Janet, her mother, and Janet's four older brothers had moved to the Philadelphia area to be near extended family after Janet's father died of a heart attack. The Gregsons lived only five blocks from the Meekers, and "it was really like one household" because the two families spent so much time together, Janet remembers. Robert had been biking home from the Gregsons' house when he was hit.

Janet believes her aunt's actions on the night of her son's death speak volumes about Eleanor's character and faith. Robert had been rallying in the hospital and the family had begun to hope that he would pull through, but he took a sudden turn for the worse. As Robert lay dying, Eleanor whispered to her son, "Just think, Robert, today you'll get to see Jesus."

After Robert died, Eleanor called Janet's mother and said, "I'm coming up there so I can read some Psalms to Jan." She spent the hours after her son's death comforting her niece.

Eleanor and Bob Meeker with
their son Robert

The Meekers interpreted the hard providence of their son's death not as irony but as the hand of God at work. Robert's death "increased our faith," said Eleanor's husband, Bob, an elder at Calvary OPC in Glenside, Pennsylvania. "We knew it was the Lord's will." Bob believes Eleanor's deep trust in Christ shone in her selection of Robert's funeral hymn, "Great Is Thy Faithfulness."

The Meekers went on to become advisors to the Calvary OPC youth group during the years when their son would have been a member. Eleanor made meals for sick people, frequently invited people into their home for meals, and continued after Robert's death to volunteer at his school, Willow Grove Christian Day School (now called Philadelphia-Montgomery Christian Academy). Eleanor and Bob also spent years driving an hour through Philadelphia traffic on Sundays to help an OP mission work in the city to grow.

Eleanor was a loving wife, and "she and Bob had a fantastic marriage," Janet said. Eighteen months before she died, her body already ravaged by cancer, Eleanor was down on her hands and knees, scrubbing floors for a relative who was moving.

Over the years, the Meekers opened their home to many people who needed lodging. Shortly after their own son's death, they offered a room every week to Bob's brother and his family, whose ten-year-old son needed treatments in Philadelphia for the stomach cancer that took his life.

Roger Schmurr, former general secretary for the Committee on Christian Education, fell into a diabetic coma near the end of his final year at Westminster Theological Seminary. When he left the hospital, the Meekers offered him free room and board so they could supervise him in case of complications. At the same time, a young Vietnam War veteran was also living there, trying to get back on his feet after the war.

"I give them credit," Roger said. "In a sense, they turned tragedy into hospitality," using the empty house God's providence had given them to benefit others.

Janet believes that opening her home to others "filled something in Eleanor that was missing. Once you've been a mother, I don't think you can just put that role away."

The Meekers' longest guest, a young woman from California, became a member of the family. The Meekers offered a room to Mardi Kopecky when she moved east in the 1970s to escape a troubled home life. Mardi adopted Eleanor as her "surrogate mother," Bob said. She has lived with the Meekers almost all her adult life, yet the Meekers didn't consider it a sacrifice.

"She's given us more than we've given her," Bob says. A licensed practical nurse, Mardi helped care for Eleanor during the long battle with cancer that claimed her life on April 3, 2015.

Eleanor and her son "are together again" in heaven, Bob says. "She loved the Lord, and she loved his people. She was one of the Lord's good ladies."

## Jean Gaffin

Jean Gaffin is a seminary professor's daughter and a seminary professor's wife, so she knows her theology. Her father was E. J. Young, an early professor at Westminster Theological Seminary in Philadelphia. Her husband, Richard B. "Dick" Gaffin Jr., is an emeritus professor at Westminster.

"I was surrounded by godly people all my life," Jean said.

All her theological preparation came to bear in 2001, when the Gaffins' 33-year-old daughter, Lisl Tyson, found a lump under her arm. She died of breast cancer three years later, leaving husband Steve Tyson and two young children, Maggie and Ben. Lisl Tyson had been an administrative assistant to Ross Graham, then general secretary for the OPC's Committee on Home Missions and Church Extension.

"I understood that God is sovereign and that I didn't have to know the reasons" for Lisl's death, Jean said. "That didn't mean that it wasn't very hurtful and painful, but it made me closer to the Lord and more aware of heaven."

Dick said that his wife was "very close to Lisl," and Jean acknowledged that, although she and her daughter had very differ-

Jean, Dick, and Lisl Gaffin

ent personalities, they complemented each other well in the mother-daughter relationship. Their closeness stemmed in part from their proximity: Lisl and her family lived less than two miles from Jean and Dick. The Gaffins had the larger house, so when hospice care became necessary, Lisl moved into her parents' house and eventually died in the bedroom that had been hers before marriage.

Jean misses her daughter deeply, but "missing her is not the same as the souring of faith," she said. She has even learned to cultivate a thankful heart: "Part of the salve in losing an adult child [who is a parent] is that you have their children." Her son-in-law remarried several years ago, but the Gaffins continue to see him and their grandchildren frequently.

Jean's service to the church has been largely in the financial realm. She was treasurer for her congregation, Cornerstone OPC in Ambler, Pennsylvania, as well as other Christian organizations, and she used to be the business manager at Phil-Mont Christian Academy.

Jean has also taught women's Bible studies for many years. Her professor husband complimented her teaching, saying it "combines solid biblical insight with addressing issues where the rubber hits the road in the Christian life."

The rubber hit the road in a very personal way in 2012, when Jean led a retreat for the women of Grace OPC in Vienna, Virginia, on the topic of grief.

"Life is a journey that sometimes takes us through deep waters," she said, describing the overall theme of that retreat. She urged grieving women to grieve openly without feigning strength. She also discussed how the church should support those who are griev-ing, explaining that it's important to allow people to talk through their grief.

"I wanted to talk about Lisl" after she died, Jean said. "I would bring it up."

As one who knew grief personally, Jean had the authority to say, and mean, the words that closed one of her retreat sessions: "On our journey to heaven, we may need to walk through the val-ley of tears, but we do not walk alone. We are in the loving arms of God and his people. Weeping may tarry for the night, but joy comes in the morning."

### Mary Eckardt

Like Jean, Mary Eckardt learned the tenets of the faith at her parents' knees. Her parents became charter members of the OPC in 1936, when she was eight. The family belonged to what is now Immanuel OPC in West Collingswood, New Jersey, which met in a movie theater after separating from the mainline denomination. Mary recalls that she and her sister loved the rocking seats even though the building had no heat.

Mary met her husband, Robert W. Eckardt, now a retired Or-thodox Presbyterian minister, when he pastored the congregation's daughter church in Bellmawr, New Jersey. The couple had three sons. Bob followed his father's footsteps and became an OP pastor, now serving at Redeemer OPC in Dayton, Ohio. Doug was the registrar at Dordt College in Sioux Center, Iowa, and Rich is a technical writer in Las Vegas.

Mary's son Bob describes his mom as having "an animated per-sonality, being passionate about things." As a churchwoman, she believes her most important contribution is prayer, and her son agrees. He said she routinely spends a couple of hours every morn-ing praying for everyone she knows.

As a mom, Mary sought to cultivate a strong family life to guard her family from the pressures of living in a pastor's house-hold, her son Bob said. She was often the mastermind of memorable family vacations.

There were times when life seemed tenuous, especially for the middle brother, Doug, who suffered grand mal seizures between ages four and nine. And on one of those memorable vacations, the whole family had a life-endangering experience. They rented a 17-foot travel trailer and drove from the East Coast to general assembly in Portland, Oregon, taking a side trip to Yosemite. They were driving up a mountain when their standard-transmission car stalled and couldn't be restarted. Mary implored her sons to pray.

"Within five minutes, ten to twelve firefighters in uniform showed up," she said. In God's providence, they had been fighting a fire on the mountain. One firefighter stopped traffic above their stalled car, another raced to the bottom of the mountain to do the same, and a third helped to back the car, with the trailer still hitched on, down the road to safety.

After the Lord's earlier preservation of their lives, it was perhaps strange providence that Doug died in a traffic accident at age 43. While riding his bike in Sioux Center, he was struck by a tractor-trailer. His wife, Greta, was left with eight-year-old twins, Zachary and Gabriella, and a 13-year-old daughter, Rachel.

Bob described Doug as a larger-than-life personality, the kind of man who would dance on the basketball court at halftime, an unforgettable figure on the Christian college campus where he worked. Doug memorized the names, faces, and family connections of all the students on campus, taking as much interest in people as his mother did. Of the three sons, Doug was the most like their mom, Bob said.

"She lost a friend and confidant and someone who really understood her," he said. "But I never heard any recriminations against the Lord."

Doug, Mary, Bob, and Rick Eckardt
in 1973

Like Jean, Mary talked about the comfort of continued ties with her grandchildren, as well as her opportunity to watch some of her family members mature in the faith.

Mary remembers the moment she received word of her son's death in 1997 as "a great shock—I almost passed out." But she soon fell back on what her son Bob describes as her natural gift of caring for people. Even in her old age at the Quarryville Presbyterian Retirement Community in Pennsylvania, she spends her time ministering to others even though she's not in the best of health herself, he said.

She now says she has come to see the hard providence of her son's death as a way to live out the words of 2 Corinthians 1:3–4: "Blessed be the God and Father of our Lord Jesus Christ, the Father of mercies and God of all comfort, who comforts us in all our affliction, so that we may be able to comfort those who are in any affliction, with the comfort with which we ourselves are comforted by God."

The opportunities for comforting began within a month of her son's death. The Eckardts were living in Massachusetts, where Mary's husband, although an OP minister, was serving as a visitation pastor for a large Christian Reformed congregation. A woman in the congregation's Bible study group was perplexed and grieving over the death of her sister's baby in spite of her prayers on the baby's behalf. Mary was able to counsel and comfort her.

"I wouldn't have been able to do that," she said, "if I hadn't been through this with Doug."

## Judy Bosgraf

Judy Bosgraf, wife of Regional Home Missionary Jim Bosgraf, is mounting her family's second battle against cancer in the past decade. She is battling pancreatic cancer; her daughter Heather Bosgraf died of ovarian cancer in 2008 at age 37.

"She fought a good fight," Judy said. Heather drove herself to chemotherapy sessions and always wore a wig because she didn't want people feeling sorry for her. Throughout her illness, she continued working for Edy's Ice Cream at the corporate level.

Heather was declared cancer-free for eight months, but the cancer "came back viciously to her brain," her mom said. It also came back without any warning. Heather played the piano at church on a Sunday and went to work the following morning. But when it became apparent at work that something was wrong again, her mom drove her to the hospi-

Judy, Jim, and Heather Bosgraf

tal to be readmitted. Doctors found ten new cancerous growths in her brain. Just two weeks later, she died.

She had two older siblings, Kim and Scott. She lived with Kim during her illness and received loving support from her church, Bethel OPC in Wheaton, Illinois. Members visited her regularly and gave her a basket containing small gifts to open every day for a month.

Church is now where the Bosgrafs often remember their daughter most poignantly, exchanging knowing glances at a line of a hymn. The pianist sometimes tells them that a particular prelude she played was "music I got from Heather."

The Bosgrafs also feel their daughter's absence at family vacations, when all their children and grandchildren are there—all but one. At those times, the family feels sad, "but we joke that we're still here and she gets to be there" in heaven, Jim said, noting that grief and comfort are intertwined for believers.

Just as Mary thinks of her son Doug, the Bosgrafs sometimes ponder God's mysterious providence in taking their daughter after sparing her. At age seven, Heather had major heart surgery that so terrified her doctors that they delayed it for three months. Doctors told the Bosgrafs that a single false move during the surgery would kill their daughter. On the operating table, however, the doctors discovered that the troublesome blood vessel had shifted position on its own.

Two months after the surgery, the family stood at the top of a ski slope on a cloudless day, the trees burdened with heavy snow. Heather's siblings took off down the hill, and she "went flying after her older brother and sister," all three screaming and laughing, Jim said. "My wife and I stood at the top and cried and wept at the goodness of God."

The same God took their child away 30 years later, yet they still acknowledge both his sovereignty and his goodness.

"The Lord gives, and the Lord takes away," Jim said. "Judy took comfort in that. The Lord says, 'Timing is mine. I am in charge.' These are hard, hard times, almost times when you can't even speak, but even then, we know the comfort of it all."

Jim believes this hard providence has increased his wife's ability to care for others. He describes his wife as a person who can be a friend to anyone. As regional home missionary, he has had contact with about 50 different congregations in the Presbytery of the Midwest. He estimates that Judy has good friends in at least 40 of them.

"She'll go to the people, especially those who are hurting in some way." Jim believes his wife's experiences give her the authority to speak comfort in a way that she otherwise couldn't.

As Judy now faces her own cancer, she prays for the strength to "be bold" in her witness for Christ when people ask how she's doing. The Bosgrafs frequently revisit their daughter's battle, marveling at her strength and endurance.

Judy says God has given her peace since the first day of her own diagnosis. "My daughter was a good example, so I have to step up to the plate."

**Rebecca Sodergren** *has been a member of seven different Orthodox Presbyterian congregations since she first began attending Covenant OPC in Grove City, Pennsylvania, as a college student in 1992. She and her husband, Jeff, have two children, Andy and Beth. Their infant son Matthew died of SIDS in 2004.*

# 50

# Margaret Falk and Shannon Baugh Onnink: "Whate'er My God Ordains Is Right"

## *Jamie Dean*

On the last day of her imprisonment in an Eritrean jail, missionary wife Margaret Falk had a surprising realization: "There was no place in the world I would rather have been than in that prison cell." That 15 x 12-foot cell—with concrete floors, no beds, dozens of other women, and a single plastic bucket—had transformed for Margaret during her four days with other Christians jailed for their faith. "It was a taste of heaven," she says.

It hadn't seemed that way just a few days earlier. Margaret had arrived at the prison on Sunday, April 29, 2007. That morning, Eritrean authorities rounded up churchgoers after morning worship at the house where her husband, Jonathan, led services as part of his work as an Orthodox Presbyterian Church missionary. Authorities sent the men to one prison, and the women to another. At the last moment, police sent Jonathan to the same prison with his wife and the women they had served in the vibrant church for the last five years.

By nightfall, Margaret and Jonathan were in separate prison cells.

For Margaret, the week ahead would prove trying and triumphant, as the Lord led her from discouragement in her circumstances to delight in his sovereignty, and blessing in the fellowship of precious saints acquainted with suffering. She would awake in the mornings on the concrete floor with an aching back, but thinking of a refrain that had proved true through many seasons of her life, as a student, a pastor's wife, a mother, and a missionary. "Whate'er my God ordains is right," she sang to her Eritrean cellmates. "Holy his will abideth. I will be still whate'er He doth; and follow where He guideth."[1]

It's a hymn another missionary's wife, Shannon Baugh, had sung during her own harrowing trial on a Haitian mission field just a year earlier. While the paths for Margaret and Shannon would end in two very different places, the central truth would remain the same: "He is my God, though dark my road; He holds me that I shall not fall. Wherefore to Him I leave it all."

## Margaret Falk

God's appointed road for Margaret Graham Falk began in Chico, California, where she was born on November 10, 1949. Margaret grew up in Lakewood, Colorado, with two brothers and a sister in a home she describes as "modern and secular."

The modern and secular collided with the eternal and spiritual when she was in the ninth grade. A friend invited her to a Baptist revival meeting, and Margaret was pierced. Convicted of her sin, she embraced Christ as he was offered in the gospel. "That's where the journey began," she says.

Margaret's journey continued in Santa Barbara, California, at Westmont College—a school she chose from a college catalog. Her young faith was growing, but she struggled with a legalistic understanding of Christianity, and strove to earn approval with God.

Within a year, she encountered another student on a spiritual journey of his own. Margaret met Jonathan Falk at a poster-making party, where he was preparing to run for vice president of the sophomore class (he won). By the next fall, the pair was dating.

---

1 Hymn 94, *Trinity Hymnal* (Philadelphia: Great Commission Publications, 1961).

They married on June 14, 1970, between their junior and senior years of college.

After graduation, the newlyweds embarked on the first of a long line of adventures. They spent a year overseas, studying Hebrew for a semester in Jerusalem, and then three months on a kibbutz—a communal farming community in northern Israel. The experience was transformative. Though they had no exposure to other Christians in Israel, Jonathan spent months reading the Bible. He had grown up in a Christian home, but hadn't embraced Christ for himself.

As he read the Scriptures, the Holy Spirit convicted Jonathan of his sin and the meaning of Christ's death on the cross. After they left Israel, the couple backpacked across Europe, and spent time at L'Abri,[2] where Margaret first encountered the doctrines of Reformed theology. She began to take special comfort in the knowledge of God's sovereignty.

After returning to the United States in 1972, Jonathan publicly professed faith in Christ and was baptized. He eventually attended Westminster Theological Seminary. During their years in Philadelphia, the couple attended an OP church plant that met at a local YMCA. They began using their gifts, and Margaret discovered a life-long love: teaching women's Bible studies. During Jonathan's final year at Westminster, Margaret gave birth to a son, Christopher. Two years later they welcomed their daughter, Katie. And nine years later the Lord gave the couple one more daughter, Emily.

After seminary, the next two decades brought fruitful service in two OP congregations. Jonathan served as pastor of Grace OPC in Sheboygan, Wisconsin, and Pilgrim OPC in Bangor, Maine.

Then, after two short-term trips to assist OPC missionaries in Uganda, Jonathan received an unexpected phone call from

---

2 L'Abri Fellowship was started in Switzerland in 1955 by Francis and Edith Schaeffer, who opened their alpine home as a place to study religious and philosophical questions and experience Christian community. "L'Abri" is French for "the shelter."

the Committee on Foreign Missions (CFM): Would he consider serving full time as a missionary in Uganda? Margaret remembers their conversations and prayers about moving to Africa hinged on a simple question: Were they willing to go? She says they prayed: "'Lord, here's our willingness, you supply everything else'… and that's exactly what he did."

As the family settled into life in Mbale, Uganda, in 1999, Margaret homeschooled their youngest daughter, and found ways to serve the women and children in local villages. She sat under a tree and taught the story of baby Moses to African children sitting on a papyrus reed mat. She enjoyed teaching Ugandan women who were often unfamiliar with stories in the Bible. "I could start the story of Esther, and they didn't know how it was going to end," she remembers. "It was really, really fun."

Two and a half years later another unexpected call came: The CFM asked Jonathan and Margaret if they would join Brian and Dorothy Wingard in the work of starting a theological college in Eritrea. Jonathan accepted the call in 2002, and the two delved headlong into a field that became one of the defining experiences of their lives. As government oppression of Christians increased in Eritrea, Margaret says they marveled at believers counting the cost for their public profession of faith in Christ: "I learned much more from them than I ever could have taught them."

Remarkable years followed, as the missionaries helped established the theological college, and the church flourished, despite opposition. Margaret taught English classes, led a women's Bible study, and tutored a boy with Down syndrome. As the mission work advanced, the restrictions from government grew. The

Margaret Falk talking with an Eritrean woman

church couldn't own a building, so the believers met in an apartment the first year, and then assembled in a house. The church wasn't allowed to display a sign, they had to close the shutters during worship, and the members entered a few at a time through a back door. Despite the restrictions, on most Sundays as many as 90 Eritreans packed into the living room and spilled down the halls to worship the Lord.

By 2007, as the Wingards returned to the United States on furlough, oppression grew. Authorities arbitrarily arrested Christians, and conscripted young people into military service out of high school. Pressure against foreigners also grew. The Falks watched as officials interrogated and expelled foreign workers who had been in the country for decades. They expected a day authorities would tell them to leave too.

Instead a very different day arrived.

On Sunday, April 29, 2007, Jonathan conducted the worship service in Asmara, as an Eritrean pastor led worship at another church. As they left morning worship in Asmara, authorities arrived at the house. The police packed the men into one set of trucks, and the women into another. They sent Jonathan to the prison with Margaret and the other women, likely trying to keep the Americans together.

As Jonathan and Margaret sat in a prison courtyard that afternoon, Margaret gave the other women items they might be able to use: hand sanitizer, chap stick, tissue, and her Bible. By evening Margaret realized she would be in jail too. Authorities escorted her and Jonathan to adjacent cells, and an extraordinary four days began.

Margaret's first night in jail was difficult. The cramped cell with concrete floors had no beds, no blankets, and no bathroom. Jailers escorted the women to three pit toilets outside their cell three times a day.

Space was tight. Twenty-five women from the church filled the cell, but since many had been imprisoned for their faith before, they knew what to do. They organized their few supplies and waited. That evening family members brought blankets, water, and food—the only way Eritrean prisoners obtain supplies.

That night Margaret shared a blanket with five other women on the hard floor, as jailers turned on a bright light that burned all night. Her sympathetic cellmates told Margaret she didn't deserve to be in jail, since she was an American. Margaret found herself agreeing, and says a cloak of self-pity and pride began to settle over her. She tried to pray, but found herself distracted. She tried to sleep, but found very little rest. She propped herself up against the wall and waited for morning.

When morning came, she formulated a plan. She learned another prisoner had a cell phone. Margaret asked to borrow it, and remembered the phone number to the US Embassy. She raced to make a fast call with limited minutes and fading battery. When Margaret reached the embassy, the operator put her on hold.

An embassy official finally answered, and said he'd come right away. Margaret's hopes revived. When the embassy official arrived, he asked to see the Americans. The jailer's reply: There are no Americans here. Unable to persuade him, the embassy official left.

It was a discouraging blow. Margaret watched her plans for an early release fade. She wouldn't be delivered by her American citizenship or rescued by an embassy worker. She faced another night in jail.

That evening the women in her cell huddled for a time of prayer and sharing testimonies. For Margaret, something changed. "It was during that time of prayer that night that the Lord just humbled me—to the core of my pride, of my trusting in myself, trusting in anything but him," she remembers. "He showed me that he was in control, and I was there because he wanted me to be. That I would be there as long as he wanted me to be there. He just flooded me with peace. It was the most marvelous experience."

The next three days were full of prayer and praise, as the women in Margaret's cell shared remarkable testimonies of enduring persecution at the government's hands. They passed around Bibles, reading favorite passages aloud. They sang hymns—sometimes two or three at a time when jailers demanded they stay quiet. Each morning, Margaret would awake with the three women who slept near her and sing the words of Lamentations 3:22: "The steadfast love of the Lord never ceases."

On Wednesday authorities interrogated Margaret, asking questions about how long she had been in the country and what kind of visa she possessed. They led her to a room where Jonathan was waiting. He was in good health, and the couple enjoyed a reunion. An hour later authorities came and said they were free to go. As they neared the gate, an official called out for them to return. They waited another two hours, until jailers escorted them back to their cells for another night in prison.

The next morning the authorities promised to release the Falks, but also gave a command: Jonathan could no longer preach or teach in Eritrea. The school was closed. The church was closed. With that, they said, "You're free to go."

Jonathan and Margaret left, but returned that evening with supplies for those they left behind. They also decided not to leave the country until authorities forced them to go. Mostly, Margaret says, "because the shepherd doesn't leave the sheep."

Five days later the order came: They had to leave their beloved Eritrea.

The Falks were sad to see their service ending, but grateful for the years of fruitful work the Lord provided. Their greatest grief: Authorities didn't release their fellow cellmates until after the Falks left the country. They never got to say goodbye.

Still, they give thanks for their remarkable time in Eritrea, and for the days they spent imprisoned with fellow believers. "If I would have gotten out when I wanted to, I wouldn't have learned anything that the Lord had to teach me," says Margaret. "I just needed this very desperately."

It was a lesson that would follow Margaret in the years ahead, as she and Jonathan spent three years opening an OPC mission field in Uruguay, until they returned to the United States to care for ailing parents. Shortly after their return to the States, Margaret faced a new trial: She learned she had breast cancer. Her thoughts immediately went back to her Eritrean prison cell. Sensing she had wasted her first day in prison with anxiety and pride, she now faced a cancer diagnosis with the prayer: "Lord, help me not to waste this."

By early 2016 Margaret enjoyed good health and a new avenue of ministry with Jonathan, where he serves as associate pastor at Falls OPC in Menomonee Falls, Wisconsin. It was a full circle moment, as the couple returned to the church where Jonathan did his first internship in the OPC. They enjoy their six grandchildren, and serving the Lord back where they began.

Whether in Uganda or Eritrea or Wisconsin, a jail cell or a sanctuary or a doctor's office, Margaret has learned the importance of contentment and purpose in whatever field of service or stage of life the Lord assigns. "I think about the idea of not looking for your circumstances to change, but accepting what God has for you," she says. "He has important lessons to teach us right where we are."

### Shannon Baugh Onnink

For Shannon Baugh Onnink, one of the toughest lessons of her life began on one of the pot-holed roads of Haiti.

Shannon didn't expect tragedy on a May morning in 2006 when her husband, OPC missionary Matt Baugh, hopped on his motorcycle to meet a Haitian pastor in the Caribbean nation he loved. But a few hours later Shannon would pass Matt's crumpled bike in the road, and hold his broken body in her arms.

She would pray and talk, as they tried to reach a hospital. Matt would look and listen, as Shannon sang familiar words: "He is my God, though dark my road …"

For the Baughs, the road to Haiti began in Alabama. Shannon Leigh Young was born on August 24, 1971, and grew up in Homewood, Alabama. She attended a Methodist church with her family and embraced faith in Christ as a freshman at Auburn University. Soon she encountered another Auburn student pursuing the Lord. Shannon met Matt Baugh through the college ministry of their church, and they married less than a year later, on September 14, 1991.

After graduating, the newlyweds moved to Southern California, where Matt attended Westminster Seminary California in Escondido. During seminary, the couple's first two children, Andrew and Laura, arrived. The family moved to Mississippi, and Matt began pastoral ministry at Tchula Presbyterian Church (PCA). The next few years were full, as the Lord blessed the family with three more children: Sara Grace, Jessica, and Margaret. Shannon homeschooled the kids and served as a pastor's wife, as Matt dove into the ministry.

During those years, Matt also began making short mission trips to Haiti, where he had spent several years of his childhood with his missionary parents. He still spoke Creole, and he loved the Haitian people.

Eventually Matt's spiritual burden for Haiti grew intense. Shannon says he had "a fire in his bones" for the nation and longed to see the gospel advance in a country where Voodoo had a stronghold. To Shannon's surprise, the Lord began directing the family's steps to the nearby country that was like a different world.

When the CFM asked Matt to help establish a mission field in Haiti, Matt and Shannon knew it was the Lord's will. But for Shannon, it also brought a mixture of feelings. She was ready to help her husband pursue Haiti, but leaving their church was hard, and she knew life on the mission field could be lonely.

It could also be difficult. After the family arrived in Haiti in 2005, their household items didn't arrive for almost two months.

Shannon and Matt Baugh and family

They slept on the floor, used paper plates, and went days without electricity. When Matt went to retrieve their belongings, he hid in a shipping container to escape flying bullets from a nearby gunfight.

But the family eventually settled into a routine, as Matt worked with a handful of churches on the mainland and the nearby island of La Gonave. Shannon homeschooled the children, and Matt often rose early to watch the sunrise over the ocean with his oldest daughter.

As the morning began on May 4, 2006, the family gathered for worship, as usual. After a hectic start to the day, Matt huddled with Shannon before he left for a meeting. "He prayed my day would get better," she remembers. "Then he told me he loved me—and he left."

A few hours later a stranger arrived at the gate with a message: The American pastor had been in an accident.

A neighbor watched the children as Shannon drove to the scene. When she passed Matt's crumpled motorcycle in the road, the sight was sobering: "I knew this was a big deal."

Shannon was right.

Matt had been traveling south on Route Nationale No. 1. As he crested a hill, a truck swerved to miss a pothole. It struck Matt head on. Witnesses took Matt to a nearby mission compound with a small clinic. He was conscious, but injured badly.

The pastor Matt was scheduled to meet arrived on the scene. He and Shannon loaded Matt into the back of the car for transport to a hospital. Shannon held onto Matt during the drive. She talked, prayed, and sang songs to him: "Whate'er my God ordains is right, holy His will abideth. I will be still whate'er He doth, and follow where He guideth."

As they neared the hospital, Matt's condition worsened. He stopped breathing. Shannon performed CPR. When they reached a hospital, doctors pronounced Matt dead. He was 37 years old.

When Shannon recounts that day, she remembers Matt's last words. They were in Creole, the language of the people he loved so much: "Gade, tande." Translation: "Look, listen."

Shannon doesn't know what Matt saw or heard in those final moments, but she's thankful he spent his final years pursuing a calling he loved in a country he loved with the family he loved.

She also remembers returning home and facing her five young children, ages two to ten. She talked with them about Job, and she told them their daddy wasn't coming home. "I said the Lord had given us this wonderful man, and that he's also taken him away," she remembers. "I saw their hearts breaking."

Over the next four days the Lord gave Shannon strength for a Herculean task, even as close friends and family arrived to help: calling loved ones, comforting children, packing the family's belongings, working through legal details, thinking about a funeral, contemplating life as a widow, and grieving a heart-wrenching loss.

After returning to the States, the family moved in with Matt's mother in Mississippi. Slowly they developed a new routine. Shannon says pursuing her calling as a mother helped her get through the hard months ahead. "I couldn't lose myself in my grief," she says. "I still had to get up."

Most importantly, she says she still found the Lord helping her, even through great loss. "It's like life loses all of its colors," she says of the time after Matt's death. "Nothing tastes good, nothing sounds good ... but the Lord meets you right there at that point, and he always carries you through."

The Lord eventually carried the family to Illinois for a fresh start. The members of Covenant OPC in Orland Park, Illinois, enfolded them into the life of their congregation. The Lord also brought another provision into the family's life: Peter Onnink, the man Shannon would marry in 2008.

A few months after Matt's death, Shannon received a letter from Peter. He had traveled to the Haiti mission to help with construction projects through his own OP church. He met Matt and Shannon, and she even has a picture of the two men working together in Haiti. Peter's letter expressed his grief over Matt's loss and his prayers for the surviving family. Shannon wrote back to thank and encourage Peter, and a correspondence developed.

Over time, Shannon says she realized God had provided a Boaz for her family, as Peter pursued her and embraced her children. They married on August 15, 2008. The couple now has two more children: Luke William Ernest (named

Shannon and Peter Onnink and family

after Matt's grandfather and Peter's grandfather) and Evelyn Mercy.

When Shannon thinks about God's providence in her life, she's struck by his goodness and his faithfulness, whatever the circumstances. "I know what it's like to do things you're afraid of doing, and what it's like to be almost crippled with fear," she says. "But I also know what it's like to have God say: 'I am enough. I am sufficient for you, and I will get you through this.' And He does."

She says her life is encapsulated by Isaiah 42:16:

> And I will lead the blind in a way that they do not know, in paths that they have not known I will guide them. I will turn the darkness before them into light, and the rough places into level ground. These are the things I do, and I do not forsake them.

**Jamie Dean** *is national editor of* World Magazine. *She has traveled to report on believers in Africa, Haiti, the Middle East, and other regions of the world. She has been a member of Matthews OPC in Matthews, North Carolina, since 1995.*

# 51

# Ruth Morton, Jane Crum, Marieta Laranjo, and Diana Cruz: Reaching the World in Our Backyard

## *Kathleen Germann Curto*

The Orthodox Presbyterian Church reaches beyond our typical English-speaking congregations to bring the gospel to those of diverse cultures, languages, and theological backgrounds. Four OP women stand beside their husbands as they minister in ways that highlight how we are all one in Christ Jesus.

### Ruth Morton: Mother to Liberians

Ruth Morton, born in 1935 and raised in North Philadelphia, has known the Lord from her childhood.[1] Providentially she attended a youth group meeting in Philadelphia where George Morton was asked to speak. George was a shy young man, but as they became acquainted over the next few months, they fell in love and married in 1955. George, a member of Calvary OPC in Glenside, was attending Reformed Episcopal Seminary. He was ordained in 1961 and served churches in both the Reformed Presbyterian Church, Evangelical Synod, and the OPC. In 1988, Trinity OPC in Hatboro called George as an evangelist to serve a congregation in Southwest Philadelphia, now known as Grace OPC.[2]

---

1 Interview, Ruth Morton, July 2015.
2 Grace OPC was called Southwest Reformed Fellowship, OPC, Southwest Philadelphia, from 1978 to 1993.

By this time the Mortons had six children: Jonathan, Joel, Jeffrey, James, Maribeth, and Jennifer, who was born with Down syndrome. Because of Jennifer's special needs, the family needed to remain in the Bucks County area so she could continue in a unique preschool program available there. When the call came in 1989 asking George to do pulpit supply at that South-west Philadelphia congregation, he agreed to go temporarily. Ruth re-

George and Ruth Morton in 1989

members telling him, "I know what's going to happen. They will hear you. They will like you, and then they will ask, 'Can the Pulpit Committee stop its search because we found our man!'" And that is exactly what happened. George turned them down initially, concerned about the need for a shepherd to live among his flock, which the Mortons were unable to do. The church's reply to George's reservations was, "You can do this. With the way you are willing to drive, you can come to us in 45 minutes!" So the Mortons said yes.

Vince Rum, a member of the congregation, often played the guitar at a Christian coffeehouse in South Philly. One Friday evening in 1998 he was approached by William Joe, a young Liberian, who asked if Vince knew of a Bible-believing church in the area that he and his family could attend. Vince invited him to Grace the next Sunday. William Joe came, and brought his family. Each week thereafter a few more Liberians came. They all stayed.

Through the example of Pastor Morton and Ruth, the Liberians were warmly welcomed into the congregation. The church began a clothing distribution ministry to Liberian immigrants in the area. Ruth and George also helped the parents enroll their children in schools and guided them through the onerous task of becoming legal citizens.

Ruth took the young women under her wing. Once she went

to the hospital with a pregnant woman, ready to deliver, who addressed Ruth as "mother." The woman explained to the hospital staff that Ruth was her "church mother," and every African in the church called her "mother." The nurses and doctor were wide-eyed at this, but when the baby was delivered, the doctor handed the baby to Ruth and said, "Here you go, Grandma!"

Sometimes the Mortons would invite their church family to their home in the suburbs. All the men sat under the trees, and all the women and children enjoyed the Morton's above ground pool. To Ruth, the church in Southwest Philly was a big family of new believers. She fondly remembers, "Their love for Jesus showed in all they said and did. They were the typical New Testament Church. They couldn't get enough of each other. They wanted to be with each other all the time."

Ruth's greatest ministry challenge was having George gone most of the time. Pastor Morton made a point to be in Southwest Philadelphia caring for his flock four to five days a week. "I tried *not* to complain because he was gone so often from the house," she said. "I tried to run a tight ship and have the house orderly when he came home at night so that *he* could relax from all the pressures of his day."

In 2012 George had a stroke. After 24 years of ministry to this vibrant Southwest Philadelphia congregation, he needed to retire. Describing his parents' service to the church, Jeffrey Morton said, "You are like that jar of oil Elijah gave to the widow and her son; your jar continues to remain full as you continually give its contents away." He reminisces, "My parents' gift to their children was a perspective of loving deferment and grace-filled openhandedness."[3]

George and Ruth now live in Dover, Delaware, and celebrated their 60th wedding anniversary on August 20, 2015. She praises God for the wonderful privilege of serving this dear church. As Ruth says, "Our hearts were in love with this congregation."

---

3 *New Horizons* 33 (December 2012): 22.

## Jane Crum: Serving South of the Border

On December 9, 1956, Jane Crum was born in Kingston, New York, to a Roman Catholic mother and an unchurched father. Her mother's vow to raise her in the Roman Catholic Church led to Jane attending Catholic Church and Catholic grade school for five years. As a teenager, a friend invited her to a Baptist church. Soon Jane attended Catholic mass in the morning and the Baptist church in the evening. Jane read and reread the Bible and finally trusted in Christ at the age of 15. "My life became full of joy and purpose as I sought to know the Lord better through his Word," said Jane. "When I read the Great Commission, I said, 'Yes, Lord!' and hoped that he would use me in missionary service."

While a student at Moravian College in Bethlehem, Pennsylvania, Jane met David Crum, who had been a Christian for only six weeks. Together with college friends in 1976, they attended Urbana, the InterVarsity Christian missions conference, and determined to pursue missionary service, if the Lord opened the door. Jane's degree was in medical technology because she thought it would be useful on the mission field.

After they married in 1978, Dave began seminary at Westminster in Philadelphia. During those years, as members of New Life OPC in Jenkintown, they grew in their understanding of the Reformed faith. With Dave's degree in Spanish, they looked for a place to serve in the Spanish-speaking world. In 1983 the Lord providentially directed their steps into missionary service in Tijuana, Mexico, through the OPC's Presbytery of Southern California. For the next 25 years the Crums lived in Tijuana, raising their family of four children, Timothy, Michael, Adrian, and Jana, and working to help the Reformed Presbyterian Church of Mexico.

Two vital ministries gave opportunities for OP young people and for churches to share in the Crums' labor. Team Baja took place each summer with as many as 36 young people from all over the United States who spent two weeks working with the Crums. The work varied from repairing and building churches to teaching VBS,

Dave and Jane Crum

visiting families, and working with children. Teams spent one week in the Crum's home, setting out each day to do local ministry. During the second week teams split up to live in church members' homes. Jane was, of course, chief cook, nurse, counselor, driver, VBS coordinator, and much more.

Weekend Witness was an opportunity for churches to help with the work. An OP congregation was invited to work on a project over a weekend. The church members were housed at the Crum home and shown warm hospitality. Friday was a time of gathering and fellowship, Saturday was a long work day at one of the churches in Tijuana, and Sunday morning the group worshipped in the church where Dave was ministering. Both of these ministries left lasting impressions on those involved. There were even marriages that resulted from time spent at Team Baja!

Although the Crums were so close to affluent Southern California, they were living in a third world city of three million people. "Life in general was inconvenient," said Jane. "All bills had to be paid in person with cash. There was no electricity or running water in many places where churches were started, and *the traffic!* One of our most difficult personal challenges included being out of phone contact with our extended family for many years." Sadly, Jane did not learn of her grandmother's death for six weeks!

Although Jane became fluent in Spanish, she was still learning to understand the intricacies of the Mexican culture and did not know the language well enough to be able to counsel or teach. She felt this inadequacy because she knew the women of the church needed to study the Bible. Rather than teaching or speaking publically, Jane "modeled" for the women what the Bible teaches about marriage and motherhood.

The Lord taught Jane so much in her years of ministry beside David. He taught her that he listens to the prayers of his people. She came to understand and practice what it means to pray without ceasing, acknowledging that praying for her husband has been her greatest ministry. She also learned that her comfort zone was not as important as she thought since she really could do all things through Christ who strengthened her.

The Crums left the work in Tijuana in 2008, and since 2009 David has served the Presbytery of Southern California as regional home missionary. Jane looks back on her time in Mexico as an answer to her cry of many years before, "Yes, Lord!"

### Marieta Laranjo: Brazil Ministry in America

Marieta Bittencourt was born on March 23, 1966, in Belo Horizonte, Brazil. Because her father abandoned the family when she was very young, her grandmother, a professing believer, raised her. From a very early age, Marieta attended church with her grandmother and heard the gospel; at 16 she committed her life to Christ. How kind God was in ordering the events of her life!

While Marieta was in college, some friends arranged blind dates for her and for Roberto Laranjo, her future husband, but with two different people. They were each introduced to "their" date, but as God intended, they found that they had much more in common with each other. A four-year, long distance relationship began, while they finished their education, culminating in their marriage on August 4, 1990. Shortly afterward, Roberto became pastor of a Presbyterian Church of Brazil congregation in Ipatinga.

Marieta had anticipated teaching school for several years before starting a family, but two months after the Laranjos married, Marieta found that she was pregnant. Their first daughter, Laura, was plagued with very serious health problems. For a year doctors tried to find treatment options, but to no avail. Several times Laura's life was in jeopardy, but their church prayed fervently for God to heal Laura's afflictions. And he did! On her first birthday, the church held a service of thanksgiving that nearly five hundred people attended. Again, Marieta had witnessed God's loving care for her and her family.

In 2007 Elder Carlos Pereira and Associate Pastor Greg Hills, of First Presbyterian Church, North Shore (OPC), in Ipswich, Massachusetts, contacted Roberto about a group of Brazilians in the Greater Boston area who needed a pastor. From that moment, the Laranjos worked towards coming to America.

On April 17, 2007, Roberto was received into the OPC's Presbytery of New York and New England to serve as pastor of the Brazilian Presbyterian Church in Melrose, Massachusetts. The congregation has experienced steady growth, not only among the Brazilian community, but among others as well because Portuguese and English are both used in their services. Igreja Presbiteriana Brasileira em Melrose became an organized church of the OPC on January 25, 2015.

Marieta struggled with some challenges in her transition to life in the States. First, she was very lonely as she found herself in the midst of a different culture with different family practices and a language she found very hard to learn. She had studied to become a biology professor and had left a good job in Brazil. Though her commitment was always to the work God had called her husband to undertake, she struggled with leaving a job and a church that she loved in Brazil. Marieta also had come from a large church in Brazil; the church plant was much smaller and required much more involvement on the part of her family. This turned out to be a great blessing for the Laranjo family, but definitely was an adjustment for Marieta.

For the Laranjos' daughters, Laura and Rebecca, moving to the States meant a new school, where

Roberto and Marieta Laranjo

they were often bullied for being different. This was particularly difficult, because in Brazilian culture those who were different, especially immigrants, were treated as very special—what a contrast to what her daughters were experiencing in America! Marieta was often reminded of the Brazilian saying that, "when a mother is on her knees, her children are standing up." She testifies that God answered many prayers of her heart when she cried out to him in the midst of her difficulties.

To understand their new culture, Marieta took English classes and volunteered as a health educator for Portuguese-speakers in the area. As a family, the Laranjos attended evening services at other area churches. Through those services and social events, they met many Americans and grew in their understanding of the language and culture.

Their church, Igreja Presbiteriana Brasileira em Melrose, the Presbyterian Church of Brazil in Melrose, now has close to 50 attending on Sundays, with 25 members, mostly Brazilian Americans. Marieta rejoices that God, even through all the obstacles, has taught her patience and trust, and has faithfully kept his promise to never leave or forsake her.

## Diana Cruz: Reforming Puerto Rico

Diana Bonilla was born on September 11, 1958, in San Juan, Puerto Rico. Her family moved to Brooklyn, New York, in the early 1960s, but moved back to Puerto Rico when she was nine. Diana and two of her brothers became members and actively participated in the work of the local Pentecostal church. After meeting Carlos Cruz Moya at church activities within their denomination, Diana married Carlos on June 19, 1982. The Lord placed within both Diana and Carlos an insatiable desire to know the truth. She remembers that "[Carlos] had determined always to be able to give a reason for his faith. He always looked for a biblical answer to questions." This desire united the Cruzes, who began to study at the Instituto Biblico Mizpa, which at the time was a theological school of their Pentecostal denomination.

As they continued to study God's Word, they became aware of the doctrines of grace and searched from church to church for sound teaching on these doctrines. Diana recalls, "We kept moving, looking now for a church of Presbyterian government that preaches and applies to our lives the truths of the Protestant Reformation ... the five solas of the Reformation (scripture, faith, grace, Christ, and God's glory)."

In 2007 Carlos Cruz established an independent Reformed church of 50 members in San Juan. That same year the Cruzes were introduced to the Orthodox Presbyterian Church through their friend Rev. Milton Villanueva, pastor of Primera Iglesia Presbiteriana Ortodoxa Jesús es la Verdad, an OP church in San Juan that began in 2006. Finding a conservative Presbyterian denomination was so exciting!

Pastor Villanueva introduced Diana and Carlos to Rev. Ben Alvira, who was born in Puerto Rico and served as an OP minister in New Jersey. Through this connection, Iglesia Presbiteriana Reformada del Caribe, the independent Reformed congregation where Carlos served as pastor, was received by the OPC's Presbytery of New Jersey in November 2007. The presbytery also received Carlos as an OP minister after consulting the 75th General Assembly about his ministerial credentials. Carlos was installed as the congregation's pastor on September 28, 2008—a joyful day for Diana and Carlos.

Since Carlos and Diana became Reformed and Calvinistic in their worldview, they have dedicated their lives to the work of the church with Carlos preaching the gospel, as Diana says, "from the rooftops!"

Diana and Carlos Cruz

It has been a difficult, but rewarding labor. Their work involves visiting towns around the island, often driving several hours to meet with people or hold services. During these travels Pastor Cruz teaches theology classes for the seminary founded by their church in 2001, Seminario Reformado del Caribe en Puerto Rico. In the past they also ran "Sola Scriptura," a literature ministry dedicated to sharing Reformation truths in Spanish.

Although Diana and Carlos are both from Puerto Rico and minister among their own people, Diana has found Reformed ministry to be very difficult. The predominant religions on the island are Catholicism and Pentecostalism, and those philosophies and world views have permeated much of Puerto Rican culture. The gospel of good works, prosperity, and the proliferation of apostles and prophets bombard their society. Because of these challenges, little change is seen in the religious culture and mentality of the island.

Despite these difficulties, young people who love the Scriptures come to the church to understand the doctrines of grace better. "I see women, young and old, whose lives have been improved and transformed, and who have also changed my life, as a result of their love of God and of the Bible as the only rule of faith and practice," Diana said. "They let go of fears, legalism, and doubts about how to manage their lives and how to enjoy absolutely everything (art, music, fashion, nature, etc.), guided by Christian principles and for the glory of God."

One of the highlights is a reading group. The women of the San Juan church meet with their counterparts in the Arroyo church, an OP home missions work about 100 kilometers from San Juan, several times a year. They read, study, and discuss books, such as the biography on Katharina von Bora, the wife of Martin Luther, to enrich and strengthen their faith.

Diana supports Carlos as he brings the message of grace and the Reformed worldview by radio and Internet throughout Puerto Rico. She has read the news on air and now handles the phone calls for the station. As Carlos begins a new facet of his work by presenting conferences to Spanish-speaking countries, her support means separation as Diana will remain at home, "missing him and praying for him!"

Diana and Carlos Cruz thank God for his blessings in leading them to a denomination that is faithful in both theology and ecclesiology. They are particularly thankful to be among the Reformed ministers, brothers, and sisters in the OPC.

**Kathleen Germann Curto** *has served as a pastor's wife, a missionary in Uganda, and now as registrar at Greenville Presbyterian Theological Seminary. A member of Covenant Community OPC in Taylors, South Carolina, Kathleen and Tony have six children and six grandchildren.*

# Kathleen Curto, Sunshine Okken, Martha Wright, and Laurie Tricarico: Four Helpmeets in Uganda

*Dorothy Brower Wingard*

## Introduction

The Orthodox Presbyterian Church's history in Uganda began in 1995 in the town of Mbale. In 2000 the work expanded to Nakaale, Karamoja, among the semi-nomadic Karimojong. Throughout this ministry, the Lord has used the wives of our missionaries to support their husband's evangelistic and diaconal work, sometimes opening up surprising avenues of service. Kathleen Curto, Sunshine Okken, Martha Wright, and Laurie Tricarico are among the women who have persevered in the challenges of the Uganda mission.

What a blessing to be a part of mission work in Africa. Dr. Brian Wingard, my husband, served as an OPC missionary, teaching pastoral students in Kenya (1994–1997); Mbale, Uganda (1998–2001); Asmara, Eritrea (2002–2007); back in Mbale, Uganda (2007–2010); and South Africa (2011–2016). Serving with Brian, I witnessed and experienced the sacrifices and service that are a part of everyday life for our missionary wives on the African continent.

During our first tenure in Mbale, we lived next door to Tony and Kathleen Curto. Brian and Tony taught at a theological college and helped the local congregations of the Presbyterian Church in Uganda. After a split in that denomination, the OPC mission subsequently worked with the congregations of the Orthodox Presbyterian Church in Uganda and established Knox Theological College.

Later the OPC started a new ministry 110 kilometers (70 miles) north of Mbale among the Karimojong, thought to be untouched by the gospel. The Karimojong were cattle raiders, greatly feared throughout Eastern Uganda because of their attacks on neighboring villages. The missionaries quickly learned how different life would be in Karamoja. During one exploratory visit, the missionary women were warned to put their heads down since some young men were bathing nude in a ditch beside the road. Once called the Naked People, now many more Karimojong wear clothes.

Slowly other things have changed in Karamoja as well. Missionary deacon Bob Wright's work on the mission compound has shifted from building missionary homes and the medical clinic to maintenance of vehicles, digging wells, and farming crops to provide work, water, and food for impoverished neighbors. Danger—while still present—has lessened. Although Karimojong warriors once could be seen walking with AK47s across their shoulders, the men no longer carry them as a result of government efforts to remove guns from the area. Communications also have remarkably improved. In the early days, Tony Curto would drive to a distant tree where he could sit on the *top* of the truck to make calls. The missionaries still call that tree "the *phone tree*." Today, one usually can get on the Internet in one's home and maybe even Skype! More foods also are available in the nearby trading center, Namalu, and cars, trucks, motorcycles, and other traffic on the dirt roads has increased greatly.

But much else is the same. Many Karimojong still face the serious challenges of chronic mismanagement of resources, polygamy, substance abuse, domestic violence, educational attainment far below the rest of Uganda, and primitive huts still made out of branches and dirt floors. Christianity is making inroads through the wide sowing of the gospel, while literacy initiatives, health instruction, and the superior medical care of the OPC clinic are supporting the evangelistic work in very practical ways.

## Kathleen Curto's Story

Kathleen grew up in a strongly Roman Catholic home and attended parochial schools. But during her teens she became rebellious and for her senior year of high school she switched to a public school. There she met and fell in love with Tony. They were in the counter-culture of the '60s in Southern California. Decisive Tony married Kathleen before he had finished high school. Soon their first son, Matthew, was born with cataracts that made him legally blind. That stopped his parents in their tracks. How could God allow such an affliction? "Jesus freaks" ministered to them in that dark time. After listening, reading the Scriptures, and coming under increasing conviction, Tony was the first to commit his life to Christ on December 31, 1971. Kathleen recalls that for the next three weeks he spent all his waking hours explaining the gospel to her. By the end of the third week, Kathleen had begun to know her sinfulness and need of a Savior. She confesses, "Because of the work of God's Spirit, I called upon Christ as my Savior."

From the time of his rebirth, Tony felt called to the ministry and soon was preaching on the streets every weekend, pastoring a small church, and studying at a small Bible seminary. Tony and Kathleen moved to New York City where again Tony preached on the streets, became Reformed in his understanding of the faith, and, at the urging of his session, began concentrated reading of the Puritans. They also encouraged Tony to go to seminary, so he first went to college in Southern California and then studied at Westminster Theological Seminary in Philadelphia.

During Tony's first eight years of pastoring in Southern California, he became convinced of Presbyterian polity. In God's providence, his church in 1988 merged with the OPC in Costa Mesa, and Tony began co-pastoring Covenant Community OPC with Greg Bahnsen. Meanwhile Kathleen cared for their three children and eventually earned her teaching degree. She taught and later served as an administrator at a Christian school. In 1994 Tony became Southern California's first regional home missionary.

Later that year, the OPC's Committee on Foreign Missions invited the Curtos to consider serving as missionaries with the Presbyterian Church in Uganda. To evaluate their request, Kathleen joined Tony on one of his evangelistic tours to Mbale, Uganda. Would she leave her hard-earned position as principal of a Christian school and proximity to her children for a small town in Africa with *iffy* water, *iffy* electricity, *iffy* security, *iffy* roads, and a dumpy open market? Her answer to Tony was NO! Then she started the trip home alone to Southern California while Tony completed his preaching commitments. En route she felt that the Spirit of the Lord was pressing upon her the spiritual needs and ministry opportunities in Mbale, Uganda. She struggled. "I stopped overnight in London and realized I could never say no. When Tony called home three weeks later from Heathrow Airport in London (the first time we had talked since I left Mbale) the first thing I said was, 'I want to go to Uganda.'"

Not only did Kathleen go to Uganda in 1995, she *thrived* in Uganda, loved the people, was fascinated by the culture, cooked and served Ugandan cuisine daily, used Ugandan fabrics and motifs in her interior decorating, and more importantly served in multiple ways to help strengthen the church and develop a Christian culture in Mbale. Kathleen came to Uganda in tears of reluctance, and left almost nine years later in tears of heart-break, for she was leaving the people and place she had grown to cherish.

Getting settled in Mbale was not easy. To get a glass of clean water meant a big pot committed to boiling water daily, followed by filtering to give an added layer of defense against pathogens. Finding a stove, even one in very bad condition, was a challenge. Yet what incredible baking and cooking she did with that tiny, poorly functioning stove.

There were many obstacles to ordinary life. Tony and Kathleen wanted a land phone (pre-cell phone days), but they were told they had to pay the outstanding bill of a previous tenant. After many attempts, Kathleen finally sought out the top administrator and firmly explained their need of a phone, their refusal to pay someone else's debt, and the business that was being lost by not granting them a phone. The answer remained no. Then, remembering the date, Kathleen tried one more appeal, "Tomorrow is my son's birthday and I will not be able to call him," at which point she unexpectedly burst into tears. The manager quickly agreed to have the phone installed by the next day.

In this country just beginning to recover from years of terror and economic collapse, Kathleen ministered through hospitality to the people of the church and short-term workers. Kathleen also took pity on the students who biked rutted, dirt roads up to 30 kilometers one-way to the classes at the theological college. Without food or drink, they returned home in the afternoon. So she prepared tea, with milk and sugar, and matooke, which is cooked, mashed, green plantains, for the middle of the day for about 17 students.

For the town and village churches, Kathleen guided their Sunday school. She loved the children, and her heart was touched by their rags, precarious health, by young children carrying only slightly younger children on their backs, and by those who balanced heavy jerry cans of water on their heads. Oh, that they might know her Savior! Kathleen encouraged pastors to find Sunday school teachers, developed a curriculum, and provided many materials. Any place where her husband went to preach, Kathleen went ready to teach the children, a huge undertaking.

Realizing the difficulty of the village women's lives and the paucity of spiritual help, Kathleen drove on rutted, dusty, or muddy roads to several villages weekly to teach the women. Husbands expected much work from their wives—collecting and carrying huge bundles of firewood, preparing and cooking meals (two a day if there was food), bearing as many children as possible, cultivating the family's subsistence garden, washing clothes, and watching the family cow if there was one and the children were too little to do it—all with little gratitude or companionship in return. Men were free to visit other women, take another wife, and get drunk.

One day in a village Bible study there was a woman whose husband had been stoned to death because he was caught stealing. This was the traditional, albeit unlawful, way of dealing with a thief. What a surprise to hear an elderly widow explain that she was not sad that her husband had died, for he used to regularly beat her, even for using too much soap washing his clothes. A wife asked how to deal with problems with her "co-wife" or "co-wives," as polygamy is common. The more Kathleen knew the women, the more she was aware of her distance from them culturally, especially the differences in how they thought. Yet, she marveled at her solidarity with these sisters in the Lord because of their relationship with Christ.

The most satisfying and most difficult ministry for Kathleen was developing a Christian school for the families of the "mother" church in town. Church families found it hard or impossible to pay the school fees in Mbale and longed for a truly *Christian* education for their children. This was perfect for Kathleen, a trained Christian educator. She formulated the kind of schooling best suited to Christian children in another culture. The initial work entailed overwhelming hassles dealing with all kinds of officials, the land owner, and builders. But she was determined. Kathleen later confessed, "If I had known how many difficulties there would be and how long it would take, I never would have been brave enough to start."

When the school finally opened in 1998, she relished teaching the children and training the teachers. Kathleen had been disappointed to leave her work as principal of a California Christian school, but teaching and administering in Uganda surpassed that joy!

A new chapter opened in Kathleen and Tony's lives when a promising pastor with whom Tony had closely worked died of AIDS, following his wife's death, also from AIDS. The couple's orphaned sons, Douglas, Isaac, and Ivan Were, in God's amazing providence, were *not* HIV-positive. Their elderly grandmother, a subsistence farmer, was overwhelmed with raising them, so, in consultation with clan and church elders, the Curtos took the boys into their home and began the long process of adoption. The grandmother (and the boys too) never thought the Curtos would keep them.

Those first days were memorable—everything was strange for the boys—the English language, Western cuisine, discipline, manners, even the Western toilet. Sometimes the boys huddled together in their shared bedroom to talk things over, with Douglas as their spokesperson. Kathleen's knowledge of the Luganda language helped in communication, since Douglas was familiar with Luganda from living in Kampala. One evening Kathleen invited Brian and me over for a birthday meal. Tony was usually very laid back at their table, but on this occasion our mouths hung open, for after the blessing, Tony and Kathleen both leapt to their feet and began serving food to the boys, helping them cut it and use utensils, correcting them as to proper etiquette, keeping their plates full, and mopping up the spills—a three-ring circus! Afterward I wondered, did Kathleen eat *anything*?

Although Douglas was nine, his school fees had been "eaten" by his uncle and he did not even know the alphabet. The others had not fared much better. What an amazing job Kathleen did with discipline and schooling. Within a few years, Douglas was reading at a ninth-grade level. Isaac and Ivan soon fit in with their peers. Even better was seeing how the Holy Spirit used the nurture of the Curto home to bear fruit that is continuing. Academically Douglas now studies law, Isaac graduated from West Point, and Ivan majors in exercise science in college. Kathleen had always wished for a large family; this was the unusual way that the Lord "gave [her] the desires of [her] heart" (Ps. 37:4).

In January 2001, the Curtos moved from Mbale to help start the mission station in Karamoja. During this time, the Lord tested and strengthened their faith. When Ivan Curto was six years old, he was accidentally run over by both axles of a trailer carrying an eight-ton tank of water. Missionary Bob Wright strapped him to a board and quickly drove to Mbale. In God's providence an

American orthopedic doctor was in town and examined Ivan. No broken bones, some internal bleeding—all which was remedied by keeping him flat in bed for six weeks. No easy task for an active young boy! As a mother, Kathleen felt emotional upheaval, questioning whether she had been irresponsible in Ivan's care and struggling with the thought that little Ivan's life could have been changed forever by this accident. When Kathleen asked Ivan what he thought about when his death seemed imminent, he replied, "I prayed that God

Kathleen Curto in Karamoja

would make me ready." What mercy, grace, and encouragement to a mother's heart!

Although Kathleen's stay in Karamoja was short, the Lord gave abiding fruit from her interactions with a Karimojong woman. Joyce had lead a "poor, bad life," as she confessed herself, and came to work for the Curtos wearing a cloth wrapped as a skirt, her only possession, which also functioned as the covering for her five naked children at night. Kathleen gave her clothing, food, a blanket, and taught her how to cook, mop, and clean. God used the Curtos' patience, example of faith, and friendship to bring the peace of Christ to Joyce's heart.

In November 2001, the three missionary families serving in Mbale left the field because of an untenable situation with the difficult moderator of the presbytery. In the hopes of continuing that ministry, the Curtos left Karamoja in December and returned to Mbale. Kathleen taught at the school for another year and a half. Then the tenuous relations that Tony had with the presbytery moderator and the local church session finally broke. Many close working associates in Mbale had swerved from the truth, loving money and power more than the Lord, proving their profession of faith hollow. Tony's very life was threatened.

Tony was forced to close the theological college and Kathleen had to leave the school into which she had poured her prayers, energy, love, wisdom, and skill. Hopes were dashed. "It taught me much about my own sin," Kathleen said, "so I was able to be more patient with others' sins."

Kathleen's nearly nine years in Uganda were a lifetime of ministry and an expression of her abiding faith in God. Kathleen now serves as registrar at Greenville Presbyterian Theological Seminary, where Tony is a professor. But she would return to Africa in a flash if the Lord gives the opportunity!

[*Born June 23, 1952, Kathleen married Tony Curto on October 2, 1970. They served as missionaries in Uganda from 1995 to 2004. They have six children: Matthew, Toby, Kristy, Douglas, Isaac, and Ivan.*]

## Sunshine Okken's Story

Sunshine and David Okken have been ministering in Nakaale since the beginning of the OP presence in Karamoja. What was striking from Sunshine's very first visit to Uganda was her willingness to do anything asked of her, even when it was completely unfamiliar. She simply counted on the Lord to enable her to do the task or ministry.

She benefitted from almost a lifetime of trusting the Lord. Sunshine's parents were "flower children" of the '60s; hence her name. When she was only four, her parents were converted. She remembers the fading of tension and the growth of love in their home. A year later she prayed with a teacher at church, receiving Jesus Christ as her Savior and Lord. During her high school and college years, Sunshine participated in a number of short-term mission trips, which were significant but did not impress her as part of *her* future. In fact, she had told herself that she would *never* marry a missionary or pastor.

Sunshine's first exposure to the Reformed faith came in attending New Life OPC in San Diego in 1998. She found it both confirming and challenging to her faith. Also at this church she met David Okken. She was the helpmate that he desired to have by his side in ministry, and she was *willing* to be that, wherever the Lord called him—including as a missionary among the Karimojong.

Sunshine and David, who married in 1999, serve in Karamoja with their three children: Caleb, Megan, and Jacob. Beyond Sunshine's responsibilities as a wife and mother, she homeschools her children and works for the mission. Her homeschooling role is the one that she finds stretching her patience. What a great blessing when missionary associates are able to help teach the children, though she does most of the teaching herself.

At the mission station, Sunshine has prepared the complicated application of the mission's renewed NGO (non-governmental organization) status with the government. She also is responsible for all of the communications with and logistics for the large number of short-termers who apply and come to Karamoja.

Living in Karamoja has many challenges. The Karimojong are "in your face" all the time, even *demanding* what you are wearing, *now*. With the dependence on one another that is part of the communal life of the mission, differences in personality, expectations, and performance easily become issues. Most of the social life revolves around the mission. While Caleb Okken, 12, plays soccer with the Karimojong boys, similar opportunities are not available for Megan. Interaction with the Karimojong girls is difficult because of their demands for clothes and the fact that most stay at home to work. Megan, nine, plays with the boys or

David and Sunshine Okken

stays home with younger brother Jacob, seven.

Although more food is available now than when the team first went to Nakaale, it still takes extra effort to plan and purchase what is needed. The heat can quickly wilt your starch, or, in the rainy season, the infamous muddy roads sometimes increase a journey to Mbale from two hours to two days. The Okkens find living so close to the Karimojong puts the evils of polygamy, alcoholism, and violence always before one's eye.

As Sunshine said, the sacrifices of being far from extended family, away from your home church, from friends, from advantages like homeschooling support groups, or all the above, are manageable when ministry and health are going well. But when the storms get big and dark, the sacrifices loom much larger. It takes grace to hang in there, trusting the Lord in all that seems to be going *wrong*.

Sunshine faced life-threatening miscarriages and was so sick simultaneously with cellulitis and malaria that she was hospitalized in Kampala for eight days—during which time her wedding ring and David's computer were stolen. Later there was some question whether they could remain on the field when Megan did not develop speech at a normal age. The Lord graciously heard and answered each crisis.

Sunshine's first miscarriage happened not long after the team moved to Karamoja in 2001. The clinic was not yet set up, and Dr. Herb Prawius and his wife were away. Missionary nurse Kristie Scott (now Freeman) remembers:

> That night I got a knock on my door from David Okken. David was slightly panicked while he explained to me that Sunshine was actively bleeding. As I assessed Sunshine, David began praying out loud for her strength and God's mercy. Within an hour or so she miscarried their first child and the bleeding increased. I took her vital signs because I was concerned about the amount of blood loss. Sunshine never complained. She was completely calm. She was also extremely pale. We put her on the couch and I started an IV while we reached Dr. Prawius on

the satellite phone.

Because it was the middle of the night, there were some concerns about traveling the roads. However, we all agreed she needed to get to a hospital as soon as possible. Tim Vanderhoff, a missionary associate, drove the vehicle while I sat in the back with Sunshine, holding an IV bag of fluids that was not doing its job, and monitoring her condition. David continued to pray the entire way, oftentimes pleading with the Lord for the life of his wife.

That night they reached CURE hospital (a hospital started by an American mission organization). Sunshine's blood levels were very low, but thankfully a blood transfusion was not needed. The next morning she was transported to the hospital in Kampala for further treatment. Says Kristie: "There was no anger, no hopelessness, no fear. No talk about 'how it would have been different if....' The Lord was and is Sunshine's strength. This was the first of several pregnancy loss trials in a faraway land for her, an enormous part of counting the cost for the work of our Savior."

Sunshine acknowledged that in such a trial she wished to just get to the *end* of it, which, she reflected, might have robbed her of the purpose God intended in the midst of a difficult situation. "I drew on the truths that I had learned but may not have *felt* at the time, keeping my eye upward," she said. "I clung to God's promises, though imperfectly, and prayed a lot. God is the One who remains faithful, who gives the strength needed at the time."

Sunshine knows that the Lord has proven faithful in all their past trials. She remains certain of the Lord's steadfast love and dependent on his grace and guidance in future difficulties and uncertainties.

[*Born January 4, 1975, Sunshine married David Okken on September 25, 1999. David, Sunshine, and their children, Caleb, Megan, and Jacob, have lived in Uganda from 2001 to the present.*]

## Martha Wright's Story

When people ask Martha and Bob Wright, "How did you know you were *called* to the mission field?" they always answer, "A phone call!"

Foreign Missions General Secretary Mark Bube called Bob twice to ask him to come to the mission field—first to Eritrea and then to Uganda. As a deacon and experienced building contractor, Bob's skills were needed in 1995 to rebuild the hospital in Ghinda, Eritrea, which was originally built by the OPC in the 1970s but later bombed during the Eritrean war for independence. Then in 2000, Bob was asked to rebuild a house that became the foundation for the OPC mission station in Nakaale, Karamoja.

Martha's journey to the mission field began with growing up in a nominally Christian home. When she was 13, her only sibling, her brother, died of leukemia and the family gave up on church and God. As a young, single woman, Martha was interested in Ireland's culture and Gaelic language. She spent more time in rustic, western Ireland than in the United States during the early to middle 1980s. Martha became so fluent in the Irish Gaelic language that she taught it both in Ireland and the United States, winning awards for speaking, writing, and singing in her adopted language. No surprise, then, that she went on to earn a PhD in educational linguistics at the University of Pennsylvania. This background prepared her for adapting to a simple life style and a different culture, as well as knowing *how* to learn a language outside a classroom. During this time, Bob, who had been a Merchant Marine and worked among Columbian Indians in South America, discovered that he too liked living overseas in a developing country.

The first time Bob met Martha in the 1980s, she was an unbeliever living very much in the world. When providentially they became reacquainted years later while playing in a band for a St. Patrick's Day celebration, much had changed. Martha had reached many of the goals she had set for herself in music and academia, but the accomplishments seemed hollow. She saw how well Bob was coping with major setbacks in his life. "Why are you like this?" she asked him. His simple answer, "Because I trust in the Lord," intrigued and mystified her. She began to read the Bible for the first time in her life and met weekly with OP Pastor David Cummings to learn about the faith. "Very gently, mercifully, the Lord opened my eyes to his truth and to the meaninglessness of my life's 'accomplishments,' and granted me faith and repentance," Martha said.

Martha and Bob married in 1990 and already had three children when they answered the call to go to Eritrea in 1996. Their family grew to five children by the time they moved to Uganda in 2000. The Lord had prepared Martha and Bob in many ways to serve him first in Ghinda, Eritrea, and then in Nakaale, Karamoja.

While visiting schools in Eritrea, Martha used her linguistic skills as part of her research for her doctoral dissertation. Five years later in Uganda, those same skills helped her to learn and analyze the Karimojong language and develop materials to teach it in the schools, where few people could read their native language. Martha also assisted with several weekly Bible studies, and joined one of the missionary pastors in teaching Bible and language in numerous public schools.

Martha also helped to develop the mission's latest initiative, KEO, Karamoja Education Outreach, which attempts to prepare Karimojong children for school with pre-literacy activities, such as listening to stories read aloud, learning letters, and counting in Karimojong, and health and hygiene. Every day the children—and teachers—hear the gospel. Due to parents' demand, preschools "under the tree" have begun in nearby Kopetatum and Moru Asia villages. The KEO staff also teach Bible and

Martha Wright with Karimojong women

literacy every week in two local public primary schools.

Homeschooling five children in rural Karamoja was a challenge because Martha and their outgoing, gregarious children all preferred classrooms filled with students. Their family has very much appreciated the missionary associates who have come to help teach their children over the years. After finishing high school in Nakaale, Rachel, their eldest, went to India to teach at a children's home and tutor missionary children, and then returned as an MK (missionary kid) tutor in Kampala before going to Houghton College in New York. Anna also went to Houghton after finishing high school at the Rift Valley Academy in Nairobi, Kenya. Mary and Christiana (Kipsy) soon followed at Rift Valley. Bobby particularly enjoyed the opportunity to be his father's apprentice for many of his school years, learning construction, vehicle repair, and agriculture. Now he is Bob's main assistant in the diaconal work. Like a city set on a hill, he has been recognized for his integrity, commitment, and winsomeness. All of this is a welcome heritage for Bob and Martha Wright.

[*Born on August 23, 1958, Martha married Bob Wright on June 23, 1990. They have served as OP missionaries in Eritrea from 1995 to 1997 and in Uganda from 2000 to the present. Their children are Rachel, Bobby, Anna, Mary, and Christiana.*]

## Laurie Tricarico's Story

In 1998 Laurie Tricarico's husband Al made a short trip to Uganda to visit our OP missionaries on behalf of the Committee on Foreign Missions and to visit members of his OP church in Vienna, Virginia, who were working there. Upon returning home, Al exclaimed, "I could live and work in Uganda." Laurie quickly replied, "Take me with you!" Although she was willing to leave the familiar to do God's work in another land, the time was not right. Six years later, Al finally received a call to serve as an evangelist in Karamoja.

During the decade the Tricaricos served in Karamoja, Laurie saw her role as support to her husband, her children, and the mission. The counseling and involvement in the lives of young women which she *relished* as a pastor's wife in the United States, did not prove transferable to Karamoja—the culture gap was *that* great. But looking at Laurie's varied work history—caterer, baker, truck dispatcher, excavating estimator, janitor, construction worker, and teacher—shows that she knew how to adapt. Despite their remote location and limited access to resources, which made it seem like a Mt. Everest situation, she continued to homeschool her children. The Lord provided ways to accomplish that goal, sometimes with the help of missionary associate teachers for certain subjects or by combining classrooms with missionary Bob Wright's children. Once the Internet came to Nakaale, libraries and art museums were suddenly accessible.

Laurie witnessed great blessings in her children's lives from growing up in such a primitive place: "What a benefit it is to observe your own culture from the outside! God has used this to help us better learn that we are called to conform to 'Christ's culture,' not a national culture." Daily they witnessed the essential nature of the faith, for death—from the very young to the elderly—was always near in Karamoja. They also saw cheetahs and baboons on the way to the grocery store, rode a boat to the source of the Nile, and stood with their feet in two countries. The kids, however, missed their friends back home, especially because it was difficult to develop deep friendships with peers in Karamoja due to the enormous cultural differences. While the Tricarico girls studied for college preparation, their Karamojan peers were already wives and mothers at 14.

On the up side, besides the Karimojong, the children fellowshipped with people from around the United States, Australia, Canada, Germany, Kenya, New Zealand, South Africa, and other regions in Uganda.

In Nakaale, Laurie saw her role as one of *modeling* the Christian life, Christian marriage, and a Christian home in a culture where the norm is polygamy, addiction, and violence. She was responsible for workers on the mission compound, so each morning she was at the gate counting the workers for payroll and lunch preparations. She kept tabs on supplies and tools and assigned workers their duties each day, from mopping and doing laundry to slashing the compound (mowing the grass by machete),

Laurie Tricarico teaching in Karamoja

and moving furniture as needed for visitors. She sought to encourage God-honoring attitudes in their work, develop their various talents, and help them understand how to respond to authority. During term breaks, 25 school boys came to work. She helped find jobs for them, such as weeding the gardens, and trained them in diligence, integrity, and completing a job up to a standard, wanting them to experience the satisfaction of hard work and earning pay, rather than begging. Modeling the Christian life included asking a worker for forgiveness when she sinned against him. "We're trying to exhibit that we're not the supposedly 'superior white people'," as Laurie puts it. "We are all the same: we all need a Savior; we all need to repent; we all need to grow in grace and godliness."

In order to create small income for a few elderly people who could not otherwise work, Laurie saved the clothing left behind by visitors or "retired" by the mission, bundled and sold it by the bag for a nominal price to these few poor people. They then took it back to their different villages to sell. Rather than being the recipients of more hand-outs, these people saw themselves as vendors whose dignity has been restored as they helped to provide for their own needs and those of their family.

One of the benefits of missionary service in Karamoja was that Al ministered from home. Although the ministry was 24/7, he was in and out of their home during the day, and available to play a part in the children's schooling. While stress came from the fish-bowl feeling of living onsite where people constantly requested help, the family felt they ministered *together* in Karamoja.

Although Laurie couldn't counsel the young women as she had in the United States, she shared her experience and godly wisdom as the speaker for a one-day conference at the Mbale mission station. The pleas of the 45 attending teens for *more* such seminars, spoke loudly of how well she addressed them about being self-controlled, wise, and godly women.

God also kindly allowed each of Laurie's children to use his or her unique gifts in this unusual setting. Kate's blog of the family's experiences had a large following back in the United States. As a result of Emily's volunteer work at the medical clinic and the medical situations to which she was exposed, she pursued a nursing degree. Maria, who studied art in college, used her artistic talent to draw pictures for the weekly village Bible lessons. After working with missionary-deacon Bob Wright on projects like well-digging, auto mechanics, construction, and solar installations, James became equipped with the vocational skills he now uses. As a budding entrepreneur, Joshua tried his hand at raising and selling doves and ducks, as well as selling crafts and locally designed jewelry.

When the children moved back to the States for college, they learned responsibility, independence, and reliance on the Lord. It was a heartache for Laurie not to meet her daughters' roommates and friends, participate in their engagements, or help them select their wedding gowns. Skype and phone calls eased the burden of distance, but did not erase it.

In December 2015 the Tricaricos moved to the Philadelphia area where Al serves as associate general secretary for the Committee on Home Missions and Church Extension. Laurie now has the opportunity once again to mentor young women.

Looking back on her time in Uganda, Laurie believes God was calling her to honor him in the small things. "God is the giver of all gifts for the building of the kingdom and he is the one who decides when and how they will be used. As the hymn encourages us, we

are to be 'content to fill a little space, if Thou be glorified.' "[1]
[*Born on March 8, 1961, Laurie married Al Tricarico on June 15, 1985. They lived in Uganda from 2005 to 2015. They have five children: Catherine (Mrs. Zachary Ritchie), Emily (Mrs. Josiah Reiner), Anna Maria (Mrs. Michael Bova), James, and Joshua.*]

\* \* \*

On the Last Day, may each of these women hear, "Well done, good and faithful servant."

**Dorothy Brower Wingard** *is a member of Calvary OPC in Glenside, Pennsylvania. She and her husband, Brian, served 22 years as missionaries in Kenya, Uganda, Eritrea, and South Africa.*

---

1  Hymn 444, *Trinity Hymnal* (Philadelphia: Great Commission Publications, 1961).

# Afterword:
# Am I Choosing the Good Portion?

### *Diane L. Olinger*

The women whose stories are featured in this book have served and sacrificed for the Lord and his church, particularly in its expression as the Orthodox Presbyterian Church. In our view, limited as it is, these women chose the *good portion*—the portion offered by Christ and received by faith. Nourished by Christ, these women then nourished others with meals, friendship, words, and even their lives. By sharing the stories of these "older women," we hope to "teach what is good" to the younger women. Scripture tells us such teaching should have a practical effect, prompting an increase in love, kindness, and action (Titus 2:3–5). In other words, we hope that reading these stories will prompt a new generation of OPC women to seek the good portion as well.

The largest individual story in this book is around three thousand words; the smallest is about a thousand; other stories were not included. These differences reflect the kind of editorial decisions that are part of any book of history, but they should not be confused with the Lord's judgment as to the relative value of anyone's service. We are reminded of this by the story of the "widow's mite" recorded in Luke 21:1–4:

> Jesus looked up and saw the rich putting their gifts into the offering box, and he saw a poor widow put in two small copper coins. And he said, "Truly, I tell you, this poor widow has put in more than all of them. For they all contributed out of their abundance, but she out of her poverty put in all she had to live on.

Jesus' point here is not to condemn the rich for the size or manner of their offerings, but to commend the widow, whose offering would otherwise have been underappreciated. Jesus weighs our gifts of service with standards that are not of this world.

And so, we acknowledge that in our quest to identify good stories, we may have overlooked great ones in the eyes of the Lord. Consider, for example, the story of Marjorie Pascoe Pine (1910–2003), a charter member of Immanuel OPC in West Collingswood, New Jersey. Although Marge's story was certainly "worthy" for inclusion, we did not add it to the book because the effects of time had already worn away detailed memories of her. Writing a full chapter of "history" would have been difficult. Marge worshipped at Immanuel throughout her life, serving as a Sunday school teacher, a women's group and missionary society leader, a member of the choir, and a presbyterial delegate. As a young woman, she longed to attend Bible college and become a missionary. But, with the Depression, Marge needed a job to support her family and fund the education of her brother, Peter, who later became an OPC minister. Though Rev. Pascoe's service in the OPC was brief (1938–44), during his time at Covenant OPC in Rochester, New York, he was the first Reformed minister of Florence Handyside, featured in chapter 11, who would later die while serving as an OPC missionary in Korea.

Tracing the line from Marjorie Pine to Florence Handyside reminds us of how God uses our humble service in ways that we cannot imagine. We must be content to fill whatever space God gives us, if he is glorified.

Many of the women featured in these pages were married to OP church officers—ministers, elders, and deacons—and this provided them with distinct opportunities for service to the church. Scripture seems to anticipate these opportunities as the households of officers are required to be well-managed, and "their wives likewise must be dignified, not slanderers, but sober-minded, faithful in all things" (1 Tim. 3:4, 11–12). But other women, including singles and widows, have also done "heavy-lifting" for the church. While the most common venues for women's service have been the

home and the pew, some used their skills as nurses, teachers, professors, therapists, musicians, authors, and administrators to serve
the church and also the wider community.

From the OPC's earliest days, women have played an important role in outreach. They have traveled to foreign mission fields,
organized and written materials for vacation Bible schools, talked
to their neighbors about Christ, and invited church guests to their
homes for Sunday dinner. In more recent years, women have been
involved in OPC efforts to bring the gospel to non-English speakers within and just across our borders, fostering diversity within the
body of Christ.

Another way that OPC women throughout our history have
participated in outreach efforts is through presbyterial auxiliaries.
"Presbyterials" are presbytery-wide women's organizations that
promote missions in the churches. The first OPC presbyterial began in 1939 in the Presbytery of Philadelphia. While at least 12
presbyteries once had women's presbyterials, only five still meet
regularly.[1] The others have been discontinued or have transformed
into retreats or other gatherings with different functions. Many of
the women featured in this book "practiced their presbyterianism"[2]
through presbyterials, but this avenue is available to few today. Are
we missing something without this institution? Has its place been
taken by something else? Or, have we lost something along the
way?

Pat Clawson and I asked Rev. John Galbraith,[3] our 103-year-
old father in the faith, what changes he had observed through the

---

1 Patricia E. Clawson, "Women's Ties across Churches," *New Horizons* 29
(July-August 2008): 10, http://opc.org/nh.html?article_id=571.
2 Wendy Thomas, a member of Grace OPC in Sewickley, Pennsylvania, and
a former president of the Ohio Presbyterial, would commend delegates for
"practicing their presbyterianism" in this way.
3 Rev. Galbraith (1913–2016), a constituting member of the OPC, served
the OPC as a pastor, general secretary of the Committees on Foreign Missions and Home Missions and Church Extension, and member of the Committee on Christian Education, among others.

years in women's service in the church. He noted the decline in church "volunteerism," with the decline in presbyterial attendance as one example. The kind of volunteerism Rev. Galbraith referred to was shown by JoAnn Vandenburg of Lark, North Dakota. Despite having a large, active household and a concern for needs close to home, JoAnn regularly journeyed to the Dakota Presbyterial, sometimes as far away as Texas. She did this because "she knew that it is too easy to relax into one's own world, so she fought that inclination by using these means given to her, in order to enlarge her heart for God's worldwide family."[4]

Do we, like JoAnn, still make time for service beyond our families?[5] Beyond our immediate congregations? Or, could it be that like Martha in Luke 10, we've filled our lives with so much busyness—whether from jobs, kids' schooling and activities, or the pursuit of physical or domestic perfection—that there's no time left for anything else? Perhaps the answer isn't so much for women to return to particular activities or institutions, like presbyterial, but to re-prioritize spiritual nourishment.[6] Only if we have received the good portion, will we have the spiritual strength to nourish others in our homes, in our churches, and in our denomination.

Over the last two years, as Pat and I worked to select, gather, and edit the stories for this book, I would sometimes talk to my

---

4 Rebecca R. D. Schnitzel, "Mabel Danzeisen and JoAnn Vandenburg: From Strength to Strength in the Dakotas," chapter 12 herein.

5 Of course, we do not want to neglect our homes! Charles Dickens humorously criticized female activists of his day who were "telescopic philanthropists." In his novel *Bleak House* (1868), the minor character Mrs. Jellyby is obsessed with the well-being of an obscure African tribe, but comically inattentive to the needs of the Jellyby household. Our Christian service extends beyond the home—but it certainly begins there. For a discussion of "housework" as a merciful service, worthy of honor and not contempt, see Margaret Kim Peterson, *Keeping House: The Litany of Everyday Life* (San Francisco: Jossey-Bass, 2007).

6 See Aimee Byrd, "Nurturing Theologically Rich Women's Initiatives in Your Church," *Ordained Servant* 24 (2015): 53, *Ordained Servant Online*, December 2015, http://opc.org/os.html?article_id=520&issue_id=110.

daughters, Katharine and Kristin, about this project. Indeed, Katharine was even persuaded to write a chapter about Charlotte Kuschke. At times, I could tell from their comments that they viewed the book as a "girl power" statement. But that's not what this is intended to be! Rather, through the efforts of the OPC's Committee for the Historian, and through the suggestions, encouragement, input, and efforts of many—both men and women—the whole church is honoring the ladies highlighted here. Just as Christ took the time to notice and comment on the widow's offering in Luke 21, we want to record our sisters' offerings and encourage others to follow their examples of service and devotion.

This book will have accomplished its goal, if after reading it, you ask, "Am I choosing the good portion?"

# Acknowledgments

Our deepest thanks to the women we have met since coming into the Orthodox Presbyterian Church decades ago. *Choosing the Good Portion* was inspired by these saints who showed by example how they applied what they have learned from Christ to live for him.

Without the whole-hearted and unflagging support of the OPC's historian, John Muether, and the Committee for the Historian, this book would never have been written. Danny Olinger, president of that committee, kept this project moving at a fast clip and answered our many questions with his legendary memory for historical detail. Special thanks to committee members David Noe and Brian De Jong whose keen abilities as readers helped us spot mistakes and improve the manuscript.

Chris Tobias's excellent cover design and Jim Scott's editing advice and layout skills brought this volume from the computer to the book shelf. They have our gratitude. Katharine Olinger's video vignettes of some of our OPC ladies and Abby Harting's design of the Historian's display at the 83rd General Assembly gave folks a first glance of what is in the book. Perhaps no one has consulted *A Ministerial and Congregational Register of the OPC 1936-2016* more than we did to get our facts straight. We are indebted to those who produced that volume and to the countless people who kindly answered our quest for facts, photos, and family stories.

The willingness and hard work of 55 women authors who researched, interviewed, and wrote about 93 special saints was phenomenal. Some lived near or shared a family connection with the women they wrote about, while others did not. Some wrote as professionals or experienced authors, some did not. We appreciated their patience with us as editors as we pushed them for specific details, more warmth, and all in fewer words.

We are especially thankful for our families as they "put up" with stacks of manuscripts around our homes and our disappearances with computers into quiet corners and late into the night over the last two years. Thanks to Douglas Clawson, who encouraged Pat to pursue her writing since the first time the words slipped out of her mouth, "I think I can do that...." Doug has supported Pat every step of the way and she couldn't be more thankful. Special thanks to Danny Olinger, who never guessed when Diane signed on to this project that it would consume so much of her time. Diane appreciates Danny's enthusiasm for these stories and for her role in bringing them to light.

Teaming up with Diane has been a joy for Pat. Not only is Diane a fine writer, she practically has memorized the *Chicago Manual of Style* on grammar and kept us moving forward. Diane notes, "It is not often that someone comes along who is a true friend and a good writer" (E. B. White, *Charlotte's Web*). Pat is both. Her lively writing style, from years of reporting, influenced our authors, making their stories come alive.

Thanks to all who prayed and lent their support to this project. We are indebted to you. Please forgive us for any mistakes in our facts for this book. All we can say is that we tried our best.

Our hearts are full of thanks foremost to our Lord who has lavished upon us this wonderful denomination!

*Pat Clawson and Diane Olinger*

# Index of Names

Falk, Margaret, 344, 405–12
Felch, Douglas, 368
Fikkert, Alison, 289
Fikkert, Brian, 289, 290, 292
Fikkert, Doris, 254, 288–92
Fikkert, Henry, 254, 288–92
Fikkert, Steve, 289, 290, 292
Finlayson, Sandy, 357
Flavel, John, 386
Folkert, Beth, 323
Frame, John, 186–87, 261
Frame, Mary Cummings, 189, 190
Freeman, Kristie Scott, 439–40

Gaffin, Harold, 73, 74, 77
Gaffin, Jean, 56, 78, 217, 355, 358, 362, 395, 398–400
Gaffin, John, 73, 75, 77, 78
Gaffin, Pauline "Polly", 3–4, 71–78, 181, 354
Gaffin, Richard B., Jr., 51, 73, 76, 77, 78, 217, 353, 354, 355, 356, 358, 362, 398–99
Gaffin, Richard B., Sr., 3, 72–78, 181, 199, 354
Galbraith, Ada, 238–40
Galbraith, John, 42–43, 48–49, 156–57, 160, 173, 238–240, 253, 451–52
Gartman, Sandra Veldhorst, 296
Gatlin, Laura, 233
Geesey, Rebecca Mullen, 354, 360
Georgian, Debbie, 279
Gerber, Dick, 248
Gilbert, Louise, 237–38
Gildersleeve, Basil, 12
Gilman, Daniel Coit, 11
Gilmore, Marian, 277–80
Graham, Robert, 32, 33, 34, 376
Graham, Ross, 248–49
Graham, Ruth, 376
Gray, Emily, 365
Gray, Richard, 365
Gregson, Janet, 396–97
Greiner, Thelma, 56
Gresham, John, 13, 15
Gresham, John Jones and Mary Baxter, 9
Griffin, Frederick John, Jr., 367, 368